BOLTON M

on request from the
Librarian

ated to the Medical Institute
 by Mr. V. J. Peel

Medicine and industrial society

A HISTORY OF HOSPITAL DEVELOPMENT IN MANCHESTER AND ITS REGION, 1752–1946

TO THE MEMORY OF MY GRANDPARENTS
IN BURNLEY AND IN MANCHESTER

Medicine and industrial society

A HISTORY OF
HOSPITAL DEVELOPMENT
IN MANCHESTER
AND ITS REGION,
1752 – 1946

John V. Pickstone

Manchester
University Press

Copyright © John V. Pickstone 1985
Published by Manchester University Press
Oxford Road, Manchester M13 9PL, UK
and 51 Washington Street, Dover,
New Hampshire 03820, USA

British Library cataloguing in publication data
Pickstone, J. V.
  Medicine and industrial society: a history of hospital development in Manchester and its region 1752–1946.
  1. Hospital care—England—Greater Manchester—History
  I. Title
  362.1'1'094273   RA987.E5

Library of Congress cataloging in publication data
Pickstone, John V.
  Medicine and industrial society.
  Bibliography: p. 353
  Includes index.
  1. Hospitals—England—Manchester Region (Greater Manchester)—History. 2. Medicine—England—Manchester Region (Greater Manchester)—History. 3. Public health—England—Manchester Region (Greater Manchester)—History.
  I. Title. [DNLM: 1. Hospital Planning—history—England. 2. Hospitals—history—England. 3. Public Health—history—England. WX 27 FE5 P5m]
  RA986.P49 1985   362.1'1'0942733   85-3090

ISBN 0 7190 1809 9 *cased*

Printed in Great Britain
by Unwin Brothers Limited, Old Woking

Contents

Acknowledgements	page ix
Note	xi
Introduction	1

Section A. Organised medicine and the Industrial Revolution

1. Small town ways and large town problems
   - Medicine and provincial society about 1750: the foundation of Manchester Infirmary — 10
   - The growth and differentiation of the Manchester Infirmary, 1752–80 — 13
   - Public health and reform in Manchester, 1780–92 — 15
2. Famine, fever, childbirth and the workhouse
   - The Manchester House of Recovery, 1796–1815 — 23
   - The Lying-in Charity, 1790–1815 — 31
   - The new Manchester Poorhouse, 1792–1815 — 35
3. Medical charities in the industrial city: Manchester, 1815–34
   - The appearance of industrial society — 42
   - Overcrowded professionals and overcrowded patients — 44
   - The spread of charity: the Dispensaries in the Manchester suburbs in the late 1820s — 51
   - The medical condition of the poor — 54
   - Ordinary and extraordinary epidemics — 57
4. Medical Charity and the Industrial Revolution in the textile towns
   - Introduction — 63
   - Dispensaries and social change — 64
   - Dispensaries in difficulties — 72
5. Medicine without charity: economism, medical services and the New Poor Law
   - Industry, indigence and independence; the debates in Manchester — 78
   - The New Poor Law and medical services — 84
   - The new workhouses — 91

CONTENTS

Section B. Voluntarism and the state in established industrial communities

6. Civic show or healing environments: Manchester hospitals in mid-century
   - *Introduction* — 98
   - *Hospitals and real estate* — 100
   - *The mid-Victorian critique of medicine* — 108
   - *Women and children: specialists and the new philanthropy* — 113
   - *New workhouses and workhouse infirmaries in Manchester* — 122
   - *The Infirmary response, 1860–80* — 127
7. Paternalism and the hospitals of the cotton towns
   - *Social structures and the new Infirmaries* — 138
   - *Urban contexts of Infirmary promotion* — 142
   - *Urban contexts of antagonism to Infirmaries* — 147
   - *Smaller towns and smaller hospitals* — 151
8. Infectious diseases and hospitals, 1860–1910
   - *The understanding of infectious diseases* — 156
   - *Infectious diseases and the workhouses* — 160
   - *Infectious diseases and voluntary hospitals* — 161
   - *Smallpox epidemics and local authority hospitals* — 165
   - *Philanthropy and economy: Bolton and the smallpox outbreaks of 1883 and 1893* — 169
   - *Completing the coverage: isolation hospitals 1890–1914* — 173
   - *The importance of isolation hospitals* — 178
9. Sciences, specialists and capital: the modernisation of Manchester hospitals
   - *Introduction* — 184
   - *Medical vs lay control and the question of the Infirmary site* — 185
   - *Scientists and specialists* — 190
   - *Science and capital* — 193
   - *X-rays and radium* — 198
   - *The Edwardian Medical School* — 202
   - *Manchester medicine and the First World War* — 205
10. Hospitals and welfare: paupers, consumptives, mothers and children
    - *Introduction* — 212
    - *The Poor Law infirmaries* — 214
    - *The hospital services for tuberculosis patients* — 225
    - *Hospitals and homes for citizens of the future* — 235
    - *Maternity hospitals* — 241

CONTENTS

11. The pattern of hospital services in the 1930s
    Introduction   251
    The voluntary hospitals   251
    The Poor Law infirmaries   256
    A sketch of the Region's hospital services in 1938   264

Section C. A regional perspective on the construction of the National Health Service

12. The Manchester Joint Hospitals Advisory Board
    Voluntary hospitals and the municipality   272
    Upgrading the municipal hospitals   274
    A public inquiry   275
    Municipal plans   276
    The birth of the Joint Board   278
    The Joint Board and the appointment of consultants   283
    The Joint Board and special services   285
    The Joint Board in retrospect   292

13. The hospital service and the Second World War: actualities and plans
    The Emergency Hospital Service in Lancashire   296
    The War and plans for the future   299
    The Medical Planning Commission   304
    The Ministry of Health and plans for hospital development, 1941   305

14. Ministry surveys and plans, 1942–5
    Introduction   316
    The North West (1942) Survey and its impact   316
    Central negotiations and compromise   327

15. Bevan and the new National Health Service
    Profession and government – a realignment   340
    The plan and the Cabinet   347
    The split between local authority and hospital services   349

Bibliography   353
Index   361

Tables

1. The growth of charity midwifery in Manchester, Manchester Lying-in Hospital, 1796–1830   *page* 79
2. The wards for the sick in the Manchester workhouse (1841)   87
3. Income of Manchester voluntary hospitals, 1922–38   252

Acknowledgements

Our first debt is to the Manchester Regional Hospital Board, the North-Western Regional Health Authority and their staffs, for the initial funding of this study. Grants from the Wellcome Trust have aided the completion of this volume and much related work. I acknowledge these debts with gratitude; they have made possible an ongoing research programme on medicine and industrial society.

The archive retrieval and listing programme which provided collateral support for the present study, was funded by the Manpower Services Commission and the Wellcome Trust. The research assistance of Karen Wood and Liz Coyne was much appreciated.

Over the past years I have received a great deal of support and encouragement from colleagues, students and friends in Manchester and elsewhere. Kathleen Farrar arranged the project and chose an awkward research fellow to whom she gave freedom and robust advice. Donald Cardwell welcomed me to the History of Science and Technology Department and encouraged history of medicine as an integral part thereof. Stella Butler and Mike Jones strengthened parts of the study from their own research. Jean Raymond read the whole and improved it; Joan Mottram gave careful and invaluable assistance in preparing the volume for publication; Emily Cooper typed almost all of it expertly, more than once. Of colleagues elsewhere, Bill Luckin, Charles Webster and especially Irvine Loudon, worked through the whole text and provided many suggestions. I would like them and all my Manchester colleagues to know how much I have appreciated their intellectual comradeship, especially during the recent institutional difficulties which have delayed this publication.

My 'feel' for this history has been deepened by interviews with some of those who made it. Most of the 'oral history' will be used in a later volume, but the more recent sections of the present study have benefited greatly from repeated interviews with Sir Harry Platt and Dr P.N. Marshall. Their patience and their honesty have added much to this book.

For help with written sources I am indebted to many librarians, archivists and other staff: at the North-Western Regional Health Authority, Manchester Royal Infirmary, Manchester Public Library, Manchester University and UMIST; in many Lancashire and Cheshire libraries and record offices,

ACKNOWLEDGEMENTS

and in many hospitals and health authority buildings; at the Wellcome Institute, the British Library, the Public Record Office and the Department of Health and Social Security in London. I can only hope the creation of a new book is compensation for all the trouble they took.

Many other colleagues and friends have assisted in a variety of ways: offering information or criticism, guiding us to records, sharing their knowledge of local hospitals. The list is bound to be incomplete and omission does not imply ingratitude: Hilda Airey, John Banks, Gail Barlow, the late William Brockbank, Mike Bury, Karen Clarke, Mark Clifford, Judith Emanuel, Willis Ellwood, the late Wilfred Farrar, Huw Francis, John Gabbay, Susan Hall, John Harrison, Jonathan Harwood, the late Reginald Luxton, Marilyn Pooley, Jim Pugh, Elizabeth Roberts, Pauline Robinson, Mike Rose, Mary Turner, Tom Wainwright, Katherine Webb, John Wilkinson, Bill Williams, Raj Williamson.

My greatest debt is to my family, especially to Vivienne.

Note

I have capitalised 'Region' when it refers to the area of the Manchester Regional Hospital Board, to distinguish this usage from less specific ones. The less specific uses of 'region' vary over historical time, because the extent and importance of the city-region so varied.

I have also capitalised terms like 'Dispensary', 'Infirmary' and 'Hospital' when they refer to institutions, especially legal entities, rather than simply buildings or facilities. This departure from normal writing practice was intended to emphasise the independence and many-sidedness of the institutions with which we shall be dealing. For example, it distinguished the Dispensary as an out-patient and home-patient charity, from the dispensary in a modern hospital; the former was a major local institution, a society as well as a facility; the latter is merely the place where the drugs are dispensed.

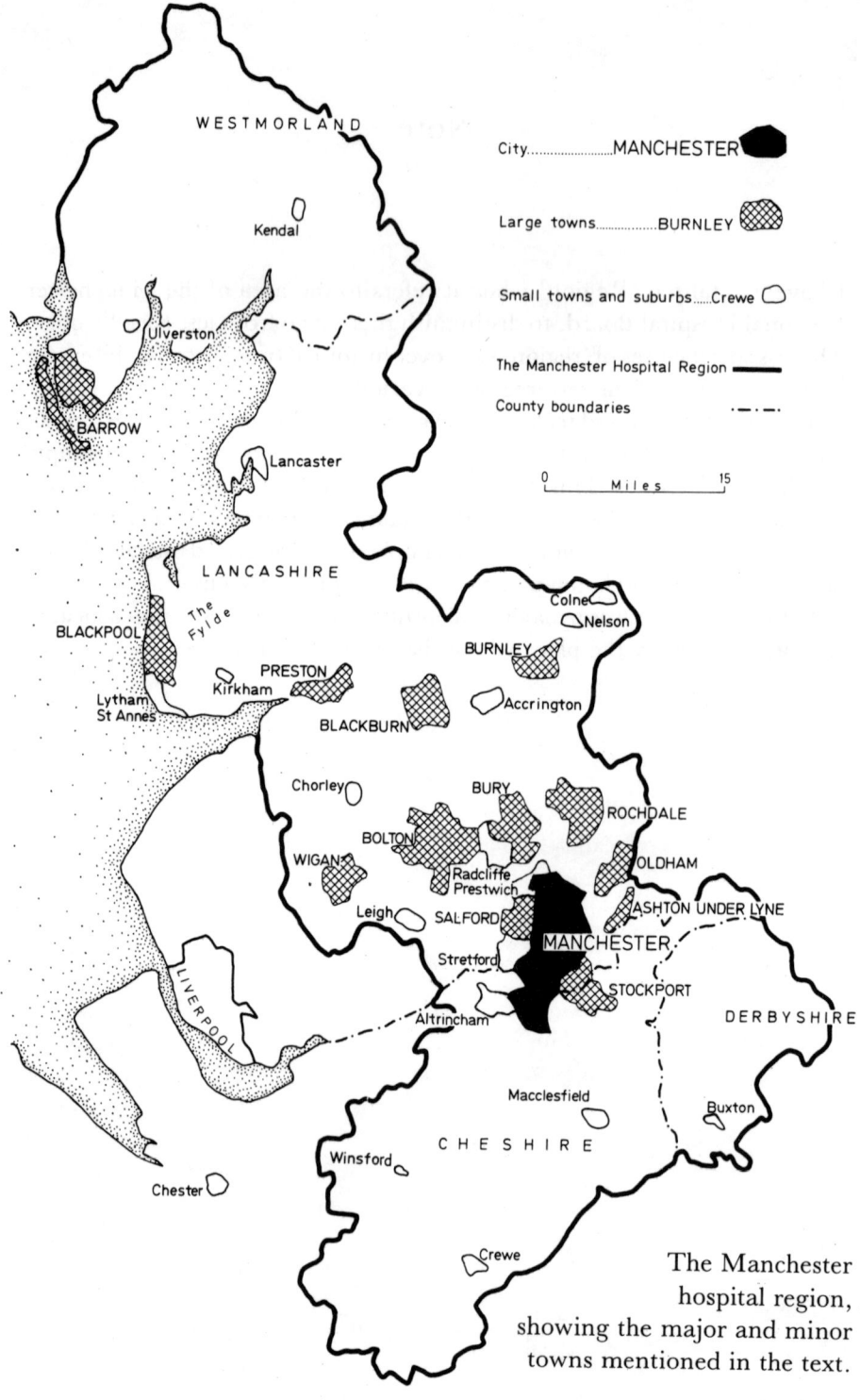

The Manchester hospital region, showing the major and minor towns mentioned in the text.

Introduction

This volume is the first of three which together will cover the development of hospitals, including mental hospitals, in the Manchester Region. The project has been long and complex; we have enjoyed considerable collaboration, within and without our research group. This introduction provides an occasion for setting out our aims and acknowledging our debts.

The whole project originated with the Manchester Regional Hospital Board which sought to record its work over the period 1948 to 1974. My colleague, Dr Kathleen Farrar, arranged for the study to be undertaken in this Department. Over the years, and on the advice of an outside referee, the 'more historical' section of the study was expanded to stand as a separate book. This is the volume which I now introduce. It does not cover mental hospitals, which will be dealt with in another book, concentrating on the NHS but also including developments over the previous two centuries. Nor does it take the story of non-mental hospitals beyond the planning of the NHS; a second further volume will review the establishment and the workings of the new service in this Region between 1948 and the reorganisation of 1974.

Thus the origin explains the scope of the present volume – in space, range of institutions and in time. In the introduction I try to show how we have used this framework; how we can justify, as historians, the treatment of all a region's hospitals over two centuries.

The geographical boundaries of the Manchester Regional Hospital Board included all the hospital centres thought, in 1947, to be more dependent on Manchester than on Liverpool or Leeds, Newcastle or Birmingham. The Region thus extended from Ambleside in the north to Crewe in the south, from Wigan in the west to Ashton under Lyne in the east. In terms of pre-1974 counties, it comprised the south of Westmorland, the east of Cheshire, a little of Derbyshire, and most of Lancashire outside the Liverpool area and the West Lancashire plain. The core of the Region was Manchester and its surrounding towns – Wigan, Bolton, Bury, Rochdale, Oldham, Ashton, Stockport and Salford. To the north was the band of boroughs running eastwards from Blackpool through Preston and Blackburn to Burnley. Further north came the rural areas and small towns like Kendal and Lancaster.

INTRODUCTION

To the south of the Manchester conurbation lay the market towns and small industrial centres of Cheshire.

These boundaries were drawn for a National Health Service based on regional 'centres of excellence'. Before then they had no formal existence and their use here is to some extent artificial. But it has a rationale, as well as an official cause. Though the inclusion of many different kinds of community has sometimes made presentation difficult, it has also served to emphasise the 'political ecology' of hospitals, and that has come to be a major concern of this study.

By 'political ecology' I mean the complex interrelations between the hospitals and the communities they were built to serve. I have tried to show how the formal and informal structures of hospitals and similar institutions were related to the economic, social and political structures of the cities or towns or villages which created them. In pursuit of these relationships, it has been useful to compare a major city, Manchester, with important industrial towns, e.g. Preston, with resort towns, e.g. Blackpool, or smaller industrial towns, e.g. Nelson, or market towns, and so on. It has been especially useful to be able to compare with each other the major cotton (and mining) towns of Lancashire and North Cheshire. Two chapters of the book are largely so based. They indicate how towns which to a distant observer might seem similar, in fact showed remarkably different patterns of medical services – differences which can be explained by, or at least linked to, their different political structures.

I have tried, as a historian of the Region, to throw some light on all its parts, but the focus and geographical balance varies considerably over the volume as a whole. The Region is sufficiently complex as to serve, in some ways, as a model of the whole country. Lancashire was an extraordinarily varied county, and Cheshire was always rather 'southern'. But no one can pretend that the Manchester Region is or was 'typical' of England. It was an industrial region, arguably *the* industrial region. Thus, though I have tried to keep the countryside in mind, it is the industrial centres which have occupied the centre of the stage – Manchester and the cotton towns. This has been an opportunity to study the historical relationships between industrialisation and institutional medical provision. I am aware that we have only made a beginning; a study designed primarily for analysis could take the issues further. But I think we can claim to have demonstrated that comparative urban history has much to offer in elucidating the determinants of medical services.

There is a second respect in which this study has been comparative: we have included all the kinds of institution recognised as 'hospitals' by the NHS.

INTRODUCTION

Three major types of hospital are described in the following pages: voluntary hospitals, Poor Law infirmaries and isolation hospitals. They differed in origin, structure and function, and have often been treated as parts of different histories. I have sought here, not only their resemblances and differences, but their relationships over time within the communities served.

Much of the first part of this volume is concerned with voluntary hospitals, especially Manchester Infirmary. These hospitals were organised as voluntary associations, funded by subscribers, served by unpaid physicians and surgeons, attending to poor patients nominated by subscribers. Dispensaries were organised on the same basis, but they contained no beds for patients; their cases were treated as out-patients or visited in their own homes. Most Infirmaries excluded infectious diseases, children and midwifery cases; Dispensaries dealt with infectious diseases as home-patients. By the end of the nineteenth century, almost all of the Dispensaries had been converted into Infirmaries or had been closed. By then Infirmaries were present in all the major towns of the Region, and were spreading into small towns. The newest charities were often called 'Hospitals' rather than 'Infirmaries'. 'Cottage Hospitals' became the preferred form of medical charity for small market towns; they were usually organised by local practitioners and expected payment from their patients. Town Infirmaries or Hospitals, plus Cottage Hospitals, continued as independent voluntary associations until 1948.

The second form of hospital then present, began as a very different kind of institution – workhouse infirmaries. Workhouses, especially after 1834, were intended as places of last resort for people incapable of gaining a living or family support. Many such people were sick or frail, but that brought few privileges; they shared a regime intended to deter the able-bodied. From the 1860s, especially in the larger cities and towns, separate buildings were provided for sick paupers. Initially they were occupied largely by chronic cases, nursed under the supervision of trained staff. Between the world wars, and especially after 1930, the proportion of acute cases rose; workhouse infirmaries came to provide the whole range of hospital care, including the chronic, medical, midwifery and psychiatric cases which were usually excluded from their voluntary counterparts.

The third kind of hospital largely sprang from the 'public health movement' – that concern with death, disease and disaffection in towns that fuelled much of the growth in Victorian government, both central and local. There were some early voluntary 'fever hospitals', indeed the 'House of Recovery', founded in Manchester in 1796 as an adjunct of the Infirmary, provided a model for English fever hospitals, including that in London. But by the mid-nineteenth century, much of the House of Recovery's earlier work had been shuffled off to the Poor Law, which in most towns was the

INTRODUCTION

only official means of isolating and caring for sufferers from typhus, or typhoid, smallpox or scarlet fever, whether adult or children. In Manchester new facilities were associated with the appointment in 1868 of a Medical Officer of Health. By 1900 most large Lancashire towns had municipal isolation hospitals, and often separate, rudimentary smallpox hospitals. They represented an increasingly technical and individual approach to disease problems that had first been seen as matters of environmental and social corruption.

In 1948, under the National Health Service, a Hospital Management Committee which took over the hospitals of a major town would usually control an ex-voluntary hospital, an ex-municipal general hospital, an isolation hospital plus a municipal maternity home and a sanatorium, perhaps with a cottage hospital and a Public Assistance Institution in a satellite town. At the time of take-over all but the voluntary hospitals had been under local authority control. Yet there was great variation between local authorities in the levels of provision, and in the balance between municipal and voluntary services. This variety reflected the economies and political cultures of the towns – in some the voluntary tradition was dominant, others looked more to 'progressive' local authorities. Corresponding balances at local, regional, national and central government levels helped determine the first structure of the NHS and indeed its subsequent history. We show here how deep-rooted the inter-urban differences could be; intra-regional patterns changed relatively little over time. Thus in the exploration of such patterns, the historian may illuminate the awesome task of the policy maker, perhaps by elevating and formalising that knowledge of the intimate and the local which is so easily neglected in 'planning by numbers'.

That hope is one justification for this long and complex hospital history, and it stands, in part, on the very material continuities of brick and stone evident in almost every town of the Region. Though in Manchester the Royal Infirmary left its Piccadilly site in 1908 and the associated special hospitals also moved, in the Region outside Manchester no major town has abandoned the premises of the late-nineteenth-century voluntary hospitals or the workhouse infirmary which was probably constructed in the same period. Some minor institutions have been replaced by new district general hospitals, especially in Cheshire, but for the most part the old buildings are still in use; adapted, converted, added to, but still housing a high proportion of the Region's hospital beds. They serve to remind even the casual historian of the material links between generations.

Here we try to show that it is not just with bricks and mortar that a generation forms the services of its successors. The periodicity of building and rebuilding is interwoven with a periodicity of concern and political culture;

INTRODUCTION

the present can now be understood against two centuries of institutional medicine.

The volume opens with a medical charity which was essentially pre-industrial. By the 1790s, the health scares of factory towns were already apparent; medical services in Manchester were being advanced by Whigs and radicals keen to improve those informal sectors of urban institutions to which they had access. The services were maintained, but not expanded, during the repressive decades of the French wars and Peterloo. They seemed to serve as barriers to infection and discontent as Manchester and its satellites grew through immigration to become classic industrial towns.

When political liberalism rose again in the 1820s, it faced the wretched industrial suburbs whose immigrant population crowded in foul conditions. The late 1820s brought a flurry of charity, spreading Dispensaries (and a few Infirmaries) to suburbs and satellite towns, but this was not the beginnings of a new philanthropic order. Rather, especially in towns like Rochdale, it was the attempt of conservatives, especially Anglicans, to hang on to a hierarchical social order of mutual obligation. The liberal reformers, by contrast, left little room for giving – evangelical missionaries and agents for provident societies penetrated the industrial masses, saving souls and saving pennies. The New Poor Law of 1834 and its Commissioners did their utmost to spread similar attitudes from the already 'economical' Guardians of Manchester, to the more casual Guardians of surrounding towns. They were resisted because they encroached on local autonomy and, in the 1840s, because the provision of 'efficient' institutions, however economical, seemed expensive compared to the accustomed squalor of township poor-houses or the paupers' own homes.

The cotton towns of south-east Lancashire probably then provided less public medical care than any comparable communities in Europe. Medical charities were unpopular with potential subscribers. In 1790 the supporters of the enlarged Manchester Infirmary had boasted that the town's poor could obtain medical services at least as good as those available to the better-off. In the 1840s that would have seemed improper, though the health costs of industry, especially the horrendous toll of accidents, fell predominantly upon the poor.

It is against this dearth of charity and meanness of statutory provision that we must see the expansion of institutional medicine that was evident in this Region from the 1860s. Its roots are many; technical factors cannot be neglected; the advocacy of trained nursing was critical in creating 'hospitals' as public healing spaces, rather than repositories for the injured. But it is perhaps in the expansion of paternalism, voluntary and statutory, that we may find the keys to hospital growth in this Region. Voluntary hospitals were, pre-eminently, community institutions. As Lancashire towns stabilised somewhat, as employing families prospered and working families reached above the bread-line, projectors of hospitals brought together conspicuous donations and work-place collections for institutions which all classes and denominations could be persuaded to support. In the same period, central government was ready to help provide elaborate institutions for those disabled sections of the population which it was not ready to support at home. Accommodation for the chronic sick was improved; out-relief was reduced.

Thus the majority of hospital construction in the Region took place between the Cotton Famine of the early 1860s and the First World War. By the interwar years, with the collapse of the cotton industry, the paternalists had vacated their positions of informal and statutory power. Their mansions were available as museums or maternity homes. Initiative in welfare matters lay increasingly with labour or progressive liberal politicians, and with women trained in the suffrage campaigns. Theirs was the task of upgrading hospitals and removing the taint of the Poor Law. Hence the high period of municipal medicine, when even the voluntary hospitals came to depend on the slow but apparently inexorable advance of local government welfare. But it was also the period in which the specialists and academics around the medical school began to incorporate not only the major teaching hospitals, but most of those within the central conurbation.

There was little hospital building between the wars, except in newer towns (e.g. Blackpool) or for newer specialties (e.g. radium treatment). The Second War followed closely after the Depression. For a time it seemed that wartime planning would bring all hospital care under local authorities. That did not happen. With Bevan all hospitals came under the central state – ministerial and parliamentary control mediated through a regional and local system where medical and 'voluntary' representatives were predominant.

The new structure weakened the link between hospitals and local authorities. Local political culture was thereby diminished and hospital planning was less responsive to local demand that it might have been. Yet, for all its faults, and many were inevitable, the NHS built on one of the great virtues of the previous hospital arrangements. It inherited the goodwill enjoyed by pre-war hospitals as community institutions. By then, at least in the more progressive County Boroughs, hospitals seemed to be provided by and for the majority of the population. The voluntary hospitals, especially in industrial towns, had come to be supported largely by the working-men and women who used them, and the taint of paternalism was diminishing. The municipal hospitals were seen as a major frontier of welfare services and stigma of public relief was fading. Among the upper classes, private hospital

INTRODUCTION

medicine was increasing, but generally, even where payments came through regular voluntary contribution schemes, the provision was for the community.

The NHS had the enormous virtue of generalising that principle, of providing a service free at the time of need. Institutional medicine was not to become a purchasable commodity, except for those who wished to pay for such an arrangement.

Hospital care in Britain, has never primarily been a question of individual purchase, because poor relief and philanthropy were replaced by local and state welfare. When most of this study was written, the continuance of that tradition seemed assured. It will be read when that tradition is in doubt. But what better time to describe how the NHS built upon and improved previous community provision? The result is a very efficient way of providing health care; experience of more private systems elsewhere makes that clear. But medicine is not just an economic question, anymore than is national defence. Institutional recognition of central values is necessary in all societies. Hospitals have been major symbolic institutions for over a century and they will probably remain so, because they now so commonly house the daily dramas of birth, sickness and death. What is at issue in Britain is the extent to which hospitals will continue to be community institutions; collective provision for the care we shall almost all require.

SECTION A

Organised medicine and the Industrial Revolution

CHAPTER 1

Small town ways and large town problems

Medicine and provincial society about 1750: the foundation of Manchester Infirmary
In 1748, there was little evidence in Lancashire that this remote and relatively underdeveloped part of England would soon be the site of the world's first large industrial society. The county was already known for its coal and minerals, the traders of Liverpool had begun to grow rich on the slave trade, Manchester textile merchants were operating nationally, but these changes appeared largely as the results of a shift of manufacturing from the south of England towards the north-west.[1] We can illustrate the situation and the ways in which it changed by concentrating on the town that was already the major textile centre, Manchester.

In 1748, the only public institutions in Manchester were the two churches (the Collegiate Church and the then new St Ann's), two chapels (Presbyterian and Independent), a free grammar school, a school and home for orphan boys and a poorhouse. The population of the township was then about 15,000.[2] The only sick people to be taken into institutions were among those destitute paupers who entered the poorhouse. For as long as money was available, sickness, like health, was a private matter, or one for family and friends. When no money was available, then sickness, like food and accommodation, was a problem which could be taken to the overseers of the poor, the parish or township officers who administered the funds collected as rates on households under the provision of the Elizabethan Poor Laws, variously amended.

The overseers of Manchester, like most of the township officers, were usually members of the Anglican church and Tory in politics. Manchester's administrative system had changed little since the Middle Ages, it was effectively ruled by a clique of burgesses working with the Mosley family, who held title to the Manor of Manchester.[3] Most of the other towns in the Manchester Region had a similar system of government, except those old chartered boroughs, including Liverpool, Preston, Lancaster and Wigan, which were ruled by corporations.

If Manchester was the mercantile centre for the growing textile trade, Liverpool was the major port. Liverpool had increased rapidly in the early eighteenth century and Manchester kept an eye on its rivals developing amenities. In 1745 a group of leading Liverpool citizens, 'clergy, physicians, surgeons, merchants and tradesmen, with some neighbouring gentlemen',[4] founded an Infirmary. Manchester followed suit in 1752, led by Joseph Bancroft, a local gentleman, and the young surgeon, Charles White.[5]

Infirmaries, at mid-century, were the newest and most popular form of civic philanthropy. They were organised, like many contemporary charities, in the form of joint-stock companies; churches were often built on the same basis, as were street improvement schemes; in each case the enterprise was controlled by the votes of the subscribers, who usually elected a management committee from amongst themselves. This was a form of giving in which the moderately wealthy could join, a small-scale, regular and communal activity for a relatively secular cause.[6] Because an Infirmary could attract support from a whole region, including landowners as well as town merchants, it was an appropriate means of displaying status and/or wealth. Because its appeal was non-denominational and non-political, it could be popular with those anxious to maintain the unity of a town's propertied classes — no small consideration in Manchester after the 1745 rebellion had thoroughly split the town's growing elite.

Manchester, like other provincial centres, was becoming fashionable; it had gained an assembly hall and other venues for 'polite society'.[7] Gentlemen, the wealthier merchants and the leading professionals developed urban cultural patterns which increasingly separated them from the ruder-mannered tradesmen and artisans. The charity to the poor which might once have been exercised through the church or simple alms-giving, was now organised through one of the instruments of 'society'.

Each Infirmary patient was admitted on the recommendation of a subscriber. An annual payment of two guineas purchased rights for two out-patients and one in-patient at any time. The patronage was direct and explicit. Anyone who sought Infirmary care first had to find a subscriber and demonstrate their need. Only then could they attend on an admission day, Monday for in-patients, Thursday for out-patients. The case would be considered by the weekly board of trustees and by either the honorary physician or honorary surgeon in attendance. When treatment was finished, or if no further benefit could be expected, the discharged patient was supposed to return thanks to the subscriber, who was then free to recommend another supplicant.[8] In a small town of growing affluence, these easily-bought rights of patronage were attractive.

If admitted to a hospital ward the patient became part of a large 'household' which, for most of the time, was in the care of two resident staff, the apothecary and the matron. The domestic servants and the nurses were supervised by the matron, who acted as 'housekeeper'. The apothecary took charge of the patients between the visits of the honorary physician and surgeons. In the nineteenth century, this was a post held for a year or two by a trainee practitioner, but in the eighteenth century one man could remain as resident apothecary for many years, so becoming a key member of the staff.

The new Infirmaries proved attractive to physicians and to surgeons, for both social and technical reasons. As towns grew larger and more prosperous the 'collective patronage' of the urban bourgeoisie could increasingly substitute for that of individual aristocrats or land owners. In as much as urban elites stressed learning, rational entertainment, cleanliness and regimen, graduate physicians were well-placed as cultural leaders.[9] Voluntary hospitals gave opportunities for conspicuous service and helped establish a physician's place in the better circles of the town. This was true for Oxbridge-educated sons of local gentry, as for Dissenters trained in Edinburgh medical school. Manchester Infirmary's first honorary physicians included both kinds.[10]

The honorary surgeons were not graduates. They were the local leaders of an occupational grouping which was much more diverse than 'physician' and, then, rather more dynamic. The distinction between surgeon and apothecary, or between either kind of practice and that of a physician, had never been clear or rigid outside of certain London circles. In the provinces, most apothecaries and most surgeons covered most of the range of medical tasks, from diagnosis to dispensing and minor surgical operations. Major operations were rare. Apothecaries concentrated on the sale of drugs; surgeons on wounds and sores, bleeding and minor operations, but this was a difference of emphasis rather than a clear divide. Physicians did not dispense, or carry out major surgery; they were traditionally learned.[11]

But in the mid-eighteenth century some surgeons were coming to realise that surgery could be developed not just as a craft but as a profession based on a detailed knowledge of anatomy. By extensive dissection, through concentrated experience in the army or the new hospitals, and by systematic teaching they were rapidly raising the scientific standing of their discipline. Invasion of midwifery was a particularly promising means of advancement. Surgeons had customarily dealt only with obstetrical emergencies; in the mid-eighteenth century, it had become fashionable for surgeons to attend normal labours.[12]

Charles White was well-placed to promote and exploit the advance of surgery. His father, the son of a Manchester attorney, had built a reputation for man-midwifery. Charles, after apprenticeship with his father, studied in London under William Hunter, one of the Scots who had pioneered obstetrics in London. At William Hunter's anatomy school, Charles met

John Hunter, then establishing his reputation as a dissector. Here was a centre not only of fashionable midwifery but for scientific surgery, both of which White was to develop in Manchester.

It is unlikely that surgeons began the Infirmary movement in Britain, but as it spread from town to town, the advantages of Infirmaries as centres of surgical teaching and collaboration must have become increasingly obvious.[13] Charles White, no doubt, was ready to advise those Mancunians who sought to emulate Liverpool Infirmary. Advertisements were placed in the newly-founded local newspaper and a meeting of Infirmary supporters was held on 4 June 1752 at the Old Coffee House. Three weeks later a new house on Garden Street had been converted into the Region's first hospital.[14]

The growth and differentiation of the Manchester Infirmary, 1752 –80
During the later eighteenth century the Manchester market came to dominate the Lancashire textile industry. Bolton was, for a time, a rival centre, as its Georgian architecture shows; Preston was the *de facto* county town and a centre of influence for the Earl of Derby. The founding of an Infirmary helped confirm Manchester's dominance, for it was a regional, not simply an urban, charity. Gentlemen in towns throughout eastern Lancashire and Cheshire subscribed; overseers from many parishes sent occasional patients; their churches took up collections.

We do not know what the patients thought of the hospital. To men and women with little schooling and little contact with the well-to-do, rough of manner and suspicious of doctors, the whole environment in the hospital must have seemed very strange – rather like entering a 'big house' or, at least, the servants' quarters. The presence of so many strangers, the separation from friends and neighbours, the discipline and regimen, the submission to doctors must all have been unnerving, especially for the ill and the relatively defenceless. On the other hand, the Infirmary offered food, warmth and attention to those for whom the alternative was solitary suffering, or a tiny room overcrowded with children. To these poor who could not afford to maintain themselves in food and fuel, let alone to buy medicines, the Infirmary might have been attractive. In a populous district it was not difficult to find enough patients for the few beds available, for the turnover was slow by modern standards; most patients stayed for more than a month and many for two months, after which they had to have special permission to remain. Some were accident cases, many were 'medical' cases barely distinguishable from those treated as out-patients, except that pregnant women, children and sufferers from infectious diseases were not admitted to the beds.

This continued to be the pattern for decades even when the hospital was well established in a new and much larger building. Not all the patients were happy with their treatment; from time to time the Board complained of ingratitude and cautioned patients that, should they leave the hospital without registering dissatisfaction, any adverse comments gossiped in town would forever preclude subsequent treatment.[15]

Whatever the patients thought of the Infirmary, it proved very popular with its subscribers. Sufficient funds were available to build handsome new premises on Piccadilly, then on the outskirts of the town. This building, which, variously enlarged, was to serve until 1908, was opened in 1755 with fifty beds, increasing to sixty in 1760. In 1763 the Weekly Board proposed to the trustees that a Lunatic Hospital be constructed next to the Infirmary building; this was funded separately and run by a separate committee, but came under the same medical staff and the same body of trustees.[16]

The development of services for lunatics will be described in a separate volume, but it would be wrong completely to divorce the topic from general medicine when the institutional links were so close. There were many precedents for the general Infirmary, but few for the Lunatic Hospital. Since the Middle Ages Bethlem Hospital in London had been the only established public provision for lunatics; over the rest of the country they were housed in parish gaols or workhouses, or, if well-to-do, confined to private madhouses. St Luke's Hospital, opened in London in 1751, signalled the adaptation of the voluntary hospital movement to the problems of lunacy; it was a subscription hospital and much more medical than Bethlem. Manchester and Newcastle were the first provincial towns to provide hospital accommodation for lunatics. The immediate stimulus may have been public concern over madhouses, raised in 1763 by an exposé in the *Gentleman's Magazine*.[17]

The readiness of the Infirmary supporters to take on the care of lunatics has to be understood in both conceptual and economic terms. The growing naturalism of polite culture allowed lunatics to appear as physically ill, rather than possessed; hospital physicians, increasingly interested in the responsiveness of living bodies, especially the nervous system, were ready, sometimes eager, to treat those 'divided in their senses'. The patients and their friends were happy to concur, not from any great faith in medical remedies, but because the new voluntary hospitals seemed more respectable and reliable than private madhouses, even those kept by doctors.[18]

Because constant supervision was expensive, lunatics were an economic burden on their families or parishes. Thus, in taking on these patients, the Lunatic Hospital was able to charge fees. Private patients paid from ten shillings to a guinea per week, depending on their means and the quality of accommodation provided. For pauper lunatics, the overseers concerned were charged five shillings a week. This was more than it would have cost them to maintain the lunatic in a workhouse, but they hoped for compensating advantages. Perhaps they expected to reduce disruption in the workhouses, certainly they were led to expect that the Lunatic Hospital, by curing patients, would reduce the total charge on poor rates.[19]

The fees covered most of the running costs and so the Lunatic Hospital required less charity money than the Infirmary. But its ability to accommodate lunatics from among the subscribing classes ensured large gifts. The benefactions were used to extend the buildings. By 1787 the Lunatic Hospital was bigger than the main Infirmary; by 1800 it had over one hundred beds.[20]

The next major venture for the Infirmary trustees met with a similar success. This was a complete set of cold, warm and vapour baths, built alongside the Infirmary, with attention to convenience and elegance. Manchester was not a spa town, the baths were a fashionable substitute. They were not cheap: a warm bath cost three shillings, about the price of six pounds of beef or cheese. For trustees the rates were lower, giving the well-to-do an incentive to charity.[21]

The success of the baths underlines the connections we have tried to draw between the new Infirmaries and the development of a polite culture which required new arenas for fashionable intercourse. The need of doctors for similar arenas is exemplified by another institutional novelty – the Manchester Literary and Philosophical Society, founded in 1781. Though this has been regarded as a forum for the new men of industry, the majority of its first members were medical; the Society was listed in the national *Medical Register* of 1783.[22]

Public health and reform in Manchester, 1780 – 92
Infirmaries were never intended as public health measures; the rules of the eigthteenth century foundations were more stringent than medieval precedents and specifically excluded children and cases of contagious or venereal disease. Rule 43 of Manchester Infirmary stated:

> That no woman big with child, no child under six years of age, (except in extraordinary cases, as fractures, or where cutting for the stone, or any other operation is required) no persons disordered in their senses, suspected of having small-pox, itch, or other infectious distemper, that are apprehended to be in a dying condition, or incurable, be admitted, or be suffered to continue.[23]

That these classes of patients were specifically excluded from Infirmaries may have made them more conspicuous. Certainly, we find them included in a variety of charities which developed in the later eighteenth century alongside or instead of Infirmaries. These include Dispensaries, Lock hospitals for venereal disease, Lying-in charities for childbirth and Fever hospitals. All four kinds were attempted in Manchester, more or less in connection with the Infirmary. In the rest of our Region, Dispensaries were eventually founded in over half of the major towns and some of the minor ones; Lying-in charities and Fever hospitals were less common.

The polite concern with cleanliness that had gained force during the middle decades of the eighteenth century did not leave the working classes uninspected. It was in the army and navy that cleanliness and regimen were first forced upon the lower orders; medical men such as Pringle and Blane played a key role and were regarded as pioneers by later physicians. Other managed populations, notably in prisons, were subjected to the same attentions and in John Howard's work on Lazarettoes this concern extended to civilian hospitals. In all these cases, typhus, the fever of camps and gaols, was the major medical target; but the movement was much more than a campaign against specific disease, it was a more or less forcible extension of patterns of behaviour already accepted by the middle classes, especially the Scottish and Dissenting groups from which so many of the physicians came.[24]

It is easy enough to see these tendencies at work in Manchester, both among the middle classes and directed at the poor. The early 1770s saw the publication of Charles White's book on midwifery which argued for cleanliness, ventilation and exercise in the treatment of lying-in women;[25] John Aikin's *Thoughts on Hospitals* was published in 1771, deriving, in part, from his contacts with White and the leading Manchester physician, Thomas Percival; in 1773 Percival and Thomas Henry, Manchester's best-known apothecary, undertook a demographic study of the local population; two years later Percival was a member of the Improvement Commission, which sought to redevelop a section of the town centre in a manner more fitting an advancing town. Percival had also been associated with an unsuccessful scheme to provide a Lock hospital.[26]

Similar concerns in other provincial towns gave rise to Dispensaries. These were institutions run in much the same way as voluntary hospitals but they had no beds. Instead they concentrated on out-patients, examined at the Dispensary building, and on home-patients who were visited at their own homes by the honorary physicians or, more usually, their paid assistants. Dispensaries were much cheaper than Infirmaries and, in terms of public health, much more effective. Their physicians became expert in the natural history and treatment of epidemic fever that every few years came to dominate the daily routine of chronic illness and sores.

A Dispensary for the Infant Poor had been founded in London in 1769, but the 'Dispensary movement' really began with the Aldersgate General Dispensary of 1770, which was closely associated with a group of Quaker physicians.[27] In London and elsewhere, Dispensary physicians were usually Edinburgh trained; they sought arenas in which to demonstrate the more scientific and social view of medicine which set Edinburgh apart from the stagnant Royal College physicians. Many were Dissenters, raised to discipline and respecting health as a means to service. They had both the ability and the incentives to lead and exploit the growing concern with public health.[28]

Many Dispensaries were set up in towns which were too small to support an Infirmary. In larger towns, where Infirmaries were already in place, Dispensaries appeared as separate charities, often because the Infirmary doctors had refused to cooperate, forcing medical 'outsiders' to found their own institutions. Both patterns were seen in the north-west. Lancaster, Kendal, Whitehaven and Workington all gained Dispensaries long before the growing textile towns; perhaps the strength of the Quakers in these districts was significant; certainly we should not forget the Georgian prosperity of the minor west-coast ports. In the larger port of Liverpool, a Dispensary was begun in 1777, quite separate from the Infirmary. Manchester did not follow this pattern. In a development of considerable interest, unique in England, a Dispensary service was built on to the existing work of the Infirmary.

In 1781 a home-patient service was introduced by assistant physicians who had been invited to join the honorary staff to help in the work of their seniors. It was probably Thomas Percival who originated this request, for it came shortly after he had been elected to the honorary staff. He felt overloaded and indeed later resigned so as to have more time for his cultural commitments and large private practice: his colleagues were both old men, who may have been relying on apprentices and the resident apothecary. The four assistant physicians elected were keen to secure their positions as likely successors and they succeeded. The home-patient service might then be seen, as can several other innovations at the Infirmary, as a measure which benefited both the institution and the younger medical men.

The service continued, even after the assistants had become full physicians, but as the Infirmary workload grew during the 1780s, home visiting was increasingly delegated to a paid subordinate, the physicians' clerk.[29]

The late 1770s and early 1780s were unsettled years. Trade was badly disrupted by the war with the American colonies; the new cotton spinning factories which began to appear in the Lancashire countryside attracted suspicion and resentment from local domestic workers. Trade depressions and conditions of factory work moved to the centre of local politics, 'relief' and 'public health' became major concerns of local magistrates and philanthropists.

In 1784, we can already see the seeds of early nineteenth century conflicts. In that year the urban poor of Manchester were so underfed that general relief measures had to be introduced.[30] In the same year Sunday Schools were begun in Manchester to keep working children occupied, to teach them to read and to behave.[31] Again in the same year, after an outbreak of fever in Radcliffe, near Bury, the Manchester Infirmary physicians were called in by local magistrates to investigate the sources of the disease. The workers saw the fever as a product of the hot and humid factory; the doctors were non-commital, but condemned the long hours which children were working; the owner, the elder Robert Peel, resented the interference. In a tense and uncertain society, medical institutions were becoming politicised.[32]

Later in the 1780s the local cotton industry boomed. Throughout Manchester and surrounding towns, new or old buildings were converted into small factories. Men with capital and men with a profession flocked into town; new residential quarters were developed. New chapels and churches were patronised by 'rich sinners' who began to take a conspicuous interest in the poor.[33] The older elite, especially the Unitarians, sought influence as their wealth increased. Their well-educated sons and immigrant professionals met in the Literary & Philosophical Society for 'rational entertainment'. They also took an interest in politics, for Manchester now mattered to the nation. It was against this background of evangelicalism and Dissenting radicalism that we must understand the development of Manchester Infirmary. It became a comprehensive health service because it was politicised – partly by concomitant campaigns on more conventional matters, partly by the recurrence of hunger and fever.

By the 1780s the management of the Infirmary had come to be dominated by the two families of surgeons, the Halls and the Whites. Charles White's son Thomas had joined the staff, first as an assistant surgeon, then as a physician.[34] The Whites and the Halls, as Anglican Tories, were well connected to the town's ruling clique. They also played a role in the new cultural institutions of the 1780s, the Literary & Philosophical Society (1781) and the College of Arts and Sciences. But these new bodies had been founded by and were identified with the opposing faction of the town's elite, the Dissenting Whigs, especially the Unitarians of Cross Street Chapel. Though their access to manorial government was limited, the Whig leaders did have considerable power in the town. For example, Thomas Butterworth Bayley, a Unitarian turned Anglican, was chairman of the Manchester magistrates, and several of the merchant families were rapidly growing very rich. As leaders of campaigns against slavery and for Dissenters' rights, men such as the merchant Thomas Walker could command majority support in the town. The influx of new professionals such as Thomas Cooper (lawyer) and John Ferriar (physician), plus the increasing ambition of men like Walker for local and national reform meant that the Whig elite had acquired a strong radical element by 1790.[35] It was these men who led a campaign for the enlargement of the Infirmary. Given their political principles, their civic and scientific interests and the exclusion of several reformist physicians from the Infirmary staff, their concern with the hospital is not surprising. Nor, given their own position and politics, is it surprising that the Halls and Whites resisted expansion. In the intensely factional atmosphere of 1788–90, the Infirmary became a major focus of local politics. It was, after all, practically the only local institution of real consequence that was 'democratic', at least for subscribers.

The details of the struggle cannot be given here.[36] It began at the end of 1788 when certain noted radicals pressed for the enlargement of the Infirmary staff; after much public debate they were outvoted, but succeeded in renovating the home-patient service by appointing three assistant physicians, two of whom had radical sympathies. In mid-1790 another Dissenting doctor, a recent immigrant who had been paying court to the Infirmary since his arrival, offered to set up a midwifery service.[37]

This further challenge to the Halls and Whites provided another opportunity for the expansionist campaign. A committee which had been set up to examine the finances of the baths was extended to review the workings of the whole hospital, including the size of the medical staff and the care of fever patients. As it became clear that the committee would favour expansion, the honorary surgeons and physicians resigned in an attempt to block reform. The issue came to a head at a large public meeting in September 1790 when the reformers won by 217 votes to 142. Their support came from an increasingly conspicuous group of evangelical Anglican-cum-Methodists, and from the backers of new candidates for the vacant medical and surgical posts.

With the reformers in charge and a new staff elected, the Infirmary service was rapidly developed. The rules were thoroughly revised, the home-patient service was increased, a lying-in service was begun, separate provision was made for in-patients found to have fever, and a new dispensary building was erected to accommodate the out-patients. This expansion proved popular and the list of subscribers grew markedly. The trustees could justly claim 'The late improvements in the Infirmary certainly render it equal, to say the least, in point of utility, to any institution of a similar kind in this kingdom'.[38]

THE INDUSTRIAL REVOLUTION

In 1752 the Manchester Infirmary had been no more than was expected of a rising provincial town. By 1790 it was unique in the scope of its services. Elsewhere, Infirmaries had changed little and Dispensaries were independent; here patients could easily be transferred from one category to another. That might seem the obvious functional requirement, but it was secured only through extraordinary circumstances. Manchester was the first British town to be transformed by industry – hence its wealth and the confidence of its Dissenters, hence too their sensitivity over public welfare and public order. In other towns traditional elites were stronger or the pressures came later, when the English reaction to the French Revolution had practically extinguished bourgeois radicalism.

Notes and references

1. Louis W. Moffit, *England on the Eve of the Industrial Revolution: A Study of Economic and Social Conditions from 1740 to 1760 with Special Reference to Lancashire*, 1925, reprinted London, 1963.
2. W. H. Chaloner, 'Manchester in the latter half of the eighteenth century', *Bulletin of the John Rylands Library*, 42 (1959–60), 40–60.
3. Arthur Redford, *The History of Local Government in Manchester*, vol. I, *Manor and Township*, London, 1939.
4. Thomas H. Bickerton, *A Medical History of Liverpool from the Earliest Days to the year 1920*, London, 1936, Ch. 2.
5. William Brockbank, *Portrait of a Hospital, 1752–1948. To Commemorate the Bicentenary of the Royal Infirmary, Manchester*, London, 1952, Ch. I.
6. On forms of charity see David Owen, *English Philanthropy (1660–1960)*, London, 1965.
7. The manners of Manchester and the social effects of 1745 were well described in John Aikin, *Description of the Country round Manchester*, London, 1795.
8. Rules and Orders of the Public Infirmary at Manchester, 1752, reproduced in W. Brockbank, *Portrait*.
9. On the values of late eighteenth century urban society and especially on the role of science, see Roy Porter, 'Science, provincial culture and public opinion in enlightenment England', *The British Journal for Eighteenth Century Studies*, 3 (1980), 20–46; Arnold Thackray, 'Natural knowledge in a cultural context: the Manchester model', *American Historical Review*, 79 (1974), 672–701.
10. Edward Mansfield Brockbank, *Sketches of the Lives and Works of the Honorary Staff of the Manchester Infirmary from its Foundation in 1752 to 1830*, Manchester, 1904.
11. Joseph F. Kett, 'Provincial medical practice in England, 1730–1815', *Journal of the History of Medicine*, 19 (1964), 17–29.
12. E. M. Brockbank, *Honorary Medical Staff* on Charles White; Jean Donnison, *Midwives and Medical Men*, New York, 1977, and n. 25.
13. John Woodward, *To Do the Sick No Harm: A Study of the British Voluntary Hospital System to 1875*, London, 1974.
14. Brockbank, *Portrait*, ch. I.
15. *Ibid.*, p. 23.
16. *Ibid.*, pp. 21–3.
17. On mental hospitals in Britain see Kathleen Jones, *Lunacy, Law and Conscience, 1744–1845*, London, 1955; William Parry-Jones, *Trade in Lunacy: A Study of Private Madhouses in England in the Eighteenth and Nineteenth Centuries*, London, 1972. On the Manchester Lunatic

Hospitals and Asylum: Nesta Roberts, *Cheadle Royal Hospital: A Bicentenary History*, Manchester, 1967.
18. Andrew Scull, *Museums of Madness*, London, 1979, gives a good account of medical approaches to insanity.
19. Roberts, *Cheadle Royal*, 11.
20. *Ibid.*, p. 29.
21. W. Brockbank, *Portrait of a Hospital*, 26–8; also discussed in Charles Webster, 'The crisis of the hospitals during the industrial revolution', in E. D. Forbes, ed., *Human Implications of Scientific Advance, Proceedings of the XVth International Congress of the History of Science, Edinburgh, August 1977*, Edinburgh, 1978, 214–23. Also C. F. Mullett, 'Public baths and health in England 16th–18th century', *Supplement to the Bulletin of the History of Medicine*, No. 5, 1946, 1–85.
22. See Porter (n. 9) who emphasises the role of previously unorganised doctors in giving a scientific bent to the town's first learned society. Thackray (1974) followed Francis Nicholson, 'The Literary & Philosophical Society, 1781–1851', *Memoirs of the Manchester Literary and Philosophical Society*, *68* (1924), 97–148, in emphasising the importance of medical men.
23. Infirmary Rules, 1752, reprinted in Brockbank, *Portrait*, 207.
24. M. C. Buer, *Health, Wealth and Population in the Early Days of the Industrial Revolution*, London, 1926 (& 1968); Michael Ignatieff, *A Just Measure of Pain. The Penitentiary in the Industrial Revolution*, London, 1978, Ch. 3, largely on John Howard.
25. Charles White, *A Treatise on the Management of Pregnant and Lying-in Women*, London, 1773.
26. There is a very well documented unpublished thesis on Percival: R. B. Hope, 'Thomas Percival: a medical pioneer and social reformer, 1740–1804', MA thesis, Manchester University, 1947. Also see the useful, if dated review by John Fulton, 'The Warrington Academy (1757–1786) and its influence upon medicine and science', *Bulletin of the Institute of the History of Medicine*, *1* (1933), 50–80.
27. Buer, *Health*, 135–6.
28. The puritan's view of the body as an instrument in the performance of duty seems to be of considerable importance if we wish to explain the place and role of Dissenting physicians in this, and other, periods.
29. The development of the Infirmary service from 1780, and the 'revolution' of 1790 are discussed and analysed in detail in John V. Pickstone and Stella V. F. Butler, 'The politics of medicine in the early industrial city; a study of hospital reform and medical relief in late eighteenth century Manchester', *Medical History*, *28* (1984). This paper extends the analysis of Webster (1977) by relating the debate to local political developments.
30. G. B. Hindle, *Provision for the Relief of the Poor in Manchester, 1754–1826*, Manchester, 1975, gives a detailed account of charity and statutory provision, especially in the 1780s and 1790s. I have used this thorough study extensively in my discussion of the period.
31. T. W. Laqueur, *Religion and Respectability: Sunday Schools and English Working Class Culture, 1780–1850*, New Haven, 1976, briefly discusses the origins of the movement and analyses developments in Manchester and Stockport.
32. Pickstone and Butler (n. 29).
33. The work of the Rev. Cornelius Bayley was particularly revealing. See his *Tracts* (Manchester Public Library) and E. A. Rose, 'Cornelius Bayley and the Manchester Methodists', *Proceedings of the Wesley Historical Society*, *34* (1964), 153–8.
34. E. M. Brockbank, *Honorary Staff*, 60–1.
35. On Manchester politics in the 1790s see Archibald Prentice, *Historical Sketches and Personal Recollections of Manchester*, London and Manchester, 1851, reprinted 1970; the rather unsatisfactory Frida Knight, *The Strange Case of Thomas Walker*, London, 1957, and

Pauline Handforth, 'Manchester radical politics, 1789–1794', *Transactions of the Lancashire and Cheshire Antiquarian Society*, 66 (1956), 87–106.
36. See n. 29.
37. The Infirmary Weekly Board minutes reveal William Simmons as a regular attender, though he was not on the staff. Also see Ch. 2.
38. *Manchester Mercury*, 28 June 1791.

CHAPTER 2

Famine, fever, childbirth and the workhouse

The Manchester House of Recovery, 1796 – 1815

'Fever' (typhus) in the later eighteenth century appeared as the major threat to public health in Britain. Fever accompanied overcrowding, in ships, army camps and prisons; it spread in the towns, especially during food shortages. Its appearance in Lancashire cotton towns in 1784, 1788 and 1795 was commonly thought to be a result of the new, large, spinning factories.[1]

Fever patients in Manchester during the 1780s came under the care of the home-patient physicians in the Infirmary, or the physician's clerk; they were not allowed as in-patients. This exclusion raised considerable problems, for fever often appeared among existing in-patients or among those attending the Weekly Boards hoping for admission. A later letter by the Infirmary secretary described the problem:

> It happened very often that in the great number of persons applying for relief, at the Infirmary, many, both in and out patients, were found on examination by their physicians or surgeons, to have feverish complaints, as well as those disorders for which they were recommended, and on that account were by the rules very properly excluded admission as in-patients, tho' the Board was always afraid that the Recommenders not knowing the cause might take offence.
>
> I have been an eye witness to the very distressful circumstances attending these cases; some of the patients being at a great distance from home, perhaps strangers in the town, and destitute of every resource here. The Boards were often at a loss with respect of the manner of dispensing of these pitiable objects. Sometimes we sent them in sedan chairs from the Infirmary to the Workhouse, where their admission was also denied on the same grounds as at the Infirmary. At other times they were conveyed to such lodging houses as could be procured, many of which having been previously receptacles for this sort of persons, were not always free from infection; and too often, when no place could be obtained, they were obliged, when able, in their miserable condition, to seek an asylum for themselves where they were regularly entered in the books and visited by the physicians as home-patients.[2]

Hilton's letter nicely shows how fever presented itself as a problem for the Infirmary, and how institutional and public health problems were bound together. One of the reforms won in 1790 was the provision of a ward for in-patients later found to be fevered; overcrowding in the waiting-rooms was relieved by building a new dispensary; the home-patient service was also improved,[3] and its flexibility was well demonstrated in the famine winter of 1791 – 2. In that year over 2,500 home-patients were visited, twice the annual total for the late 1780s.[4] At this time John Ferriar, who had made a close study of the 1788 – 9 fever outbreak, began to publicise his advice to the Police Committee and to the poor of Manchester, directing attention to the cellar dwellings and the common lodging houses.[5] Cellar dwellings were damp, unventilated and often contaminated; lodging houses were filthy and often contained fever cases. Without better housing the spread of typhus among the poor was inevitable. Ferriar was ready to use the consequent threat to the health of the bourgeoisie to try and force such action as compassion alone should have secured.[6]

One of the apparent reasons for the success of the Infirmary reform had been the new-found interest of evangelicals and Methodists in the condition of the poor. The Methodist interest was institutionalised in 1791 in the Strangers' Friend Society, a charity devoted to searching out and relieving the needy poor who had no claim on local poor rates.[7] This investigation of the condition of the poor was an important part of the brief; the Society's visitors, like the Infirmary physicians, became experts on the poor. Such expertise became crucial as the political and economic climate deteriorated rapidly during the war with France that began in 1793. Since 1784 emergency relief committees had operated in Manchester during famine years. In the 1790s they were joined by these more permanent, expert agencies, including a new Police Commission. In this more complex response to hunger and fever, the fear of unrest showed more and more strongly through the surface of charity.

The collapse of the cotton trade at the end of 1792 led to the formation of the first Manchester Poor Committee, comprised of business men, the managers of the Strangers' Friend Society, and the churchwardens and overseers.[8] They used the new Police Act to solicit subscriptions, and called for charity sermons in the churches. The local elite pointed to this relief work as they sought to reduce political agitation among the unemployed artisans. At the time, Benjamin Booth, 'one of the New Patriotic Society', was being tried for sedition.[9]

During 1795 and 1796, commercial stagnation coincided with exceptionally high grain prices, and increased political repression. The severe food shortages increased the incidence of typhus fever which had been endemic in the poor quarters for some years, and the usual charity fund for the provision of food and fuel to the poor was now directed particularly at the 'Sick Poor afflicted with Epidemic Fever'. A committee set up in December

1794 included the Strangers' Friend Society representatives and took advice from the Infirmary physicians. The committee ventilated and whitewashed houses, and where necessary supplied beds, clothes and food, including fresh meat 'as far as the Funds of the Town would permit'. This last phrase betrays a consciousness of financial restraints; the expenditure of Town monies was being resisted by an association of rate-payers.[10]

Perhaps it was for that reason that the charity had been aimed at the sick poor; certainly the Infirmary Board now took the lead in setting up another relief committee (Jan. – March 1795). The Board believed that many of the poor who requested admission to the Infirmary only wanted and needed food, clothes and fuel. But many became ill 'by being exposed to Hunger and Cold; and ... the Extension of Disease might be essentially lessened by defending them against those Evils'.[11]

The hard winter gave way to a summer of grain shortage, and a new relief committee was set up along similar lines (Oct. 1795 – ?1796). By the end of 1795 the fever was again increasing, and rumours began to circulate about a particularly terrifying 'low contagious fever' in Ashton under Lyne. Ashton, like Bury, was an area in which many new factories had been constructed; in such diffuse, rapidly growing industrial communities, fever was more conspicuous than in the poor quarters of Manchester. Contagion was perhaps more obvious; certainly rumours from Ashton raised fears that Manchester might be subject to the same plague.[12]

The Infirmary physicians, already deeply involved in the relief programmes, now initiated a more specific and technical attack on fever – they pressed for a Fever hospital or House of Recovery. T. B. Bayley, the leading magistrate, chaired a public meeting in December 1795, when a malignant fever raged with great violence in the [poor] house.[13] As a result of the public meeting a Board of Health was set up, including all local magistrates, all the physicians, surgeons and apothecaries of the neighbourhood, the Committee of the Strangers' Friend Society, the leading clergymen and ministers, and many of the leading manufacturers and gentlemen. The reforming physicians had now gained the support of a wider spectrum of middle-class leaders, as poverty, disease and fear increased. During 1796, a year punctuated by food riots and spinners' strikes, the apparatus for epidemic control was set up.

Ferriar, Percival and their associates used their opportunity well. They publicised their views on the social causes of fever; they circulated the opinions of their medical friends in other towns, notably Dr Haygarth of Chester, who had considerable experience of fever; they sent enquiries to notable manufacturers elsewhere, including David Dale of New Lanark. The material they collected remains as a socio-medical source book of international significance, for theirs was the first major response to the emerging health problems of the industrial city. Manchester, which less than fifty years earlier had followed the county towns of agricultural England in building an Infirmary, was now facing unprecedented problems of medical and social order. Its innovations were to guide later practice, even in London. And the chief of these inventions was the Fever Hospital or House of Recovery, opened in three houses near the Infirmary, in May 1796. Haygarth had operated a fever ward in the attic of Chester Infirmary, but Manchester's was the first institution to be set up in this country in order to stem a fever epidemic. It was the embodiment of the theory of infectious disease which dominated progressive medical circles at the time.

To Percival and his medical friends the common fear of the contagion of fever was misguided. The theory that the air was generally tainted, or that any approach to the sick was dangerous, increased apprehension and restricted salutory action. Fear of contagion seemed to be increasing during the 1790s;[14] the Board of Health collected their many reports so as to counter-attack. They claimed that action was possible without strict isolation, because the poison of fever could not, in fact, be propagated over more than a foot or so under conditions of adequate ventilation. Given fresh air and lots of clean water in which to wash clothes, the generation and spread of the contagion could be prevented.[15] Hence the importance of the Fever Hospital, to which patients could be removed from filthy, overcrowded and under-ventilated cellars and lodging houses.

The Fever Hospital was not established without a fight. The owners and occupiers of property near the assigned buildings objected, claiming that the neighbouring inhabitants would be put at risk. They gained the support of the Mosley family and the technical backing of the surgeon Charles White. But this Tory rump was even less successful than the 1790 movement against Infirmary reform. Their alternative proposal was to build a Fever Hospital near the poorhouse, to serve paupers and non-paupers alike.[16] This was too remote and expensive a prospect to have much appeal; the Board of Health deprecated attempts to associate fever victims with paupers; they represented their opponents as motivated by private interest and out of step with best medical opinion; most of all they contrasted the likely salubrity of the new hospital with the fever-ridden lodging houses in the same district. The hospital would not bring contagion to a virgin district, it would be a means of extinguishing the contagion already there.[17]

It was May 1796 before the Fever Hospital was opened. In the first year it admitted 371 patients, of whom forty died. Only seven patients remained in the house by 1797, and the new institution was generally given credit for extinguishing the epidemic and for the relatively low levels of fever over the next few years. Its real effect is difficult to judge, for fever epidemics usually declined with the coming of spring, and not until 1800 – 2 was there another severe food shortage.[18] It is almost impossible to gauge efficacy, because there are no proper standards for comparison; that there appeared to be no cases of infection spread from the Fever Hospital to the Infirmary or to surrounding houses may suggest that the House of Recovery was well-managed.[19]

As far as we can see, the potential patients offered little resistance when it was suggested they should be sent, closed in sedan chairs, to the House of Recovery. Some opposition to a proposed Fever Hospital had been manifest in Ashton, but the Manchester Infirmary physicians, massively experienced in dealing with home-patients, were confident of acquiescence, partly because it was only intended to hospitalise a small proportion of the total fever patients. The first House of Recovery had twenty-eight beds; when it was proposed there were already 178 cases of fever on the Infirmary books; only those from the worst or most overcrowded premises were to be moved.[20]

As we have seen, the history of the Infirmary during the 1790s, and the measures against fever, may be seen as a series of responses to recurrent and intensifying crises. The next came in 1801 when the price of wheat reached three times its level in 1797 – 8.[21] Another major typhus outbreak overloaded the Fever Hospital and put enormous strains on the Infirmary home-patient service, which took almost 5,000 new cases in the year. Arrangements were made to employ temporary assistants to the physicians' clerk,[22] but even so James Jackson, one of the four honorary physicians, complained that he was spending four hours per day on the task, and still was unable to do half of what he ought:

> I have felt it disagreeable in the extreme to be going so much into such dirty cellars, and coming out with my clothes sullied with filth and covered with vermin. Of the imminent and terrible danger attending the office you have lately had a sufficiently alarming proof in the person of one of your Clerks. Finally, the circumstances and conditions of most of the patients preclude almost every chance of my assistance being of material benefit to them.[23]

Jackson temporarily resigned his home-patient duties in protest against the rearrangement of the districts. The physicians collectively pressed for more fever wards to be made available by taking over the Lunatic Hospital. This had become overcrowded and unsuitable and the physicians argued for a new asylum to be built outside the town.[24]

This proposal for more fever wards was opposed by the surgeons, apparently from fear of infecting the Infirmary. It was almost certainly opposed by the powerful treasurer, the industrialist J. L. Philips, and though raised again in 1802 it was rejected. Instead a plan was devised to build a new House of Recovery, completed in 1803, with one hundred beds.[25]

The failure of the expansionist party in 1801–2, after their successes of 1790 and 1796, seems to reflect a hardening of attitudes and the loss of the reforming impetus within the Infirmary. Certainly there were marked contrasts between the patterns of response to crisis shown in the 1790s and those evident in the 1800s.

As we have seen, the fever services in 1795–6 were closely linked to measures of general relief but both the relief and the linkage changed with the century. Relief became standardised in the form of soup kitchens, promoted by the (national) Society for Bettering the Conditions of the Poor and introduced into Manchester in 1799 by the magistrate T. B. Bayley.[26] Initially the Infirmary physicians and their clerks could give patients tickets that entitled them to free soup. But in January 1801 that measure was discontinued, because, it was claimed, the physicians' clerk was spending far too much of his time on the task and that many patients were getting recommendations as out-patients or home-patients simply to gain soup-tickets.[27]

The number of home-patients, which had shown such enormous peaks in the period 1792–1802, remained almost constant for the next decade. This was largely due to the lack of any severe fever epidemic, but the mortality figures for home-patients caution against such a complacent explanation. As the population grew and the price of wheat rose to peak in 1812, the percentage of home-patients dying also rose. In 1808, 27 per cent died, a fact which drew no comment at any Infirmary meetings.[28] This very high figure, over three times the average for 1791–1801 might possibly be a reflection of a severe measles epidemic which affected most large towns in that year;[29] it is certainly a reflection of the limitation of the home-patient service. Not until 1816 did the number of home-patients increase appreciably, even though new arrangements had been introduced in 1810 to extend the geographical limits of the service.[30]

The years of the Revolutionary wars, 1793–1801, had transformed Manchester and its medicine. The Fever Hospital had its roots in the generous civic spirit of the 1790 reforms, but by 1796 the radical element of this reform movement had already been suppressed and the more 'moderate' Infirmary physicians found themselves leading the response to commercial and agricultural crises.[31] Relief and the isolation of fever patients were demanded by charity and a sense of community, but they were achieved in large measure because of fear; free provisions and soup for the necessitous were arguments against working-class radicals; to pay a shilling for information on the first fever case in a neighbourhood[32] was to set spies against

FAMINE, FEVER, CHILDBIRTH AND THE WORKHOUSE

a contagion which also threatened the middle classes. Manchester, which in 1790 had been incredibly prosperous, by 1801 was among the most troubled towns in the kingdom. Treason trials and militia men had become commonplace; medical welfare schemes which once had been ventured in spite of the conservative oligarchy, now gained support as means of defending the socio-economic order; they were the philanthropic, progressive aspect of social control: 'the exercise of their generous feelings may be indulged to their own gratification – to the rescue of the poor from want and disease, and to the support of *civil society* which is always exposed to violent shocks from the presence of temporary scarcity'.[33] The local clergy showed themselves increasingly ready to attribute famine to the impiety of the poor; the middle class became increasingly interested in forming volunteer regiments, only partly as a precaution against invaders. Manchester raised £25,000 in 1797–8 against a possible invasion;[34] a figure which puts into perspective the £500–3,000 sums raised by the various relief committees.

By 1803, when the wars with France resumed after a short peace, the Infirmary authorities felt beleaguered. During the next decade the building was often reported to be full,[35] but there was little hope of any extension. The population (of the parish) which had seemed astonishingly high when the results of the 1801 census were published (102,000), leapt upwards during the peace and then continued to climb to reach 136,000 by 1811. As the demand increased, the average length of stay of in-patients began to fall and the number of in-patients treated crept slowly upward. Inflation meant that each in-patient cost about four guineas, though a subscriber could recommend an unlimited number, provided there was no more than one at any time.[36] By charging a shilling for recommendation forms,[37] by raising the subsistence charge for soldiers and servants,[38] by constantly entreating restraint and careful enquiry into the circumstances of patients,[39] J. L. Philips tried to keep the costs down.

Under these circumstances it was the out-patient service which grew most rapidly. From a peak of 5,500 new admissions in 1793, just after daily sessions had been instituted, the annual number had fallen to little over 3,000 in 1803; thereafter it rose rapidly with the population, exceeding 8,000 by 1815. This curve is closely followed by that of accident cases, treated as emergency cases without recommendations, usually as out-patients, which would suggest that the out-patient curve was due to changing demand rather than constraints on recommendations. Certainly, the relative importance of out- and home-patients changed notably. In the 1790s the average number of out-patients was about twice that of home-patients; roughly equal in crisis years. After 1802 the rise in out-patients meant that the ratio reached 4:1 by 1815.[40]

THE INDUSTRIAL REVOLUTION

During the 1800s the Infirmary was firmly under the control of J. L. Philips, who had become treasurer in 1793. He was one of Manchester's largest manufacturers, a cultivated man who in his youth had been friendly with the local radicals in the Literary & Philosophical Society. He had continued to patronise science and the arts, but had become known chiefly as a fervent loyalist and a commander of the local volunteers.[41] He saw his task at the Infirmary as defensive rather than expansive. He was remarkably diligent in attending almost all Weekly Boards (except when on military duties), but was opposed to extension schemes. In 1801 and again in 1802 he resisted the conversion of the Lunatic Hospital to fever wards;[42] more generally he tried to keep the Infirmary separate from the Board of Health and the House of Recovery;[43] in 1803 he presented a whole series of arguments against changing the rules to admit venereal in-patients.[44]

But these were not the major points of argument during that decade. From 1800 to 1806 and occasionally afterwards, the Infirmary was the scene of recurrent disputes between the honorary medical staff, the salaried medical men and the lay trustees. These disputes frequently erupted in the press, in pamphlets and at General Board meetings. The details are tedious but taken together the disputes are important, and informative. About 1790, Robert Owen, then a cotton mill manager, had seen the leading medical men of Manchester as the local aristocrats;[45] by 1800 their successors at the Infirmary, especially the surgeons, clearly felt that they were being treated like hired hands. They were denied the right to pass judgement on potential house surgeons (1800 and 1804); their 'medical committee' which had met monthly since 1795 was denied official status (1800); they were sensitive about the responsibilities of the house surgeon (1804). In 1804, four of the six surgeons resigned, and were soon replaced.[46]

Because some pamphlets survive with annotations by Philips we can be sure he was not impressed by claims of medical altruism. He regarded the Infirmary surgeons and physicians as self-interested. Philips was convinced that the best interests of the hospital were represented by its lay trustees.[47] Some physicians, notably Ferriar, seem to have accepted this view; but then Ferriar was doubtless accepted by Philips as a cultivated man. So too was P. M. Roget, the author, once a tutor to Philips' sons, and from 1804 to 1808 an Infirmary physician. But Manchester, for its size, had few high status physicians. The repute of Percival and Ferriar may have deterred competitors; more likely the 'horrible, dirty and black town' repelled young gentlemen. Certainly the vast majority of the practice was in the hands of surgeons or Scottish-trained practitioners;[48] those attached to the Infirmary hoped to be treated as public benefactors, they felt themselves treated as employees.

FAMINE, FEVER, CHILDBIRTH AND THE WORKHOUSE

The conflicts were dampened when, after 1804, the posts of house apothecary and house surgeon were separated and limited rights were accorded to the Medical Committee.[49] But resentment continued and gave rise to factional disputes. For such debates and, of course, for elections, subscribers would attend. Otherwise the week to week business was carried on by Philips, regularly aided by Dr Barnes, the Unitarian leader and Roland Broomhead, the liberal and philanthropic Catholic priest.

In 1810, after a short boom in the cotton trade, the Infirmary managed to increase markedly the number of subscribers, and to extend the home-patient service; but Philips finally resigned in 1811, bitter about the failure of his fellow capitalists to take a real interest in the Infirmary. He had been appointed treasurer in the wake of the 1790–2 expansion, when a decade of prosperity had funded a generous elaboration of real services; he had grown narrower and more autocratic as fifteen years of war and trade depression had fixed the Infirmary's place in the class-divided town. As 1812 made clear, the quiescence of the Manchester working class was to be secured, not by the elaboration of medicine and relief schemes, but by the now customary mixture of soup and troops.

The Lying-in Charity, 1790–1815
We have already referred to the reputation gained by the White family as men-midwives, and to the training which Charles White had received from the leading men-midwives of London. Charles White's well-known text on the management of pregnancy was published in 1773, but it was not until 1790 that attempts were made to develop a lying-in charity for poor women, along the lines which had proved so popular in London. There, in 1747, the Middlesex Hospital had arranged a midwifery service for in-patients; the other general hospitals did not follow suit but continued to exclude pregnant women. Instead, a series of special maternity charities were founded over the next thirty years. Most of them were Lying-in hospitals, concentrating on institutional deliveries; some provided midwives and surgical cover for the delivery of poor women in their own homes. The latter were the special analogues of general Dispensaries; in the case of the Westminster General Dispensary, the maternity department was added on to an existing general service.[50]

In Manchester, one of the elements of the Infirmary crisis of 1790 was the offer by William Simmons to develop a midwifery service within that premier medical institution. Simmons was a newly-arrived Scottish surgeon, so this was a direct challenge to the reputation and practice of the White family and their friends the Halls. They reacted by forming a separate lying-in charity of their own. Even before they had resigned their Infirmary positions the new charity was opened, in May 1790.[51] The surgeons had the active support of a few leading citizens, especially John Kearsley; they engaged the interest of the Anglican churches and encouraged the taking of collections on behalf of the new charity; from the beginning they were assisted by the officers of the neighbouring regiments.[52] This loyalist support was sufficient to establish the institution; as it became an accepted part of a spectrum of medical services, so the basis of its support grew; prominent Dissenters began to contribute, chapels to take up collections. The Methodists were collecting by the late 1790s, though not the Unitarians.[53]

The new Charity appealed particularly to female subscribers, partly because it met some of their needs as well as those of poorer women. A register of wet-nurses was kept so ladies could take their choice.[54] The Charity trained midwives, both by lectures and by practice and it offered experience of domiciliary confinement to the male pupils of men-midwives. It also gave board and lodging to women who wished to train as nurse-tenders – private nurses for well-to-do ladies.[55] In all these ways the Charity extended its usefulness, both geographically and socially; it served the larger region and it helped the higher classes on whose support it depended.

Within the strained hierarchy of Manchester medicine, the Lying-in Charity was overshadowed by the Infirmary. Perhaps this was why its medical committee was open not just to its own honorary staff but to any apothecaries who paid subscriptions.[56] In this way the tradesmen of medicine, traditionally subordinated to physicians, could be brought into a mutually satisfactory relationship with surgeon-midwives.

The service offered to the poor was always chiefly domiciliary. Yet from the beginning the activists had also wanted an in-patient facility. They had hoped to buy a building as soon as £2,000 was raised; interim arrangements were made as that target proved unreachable. This first accommodation, a house at Salford Bridge, was given up in 1795 when the Charity purchased a large building intended as a hotel, the Bath Inn, Stanley Street, Salford. This bargain purchase proved to be more than the Charity could afford; it was abandoned in 1813. But in 1795 it had been a mark of confidence in Manchester's second medical institution.

The in-patient accommodation was intended for women who had been deserted or recently widowed or whose homes were unfit for childbirth. To accommodate such women for several weeks[57] around childbirth was expensive, but it gave the Charity an obvious focus and the destitute mothers constituted a more dramatic appeal than the routinely poor. The contrast between the squalor from which they had come, and the wholesome, moral atmosphere of the hospital, could be projected in printed appeals:

FAMINE, FEVER, CHILDBIRTH AND THE WORKHOUSE

May Simcock, whose husband had left her to procure work at Macclesfield, was delivered in a cellar in Elbow St, unassisted and alone, not being able to make her distress known to her neighbours for some time. She and her child lay upon the cold flag floor upwards of half an hour before any assistance could be obtained. She had neither fire, candles, meat, drink nor clothes sufficient to cover herself or the child, having disposed of part of her own, and those she had provided for the child at a pawn-broker's shop, for present subsistence. Clothes were sent from the charity and likewise the slings; by which, with the assistance of two men, she was conveyed to the Hospital, and at the expiration of the third week, she and her child were discharged in perfect health.[58]

The hospital also took in women who were so deformed that labour was bound to be difficult, and a number who came from outside the normal boundaries of the charity. This last provision was an incentive to distant subscribers, but it proved too expensive to maintain.[59] Of eighty women 'received into the House' in 1791–2, twenty-four had been deserted, three had been widowed in pregnancy, nineteen had husbands who were sick or lame; two were wives of prisoners, seven of soldiers, four of apprentices; six women came from beyond the limits, one was travelling by pass (from poorhouse to poorhouse); two wives had consumption. Only one was classed as a difficult labour.[60]

The number of in-patients reached its maximum, 177, in 1799–1800. By then the annual total of home-patients was exceeding 800, and this figure continued to rise (to 1,415 by 1815) as the number of in-patients was reduced. Most of the women delivered at home were attended only by midwives, each selected by the patient from the list of trained midwives attached to the charity. For each delivery the midwife was paid two shillings and sixpence[61] (later three shillings). The midwife was also responsible for presenting the patient to the Weekly Board on conclusion of treatment, though probably a third of the patients were never officially discharged.[62] One can only guess the number who obeyed the injunction to thank the subscriber, and who gave public thanks in their normal place of public worship; these were official conditions for future benefit, but their effectiveness was never discussed.[63]

The Lying-in Charity had its own peculiar relationship to the war effort. We have seen that the local regiments assited in its foundation. When the war against France began and large numbers of Lancashire men were recruited, many pregnant women were left to apply to the Charity for help in childbirth. In 1798 it was claimed that a quarter of the women assisted since 1790 were wives of soldiers, sailors or militia men, and frequent appeals were made to the patriotism of subscribers.[64]

The war may also have strengthened the argument, founded in mercantilist economics, that the strength of the nation depended on the increase in numbers of its inhabitants.

> That end will in some measure be promoted by this species of well-judged charity, for does it not encourage the poor to enter into the married state when they consider, that the person, on whose safety their happiness so greatly depends, will be assisted in the most effectual manner, at the public expense, when the pains of death would otherwise surround her.[65]

But by 1803 the Charity still owed £900 on the building purchased in 1795 and the current funds were in deficit. The use of the hospital by patients from a distance had been curtailed, benefactions were still being used for the payment of expenses, and the management was being threatened with legal action over the debt.[66] By 1806, the Charity had restricted in-patients to six at any time, and in 1811 they decided to admit no more in-patients. For years it had been claimed that the in-patient service, though expensive, was not extravagant, for only mothers whose home situation was intolerable were admitted; but the supporters seemed unconvinced. Bowing to necessity the Charity reminded the public 'that it is the great object of this Institution to afford, at the least possible expense, the necessary professional aid at their own homes, to those who are not in a situation to pay for it'.[67]

The numbers of domiciliary patients increased rapidly; by 1814–15 there were over 1,400 per year. The Charity also vaccinated large numbers of babies; Jenner's cowpox vaccine had replaced smallpox inoculation by 1806, and by 1806 the Charity referred to 'the inestimable benefits of that modern now general practice'.[68] In that year over 2,000 babies were vaccinated but the number tended to fall thereafter.

The Lying-in Charity was purely domiciliary from 1811 to 1850, with but one exception. In 1812 and 1813 the wards were re-opened for the admission of soldiers' wives.

> Great numbers of military men are in town, or encamped in its immediate neighbourhood. They are principally regiments of militia, and many of the men have their wives and families with them. The temporary accommodation, that soldiers can command, are ill adapted to the exigencies of situations such as the Lying-in Hospital provides for, and still less does a camp afford them. These men are here on severe duty as our protectors from the misguided, the lawless and the unprincipled, and well would it become the generosity of the town and neighbourhood to stand forward to make some return to them, by providing for their wives and young children in a point, where even common humanity demands our aid.[69]

It was not only the soldiers' wives who suffered. The poor of Manchester were generally so desperate that on the recommendation of its newly-formed Ladies' Committee, the Lying-in Charity began to supply free gruel and linen to those newly-delivered mothers who were in greatest need. For medical charities to supply food was rare and sensitive, though probably very beneficial. The practice was stopped in 1813, on grounds of economy.[70]

FAMINE, FEVER, CHILDBIRTH AND THE WORKHOUSE

The new Manchester Poorhouse, 1792–1815

By the end of the eighteenth century, many towns of over 10,000 population, and some below, had Dispensaries or Infirmaries. In towns without medical charities and throughout the rural areas, the sick poor had to rely on the Poor Law. In the agricultural south, medical relief was regularised in the form of parish surgeons, paid by case or contract, to attend to the paupers of the parish. In the north, the medical relief appears to have been less common and less organised. Most records of poor relief include monies disbursed by overseers to doctors, or midwives, or for patients sent to distant hospitals, but the parish surgeon contract system developed later than elsewhere. Evidence is thin, but we know that in Blackburn the system was in force before 1820.[71]

Even in the case of Manchester we know relatively little about the medical relief of paupers living at home. In 1815 the 'House Surgeon and Apothecary to the Workhouse and visiting Apothecary to the Out Poor' claimed that his domiciliary work had been increasing rapidly. There is evidence that he visited all the sick paupers who lived beyond the limits of the Infirmary home-patient scheme.[72] Within these limits, paupers seem to have been eligible for Infirmary care, so that charity rather than statutory provision dominated the domiciliary services of the town. That seems to have remained the case until after the introduction of the New Poor Law in the late 1830s.

Generally, medical charities before the 1830s, drew some of their support from the poor rates, and that helped cover the cost of paupers visited. But paupers were not, generally, taken as in-patients, unless special payments were made on their behalf. At the Lying-in Charity, pregnant paupers were excluded unless the township subscribed two guineas annually and agreed to pay three shillings and sixpence a week for the subsistence of the patient.[73]

In general, sick paupers who could not be cared for at home were removed to the sick wards of the workhouse or poorhouse. Poorhouses had developed to accommodate paupers who had nowhere else to go. 'Workhouses' became popular in the eighteenth century, when it was hoped that paupers, by working in this 'house of industry' would both pay for their keep and learn good habits. Kendal, a well-organised town, had a notable workhouse which for a while was run at a profit. But more commonly, work in the poorhouse was a means to discipline the able-bodied, or to deter them from entering.

For most poorhouse inhabitants, the question of work was irrelevant. Many were aged or chronically sick, or unmarried mothers with small children; some were mad or mentally handicapped. It is likely that in the eighteenth century, as for most of the nineteenth, the concentration on the able-bodied pauper helped disguise the extent to which the poorhouses were receptacles for the feeble and the sick.

THE INDUSTRIAL REVOLUTION

The early history of the house of correction and/or poorhouse and/or workhouse in Manchester is obscure, but certainly by 1773 there was a poorhouse in Cumberland Street, off Deansgate, and there were then ninety-two inmates. By 1784 there were proposals for enlarging the workhouse, but no action was taken. Poor Law provision had been a subject of contention in Manchester since at least the 1730s when an ambitious scheme linking a new poorhouse with reform of local government had been blocked by the Tory oligarchy. Between 1784 and 1791 the poor rates had doubled to about £9,000, and the number of inmates had risen to about 200. One can only presume that gross overcrowding forced the churchwardens to provide a new poorhouse. They did so under the Manchester Poor House Act of 1790.[74]

This Act was canvassed locally from December 1789 through to June 1790, when the town was strongly politicised by the Anti-Slavery Campaign and especially by the unsuccessful attempt to repeal the restrictions on the rights of Dissenters. Though certain Dissenters lent their support, the measure was initiated and controlled by the Tory-Anglican faction which operated the Poor Law machinery. By this Act and by the Police Act of 1792 they consolidated their control over the local statutory services,[75] at the same time as the Dissenting radicals had come to dominate the voluntary Infirmary.

The new poorhouse was large and well situated, above the Irk at Strangeways. It cost £4,000, raised by several, large annuities and loans, and was opened in 1793. Though seen as an ornament to the town, the workhouse attracted little close attention. The overseers were lackadaisical and the new building rapidly became 'a mere receptacle of filth, vice and disease'. Some forty years earlier, it had been written of the Manchester workhouse 'He that hath seen this place will never come here till his limbs or his reasons fail him'. The new building was little better until a long campaign led to a much tighter, and tougher, regime after 1808.[76]

Our information about the sick poor is generally scrappy: there was a sick ward in the new poorhouse, the sick received a better diet than the rest, whose food was at times quite inadequate; the house apothecary arranged for the nursing by employing four aged paupers at eight pence per week.[77] But we do have some better information for 1795, the year in which Sir Frederick Eden (or his assistant) visited Manchester during his survey of the country's poor,[78] and the year when Samuel Bamford's father became workhouse master.[79]

The year was one of severe shortages; unemployment was high and many women had been left destitute by husbands joining the services. The cost of poor relief in Manchester set a new record of about £20,000, and because the parochial administration was incompetent and corrupt, there was considerable dispute about this charge.[80] It was also the year of a major typhus epidemic; the poorhouse had no provision for isolating fever patients and many inmates died, including Bamford's mother and uncle; Samuel and his father recovered but during this difficult year, and until 1799, the workhouse was well-managed. When Eden visited, its 319 inmates were mostly old women and children. Bamford later recalled the hard-working tenderness of some of those who attended him in fever, but also the horror which a drunken attendant induced. He also left his memories of the 'apothecary' whose official salary was £25 *per annum*.[81]

> The dispenser of medicine was a little cheerful old man, dressed in black, with thin grey hairs on his head, a white cravat and a dusting of snuff on his waistcoat; his walk was almost a kind of dance, it was so lightsome, and he went tripping round to his patients, as he called them, every morning, with a small saying or a cheerful word for every one. He was a native of London, and had moved there in a respectable mercantile sphere, but being suddenly ruined and abandoned by those on whom he thought he had claims of gratitude, he left the place in disgust of mankind, and almost of life, and having, scarcely knowing how or why, wandered into Lancashire, he took a humble situation in a tea warehouse at Manchester, when, his health failing, he was transferred to the workhouse, and on his recovery became attendant on the physician, and a kind of house apothecary, in which situation, having a small salary and comfortable maintenance, the old gentleman seemed to have become quite happy, and forgetful of his former condition, seldom indeed even alluding to it.[82]

Bamford, as a child, also got to know many of the lunatics in the workhouse: 'Some who were fierce and dangerous towards all others would permit me to approach them, and seemed pleased by my confidence', 'Some unmitigably mad, and untamed as wild beasts'. Others were harmless and allowed to go about the yard; one who imagined himself the Duke of York would play soldiers with Bamford and the pauper boys.[83]

This good order was fragile; it depended on the motivation of honest, unassuming men like Bamford's father. The recollections may be idealised, yet the 'family of poverty' in which behaviour was regulated by accommodations between those who knew each other well, is an attractive if elusive model. The alternatives were more usual: unleavened squalor or the later imposition of a harsh and segregating discipline.

If the wars depressed the contributions to medical charities, they forced massive increases in poor-rate expenditure. In 1790, the charge on the Manchester poor rates, had been about £8,000, roughly the amount of the Infirmary's annual income from 1792 onwards.[84] But while the Infirmary income decreased in years of crisis, the charge on the poor rate increased hugely. We have seen that in 1795 the expense of poor relief topped £20,000; during the Napoleonic wars, in a series of cyclical rises, the annual expenditure rose to almost £60,000 by 1815–16. The accommodation in the poorhouse came to be greatly overcrowded; it had been built for a total of 400–500 inmates; in 1813 the *average* number over the year was 513; 526 in 1816–17.[85]

For the first five years of the renewed war the Poor Law administration and the condition of the house were as corrupt and foul as they had been in the early 1790s. The reform was in large measure attributable to the pamphlet campaign of Thomas Battye, begun in 1794 and continued to 1807.[86] He exposed the miserable diets which the paupers of Manchester were receiving about 1800, and the obfuscation of the death-rates; he revealed gross corruption in the bastardy accounts and in handling monies gained by giving lodging to paupers from other parishes: 'Bed-ridden old women and ... wild lunatics are boarded and taken every care of, at two shilling a week', well below the real cost to the Manchester township.[87]

From 1808, the affairs of the churchwardens and overseers were put in order, and discipline in the poorhouse was increased. From 1810 Manchester local government was dominated by the Tory strong-man Fleming who headed the Police Commission, and by Joseph Nadin, the deputy constable; both were detested by the working class. Whereas in the 1790s[88] most of the inmates had been women, by 1816, at the end of the war, the workhouse contained many able-bodied men. A Mr Waddington, of London, who may have exaggerated the number, claimed to have seen 400 men 'march two by two, in silent and gloomy procession to the workhouse; it was an appalling sight, such as Englishmen should not suffer'.[89] The traditional Tory-Anglican ruling group which had been effectively challenged before the war, at least in the non-statutory areas of medical charity, was firmly back in charge.

Notes and references

1. R. B. Hope, 'Dr. Thomas Percival; a medical pioneer and social reformer, 1740–1804', MA thesis, Manchester University, 1947, pp. 105–25.
2. 'Copy of a Letter from Mr. Hilton addressed to Mr. Meadowcroft, Treasurer for the Board of Health', 1 June 1796. This letter was not included in the *Proceedings of the Board of Health of Manchester* as printed in 1806, but is to be found in a manuscript volume relating to the Manchester Board of Health in the University of London Library, pp. 80–1. Hilton resigned as Secretary at the annual meeting in 1792.
3. *Manchester Mercury*, 28 June 1791, and Infirmary Rules, 1791.
4. Figures from Annual Reports.
5. See J. Ferriar, *Medical Histories and Reflections*, 3 vols., Warrington, 1792–8, esp. I, pp. 218–48; II, pp. 177–214; III, pp. 41–92. J. E. M. Walker, 'John Ferriar of Manchester, MD: his life and work', MSc thesis, UMIST, 1973, is a convenient collection of the material on Ferriar.
6. E.g. *Medical Histories and Reflections*, I, pp. 246–8.
7. G. F. Hindle, *Provision for the Relief of the Poor in Manchester, 1754–1828*, Manchester, 1975, pp. 78–89.

8. Hindle, *Relief*, 111–12; G. W. Daniels, 'The cotton trade during the Revolutionary and Napoleonic wars', *Transactions of the Manchester Statistical Society* (1915–16), 53–84.
9. Hindle, *Relief*, 111–12.
10. *Ibid.*, p. 113.
11. *Ibid.*, p. 114.
12. *Proceedings of the Board of Health of Manchester*, Manchester, 1806; Ferriar, *Medical Histories and Reflections*, III, pp. 43–92. The following passages on the Fever Hospital derive from these two sources, unless stated otherwise. A thorough description is given in Hope (n. 1), 121–60. Also see Charles Webster, 'The crisis of the hospitals during the industrial revolution', in E. G. Forbes, ed., *Human Implications of Scientific Advance, Proceedings of the XVth International Congress of the History of Science, Edinburgh, August, 1977*, Edinburgh, 1978, pp. 214–23. Frank Renaud, *A Short History of the 'House of Recovery' or Fever Hospital in Manchester*, Manchester, 1885, and S. E. Maltby, *Manchester and the Movement for National Elementary Education, 1800–1870*, Manchester, 1918.
13. F. M. Eden, *The State of the Poor*, London, 1797, II, p. 343.
14. Hilton's letter (n. 2) is suggestive of a change of opinion among the Infirmary's medical staff: 'Perhaps they were not then so apprehensive of contagion as it seems they are now'.
15. See for example, the article on 'Contagion' in Abraham Rees, *Cyclopedia or Universal Dictionary of Arts, Science and Literature*, 39 vols, London, 1819. Eighteenth-century theories of fever and contagion require more historical analysis. There is some pertinent material in Margaret Pelling, *Cholera, Fever and English Medicine 1825–1865*, Oxford, 1978.
16. *Proceedings*, 91, and Eden, *Poor*, II, p. 343.
17. *Proceedings*, especially 96–7.
18. The annual returns of the House of Recovery (1796–1817) are given in Dr Holme's evidence in the *Report of the Select Committee appointed to examine the state of Contagion Fever in the Metropolis* ..., 1818, pp. 48–9.
19. *Proceedings*, 184.
20. Ferriar, *Medical Histories and Reflections*, III, p. 44; *Proceedings*, 101–2 and on 126: 'Respecting the objections to the removal of fever patients from their own houses, we wish to observe, that those objects whom the infirmary physicians mean to remove, will be found very willing to exchange their situations. At Ashton there is no hospital, and the poor have a sense of nicety, even on the subject of relief from the parish, which does not subsist in Manchester.'
21. Daniels (1915–16), Appendix.
22. For example, Weekly Board, 11 May 1801.
23. Letter of James Jackson, Weekly Board, 28 September 1801. It was common for physicians' clerks to contract 'fever'; in several cases the clerk died.
24. Weekly Board, 7 September 1801; Quarterly Board, 24 September 1801; Special General Board, 2 December 1802. (F. Renaud in his *Short History of the Rise and Progress of the Manchester Royal Infirmary*, Manchester, 1898, conflates the events of 1801 with those of 1802.)
25. *Ibid.*, and *Proceedings of the Board of Health*.
26. Hindle, *Relief*, 90–104.
27. Weekly Board, 19 January 1801.
28. It was the thesis of Mrs Rita Darling which first drew my attention to these figures: 'The role of the medical profession in Manchester, 1790–1815', BA, Manchester University, 1977.
29. Charles Creighton, *A History of Epidemics in Great Britain*, 2 vols, London, 1891–4, reprinted 1965, II, ch. 2.
30. Quarterly Board, 27 September 1810.
31. On the overt repression in Manchester, including Walker's trial, see Frida Knight, *The Strange Case of Thomas Walker*, London, 1957. Also Hope (n. 1), p. 134 who notes that

Percival had been overshadowed by Ferrier in the fever campaigns of 1790–4. V. A. C. Gatrell, 'The commercial middle class in Manchester, c. 1820–57', PhD thesis, Cambridge University, 1972, gives an excellent account of the radicalisation and suppression of the 'Lit. & Phil.' elite, esp. pp. 190–7.
32. Propositions submitted by Dr Percival, 13 April 1796, to the Board of Health, *Proceedings*, 108–10.
33. Hindle, *Relief*, 121.
34. *Ibid.*, p. 119.
35. Annual Report, 1802, 1807; Weekly Board, 1 April 1805, 31 August 1807.
36. See the correspondence with Sir Oswald Mosley, Weekly Board.
37. Weekly Board, 27 April 1801; Annual Board, 18 June 1801.
38. Quarterly Board, 22 March 1798.
39. For example, Annual Report, 1798.
40. Figures from Annual Reports.
41. F. J. Faraday, 'Selections from the correspondence of Lt.-Colonel John Leigh Philips, of Mayfield, Manchester, Pt. I', *Memoirs of the Manchester Literary & Philosophical Society*, 4th ser., *3* (1890), 13–54, also Pt. II (by W. B. Faraday), *44* (1900), 1–51.
42. See n. 25.
43. Quarterly Board, 22 December 1803.
44. *Ibid.*
45. Quoted in M. C. Buer, *Health, Wealth and Population in the Early Days of the Industrial Revolution*, London, 1926 (& 1968), p. 122.
46. Renaud, *Infirmary* (1898) gives sufficient detail.
47. The Infirmary and Manchester Public Library and Manchester Medical Library have collections of the various pamphlets, some of which are discussed briefly in W. Brockbank, *Portrait of a Hospital, 1752–1948*, London, 1952, and in Rita Darling's thesis (n. 28). Note specially, James Jackson, *A Letter to the Trustees of the Manchester Infirmary, Dispensary, Lunatic Hospital and Asylum*, Manchester, 1804 (Public Library copy).
48. D. L. Emblen, *Peter Mark Roget: The Word and the Man*, London, 1970, pp. 64, 90.
49. (Published) *Report of the Committee*, 17 December 1804.
50. Buer, *Health*, 141–4; J. Donnison, *Midwives & Medical Men*, New York, 1977, pp. 25–8; M. C. Versluysen, 'Midwives, medical men & 'poor women labouring of child': lying-in hospitals in eighteenth century London', in Helen Roberts, ed., *Women, Health & Reproduction*, London, 1981.
51. The Lying-in Charity became St Mary's Hospital and has been chronicled in two books: J. W. Bride, *A Short History of the St. Mary's Hospitals, Manchester*, Manchester, 1922, and J. H. Young, *St. Mary's Hospitals Manchester, 1790–1963*, Edinburgh, 1964.
52. See the early minutes from the Weekly and Quarterly Boards (at St Mary's Hospital).
53. Annual Reports.
54. Annual Reports, 1791, 1801.
55. *Ibid.*
56. Annual Report, 1793.
57. No figures are given for duration of stay, but from a sample of patients named in the 1791–2 Weekly Boards, it appears that domiciliary patients usually remained on the books for six to fourteen weeks.
58. Annual Report, 1792.
59. Annual Report, 1801.
60. Annual Report, 1792.
61. Calculated from statistics in Annual Report 1791. In 1790–1, twenty-eight of 135 patients were also attended by surgeons. Also see Quarterly Board, 19 June 1812.
62. Rule 24, 1790. Comparing the lists of patients admitted and discharged in 1791–2 with the figures in the Annual Report, it seems that about a third of the domiciliary patients were not officially discharged.

63. Rule 15, 1790.
64. Annual Reports, 1798 and 1800.
65. Leaflet in Manchester papers, 26 January (1796?) bound with the Annual Reports (St Mary's Hospital).
66. Annual Reports, 1801, 1803, 1804.
67. Annual Report, 1813.
68. Annual Report, 1804, 1806.
69. Annual Report, 1812.
70. Quarterly Board, 19 June 1812, 25 June 1813.
71. See the discussion below of the foundation of Blackburn Dispensary in 1824 which was partly based on the previous Poor Law service.
72. Letter from Henry Dadley to the Weekly Board, 20 January 1815, Manchester Poor Law Papers (Manchester City Archive M/3/4/2B). I owe this reference to Hindle's book. Also see *Manchester Guardian*, 27 April 1827, Report of Infirmary election, speech in favour of Mr Whatton.
73. Lying-in charity, Rule 47, Annual Report, 1800.
74. Hindle, *Relief*, 26–7.
75. The 1792 Act is discussed, in the context of post-Revolutionary repression in Gatrell, 1972, 195–6.
76. Hindle, *Relief*, 28–9.
77. *Ibid.*, p. 49.
78. Eden, *Poor*, II, pp. 342–59.
79. Samuel Bamford, *Early Days*. I used the Dunckley edition (which also includes *Life of a Radical*), 2 vols, London, 1893, I, Chs. 5–8.
80. Hindle, *Relief*, 68.
81. Eden, *Poor*, II, p. 354.
82. Bamford, *Early Days*, 70–1.
83. *Ibid.*, pp. 73–5.
84. Hindle, *Relief*, 68.
85. Figures are given in J. Aston, *A Picture of Manchester*, Manchester, 1816. J. Wheeler, *Manchester: Its Political, Social and Commercial History*, Manchester, 1836, pp. 331–2; Daniels (1917–18), Appendix III.
86. Hindle, *Relief*, 53–76.
87. *Ibid.*, p. 69.
88. A. Redford, *The History of Local Government in Manchester*, I, Manchester, 1939, especially 240–75; Gatrell (1972), 191–7.
89. Hindle, *Relief*, 41.

CHAPTER 3

Medical charities in the industrial city: Manchester, 1815 – 34

The appearance of industrial society
The end of the Napoleonic wars gave occasion for national rejoicing and for boosting the funds of medical charities, but it did not bring prosperity. Severe shortages continued until the end of the decade; working-class radicalism which had grown up covertly during the wars now became overt. In 1817 the 'Blanketeers' marched from Manchester attempting to bring their grievances to the attention of metropolitan government. In 1819, at St Peter's Field, an assembly of the working class was charged by the local volunteer cavalry; the massacre of Peterloo was to echo through the class struggle of the next thirty years.

The early 1820s were prosperous and political tensions lessened. Manchester grew at an astonishing rate as young people came to work in factories that now housed power-looms as well as spinning mules. For a while, the economy could also support hand-loom weaving, but in 1826 came the first great commercial collapse and there were riots in several Lancashire towns. The economy remained depressed through the political and health crises of 1831 – 2. Though the mid-1830s saw a short boom, commercial difficulties returned and persisted through most of the 1840s.

It was during the 1820s and 1830s that Manchester became the paradigmatic industrial city; the many surviving descriptions by British and foreign visitors demonstrate its central place in contemporary visions of economic and social change. Of these visitors, Alexis de Tocqueville was perhaps the most incisive. He saw the contrast between the technical prowess of Manchester's industrialists and the subjection of its working class.

> Look up and all around this place you will see the huge palaces of industry ... These vast structures keep air and light out of the human habitations which they dominate; they envelop them in perpetual fog; here is the slave, there the master; there the wealth of some, here the poverty of most; ... Here the weakness of the individual seems more feeble and helpless even than in the middle of a wilderness; here the effects, there the causes.[1]

Between the censuses of 1821 and 1831 there was a 47 per cent increase in the population of Manchester, Salford and suburbs – from 162,000 to 238,000 – while the population of England and Wales as a whole rose only 16 per cent. The growth was especially dramatic in the outer parts of Manchester's township and in adjacent townships where new industrial districts were bordered by middle-class residences. The census district which included Ancoats was barely inhabited in the 1790s; it housed 21,000 people in 1821; 32,000 in 1831. Immediately to the south, Ardwick was still a genteel suburb.

The township of Chorlton Row, which in 1801 had only 675 inhabitants, had 8,000 in 1821 and 21,000 in 1831.[2] It contained several very large factories, some owned by the Birley family, and the great bulk of its inhabitants were factory workers. But to the south of the township, around All Saints Church (1820) was a series of 'spacious well-formed streets, inhabited by those who carry on business nearer the [cotton] Exchange, or by those who live independent of trade'.[3] Similar developments were taking place in Salford, parts of which were favoured as residential districts by major industrialists, while other parts were compounded of factories and poor housing.

Such is the essential economic, social and geographical background for the study of medical services. Medical charities linked the subscribing of the middle class to the suffering of the working class as these class differences grew deeper and more self-conscious. In medical charities we can see middle-class images of their supposed inferiors; we can also see the indisputable misery of much of the working population.

The medical charities of the city centre continued throughout the period, but generally grew much more slowly than the population they served. The Infirmary was enlarged in the 1820s but not before its condition had deteriorated substantially. The Lying-in Charity continued as a domiciliary midwifery service. New institutions arose, both centrally and in the suburbs – both kinds evidence of differentiation within a larger and more complex community.

The new central institutions were specialist charities and medical schools, set up by young doctors of good education seeking to make a mark in an increasingly crowded profession. The suburban institutions were Dispensaries, set up by middle-class groups in the new residential districts. Their supporters were often members of the Select Vestries of the suburban townships, responsible for poor relief in some of the newer working-class districts; the Dispensaries reproduced this pattern at the level of charity. For the middle class Dispensaries were a way to local influence; for many doctors a first honorary post which might lead to an Infirmary career. At the Infirmary, home-visiting had long been a chore for paid juniors. The new suburban

Dispensaries once again brought independent practitioners into regular and intensive contact with the sick poor. It is to these doctors that we owe much of our knowledge of the new industrial working class.

Overcrowded professionals and overcrowded patients
The number of medical men in Manchester increased very rapidly in the years after the wars. In 1815 there were fifty-one practitioners advertised as physicians, surgeons and/or apothecaries in the *Manchester Directory*; by 1820 there were seventy-eight, and by 1825, 122. Over this decade, though the population of Manchester and Salford rose by about 40 per cent, the population to doctor ratio fell from about 2,500 to about 1,500. For comparison, in 1959, the average list for a general practitioner was 2,270.[4]

We lack the data to show how typical Manchester's experience was, but other Lancashire towns show similar ratios and a similar fall in the patient/doctor ratio in the early part of the century. In Liverpool, where the number of practitioners increased from sixty to ninety between 1815 and 1821, the ratio fell from 1,700 to 1,200. In Leeds, then a much smaller city, the ratio only fell from 2,600 to 2,300.[5] One reason for this increase was the return of army surgeons; another was the large increase in medical students during the 1820s. We learn something of the immediate post-war pressures from the filling of the post of workhouse surgeon in Manchester in 1816. The job involved the care of the sick poor in the workhouse plus visiting the out-door sick beyond the area served by the Infirmary. There were seventy-two candidates.

For young men establishing practices in Manchester around 1815 there were few institutional aids to professional advancement. None of the Infirmary staff appeared close to retirement; the Lying-in Charity had recently abandoned its in-patient accommodation and was trying to find a cheaper building. In these circumstances, two of the surgeons newly settled in Manchester took the initiative in founding two specialist charities, the Eye Institution and the Lock Hospital.

Special hospitals had been pioneered in London in the eighteenth century; a few more were established there and in other cities during the wars with France. The first Eye Infirmary in England was founded in 1805 in London by J. C. Saunders, a surgeon, partly because of a severe epidemic of purulent ophthalmia which had particularly affected soldiers. Saunders' Infirmary admitted medical students from 1811, and thus developed a group of surgeons who claimed particular expertise in the treatment of eye diseases. One of Saunders' pupils began a similar institution in Exeter; another, William James Wilson, in 1818, initiated the Manchester Institution for Curing Diseases of the Eye, which was to develop into the Manchester Royal Eye Hospital.[6]

Wilson had grown up in Leeds, and was apprenticed in Lancaster and Chester before studying in several London hospitals. He took his Membership of the Royal College of Surgeons and in 1813 settled in Manchester. In the following year he interested several manufacturers and merchants in the possibility of setting up an Eye Institution. This proposal was put to a public meeting held in October 1814. Officials were appointed, notably Benjamin Wilson, calico printer, as treasurer; a house in King Street was rented; and in the first year almost two thousand patients were treated as out-patients.[7]

The Manchester Eye Institution is a classic illustration of the place of special medical charities in early nineteenth-century England. Unlike general hospitals and Dispensaries, special institutions were almost always promoted by doctors, usually young men whose particular expertise offered them the chance of by-passing the queue of aspirants of honorary appointments in general hospitals. In special hospitals trustees were seen as facilitating the work of the medical men, whereas, as we have seen, the situation at the Infirmary was sometimes held to be the converse.

That the Infirmary resented Wilson's initiative was made clear in their minutes, when the Weekly Board rebutted any suggestion that they were failing or would fail to meet the demands of eye cases. Not surprisingly, Wilson's earliest links seem to have been with the Lying-in Charity rather than the Infirmary: John Hull, physician to the Lying-in Charity, was appointed to a similar post in the Eye Institution; Wilson himself soon became a surgeon at the Lying-in Charity. The other medical man at the Eye Institution, Dr Ward, had resigned from the Infirmary in the dispute of 1804. Nonetheless, the Infirmary did eventually come to recognise Wilson's merits; he joined its honorary staff in 1827.[8]

The establishment of the Eye Institution reflected the dispersion of Manchester civic life which had taken place during the wars and was evidenced as soon as the wars drew to a close. The proliferation of religious congregations, especially those of the Methodists and Congregationalists, was probably the major expression of this dispersion, but it was soon manifested in many fields. Rather than fight their way into the major civic institutions, new men wanting to make a mark, found it easier to begin groups or societies of their own. The growing middle class was becoming multi-nucleate.

The Manchester Lock Hospital, for the treatment of venereal diseases, began in 1818.[9] Again we are dealing with a group of patients whose needs were rather neglected; again the impetus came from a young surgeon, in this case Joseph Jordan. Jordan was not an immigrant, he had been apprenticed to the Infirmary, indeed he had there been reprimanded for hanging about the nurses' kitchen;[10] but he chose to advance his career through independent institutional initiatives, of which the Lock Hospital was one. In this case, as in the Eye Institution, Quaker philanthropists were prominent: David Holt, a manufacturer, played a similar role to William Fox, the banker. In both cases, aristocrats were persuaded to become (decorative) officers.

The Lock Hospital was not a threat to the Infirmary, which had consistently refused to take venereal cases as in-patients. Its patients were too offensive to be fought over, and the Lock Hospital had to struggle against the common feeling that the patients deserved their sufferings. It began with a few beds and many out-patients, it was regularly in financial difficulties, but it survived. By the late nineteenth century, a softening of public attitudes to prostitution and a number of large legacies eased its position; but like all Manchester hospitals, it was constantly faced with increasing demand from an ever-growing population.[11]

When Joseph Jordan helped found the Lock Hospital he was already well known as a teacher who had opened Manchester's first anatomy school. He had returned to Manchester in 1812 after studying in Edinburgh and London, and spending five years as a surgeon in the Royal Lancashire Militia. He was briefly in partnership with two Manchester practitioners, one of whom later helped him found the Lock Hospital. Then in 1814, as the country adjusted to peace, Jordan advertised his new Anatomy Rooms.[12] Anatomy teaching, like special hospitals, was a means to a career in medicine; both reflected critical changes in the structure of the medical professions.

Formal lectures as a means of supplementing a surgical apprenticeship had been growing in importance from the mid-eighteenth century. At the time of the Manchester Infirmary's foundation, Charles White could boast of his attendance at William Hunter's lectures in London; William Simmons, to whom Jordan had been apprenticed at the Infirmary, had earlier spent two winters studying with John Hunter, William's younger and even more famous brother.[13] The business of the London anatomy schools had increased greatly during the wars because of the demand for military surgeons, but residence in London was expensive and many northern parents feared for the morals of their sons. Jordan saw his chance to extend the anatomy business to the provinces.

He did so as parliament was considering proposals which became the Apothecaries Act of 1815. This Bill failed to meet the wishes of the general practitioners who had been its chief promoters, for it left midwifery and surgery unregulated, and allowed druggists to continue to undercut the charges of apothecaries. It also raised problems about the qualifications for practice of those general practitioners who were in fact the best educated, those with Scottish degrees. By strengthening the rights and privileges of the London Society of Apothecaries it tended to perpetuate the old divisions of the medical hierarchy which had been substantially eroded in provincial practice during a quarter century or more. Even so, the Act was the first to require aspirant medical practitioners outside London to provide evidence of a completed apprenticeship, attendance for six months in a public hospital or dispensary, and attendance at medical lectures.[14]

Before 1815 many Infirmaries, including Manchester's, had progressively increased the formal qualifications required for paid resident staff and for honorary staff. Such qualifications had not mattered much in the mid-eighteenth century, but as the city and medical competition grew, as medical men arrived as strangers to make careers, qualifications began to count. In 1797, J.L. Philips had reminded an aspirant honorary physician that

> ... it would be extremely unpleasant to liberal men to be at any time under the necessity of co-operating with men of no respectability, who in a populous neighbourhood like this might possibly find means to foist themselves into practice, or at least into society to which they have no pretensions.[15]

A few years later the qualifications of the house surgeon and house apothecary were the subject of a major dispute.[16]

Jordan's school provided the first formal medical education in the English provinces. The Manchester Literary & Philosophical Society had tried to sponsor a College of Arts & Sciences in 1783, and that included some medical lectures. Occasional lectures had been given later, for example by the Whites in 1787–9, Roget and Gibson in 1805–7 and Ainsworth and Ransome from 1811 and in 1815–16.[17] The students were the apprentices of local surgeons and the pupils of the physicians, plus those apprenticed to the Infirmary and under the supervision of the resident staff. About ten apprentices and pupils were attached to the hospital in 1803, others paid to see ward rounds, others were attached to the Lying-in Charity. The Infirmary had a large library which apprentices and pupils could use, albeit under increasingly severe restrictions.[18] The Lying-in Charity had taken Charles White's extensive anatomy museum and that provided material for some lectures.[19] But until 1814, anyone wanting systematic lectures had had to go to London.

Jordan's 'School of Anatomy' proved successful, and from 1821 his certificates were accepted as evidence of instruction in anatomy and surgery under the Apothecaries Act; Wilson, in 1821–2, was the lecturer in surgery. Success encouraged imitation and in 1824, Thomas Turner, from 1817 to 1820 the house surgeon of the Infirmary, opened a course on anatomy, physiology and pathology at the rooms of the Manchester Literary & Philosophical Society. Soon afterwards he acquired his own lecture theatre in

Pine Street and began to develop a 'preparatory school of medicine and surgery'. In turn Jordan collected a group of lecturers and expanded his own school. A third school, in Marsden Street was opened in 1829 by some of Jordan's former colleagues. So was established the pattern of nineteenth-century provincial medical education: proprietary schools run by local practitioners, competing for students, more or less closely associated with the local Infirmary. The students usually qualified through the Society of Apothecaries or the Royal College of Surgeons; the more ambitious moved on to the hospital schools of London.[20]

The core of the education was anatomy, especially the dissection of human corpses, and in the early 1820s both Jordan and Turner boasted of the facility with which corpses could be obtained in Manchester; Jordan was said to supply bodies to Edinburgh and London. But by the late 1820s, even in Manchester, bodies were expensive and grave-robbing common. Seventy to eighty students were then restricted to about fifty bodies a year.[21]

Dissection was, for Jordan, an almost religious activity; the mastery of the corpse was the hallmark of a good practitioner. The body rather than the discursive patient was becoming the real object of medicine. In Manchester, this attitude was established by men like Jordan, Wilson and Turner who had come to prominence in the years after Waterloo. All were from definitely middle-class backgrounds, sons respectively of a Manchester calico printer, a Leeds solicitor and a Truro banker; all were ready to begin their own institutions – schools and special medical charities; all by doing so established a new route to the Infirmary, relying less on the approbation of a cultured elite than on a reputation among the town's practitioners. All three were active in the Provincial Medical and Surgical Association after its foundation in 1832. Thus new professional forms were developed alongside a new form of medical knowledge. Jordan was a regular visitor to Paris, where such attitudes had developed rapidly following changes wrought by the Revolution in the control of medical education and hospitals.[22]

The hospitals of England experienced no revolutionary change, but here too the new attitudes took root. Dissection, in hospitals and in medical schools, became controversial as young doctors came to see mastery of the corpse as part of their professional identity. In Manchester, in 1818, the house surgeon of the Infirmary was reprimanded for dissecting the body of a girl patient without the parent's permission. Joseph Jordan had been guilty of a similar offence when a military surgeon in Kidderminster; his anatomy school in Manchester was frequently the object of public suspicion.[23]

Many working-class Mancunians, and perhaps especially the Irish immigrants, saw the institutions of medicine as a threat; part of the machinery of exploitation. In 1819, after Peterloo, the Infirmary was the subject of a propaganda campaign by the radicals. It was alleged that the Infirmary beds had been emptied before the massacre, in anticipation of injuries, and that one of the injured demonstrators had been refused treatment. The authorities found no truth in these claims, but their propagation alone is evidence of working-class hostility towards the hospital.[24]

Peterloo was a major political landmark of the Industrial Revolution; decades of harsh repression had failed to contain political unrest. From the early 1820s, in Manchester and elsewhere, middle-class radicals re-appeared to argue for more liberal policies.[25] Their major concern was trade and local political representation; in that they resembled their predecessors around 1790. As in the previous generation, attempts were made to develop the Infirmary, but these were now weaker and much less successful. The hospital became increasingly overcrowded during the 1820s but new buildings were minimal and late; proposals to extend the service were easily defeated.

Though the population serviced by the Infirmary increased very rapidly between 1815 and 1825, the number of out-patients and in-patients hardly changed, and there was no overall increase in home-patients until the crisis of 1826. There was, however, an increase in the number of accident cases; these rose in the later 1810s from about 1,200 to 2,200, then again from 1825. This increase put more and more pressure on the Infirmary, since many of the accidents were serious and could not easily be turned away. Because accident cases were admitted without a subscriber's recommendation, the numbers were more independent of the total monies subscribed.

The increase in the number of accident cases shifted the balance of the Infirmary towards surgical work and there was a corresponding increase in the mortality of in-patients; this rose from about 3 per cent in the early 1810s to about 6 per cent in the early 1820s. By 1820 the medical and surgical staff were asking for a new and larger operating theatre. In 1823 erysipelas was rife and a sulphur fumigation apparatus was purchased in an attempt to stem this characteristic 'hospital disease'. In 1824, the Quaker surgeon, J. A. Ransome (1779–1837) complained of the shortage of accommodation and the fact that many urgent cases were being refused admission. The trustees agreed to extend the premises to provide another sixty beds, but even after several years of prosperity, the money proved difficult to raise and there were complaints about the Infirmary encroaching on adjacent land. The plan had included elaborate porticoes and stone-facing; these ornamentations were abandoned as the appeal fell short of its target, £7,000.

By 1828 the building had been remodelled and extended to include a reception room for accidents and better domestic accommodation. The total number of beds was now 178, 110 for males and sixty-eight for females, 108 for surgical cases and seventy for medical. Most of the wards were small;

for example the thirty-seven surgical beds for females were contained in five wards, the largest of ten beds and the smallest of four. No ward appears to have taken more than thirteen of the beds which were now made of iron rather than wood. There were nine nurses regularly employed during the day: one for the thirty-one female medical beds and one for the thirty-nine male medical beds; the surgical cases required more attention, two nurses attended the thirty-seven female beds and four nurses (one of them male) the seventy-one male surgical beds. On average then, a nurse would probably have been responsible for one larger and two smaller wards.[26]

The additional sixty beds were fully utilised by 1830. The number of accidents increased rapidly about then. In 1833-4 over 4,000 such cases were seen at the Infirmary, and 542 were admitted, about a third of the total in-patients. Many of these were serious factory accidents and they were the cases which impressed visitors: 'So we saw feet torn off from legs, and arms severed from bodies, and hands literally crushed, and heads laid open to the brain'.[27] Manchester was known for 'factories, schools, churches, chapels, hospitals' and for cultural societies: the hospitals were seen, in part, as the necessary complement to the factories.

The expansion of the Infirmary buildings was accompanied by a dispute about extending the honorary staff, an issue which, as in 1788-90, appears to have been a question of party. In February 1827 an election for the paid resident junior post of physician's clerk annoyed the local reformers. Their candidate lost to a Manchester youth, in spite of apparently better qualifications. The *Manchester Guardian*, the newly established Liberal organ, regretted that 'there should have been any circumstances tending to make it appear that the votes of any of the trustees were determined rather by personal than by public motives'.[28] Soon afterwards Thomas Harbottle, a Salford mill-owner and Presbyterian (whose mill was to be burned down in the unrest of 1829), proposed to the Weekly Board that the honorary staff be increased. The retired physician and well-known Tory, Dr S. A. Bardsley, tried to block the move but failed and the issue was referred to a special meeting. In the meantime came an election for a vacant post of honorary surgeon, one of the most intense contests in the history of the Infirmary.[29]

It was then fifteen years since the last surgical vacancy; in the interim many surgeons had established themselves, including Wilson at the Eye Dispensary, Jordan and Turner in their medical schools, and John Roberton recently appointed a surgeon to the Lying-in Charity. At least eleven surgeons expressed interest and advertised for support and seven persisted to the election, though at least two of the seven did not canvas. Almost 700 people voted in the election, which was held in the dining room of the Cotton Exchange and was overcrowded past the point of confusion. In spite of claims that he would be more useful remaining at the Eye Dispensary, Wilson was elected with 321 votes. His proposer was Francis Philips, then notorious as the defender of the Peterloo magistrates and a major supporter of the Stockport Dispensary. He argued that the appointment of Wilson would encourage auxiliary charities in the hierarchy of Manchester medicine.[30]

The proposal to increase the staff was taken up in the following week. Again it was opposed by Samuel Bardsley who argued that six physicians and six surgeons was plenty, even though the work-load was increasing; when the staff had been increased to twelve in 1790 there had been insufficient work, surgeons had regretted the sparsity of major operations; Bardsley, with Ferriar and Holme had easily handled the home-patients, even during epidemics. Though a committee was appointed, no increase in staff took place.[31]

One of the suggestions of the expansionists had been that the Infirmary should establish branch Dispensaries in Salford and Ancoats. Instead these Dispensaries, like the earlier one in Chorlton on Medlock, were set up as independent institutions. It is to their development and to the medicine of the new industrial suburbs that we now turn.

The spread of charity: the Dispensaries in the Manchester suburbs in the late 1820s

The growth of industrial and residential suburbs in and around the old township in Manchester raised obvious problems for the central medical charities. Not only were there more potential patients, many of them lived beyond the limits of convenient house-visits. Since 1810 the Infirmary had operated a system under which those patients who lived beyond the town centre were visited only by the physicians' clerks: two junior, salaried and resident practitioners.[32] In 1820 the Lying-in Charity extended its area to include Hulme, Chorlton Row, Ardwick, Miles Platting, Collyhurst and much of Salford. To do so they appointed three men-midwives to the out-districts (in addition to the ordinary men-midwives) and also increased the number of female midwives.[33]

But these arrangements did not satisfy the ruling groups in the surrounding townships, where the population was increasing very rapidly. In 1825 the leading citizens of Chorlton Row, to the south of central Manchester, began to consider forming a Dispensary. The immediate stimulus appears to have been a fever epidemic in 1825, which, no doubt, particularly affected the Irish immigrants crowded in the low-lying areas by the River Medlock. This was probably an instance of a more general pressure on the Chorlton Select Vestry, the body responsible for the administration of the Poor Law within the township. The Select Vestry, which included all the leading ratepayers,

[51]

probably devised the scheme for a Dispensary; the Vestry would make a contribution, as payment for medical care of paupers, but the Dispensary would also be supported by subscribers who could refer non-paupers. The Dispensary in Blackburn, founded the previous year, had certainly begun as an extension of the parish surgeon's work, and the largest mill-owners in Chorlton, the Birleys, had strong business connections with Blackburn. Hugh Hornby Birley, who had led the charge of cavalry at Peterloo, was the first President of the Chorlton Dispensary.[34]

In October 1825 an approach was made by the Township to the Infirmary, but the Board felt unable to take on any further commitments; they were still trying to raise funds to extend the Infirmary building and they thought the home-patient districts were already large enough to tax all the resources of the professional staff.[35] After this refusal, the ministers, overseers and leading citizens of Chorlton called a meeting and decided to start their own Dispensary. It was another institution to set alongside the several churches and chapels in the township; soon it was housed in the classical Town Hall which followed the Chorlton Improvement Act of 1832. At about the same time, a separate Dispensary was founded in the adjacent township of Hulme, a very small institution from which no records have survived.[36]

When, in 1827, the expansion of the Infirmary was again discussed, the possibility was raised of opening branch Dispensaries in Ancoats and in Salford. Again it was decided that any such institution had better be independent of the Infirmary.[37] Very soon thereafter the Salford and Pendleton Dispensary was founded, under the presidency of Mr William Garnett of Lark-hill, a gentleman who was to be the repeatedly unsuccessful Tory candidate for the Salford seat after the parliamentary reform of 1832. The Boutflower family of surgeons provided members of the honorary staff over several decades; they were Tory Anglicans related to major Dispensary supporters in both Bolton and Bury.

Economically and socially Salford was a suburb of Manchester, but politically it was an independent borough with its own ruling group and its own administrative system. Many of the richest manufacturers of the conurbation lived within its limits and interested themselves in its affairs. Hence it proved relatively easy to raise money for a new institution. In 1830 the foundation stone was laid for a purpose-built Dispensary which was also intended to supply some in-patient accommodation. But money proved difficult to raise and it was 1845 before patients were admitted to the ten beds provided; almost all of these in-patients were surgical, most of them accident cases.

In 1828 the third major suburban Dispensary was opened, to serve Ancoats. Its formation had been strongly urged by the Infirmary Board, who seem to have calculated that they spent far more in treating poor residents of Ancoats than they gained in subscriptions from that area. This was hardly surprising, for Ancoats was a district of factories and close-packed housing; it was a 'peculiarly dependent' district; a great deal of wealth was created there but little passed through the hands of its inhabitants.

The newspapers hoped that a local institution would stimulate local response by placing responsibility on the employers and the inhabitants of the neighbouring residential districts. The churchwardens of Manchester gave £25 *per annum* (raised to £50 in 1831) but most of the subscriptions were obtained from manufacturers, including some of the richest in Manchester, who subscribed £2 or so each year, with occasional donations. The President, George Murray, was a self-made Scot; like several of his fellow subscribers and Scots he attended the affluent Independent Chapel in Mosley Street where the congregation included several doctors interested in social questions. The successive secretaries of the Ancoats Dispensary were all to be ministers.[38]

All these Dispensaries took accident cases without recommendations but Ancoats and Salford took a larger proportion of accident cases than Chorlton. Around 1830 the fraction was about 25 per cent for Ancoats, 20 per cent for Salford and less than 15 per cent for Chorlton which called itself a Medical Dispensary. The total number of out- and home-patients per year in the early 1830s ranged from about 4,200 at Salford, about 3,000 at Ancoats, to about 2,500 at Chorlton. For comparison, the Infirmary was treating about 4,000 home-patients and about 13,000 out-patients, about twice the total of the other Dispensaries combined, though more heavily weighted to home-patients.

Besides these general Dispensaries a number of more specialised medical charities were founded. In 1829 two general practitioners, John Alexander and W. B. Stott, began a Dispensary for Children.[39] It was a small institution, where until the 1850s admissions seem to have fluctuated between 800 and 1,600 children per year. The inspiration was probably the Universal Dispensary for Children founded in London in 1816, by J. B. Davis who got the idea from Paris. Certainly the treatment of children was an obvious gap in the range of medical charities: they were formally excluded from admission to hospitals as in-patients; they were not so excluded from Dispensaries, but children rarely appeared as Dispensary patients. Exactly why we do not know. Davis maintained that parents did not take children to Dispensaries because they expected them to be neglected there.[40] Carbutt in his review of the medical cases in Manchester Infirmary and Dispensary in the late 1820s, remarked that children's infectious diseases were very few – 'for causes sufficiently obvious to practitioners'.[41]

The children's Dispensary survived to become a major children's hospital, but other ventures by medical entrepreneurs were short-lived. A Lying-in Charity was begun in Chorlton in 1833, against some opposition from the Manchester Lying-in Charity. It seems to have emerged from competition between medical schools; an attempt by a lecturer in midwifery to secure more clinical experience for his pupils. A 'Hospital' for the Treatment of Skin Diseases opened briefly in 1835; one of its surgeons, Edward Stephens was the nephew and former apprentice of Joseph Jordan who had founded the Lock Hospital, to which the other 'skin' surgeon, George Plant, was also attached. Thus it seems likely that the Skin Hospital was an offshoot from the Lock Hospital which may have been treating non-venereal cases of skin disease.[42]

The short lives of these medical charities is one indication of the increasing difficulty of founding and maintaining hospitals and Dispensaries. After 1831 there were no lasting foundations in Manchester until after 1850. As we shall see in the next chapter, charity had become unpopular with reformers who increasingly placed their faith in 'political economy'.

The medical condition of the poor
The honorary medical staff of the Dispensaries became the experts on the condition of the poor. Soon after the suburban Dispensaries were founded around Manchester, that expertise was called on by civic authorities worried by the approach of a new epidemic disease, cholera. The health crisis of 1831–2 coincided with the political crisis over electoral reform; both are better understood against the background of endemic poverty and disease – the year to year suffering of families in the new industrial suburbs.

A major component of disease and death was markedly under-represented in Dispensary reports, because children were rarely treated by general medical charities. Over half of those dying in Manchester then were children under ten; children's diseases probably accounted for over half the cases of the average practitioner, but in a physician's account of four years' practice in the various departments of Manchester Infirmary in the late 1820s, there were only eight cases of measles and twenty-four of scarlet fever, twenty-one of whooping-cough and three of infantile convulsions, from the total of 5,833 cases.[43]

This proportion may be exceptionally low, but figures are few. The scarlet fever cases in the House of Recovery between 1826 and 1831 varied from five to twenty-nine per year. In 1833 Chorlton Dispensary had sixty-one cases of scarlet fever; in 1847 it had fifty-eight cases of scarlatina and measles, and twenty of whooping-cough and croup, out of a total of 1,375 cases.[44] But even the higher of these figures are small compared to the deaths caused by these children's diseases: in April 1821 – April 1825 at Rusholme Road Cemetery there were about 3,670 burials, of which 299 were caused by measles, eight by scarlet fever, 150 by chin cough and forty-one by croup. Moreover, these specific diseases were by no means the most important causes of infant and child deaths; almost half of the deaths under ten recorded in the Rusholme registers were due to less specific complaints, mostly arising from the 'first passage' (convulsions 332, tooth fever 181, infantile decline 260, bowel complaints eighty-five, etc.). These were the diseases of babies and they are hardly mentioned in Dispensary reports.[45]

For adults, where the records are more representative, the non-specific, gastro-enteric diseases are prominent in Dispensary case-loads. At the Infirmary, in Carbutt's list, about 15 per cent of cases were typhus; catarrhal fever added another 10 per cent or so, so did rheumatism, and so did coughs, asthma and dyspnoea together. Phthisis accounted for only 4 per cent of the cases, dropsy for 2 per cent, pleurisy and pneumonia together far less than 1.5 per cent. No other disease was responsible for more than 1 per cent of the cases, except disorders of the bowels. Gut disorders were diagnosed in 26 per cent of the Infirmary's patients; of these about half were suffering from constipation.[46] Other sets of records show the same pattern. Physicians in medical charities were concerned largely with fevers, lung disease, rheumatism and, especially, disorders of the bowels. Winter brought catarrhs, coughs and fevers, asthma and dyspnoea; summer brought dysentery.

The complaints of adults were, in large measure, direct results of the conditions under which they lived: the damp cellers, the filthy undrained streets, the foul and contaminated atmosphere and the miserable diet of the poorer workers. J. P. Kay, in 1830, discussed the 'morbid sensibility of the stomach and bowels' occasioned by the habitual diet of the Ancoats' poor.

> The whole population employed in the various branches of the Cotton Trade, (and amongst them, those lower classes from whose diet and habits the disease which we have attempted to describe takes its origin) rises at five o'clock in the morning, works in the mills from six till eight o'clock, and returns for half an hour or forty minutes to breakfast. This meal generally consists of tea or coffee, with a little bread. Oatmeal porridge is sometimes, but of late rarely, used and chiefly by the men, but the stimulus of tea is preferred and especially by the females*. The operatives return to the mills and work shops until twelve o'clock, when an hour is allowed for dinner. The dinner is greedily devoured. It generally consists (amongst those who obtain a low rate of wages, and with whom alone we are here concerned) of boiled potatoes. The mess of potatoes is put into one large dish, melted lard and butter are poured upon them, and generally a few pieces of fried fat bacon are mingled with them, and but seldom a little meat. The family sits round the table, and each rapidly appropriates his portion on a

plate, or, they all plunge their spoons into the dish, and, with an animal eagerness, satisfy the cravings of their appetite. Some families provide a greater proportion of bacon or other animal food, but those who are most subject to gastralgia seldom taste flesh meat; and the quantity consumed by the labouring class in general is not great. At the expiration of the hour they are all again employed in the work shops or mills, where they continue until seven o'clock or to a later hour, when they generally again indulge in the use of tea, often mingled with spirits, accompanied by a little bread. Oatmeal or potatoes are, however, taken by some a second time in the evening.[47]

* The tea is almost always of a bad, and sometimes of a deleterious quality; the infusion weak, and little or no milk is added.

For these patients Kay prescribed the following diet:

three meals in the day – a breakfast consisting of milk or rice milk, and stale wheaten bread, at the usual hour – a dinner, of a few ounces of animal food, and stale wheaten bread, without any vegetable – and, in the evening, a supper of milk and bread. These directions are of course occasioned by the incapacity of the poor to afford any other diet, which could be obtained with equal ease, and would be equally simple, mild and nutritious.[48]

It should be emphasised that Kay was discussing men and women at work: card-room operatives, hand-loom weavers and especially the Irish. Many of these patients were unable to afford the diet suggested; but unlike some earlier Dispensaries (e.g. Wigan in the 1790s), Ancoats Dispensary did not provide food. The leading industrialists and gentlemen of Ancoats and Ardwick each gave one or two guineas *per year* to the Dispensary.

The appalling prevalence of these lingering complaints led the more socially-minded of the Manchester medical men to picture the life of the new industrial proletariat as one of chronic ill-health. It was an image soon to be boldly outlined in the works of the surgeon Peter Gaskell who referred to the 'stunted, enfeebled and depraved' mill-workers, contrasting them with the rural population, who had hardly a day's illness. Here was the medical aspect of the country–town antithesis. In the country life was vigorous and so was disease; death, when it came, was rapid. In the town, life was one long disease, and death the result of physical exhaustion.[49]

This contrast became familiar in writings on the sanitary conditions of large cities. It appears to have originated in the writings of John Roberton, who mobilised the argument to those political economists, including Nassau Senior, for whom falling mortality rates demonstrated the success of the industrial system. Roberton argued that mortality rates were no measure of health; in a pamphlet of 1831 and in a letter to the *Manchester Guardian* he argued that health and happiness, not wealth, were the true test of political economy. On this test, as applied to Manchester, the industrial system failed.

The evidence as to the quantity of disease came from the Dispensaries. Roberton stated that in 1830 there were 22,626 admissions of out-patients and home-patients to the four great general Dispensaries (a figure which would appear to exclude accident cases).[50] Kay, calculating for 1832, concluded that the medical charities of Manchester together admitted over 40,000 patients, about a sixth of Manchester's population.[51] Kay, as we shall see, was arguing that medical charities were abused, Roberton was illustrating the level of disease. He claimed that, if one added Poor Law, private and domestic medicine to the case-load of medical charities, then 'not fewer perhaps than three fourths of the inhabitants of Manchester annually are, or fancy they are, under the necessity of submitting to medical treatment'.[52]

Ordinary and extraordinary epidemics

If chronic disease and its yearly cycles were the grey background of Manchester life as seen from Dispensaries, in the foreground were the comings and goings of epidemics which, though less predictable than bronchitis in winter and dysentery in summer, were believed by many to be linked to the 'constitution' of the year: the balance of seasons, the sequence of climatic conditions. Some years, like 1830, were 'not particularly notable for sickness'; others, like 1831, were marked by a whole series of medical crises. This is important, for the medical difficulties of 1831 were the prelude to the cholera epidemic which spread over most of England in 1832. For medicine as well as for politics these were years of crisis in which the shape of capitalist, urban England became obvious: the power of the urban bourgeoisie and the wretchedness of the urban proletariat, both of which could be seen most clearly in Manchester.

We can quote here the summary of 1831 given in the Annual Report of Chorlton Dispensary:

> In the spring, whooping cough, the first which appeared shewed a strong tendency to pass into inflammation of the lungs, a disease so highly dangerous to children: in the summer and early part of the autumn, after the disappearance of whooping cough, diarrhoea affected very great numbers, so that in one month (August), three hundred patients were admitted, a great proportion of whom were labouring under this disease. Its cessation was followed by an epidemic fever, of a distinctly typhoid character but happily not malignant in its degree, which ... declined in the month of December.

Between June 1830 and June 1832, over 1,200 cases of continued fever (mostly typhus) were admitted to the House of Recovery, and the mortality rate in the second year was high. Similarly the admissions at the Infirmary were increased. In 1831–2 out-patients were 10 per cent above what might normally have been expected; home-patient admissions reached 5,400, against a previous peak (1827–8) of 4,157.[53]

But these were not the only institutions under pressure: at the Lying-in Charity midwives and surgeons, who, as we have seen, were dealing with a growing proportion of the rapidly increasing births, experienced an epidemic of puerperal fever. It appears to have arisen in the practice of one midwife who, between 4 December 1829 and 4 January 1830, delivered thirty women of whom sixteen caught the disease and died of it. The midwife was suspended and sent 'into the country', but the disease became common during the spring, killing hundreds of mothers, mostly among the poor. John Roberton, looking back after twenty years, recorded this epidemic as the most traumatic in his experience.

> In company with my colleague, Mr. Fawdington, I was in the habit of wandering till midnight, and sometimes later, from home to home, visiting patients of the Lying-in Charity stricken with this malady; and some of the most heart-rending scenes that I have ever chanced to witness were in these perambulations. As an ordinary specimen, one night we entered a cottage in Copperas-street: the sleeping apartment was roomy, with a fire lighted in it; and around this the father was undressing five young children, while the mother, having an infant by her, was sitting up in bed giving her directions as though little were amiss with her. We could at once perceive, however, from the countenance and the hurried breathing, that she laboured under the prevailing fever, and would probably sink before morning. She did not survive many hours.[54]

As we shall see, it was during this epidemic that Roberton had to defend the Lying-in Charity against a public accusation that it injured the poor by undermining their independence. Soon afterwards came the new threat of cholera, then spreading across Europe from India. It evoked concern and regulations from the government in London, and some of those regulations were to be applied in the towns.

The Central Board of Health was set up by the Privy Council on 21 June 1831 at the same time as it invoked quarantine regulations, partly as a result of reports from Russia where cholera was widespread. In July 1831 the Borough Reeve and constables of Manchester called a ratepayers meeting and produced a circular advocating careful attention to cleanliness in both factories and homes – cholera as such was not mentioned, the meeting had been 'to take into consideration such measures, as may appear most proper to be adopted, for preserving the health of the working classes'.

The summer and autumn of 1831 were traumatic: throughout the country, massive meetings of local capitalists and of artisans pressed for parliamentary reform; in Bristol and elsewhere the temporary failure of the Bill provoked riots. Rick burning and strikes were common and the newspapers were full of reports of the approach of cholera. In November 1831, soon after the outbreak of cholera at Sunderland, a Special Board of Health was set up in Manchester, under government regulations of October which recommended the setting up of isolation hospitals. In Manchester, such measures had precedent in the Board of Health begun in 1796; but now the local committee was working under national direction.[55]

The Manchester Board moved quickly, submitting a list of particularly filthy streets which needed to be cleansed, persuading the churchwardens that the expenses of the Board should be met out of the poor rates, setting up district committees and inspectors to report on the streets and the homes of the poor. Attempts to clean even the worst districts met with opposition or inertia, but we are here particularly concerned with two 'hospitals' set up in Knott Mill, Deansgate, and in Swan Street, Ancoats, to deal with cholera victims. Both were industrial buildings, converted temporarily into hospitals.

When cases of cholera occurred among the richer citizens, the patient remained at home. Victims in the poorer classes were transported to cholera hospitals in special carts kept for the purpose. Though the use of the House of Recovery had long been familiar to the Manchester poor, the cholera hospitals provoked great opposition. The Fever Hospital was part of the Infirmary service, which, in any instance, was requested by those concerned: the cholera hospitals were part of a system which involved close and daily inspection of all the families in the poorer quarters. Fever was understood, cholera seemed to many an invention of the middle class and the doctors; of course the symptoms were obvious enough, but dysentery and diarrhoea in the slums did not normally attract much attention.

Even some local medical men were opposed to the fever hospitals. Henry Gaulter was sure that cholera was not contagious; that the disease was bred of dirt and that isolation was futile.[56] His alienation from his fellow medical men enabled him to picture the horror which cholera patients experienced when transported in a hearse-like van, across the pitted streets of Manchester, to a converted factory. If they were not in shock when they began the journey, they frequently were at its end.

The hospitals and medical men also interfered with death. Cholera corpses were quickly buried in ground near the workhouse; no time was allowed for the comforting ritual of wakes and normal funerals. Even worse was the threat of dissection; after years of publicity over the supply of corpses to medical schools, fear was widespread and very real.

For all these reasons, the cholera hospitals were the foci of discontent. Cholera appeared in Manchester in May 1832 but was not publicised until 13 June. Very soon afterwards there were disturbances outside the cholera hospitals. The cholera vans and stretcher bearers were frequently impeded and were given police protection. Police were stationed at the hospitals to protect the medical men who were often jostled and abused. In mid-August, at the height of the epidemic, visitors were banned from the cholera hospitals. In September, the discovery that a child dead from cholera had been decapitated led to a full-scale riot, and greatly embarrassed the authorities. The crime was blamed on a medical student dispenser who had conveniently disappeared.

It was reported, probably correctly, that most of those involved in the rioting, were Irish immigrants. The working-class press, then just beginning to gain influence, agreed with the doctors that hospitalisation was necessary. But whether the response of the poor was an emotional reaction to the fear of dissection or more grounded in analysis of the new industrial economy, the hostilities cholera aroused are evidence of the gap between the middle-class authorities and those they governed through emergency measures.

In the 1790s it was John Ferriar, the physician, who claimed that in enforcing aid to the poor, disease merely underlined moral obligations. In 1832 the *Poor Man's Guardian* ridiculed a fustian manufacturer in Salford who had contributed £20 to the relief fund but was simultaneously reducing the wages of his workers.

> Those who have always been deaf to the calls of humanity, appear now most sensitively alive to the whisper of cholera; and that which neither humanity, justice, nor religion could effect, has been most triumphantly achieved by the *cholera morbus*.
>
> The Mssrs. Rostron, we are informed, employ upwards of one hundred hands as cutters; so that one week will make up half, at least, of this liberal donation. The process seems to be, to deprive the poor wretches of wages, that Mr. Rostron may gain the credit of being liberal and benevolent in giving them back a portion of their own earnings in the shape of alms ...
>
> This town is to be exposed to all the horrors of this terrible disorder, that the avarice and ostentation of Mr. Rostron may be gratified.[57]

Notes and references

1. A. de Tocqueville, *Journeys to England and Ireland* (1835), London, 1958, p. 105.
2. J. Wheeler, *Manchester: Its Political, Social & Commercial History*, Manchester, 1836, pp. 245–9.
3. E. Lyon, 'Sketch of the medical topography & statistics of Manchester', *North of England Medical & Surgical Journal*, 1 (1830), 1–31, p. 18.
4. A. Lindsey, *Socialised Medicine in England & Wales*, North Carolina, 1962, p. 207.
5. The data are from Directories and Census Reports. Dr Irvine Loudon has recently compiled national ratios. See his forthcoming book on the development of medical practice.
6. F. S. Stannicliffe, *The Manchester Royal Eye Hospital, 1814–1964*, Manchester, 1964; George Rosen, *The Specialization of Medicine with particular reference to Opthalmology*, New York, 1944, p. 39.

7. Stannicliffe, *Eye Hospital*, Ch. I.
8. E. M. Brockbank, *Sketches of the Lives and Works of the Honorary Medical Staff of the Manchester Infirmary 1752–1830*, Manchester, 1904, pp. 269–72, & n. 30.
9. T. J. Wyke, 'The Manchester and Salford Lock Hospital, 1818–1917', *Medical History*, 19 (1975), 73–86.
10. Manchester Infirmary Weekly Board Minutes, 14, 21 July 1806.
11. Wyke, 'Lock Hospital'.
12. F. W. Jordan, *Life of Joseph Jordan*, Manchester, 1904; E. M. Brockbank, *Medical Staff*, 227.
13. E. M. Brockbank, *Medical Staff*, 170.
14. S. W. F. Holloway, 'The Apothecaries Act, 1815: a reinterpretation', *Medical History*, 10 (1966), 107–29, 221–36.
15. Manchester Infirmary Weekly Board Minutes, 22 May 1797.
16. *Ibid.*, 26 November 1804.
17. E. M. Brockbank, *The Foundation of Provincial Medical Education in England*, Manchester, 1936, Ch. IX; Lying-in Hospital, Annual Board, 11 May 1811; Special Board, 4 December 1811.
18. Manchester Infirmary Weekly Board, 1, 8 August 1803.
19. Lying-in Hospital, Quarterly Board, 3 February 1808; Special Board, 18 February 1808; Annual Board, 1 May 1811; Special Board, 4 December 1811.
20. F. W. Jordan, *Joseph Jordan*, Ch. II. Also see *Memoir of Thomas Turner*, by a relative, London, 1875. Mrs Katherine Webb who is writing a (UMIST) PhD thesis on Manchester medical men, has corrected some details.
21. F. W. Jordan, *Joseph Jordan*, 33; *Thomas Thurner*, 86; M. J. Durey, 'Bodysnatchers and Benthamites: The implications of the Dead Body Bill for the London schools of anatomy, 1820–1842', *The London Journal*, 2 (1976), 200–25. 'Resurrectionists' feature in a number of local town histories, e.g. W. Chadwick, *Reminiscences of Mottram*, Glossop, 1870, reprinted 1972, pp. 72–82 (I am indebted to R. Williamson for this reference).
22. F. W. Jordan, *Joseph Jordan*, 81; on Paris medicine see E. H. Ackerknecht, *Medicine at the Paris Hospital, 1794–1848*, Baltimore, 1967, and Michel Foucault, *The Birth of the Clinic*, London, 1973.
23. F. Renaud, *A Short History of the Rise and Progress of the Manchester Royal Infirmary from the year 1752 to 1877*, Manchester, 1898, pp. 86–7; F. W. Jordan, *Joseph Jordan*, 23, 33–5.
24. W. Brockbank, *Portrait of a Hospital, 1752–1948*, London, 1952, Ch. 5.
25. On Manchester radicalism see A. Prentice, *Historical Sketches and Personal Recollections of Manchester*, London & Manchester, 1851, reprinted 1970.
26. See Renaud, *Infirmary*; Brockbank, *Portrait*; Infirmary Annual Reports.
27. Anon. 'A week at Manchester', *Blackwood's Magazine*, 45 (April 1839), 490. For local data on the nature of factory accidents see S. Gaskell, 'Tables of accidents brought to the Stockport Infirmary, and attended by the house-surgeon, in the years 1833, 1834, and 1835', *Journal of the Royal Statistical Society*, 8 (1845), 277–81.
28. *Manchester Guardian*, 3 February 1827.
29. *Ibid.*, 7 April 1827.
30. *Ibid.*, 21 April 1827.
31. *Ibid.*, 28 April 1827.
32. Manchester Lying-in Charity, General Quarterly Board, 27 September 1810.
33. J. H. Young, *St. Mary's Hospitals Manchester, 1790–1963*, Edinburgh, 1964, p. 26.
34. Chorlton-upon-Medlock (or Chorlton Row) Dispensary, Annual Reports; *Manchester Guardian*, 3, 10 December 1825.
35. Manchester Infirmary, Weekly Board, 17, 24 October 1825. This may have been the first suggestion in Britain of a 'branch dispensary'; such 'branch dispensaries' were set up in Birmingham and elsewhere from the 1860s.
36. Wheeler, *Manchester*, 825.

37. *Manchester Guardian*, 28 April, 5, 12 May 1827; Salford Dispensary Annual Reports; Lyon, 'Sketch' (1831), 147.
38. Ardwick & Ancoats Dispensary Annual Reports; *Manchester Guardian*, 9 August 1828.
39. Lyon, 'Sketch' (1831), 147.
40. I. S. L. Loudon, 'John Bunnell Davis and the Universal Dispensary for children', *British Medical Journal*, 1 (1979), 1191–4.
41. E. Carbutt, 'Observations on disease', *North of England Medical & Surgical Journal*, 1 (1831), 27.
42. F. W. Jordan, *Jordan*, 130; Wheeler, *Manchester*, 425.
43. Carbutt, 'Observations' (1831), 26–7.
44. Annual Reports.
45. J. Roberton, *Observations on the Mortality & Physical Management of Children*, London, 1827, esp. pp. 18–19, 79.
46. Carbutt, 'Observations' (1831), 26.
47. J. P. Kay, 'Gastralgia & enteralgia, or morbid sensibility of the stomach and bowels', *North of England Medical & Surgical Journal*, 1 (1831), 225–7.
48. *Ibid.*
49. Peter Gaskell, *Artisans & Machinery*, London, 1836, p. 204.
50. J. Roberton, *General Remarks on the Health of English Manufacturers*, London, 1831; *Manchester Guardian*, 16 June 1831.
51. J. P. Kay, *Defects in the Constitution of Dispensaries with suggestions for their improvement*, London, 1834.
52. Roberton, *Health of English Manufacturers*, 13.
53. Annual Reports.
54. J. Roberton, *Essays and Notes on the Physiology & Diseases of Women, and on Practical Midwifery*, London, 1851, p. 439.
55. The first cholera epidemic is covered in several good recent studies: R. J. Morris, *Cholera 1832: The Social Response to an Epidemic*, London, 1976; M. Durey, *The Return of the Plague: British Society and the Cholera, 1831–2*, Dublin, 1979; M. Pelling, *Cholera, Fever and English Medicine, 1825–1865*, Oxford, 1978. The epidemic in Manchester has been examined in at least two theses: T. Jones, 'The cholera in Manchester', BA thesis, University of Manchester, 1948; M. Clifford, 'Medicine, politics and society: Manchester's 1832 cholera epidemic', BA thesis, University of California at Berkeley, 1979. For details on the Manchester riots from a Catholic viewpoint see G. P. Connolly, 'Little brother be at peace: the priest as holy man in the nineteenth century ghetto', in W. J. Sheils, ed., *The Church and Healing. Studies in Church History*, Vol. 19, Oxford, 1982.
56. The major primary source on Manchester's cholera epidemic is H. Gaulter, *The Origins & Progress of the Malignant Cholera in Manchester*, London, 1833.
57. *Poor Man's Guardian*, 3 March 1832. I owe this reference to Mark Clifford's thesis.

CHAPTER 4

Medical charity and the Industrial Revolution in the textile towns

Introduction
So far in this work we have focused on Manchester and Salford – the core of the textile districts of Lancashire and Northern Cheshire. We have followed three periods of development in local medical charity: the foundation of the Infirmary in the mid-eighteenth century, the struggles around 1790, and the weaker reform and extension movements of the later 1820s. The first took place in a centre of domestic industry; the second was a radical response to the health and political consequences of early industry. The third took place as boom once again gave way to depression, but control now lay with conservatives and loyalists; liberal-radicals showed little interest in medical charity; by the early 1830s, as we shall see in the next chapter, they were arguing against direct charity by advocating economic independence.

In this chapter we cover the period from the 1780s to 1830 – the formaive half-century of industrial society – but we look outside Manchester itself to the range of towns around it, to the ring of towns which now form Greater Manchester – Wigan, Bolton, Bury, Rochdale, Oldham, Ashton, Stockport; to the major towns of mid-Lancashire – Preston & Blackburn; to the smaller, more slowly industrialised towns in the north of the Region – Lancaster and Kendal. They were all, in some sense textile towns, but they differed in many ways – in pre-industrial structure, in speed of industrialisation, in size, in proximity to Manchester, etc. To treat them all, for a period of fifty years, yields a complex matrix. Yet such comparative urban studies can be most rewarding, as recent work in the general social history of Lancashire has begun to show.[1] More general work of this kind is required before we can be sure of the explanation of specific phenomena such as medical charities. But meanwhile, and as a contribution to that more general social history, we can outline a preliminary argument about the geographical and historical factors which advanced and retarded medical charity during this critical period.

By presenting brief histories of the various institutions in their local contexts, I shall be arguing that Dispensaries cannot be seen as a product of 'need' arising from 'industry'. They were founded first and worked best in small towns with developed pre-industrial structures: the paradigmatic new factory communities did not support medical charities until after 1850, when they were already large towns. Dispensaries, it seems, were popular in the 1780s for some of the same reasons as Infirmaries were established earlier and in larger towns. They afforded a cheap means by which middle-class 'society' could associate together to receive the patronage of the local land-owners and to dispense patronage to the poor of the town whom they knew as individuals. Leadership was sometimes provided by medical and social reformers akin to those active in Manchester around 1790. As in Manchester, the threat of typhus fever could be a major stimulus to a Dispensary foundation, and that in turn might lead to a Fever Hospital or 'House of Recovery'. Again as in Manchester, the fear of unrest and of epidemic disease becomes more obvious in the 1790s.

We have argued, for Manchester, that medical charity became more restricted and more conservative during the early nineteenth century. In the surrounding towns we find a similar pattern. Where towns remained small and industrialisation was slow, the Dispensary prospered; where towns which already had a Dispensary began to grow rapidly, the charity rarely grew proportionately; in some cases a limited reform and extension was attempted in the more liberal 1820s. Where no Dispensary had appeared before 1800, the new foundations were usually conspicuously 'loyalist'; those of the late 1820s were closely associated with Anglican-Tory groups in towns which were coming to be dominated by Dissenters. Dispensaries then appeared as a means of re-establishing traditional social hierarchies; they could no longer be projected as representing the generality of the local middle class.

Dispensaries and social change
Significantly, the first Dispensaries founded in our area were in Lancaster (1781) and Kendal (1783) rather than in the textile towns nearer Manchester. These ancient market towns had long been governed by corporations; there were well-established urban elites and many traditional charities for the poor. Lancaster especially was thriving as a port. The towns were too small to support Infirmaries, but with populations of about 8,000[2] they were large enough to support Dispensaries which did not require large buildings and were much cheaper to maintain. But Lancaster and Kendal were more than well-established corporate towns; they were situated in a district, where Lancashire, Yorkshire and Westmorland came together, that was a major seedbed of late eighteenth century Enlightenment, in large measure because

of the numerous families of prosperous, highly literate and public-spirited Quakers who lived there.

This philanthropic culture was well expressed among the physicians who came from or were educated in the area. John Fothergill (1712–80) who became one of London's most successful physicians, was born into a Quaker family in Wensleydale, and was educated at Sedbergh. He spent most of his money on natural history collections and philanthropy; his friend Benjamin Franklin said of him: 'I can hardly conceive that a better man has ever existed'. Anthony Fothergill (1732–1813) who was a friend (not a relation) of John, came from Sedbergh and also became well known as a philanthropic physician especially for his work on asphyxia. Both men were friends and advisers to the Quaker, John C. Lettsom, who in 1761–6 was an apprentice to a surgeon-apothecary in Settle. In 1770 he moved to London and, assisted by John Fothergill, helped found the Aldersgate Dispensary, the first of the major subscription Dispensaries. John Haygarth (1740–1827) who at Chester pioneered the use of fever wards also came from the district and was educated in Sedbergh.[3]

All these men knew each other well, as they did Thomas Percival in Manchester and James Currie in Liverpool; they were key members in a network of scientific, philanthropic physicians. Since this web was so well-rooted in the dales around Kendal and Lancaster, it is not surprising that there were laymen and physicians there interested in following up Fothergill's Aldersgate initiative.

The Lancaster Dispensary was begun by Dr David Campbell, an Edinburgh graduate, who later provided evidence on fever when the Manchester House of Recovery was being set up.[4] The Kendal Dispensary was apparently begun by the Dissenting physician James Ainslie and it owed much to the local Quakers who were conspicuous in the schemes to provide provisions for the poor, in 1782 and in 1800.[5]

When Eden visited the north in 1795, both Lancaster and Kendal were prosperous, confident towns, not greatly depressed by the wars. Besides their Dispensaries, each had a relatively new workhouse (Kendal 1769, Lancaster 1787), and these were well kept. Friendly Societies, including some for women, had developed since mid-century, and especially during the 1780s. Lancaster had eighteen and Kendal twenty, and since the male membership of Lancaster societies was over 1,100, and the number of families in the borough probably about 2,000, a high proportion of those families must have been insured against the sickness of their wage-earners, a conclusion which remains true even if we assume that many of the Friendly Society members came from outside the borough. Lying-in-charities were established in Kendal in 1794 and in Lancaster about 1807.[6]

THE INDUSTRIAL REVOLUTION

By the end of the Napoleonic wars, Lancaster's trade had stagnated, but in the early 1820s the Dispensary continued to treat between 1,000 and 1,500 cases per year. In 1815 a Board of Health and a House of Recovery had been started on the initiative of the Dispensary committee and the Dispensary medical officers were responsible for the care of in-patients. In 1832 a new building was provided to house both fever patients and the Dispensary operations. This combined General Dispensary and House of Recovery took some surgical in-patients, at least from 1841. From about the same date the number of Dispensary patients also rose considerably, approaching 3,000 *per annum* by 1850, about 20 per cent of the population of the borough. By contemporary standards Lancaster was well-equipped with medical institutions and these enjoyed general support.[7]

In Kendal too, the population grew comparatively slowly during the early nineteenth century. The long-established Dispensary took a high proportion of the local sick, paupers and non-paupers, and the town was well-endowed with other charities, including a Ladies Visiting Sick Society founded in 1811. As in Lancaster, though rather later, a House of Recovery was set up (*c.* 1829) in association with the Dispensary and alongside the workhouse. In 1829 the Kendal poor were 'more comfortable than in those of other manufacturing towns, though the evil effects of too much machinery was gradually diminishing their wonted prosperity'.[8]

The only other corporate town in our region also founded a Dispensary relatively early, in 1798. Wigan was then a market town dominated by local gentry including the rector who doubled as lord of the manor. Robert Holt Leigh, later Wigan's MP, was told about the Dispensary in the newsy letters from his sister:[9]

> 19 March 1797
> A dispensary is in agitation and Mr. Bankes [of Winstanley Hall] is President, Mr. Latham Treasurer.
>
> 26 March
> I will tell you another secret ... that Mr. President (Self appointed President) Bankes only thinks of giving half a crown a month towards the Dispensary. It is a farce to disturb the muscles of a judge to see a man so active and zealous to gain supporters of a cause, and when his own shoulder should be set to the wheel to give only the help of one little finger.

When he proposed the Dispensary, Bankes thought they would be dealing with about 1,000 patients per year at a cost of about £53, a calculation based on the Liverpool Dispensary accounts for 1795. In fact the work was less and the cost much more.[10] We have figures only for 1806, when 332 patients were admitted, at a cost of £220 but this seems to have been about the average from 1798.[11] The cost per patient was very high, considering that no resident surgeon or apothecary was employed and the local physician and surgeons gave their services, but the Wigan gentry and tradesmen could afford it, and the Dispensary continued to treat a few patients on two days each week until a reform in the late 1820s.

The immediate reason for the Dispensary foundation was revealed in a note sent round to all in the district who seemed likely to contribute. It emphasised the benevolence of the age and the 'miserable situation of a family labouring under the complicated misfortunes of sickness and poverty'. Typhus was rife: 'a low fever which lately prevailed to an alarming degree was increased and its dreadful effects widely diffused from the sick and poor being unable to obtain medical assistance or to observe the directions of the Faculty when obtained'. It was the 'destructive ravages of this disease' which had 'given birth to the idea of a Dispensary, ... for the general relief of the sick poor unable to pay either for medicines or advice or the necessary support recommended by the Faculty'.[12]

We have seen that in Manchester the Infirmary physicians had the power to recommend patients for free provisions during those emergencies when special subscription funds were in operation. The Wigan Dispensary was perhaps unique in the Region in making the supply of provisions on medical advice an explicit feature of the service;[13] the context was revealed in another note to the MP: 'The poor if one may judge from the number of petitioners want support somehow for your door is never free'.[14]

As these letters make clear, the Dispensary was not the only project to occupy the Wigan gentry in 1797; they were also raising a troop of volunteers. Here, as in the cities, the two were closely associated as middle-class responses to the threat of invasion or insurrection which the food shortages of the 1790s exacerbated. These initiatives could be separated by a Quaker, Mr James Neville, who wrote to Leigh urging support for the Dispensary and an end to the Volunteers,[15] but for most of those with property, the projects were complementary.

Wigan Dispensary continued as a small-town institution until the 1820s. Until then it opened only a few days each week, there was no resident practitioner, and it counted its patients in hundreds per year rather than in thousands. In 1824 a committee was set up by the Quakers William and James Neville to improve the Dispensary. As a result, the opening hours were changed, surgical instruments and new drugs were purchased; most importantly, a resident apothecary was appointed. There may even have been plans for an Infirmary. In 1829, the year of a typhus epidemic, annual admissions reached almost 3,500, a high figure by the standard of much larger towns, about 14 per cent of the Wigan population, and a figure that was not maintained.[16]

The only other town in the Region to found a Dispensary before 1800 was Stockport, which had an unusually close relationship with Manchester and closely followed the pattern of medical charity established there. Both the Manchester Strangers' Friend Society[17] and the House of Recovery were rapidly imitated in Stockport. It was a Unitarian manufacturer, Peter Marsland, who gave the site for the Fever Hospital; and this building was later used as wards for the Dispensary. The Dispensary itself had been opened in 1792, but though this might suggest links with the Manchester Infirmary reforms and the (Methodist) Strangers' Friend Societies, it appears to have grown from the practice of Dr Briscall, a relation of the Rector of Stockport, who had for some time been treating poor patients gratuitously at his house.[18]

Such a mixture of religious denominations (Anglican, Methodist, Unitarian) and of motives to medical charity (traditional, evangelical, prudential) is not surprising for the early 1790s; similar cross-denominational initiative had characterised the early Sunday School movement, which was notably successful in Stockport. In the early nineteenth century, the Sunday Schools movement had broken into denominational factions, and medical charities, especially new ones, could less easily present themselves as above party and sectarian conflict.[19]

Thus as the social consequences of industrialisation became more serious, the will to charity declined. In Stockport, as in Salford and some other towns, the conspicuousness and frequency of serious factory accidents led to proposals that the Dispensary should be extended to provide hospital beds. In Stockport, the plan for an Infirmary was conceived as early as 1816 but it took fifteen years to materialise. In spite of a subscription in 1821 for the coronation of George IV and the unparalleled prosperity of the following years, the fund grew slowly and the Dispensary was persistently in debt. As a makeshift, from 1823, the victims of serious accidents were admitted as in-patients to the House of Recovery. In 1827 the Dispensary was subject to public criticism for extravagance: lay supporters, it was said, had lost interest and left the management in the unsuitable hands of medical men. At about the same time Francis Philips, the brother of the former treasurer of Manchester Infirmary, renewed his interest in Dispensary affairs. He revived the Weekly Board to increase lay participation and to decrease the number of patients, especially the surgical in-patients. By these means and by employing a regular collector, the debt was reduced and in 1832 the foundation stone for a new Infirmary was laid.[20]

Stockport Dispensary was well enough established to survive criticism and erect a new building. That it did so can be attributed to a handful of interested and powerful men of whom Francis Philips was the best known.

MEDICAL CHARITY: THE TEXTILE TOWNS

As a member of the conservative wing of a rich family of industrialists, he, like his brother, felt responsible for civic affairs. He had succeeded to family estates and had the time for Dispensary commitments; he had been the most outspoken defender of the Peterloo magistrates and was committed to the maintenance of a society in which everyone knew his place.[21]

In these efforts he was aided by James Heald, a prominent Tory Wesleyan, and by Dissenting ministers, including N. K. Pugsley, whose prolix prefaces to the Annual Reports presented inequality of rank and fortune as 'the general order of the Universe' and 'one of the most beautiful features of civilised society'. It was inequality which made possible charities like the Dispensary.[22]

It is instructive to compare the calm and secular prefaces of the Lancaster reports with the often religious and overtly political propaganda in Stockport, where the Dispensary was used as an argument against 'the advocates of infidelity' and where the influence of charities was claimed to be a cause of 'the comparative quietness and resignation which have reigned amongst us at the late awful crisis' of 1826.[23]

In terms of size and importance, Stockport in the early nineteenth century ranked not with Lancaster or Wigan but with Preston and Bolton, but in these latter towns, medical charities did not appear until the Napoleonic wars. Both provide evidence that Dispensaries were increasingly being promoted as a means of strengthening loyalist and traditionalist elements in town. With Stockport, they provide further evidence that the care of factory victims was not a popular cause.

Preston in the eighteenth century had been an affluent agricultural and administrative centre with a small port. It was in many ways the *de facto* county town, well equipped with professional men. The Earl of Derby had property nearby and kept a town house in Preston. The county justices met there and the important post of Deputy Clerk of the Peace was monopolised by a firm of Preston solicitors. The prison, which had been strongly criticised by John Howard, had been replaced in 1789, partly because a typhus outbreak in 1783 was thought to have spread from the prison, partly because T. B. Bayley, the Lancashire magistrate, had secured legal reforms in 1784.[24]

Though Richard Arkwright, the originator of the factory system in cotton spinning, had been a Preston barber, resistance by local workers ensured that factories came later to Preston than to the Manchester district. Not until 1791 did the Horrocks family build their first mill there, but they rapidly became powerful enough to challenge the control of the Earl of Derby over the parliamentary representation of the borough. In a compromise of 1801, the two seats were divided between the two families, nicely symbolising the accommodation of rising manufacturing interests to the traditional rulers. This pattern of deference was repeated at a lower level; compared to Bolton workers, the employees of Preston were reckoned to 'want spirit'.[25]

The Preston Dispensary certainly accorded with this relatively traditional and hierarchical outlook. It was founded in 1809 to celebrate the Jubilee of George III. Its honorary staff included only physicians; surgeons were excluded until the 1830s.[26] The leading physician was also the medical attendant of the volunteers; his tombstone in the Parish Church records his spirited exertions for king and country.

The services of Preston Dispensary proved much more popular than those of Wigan, or even Stockport. The yearly attendance continued to be about a tenth of the rising population of the borough. This ratio was about the same in Lancaster, though there the population rose very little during the wars. The ratio in Stockport was about 1:20, in Wigan, about 1:30.

The Preston Dispensary was also successful in prompting other medical services. A Ladies Charity which provided medical aid as well as clothing, sheets etc., was begun in 1810 by the wives of the Dispensary leaders, especially the physicians' wives.[27] In 1813, the Corporation of Preston provided a House of Recovery which was run in connection with the Dispensary.[28] Thus, by the end of the wars, Preston was roughly on a par with Lancaster, though it was by then a much larger town. The industrial growth which had occurred during the wars was being contained within the social machinery of a county town; under these circumstances a Dispensary was attractive to the middle classes, anxious to make a mark socially, and acceptable to a working class trained to its place.

Preston Dispensary was one of the few in which the numbers of patients seen rose parallel with the population figures; annual attendance between 1810 and 1830 was usually about 8 per cent of the population. But by the 1820s the Dispensary and allied operations were becoming more contentious. In 1821 several local surgeons tried to get on to the Dispensary staff, so far restricted to physicians. They failed, so that surgeons (other than the resident) continued to serve only as men-midwives, for which they were paid seven shillings per case. In 1823 the overseers were challenged over their financing of the House of Recovery and this also put the Dispensary at risk; evidently the sick poor were proving unwilling to enter the House. Reforms came at the end of the decade: a new House of Recovery was built in 1829, at the time of a typhus epidemic. The following year the local surgeons gained entry to the Dispensary staff, partly because the overseers wanted more medical attention for the workhouse inmates. At first the surgeons had to agree to do home-visits, but this requirement was soon dropped and surgeons were recognised as the equals of physicians.

MEDICAL CHARITY: THE TEXTILE TOWNS

There is scope here for more investigation of local politics, and especially the conflicts surrounding the overseers. But even with our present information, the transformation of the Dispensary from an institution dominated by physicians to one more representative of the medical professions of a growing industrial town appears to parallel the political changes in Preston. In 1826 there ended a long standing alliance between the Earl of Derby and the Horrocks family, owners of Preston's largest mills, who had divided Preston's two parliamentary seats between them. In 1830 the radical Henry Hunt was elected and in 1835 the Earl of Derby abandoned his Preston house. By then Preston had ceased to be a 'county' town and had become one of the cotton towns, albeit with a rich agricultural hinterland and an unusually large professional class.[29]

By the end of the wars, the cotton towns around Manchester had grown very considerably. Blackburn, Oldham and Bolton all had populations of over 18,000, twice the size of Lancaster or Kendal. But though there were plenty of sick poor in these newer towns, there was relatively little pre-industrial structure and little sympathy among the middle classes for those ideas of social obligation which had motivated Dispensaries in the older towns. Neither the open, rational, utilitarian philanthropy of a Percival, nor the respect for traditional rights and obligations evidenced in the annual reports of Preston Dispensary, had much purchase in the 'frontier towns' of the cotton industry. Those groups whose religion and politics led them to value medical charities as symbolic of the obligations of hierarchy, found it difficult to project their views.

Such was the case in Bolton, where a Dispensary was begun in 1814 to celebrate the victory over France. It soon became clear that the major supporters of the charity were the energetic high-church Rector, Canon Slade, and a family of manufacturers and surgeons into which he had married. This same family, the Bollings, later provided a Tory MP for Bolton. The Dispensary got off to a good start, but after about 1817 financial support and finances gradually fell away until the later 1820s.[30] In spite of the rapid growth of the town from 25,000 in 1811 to 60,000 in 1851, the amount subscribed hardly rose at all; only in years of special collections did the income exceed £500 *per annum*. The Dispensary supporters opened purpose-built accommodation in 1827, after using two cottages for thirteen years and collecting for four. They wanted to follow the normal pattern and establish an Infirmary for surgical cases and accident victims, but not until 1838 were funds raised to build this accommodation and employ a resident nurse. The wards were meant to house thirty beds, but there was no money to use more than six; the rest of the building was rented out. The number of out-patients had fallen notably in the early 1820s; it then rose until 1838, but in the new building numbers were again reduced to little more than 2,000 *per annum*, a figure reached in the late 1810s when the Dispensary was new and the town half the size.

Again, as in Stockport, the Dispensary Annual Reports were markedly religious. In both places particular efforts were made to attract more and larger subscriptions from the large manufacturers. These efforts were not particularly successful. Stockport Dispensary and Infirmary relied heavily upon large donations from owners of nearby estates; Bolton was less fortunate.[31]

Dispensaries in difficulties

So far we have drawn a contrast between the settled towns of the north which naturally supported a range of medical charities and the larger expanding textile towns which gave very little, even when there was some tradition of medical charity. In Blackburn we shall see a 'new town' without that tradition initially following the older parts but soon encountering difficulties. In the towns to the north and east of Manchester – Bury, Rochdale, Oldham and Ashton we shall see how new industrial communities could be even less hospitable to the ideas of medical charity.

Blackburn, to the east of Preston, was marginally smaller but considerably less established. It did not have the aristocratic connections or the professional groupings prominent in Preston, rather it was dominated by several former yeoman families who had invested in the textile trades and grown very prosperous, notably the Pilkingtons, the Hornbys and the Fieldens.

The overseers of Blackburn had employed a surgeon to attend paupers since at least 1794. In 1824, during a period of prosperity for both factory owners and hand-loom weavers, the leading citizens decided that the service to paupers could be incorporated into a charity Dispensary that could also care for the non-paupers. Blackburn was following the example of Preston and Bolton, but it had greater ambitions, and plans were mooted for an Infirmary to serve the whole of north-east Lancashire. The Dispensary, which paid particular attention to epidemic disease, was liberally supported from the poor rates, but the Infirmary fund relied on donations and the proposal soon lapsed. After 1826, a year of economic collapse and of weavers' riots, it proved difficult to raise funds and when in the early 1830s the governors tried to collect enough to start the building, their application, even to individuals who had already promised help, were 'either unnoticed or answered in unfavourable language'. Here, as in Preston, when the economic difficulties of the later 1820s first made plain the recurrent problems of industrial society, the response was not an increase in facilities but increasing suspicion of the existing means of medical and poor relief.[32]

MEDICAL CHARITY: THE TEXTILE TOWNS

Yet, if Blackburn and Preston had become major industrial centres with clear and conscious class divisions, some of the smaller towns around still showed older patterns of deference. One such was Chorley where a Dispensary began in 1828 and proved very successful, serving about 10 per cent of the population each year on an income of £100–150 per annum. It drew support from all the churches and chapels including the Roman Catholics, but the initiative and leadership seems to have come from the Anglicans, especially the Masters family who were patrons and occupants of the living of Chorley, then worth over £1,000 per year.[33]

Small towns could still found successful Dispensaries, large towns in Lancashire could not. After the mid-1820s the only new foundations were in Rochdale and Bury and neither managed to be much more than an annexe of the parish church until after 1850. Rochdale shared with Ashton and Oldham, a reputation for radicalism, both at middle-class and working-class levels. In all these towns the Anglican Tories were already a defensive minority – the weakness or absence of medical charity was a mark of the impotence there of traditional appeals to social hierarchy.

We know relatively little about the Rochdale operation. It was begun in 1831 and was associated with the parish church where the Rector during the 1830s was the Rev. W. R. Hay, previously the magistrate in the Peterloo trials. The Dispensary appears to have developed from a Benevolent Society, also attached to the church. The main founder, Clement Royd, was a banker and member of Rochdale's leading Tory family.

The Dispensary had a resident apothecary but it remained a small charity, probably in improvised accommodation, until the late 1850s. Through the 1830s it rarely served more than 1,000 patients per year, though its income was often about £300 *per annum* and the town's population was about 25,000. During this period one of the major issues in Rochdale politics was the Dissenters' opposition to compulsory payments in support of the parish church. In 1840 John Bright, later to be the joint leader of 'Manchester liberalism' confronted the new Vicar in Rochdale churchyard. When church-rates were refused, the parish clock was stopped, the bells silenced and the Dispensary closed.[34]

In Bury, the Dispensary had been founded two years earlier in 1829, and because it was frequently the object of controversy, we are relatively well-informed about its work. It was begun by the Reverend H. C. Boutflower, a very busy clergyman who was also headmaster of the Bury Grammar School, a long established charity by then turned to the service of the local middle class and the profit of its staff. Boutflower was 'father, son and brother to doctors', some of whom were involved with the nearby Salford Dispensary begun in 1827. In Bury he managed to obtain some support from the leading citizens and the Rector chaired the necessary public meetings, but funds did not prove sufficient to pay a house apothecary and for several years a variety of other patterns of work were tried. One method involved the local practitioners attending in rota and supplying the medicines themselves at six shillings per case. This Boutflower found too expensive and eventually a house apothecary was appointed. Even then controversy continued: the resident was accused of practising without directions from the honorary surgeon, who frequently failed to attend at the Dispensary; a later resident was accused of damaging the practices of other surgeons in the town.

It is clear that from the beginning most of the local surgeons were intensely suspicious of the Dispensary. They were prepared to tolerate it only if its assistance was restricted to cases deserving relief, and no practitioner gained an advantage over his fellows through attachment to the charity. The radical surgeon Matthew Fletcher, who led local campaigns against the New Poor Law and later for the People's Charter, left a very graphic account of his objections to medical philanthropy. He believed that the growth of industry was impoverishing the mass to the benefit of the few and that clergymen like Boutflower ought to be speaking out against that system rather than engaging in ostentatious but trifling charity, partly at the expense of surgeons. He particularly objected to Boutflower's attempts to include factory accidents within the Dispensary's scope and so attract support from cotton masters. That for Fletcher was a clear example of how 'charity' shifted responsibility from the employers and at the same time undermined the returns to surgeons. This particular scheme of Boutflower's failed: Bury Dispensary, like Rochdale later, did not take factory accidents.

In later controversies the same themes recurred: medical charities might be acceptable in large towns where medical practitioners were often paid five to ten shillings per visit, but in towns like Bury even the rich bore medical fees 'in a grumbling way'. Surgeons in small towns could not afford charity, and they were afraid that Dispensaries and hospitals, by creating a hierarchy within the local profession, relegated those not attached to the institution, to the status of 'useless men, professional mongrels or old women'.[35]

The reasons why Bury Dispensary remained a very small charity until the late nineteenth century are both geographical and historical. Bury's major employers – the Peels, the Grants and the Gregs – were not 'Bury based'; they were industrialists of regional or national standing. They often preferred to send accident cases to Manchester than have them treated by local surgeons. The Earl of Derby owned much of the land, but he had never lived at Bury as he had, occasionally, at Preston. The middle class of Bury could call on professional services from Manchester so the local medical profession consisted almost entirely of hard-working surgeon-apothecaries.

If these factors had made 'charity' unprofitable in 1790 or 1820, by 1830 the climate was even less favourable. Bury, like Rochdale, was strongly divided by religion and political party, and such vertical divisions considerably interfered with the projection of charities as 'quasi-municipal'. By 1830 too, the deeper, horizontal divisions were also apparent, and civic philanthropic activities were bound to reflect the polarisation between 'masters' and 'hands'. The masters were often suspicious of 'charities' begun by clergymen and bankers; the more conscientious preferred to employ their own factory surgeons and to use Manchester charities, the majority saw no need for charity. The mill-hands, or at least their articulate leaders saw through the emollients. Men like Fletcher, who felt their own professional independence draining away as independent artisans became factory workers, were unwilling to join the small clergymen and bankers in toadying to the large employers.

Much the same reasons probably explain why no medical charities at all were begun in Oldham or Ashton before mid-century and why an attempt in Ashton in 1843 failed. These rapidly growing towns never passed through a stage when employers, landowners and professionals felt themselves to be the summit of a civic hierarchy, or when any such feeling was returned by the growing army of textile workers. Most of the working population, at the beginning of the century were hand-loom weavers who were traditionally independent. That democratic spirit carried over into the early organisation of industrial politics. There was no urban hierarchy around which industrial politics could grow as it did, for example, at Preston. Oldham politics in the 1830s was dominated by the radicalism of small masters and operatives; they effectively controlled local government through their influence over shopkeepers and the lower middle-class voters.[36]

It was from such towns that Anglican clergymen called for help to stem the barbarism of operatives and the Dissent of cotton-masters. Government aid was forthcoming to build churches and primary schools. Without any such aid for medicine the effort of beginning a Dispensary must not have seemed worthwhile, for it would certainly be factional, and suspected of 'jobbery', especially by medical men. By the early 1830s, as worries mounted over the cost of poor rates, charity was very definitely out of fashion.

Notes and references

1. John Foster's powerful work on Oldham has stimulated considerable debate: J. Foster, *Class Struggle and the Industrial Revolution*, London, 1974; D. Gadian, 'A comparative study of popular movements in north-west industrial towns, 1830–50', PhD thesis, Lancaster University, 1976; R. A. Sykes, 'Some aspects of working-class consciousness in Oldham, 1830–1842', *Historical Journal*, 23 (1980), 167–79. Most of my basic data on early nineteenth-century towns is derived from Directories, especially E. Baines,

History, Directory and Gazetteer of the County Palatine of Lancashire, 2 vols, Liverpool, 1824–5, reprinted by David & Charles, 1968.
2. Populations given in the relevant parochial reports in F. M. Eden, *The State of the Poor*, 3 vols, London, 1797, reprinted 1966.
3. Entries in the *Dictionary of National Biography*, and the very useful article by C. C. Booth, 'Doctors from the Yorkshire Dales', *Proceedings of the 23rd International Congress of the History of Medicine*, London, 1972, pp. 998–1001. I owe this reference to Catherine Crawford.
4. 'David Campbell', Biographical notes, Lancaster Public Library.
5. Francis Nicholson and Ernest Axon, *The Older Non-Conformity in Kendal*, Kendal, 1915, pp. 351, 515; newspaper cutting in Kendal Public Library (42/362.5) 'The origin of the soup kitchen in Kendal, 65 years ago' quoting the *Cumberland Pacquet*, 24 December 1782 and the *Carlisle Journal*, 18 January 1800.
6. Eden, *Poor*, reports on Kendal and Lancaster, also Baines, *Lancashire*, on Lancaster.
7. *Royal Lancaster Infirmary; an Epitome*, 1922; W. Parson and W. White, *History, Directory & Gazetteer of the Counties of Cumberland & Westmoreland*, Leeds, 1829, p. 644; Annual Reports of the Lancaster Dispensary.
8. Parson and White, *Cumberland and Westmoreland*, 639, 644.
9. See Baines, *Lancashire*, II; Holt Leigh Papers (Wigan Borough Archives). Letters of Miss J. H. Leigh to Robert Holt Leigh, 1797.
10. J. H. Leigh to Robert Holt Leigh, 1 April 1797.
11. Wigan Dispensary – Annual Report, 1806 (Wigan Borough Archives). In most Dispensaries the total number of patients over several years was obtained by adding the annual gross totals, so that those 'on the books' at the end of each year were counted twice.
12. J. H. Leigh to Robert Holt Leigh, 1 April 1797.
13. Notice, Wigan Dispensary, 9 November 1797 (Wigan Borough Archive) 'That, besides medicine, those patients whom the medical gentlemen think especially in need of wine, or other sustenance, be granted (so far as the funds of the Charity will allow) *Diet Tickets*; which shall enable them to obtain it from such vendors as the committee may find charitably disposed to afford it on the most reasonable terms'.
14. Holt Leigh papers, 16 May (1797).
15. Holt Leigh papers, 24 July 1798.
16. Wigan Dispensary Minutes (Wigan Borough Archives).
17. G. B. Hindle, *Provision for the Relief of the Poor in Manchester*, Manchester, 1975, p. 82.
18. Charles Smith, *Stockport Infirmary: A Short History*, Stockport, n. d. (*c.* 1947), pp. 1–8; also J. Ferriar, *Medical Histories and Reflections*, III, Warrington, 1798, p. 92 note.
19. W. I. Wild, *The History of Stockport Sunday Schools*, London, 1891; Henry Heginbotham, *Stockport Ancient and Modern*, 2 vols, London, 1882–92, I, pp. 349–50; II, p. 385 *et seq*; T. W. Laqueur, *Religion and Respectability. Sunday Schools and English Working-Class Culture, 1780–1850*, New Haven, 1976; on Anglicans and Dissenters in the Manchester region, see W. R. Ward, *Religion and Society in England 1790–1850*, London, 1972.
20. Stockport Dispensary and Infirmary, Annual Reports and Minute Books; G. N. Jackson, 'The House of Mercy: a short history of Stockport Dispensary and House of Recovery', thesis, Elizabeth Gaskell College of Education, 1969, (Stockport Public Library); *Stockport Advertiser*, 23 February 1827.
21. [Francis Philips], *An Exposure of the calumnies circulated by the enemies of Social Order and reiterated by their Abettors against the Magistrates and Yeoman Cavalry of Manchester and Salford*, Manchester, 1819; *A Dialogue between Thomas, the Weaver, and his Old Master*, Manchester, 1817.
22. Annual Report, 1823–4.
23. Annual Reports, 1822–3, 1825–6.
24. See Baines, *Lancashire*; A. Hewitson, *History of Preston*, Wakefield, 1883, reprinted 1969; A. F. Davie, 'The government of Lancashire, 1798–1838', MA thesis, Manchester University, 1966, esp. p. 27.

25. Baines, *Lancashire*: Gadian (1976), esp. pp. 96–7, quoting *Manchester & Salford Advertiser*, 10 December 1836: 'there was always a want of spirit among the men of Preston'.
26. The early years of the Preston Dispensary are unusually well documented by letter books covering 1809–37 (originals in the Lancashire CRO). I thank John Wilkinson of the Pathological Laboratory, Preston, for helping me to study these manuscripts.
27. See esp. report of 11 April 1810.
28. Baines, *Lancashire*; Preston Dispensary Annual Report, 1814.
29. Preston Dispensary Minutes & Correspondence; Hewitson, *Preston*.
30. See Baines, *Lancashire*; Bolton Dispensary Annual Reports (Bolton Record Office); J. A. Atkinson, *Memoirs of the Rev. Canon Slade*, Bolton, 1892.
31. Bolton Dispensary Annual Reports.
32. Blackburn Dispensary Annual Reports; W. A. Abram, *A History of Blackburn, Town and Parish*, Blackburn, 1877, pp. 382–3; G. C. Miller, *Blackburn, the Evolution of a Cotton Town*, Blackburn, 1951, esp. pp. 110–23; T. A. I. McQuay, 'The Blackburn General Dispensary 1824–1838', *The Practitioner*, 196 (1966), 716–20. On politics and industrial relations in Blackburn (& Preston) see H. I. Dutton and J. E. King, 'The limits of paternalism: the cotton tyrants of North Lancashire, 1836–54', *Social History*, 7 (1982), 59–74.
33. Chorley Dispensary Annual Reports. Also John E. Harrison, 'The development of medical care & public health in nineteenth century Chorley', MSc thesis, UMIST, 1983. The values and patronage of Lancashire livings are given in James Wheeler, *Manchester: its Political, Social and Commercial History*, 1836, p. 377.
34. 'The story of Rochdale Infirmary', *Souvenir Programme*, 1962; Rochdale Public Library Scrapbook on Infirmary; John Vincent, *The Formation of the British Liberal Party 1857–68*, Penguin, 1972, pp. 131–53.
35. Bury Dispensary Annual Reports; Printed letters about the Dispensary by Wm. Goodlad (1837), Dr Chadwick (1845), Robert Harris (1845). Fletcher's letters were published in the *Bury Mercury and General Investigator*, 2 and 3, 1831. (Bury Public Library)
36. See n. 1.

CHAPTER 5

Medicine without charity: economism, medical services, and the New Poor Law

Industry, indigence and independence: the debates in Manchester
When, in 1829, the Manchester Children's Dispensary was launched, a short article appeared in the *Manchester Guardian* requesting support. It contained the following awkward but revealing sentence:

> The originators of the Dispensary are sensibly aware of the blessings which flow to the poor from those noble monuments of public benevolence which already exist amongst us; but to a community which from being essentially a manufacturing [one] must, amongst its operative branches, be of necessity, an indigent one, there has still been wanting an asylum open exclusively to the cries of the helpless child, suffering from the inflictions of the varied diseases which are the common lot of early years.[1]

It was here assumed that industry implied indigence and indigence necessitated medical charity. But two years later, in the same newspaper, very different views were to be put forward.

In 1830 a number of leading medical men in Manchester and other cities began the *North of England Medical and Surgical Journal*. This was a distinctly provincial initiative, following the example of Dr Charles Hastings, the founder of the Provincial Medical & Surgical Association, who had begun a similar periodical in the Midlands. The *Journal*, which was probably edited by J.P. Kay, was a token of the scientific and professional ambitions of medical men who were well educated, often at Edinburgh University, and who were well aware of the latest developments in medicine, and anxious to establish that even in provincial general practice they could contribute to medical knowledge. We have already discussed how articles in the *Journal* presented the medical experience of Dispensary and Infirmary physicians. Inevitably, articles based on experience in local medical charities were, to some extent, discussions of the operations and effects of those charities. In this way, the new *Journal* proved controversial.

In the November 1830 number, Edmund Lyon, a Manchester Infirmary physician, questioned the usefulness of the Lying-in Charity. Pregnancy was not an accident and 'whatever teaches the labourer that he need not provide

[78]

for the natural and ordinary casualties of life, and so destroys in him the inducement to forethought and frugality, leads directly to his degradation in the scale of society'. Lyon saw the financial difficulties of the Lying-in Charity as evidence that his opinion was widespread.[2]

The following year the issue became public when, in the next number of the *Journal* John Roberton published an article including a table showing

Table I The growth of charity midwifery in Manchester, Manchester Lying-in Hospital, 1796–1830

Dates	Pregnant married women admitted into the Hospital	Ditto delivered at their own homes	Out-patients with diseases peculiar to women and children	Admitted for vaccination	Total
1796–7	124	580	129	—	833
1798	133	655	146	—	934
1799	177	623	253	—	1,053
1800	192	852	99	—	1,143
1801	164	874	426	—	1,464
1802	99	785	320	—	1,204
1803	120	748	374	—	1,242
1804	157	871	33	875	1,936
1805	89	754	23	1,189	2,055
1806	129	810	12	2,222	3,173
1807	114	851	13	1,047	2,025
1808	123	983	39	1,353	2,498
1809	138	1,148	45	1,545	2,876
1810	88	887	55	1,143	2,173
1811	29	1,112	44	1,070	2,255
1812	5	1,148	39	1,220	2,412
1813	56	1,251	51	1,303	2,661
1814	1	1,253	21	951	2,226
1815	—	1,433	8	1,030	2,471
1816	—	1,512	6	1,787	3,305
1817	—	2,164	14	1,408	3,586
1818	—	1,910	14	1,273	3,197
1819	—	2,276	11	1,487	3,774
1820	—	2,446	19	1,046	3,511
1821	—	2,440	27	973	3,440
1822	—	2,654	30	1,034	3,718
1823	—	2,706	47	872	3,625
1824	—	2,989	10	1,263	4,262
1825	—	3,120	7	500	3,627
1826	—	3,443	11	551	4,005
1827	—	3,632	4	724	4,360
1828	—	3,739	16	416	4,171
1829	—	4,108	12	337	4,457
1830	—	4,356	23	524	4,903
Total	1,938	61,113	2,381	29,143	94,575

the growth of charity midwifery in Manchester. The number of deliveries had risen since about 1815 much faster than the growth of population.[3]

At the suggestion of a correspondent this table was reprinted in the *Manchester Guardian*, when the editor gave his own views on 'forethought, economy and care', before adding 'To us it seems utterly improbable but that a large proportion of those who appear to have received the benefits of charity, within the last few years, must have been of a class that might and ought to have provided for the necessities of these periods, without recourse to public charity.[4]

The Lying-in Charity was peculiarly exposed to criticism. Some who valued the power of the lay administration at the Infirmary, thought the Lying-in Charity was unduly controlled by doctors. Some doctors suspected that the charity midwives sought out cases to gain the fees, and that some of these cases could have afforded private surgeons. When Malthusian doctrines were in vogue and fear of over-population was general, then a Lying-in Charity might be seen as anti-social. But, as the later disputes were to show, the main arguments about need and effects applied to all medical charities.

On the question of need, Roberton replied to the *Manchester Guardian* from five years' experience as a surgeon at the Lying-in Charity.

> That some – I will even allow that several hundreds out of the 4356 – might provide well enough against the period of delivery, maybe true; but unhappily an overwhelming majority is in a state of incredible destitution ... their families are of a *very poor* description, destitute of every comfort and convenience, and generally even of necessary articles. Few of them, probably not one in a hundred, rent an entire cottage. A great proportion live in cellars, and those that live above ground are chiefly lodgers; a single family, however numerous, occupying commonly one apartment.[5]

Roberton estimated that about two thirds of the population of Manchester was in 'so destitute a condition, (or if you will – so degraded), as to have their offspring brought into the world by the aid of a public charity!'. He initially guessed that a majority of the cases were Irish, but corrected himself – the majority were English. Later counts at the Charity showed that less than a quarter were Irish.[6]

Later in 1831, Roberton again used the *Manchester Guardian* to argue that the operative population of Manchester was nowhere near so well or well-off as commonly assumed. Nassau Senior, the political economist, had claimed that falling national death-rates proved that industry, in general, was not productive of disease. Roberton, pointed to the enormous scale of medical charity in Manchester as evidence of chronic sickness. His calculations were very general; the important point is that Roberton, knowing that medical charities were not greatly abused, was ready to use their extent as evidence of real need – medical and financial. Such a state of affairs in his eyes condemned as a failure the 'experiment' of industrialisation.[7]

His policy was made clear in his defence of the Lying-in Charity. Subscribers should certainly enquire personally into cases asking for recommendations – that would prevent abuse and it would also strengthen bonds between classes. He wanted the Charity to exclude first pregnancies, so as to reduce the incentive to improvidence. But generally one had to recognise that the majority of the working class were in no condition 'to lend an ear to such phrases as "forethought and economy"'. Yet even the destitute deserved the best obstetrical attention. Left to themselves they would have only those untrained midwives who would work for little or no fee. The Lying-in Charity was necessary as a source of trained, efficient midwives, backed by experienced surgeons. Under these conditions maternal and infant deaths were rare, and so was damage to the mother or the baby. Roberton agreed that for mothers to pay the midwife's fee (three shillings) themselves would be preferable but that was a situation 'to be wished for, rather than hopefully anticipated'. Roberton's letters were reprinted and circulated in an attempt to reduce the damage to the Lying-in Charity's funds.[8]

The state of the Manchester poor became a national concern with the publication of J.P. Kay's book on the *Moral & Physical Condition of the Working Classes* (1832). He sought to break the complacency of Manchester employers and to advertise the investigative methods and political remedies favoured by his circle of reformers. In 1833, with the Greg brothers, the Heywoods and other industrialists and bankers, Kay helped found both the Manchester Statistical Society and the District Provident Society. The paid investigators of the Statistical Society collected data on social conditions; the assistants of the District Provident Society visited the poor to collect small savings. They were to teach the working classes the benefits of thrift.[9]

At the same time other institutions were founded to take different remedies from door to door. Several Christian missions attached to middle-class congregations began in the early 1830s. Roberton, whose social concerns were motivated by a traditional Christian piety, suggested that these missions should be combined into a city-wide charity which could be better organised. He was later to serve as an honorary medical officer to the Manchester & Salford Town Mission, begun by evangelical Quakers.[10]

In 1834 Kay resigned from his post at Ancoats Dispensary and joined the service of the New Poor Law. His health had suffered from overwork and he sought retirement from the city.[11] But before leaving Manchester he published his views on Dispensaries in the form of a letter to George Murray, the Ancoats industrialist. Kay used Roberton's statistics to show the disproportionate growth of the midwifery charity and then generalised his attack by including the Infirmary and the Dispensaries. He was able to show that the dependence on medical charities had been increasing much faster than the population.[12]

There is little doubt that this was indeed the case between 1825 and 1832. Around 1810 the annual number of cases relieved by Manchester and Salford medical charities was about 9 per cent of the population. In 1825 the proportion was very similar, but by 1831 it had risen to about 17 per cent, partly because of the opening of new Dispensaries, partly because the Infirmary and the Lying-in Charity were taking far more out-patients and domiciliary cases respectively.

Kay also gave the expenditure of the various charities to show that they too had increased considerably over the decade, though less than the numbers of patients. In fact a high proportion of the expenditure was on in-patients at the Infirmary, whom Kay recognised as legitimate objects of charity. Dispensary attendance was cheap. Over 1830–2, at Chorlton, Salford and Ancoats Dispensaries, the expenditures per patient were respectively 5s 3d, 3s 9d, and 3s 0d. William Farr, the medical statistician, estimated that the average cost per patient of medicines supplied by Dispensaries was about 2s 1½d.[13]

At the end of his pamphlet Kay listed the wages for the various classes of Manchester operatives, to support his view that they were capable of paying for medical services and were being weakened by not doing so. He wanted the Ancoats Dispensary linked to the District Provident Society and supported by the weekly subscriptions of the patients, a plan advocated nationally from 1830 by the Society to Promote Self-Supporting Dispensaries, and one which continued to be advocated into the 1840s. There were a few such institutions, mostly in the Midlands, but generally it was not until the 1870s that the working classes proved able and ready to support Provident Dispensaries. The better-off workmen did join Friendly Societies and some of these provided medical services. But doctors disliked them, for the contract-practitioner was employed by his patients: Provident Dispensaries usually had enough middle-class patrons to protect the doctor.[14]

If Kay's argument against the Ancoats Dispensary was part of a very general 'economic' critique of philanthropy, it was also a personal response to the conditions under which he as a Dispensary physician had worked. The large numbers of patients meant that little time could be spent with each and that there was little privacy. Roberton indeed claimed that women with 'women's diseases' were loath to attend general Dispensaries or to disclose their true symptoms if they did attend.[15] It was difficult to practise good medicine there. It was also unrewarding because Dispensaries like the one in Ancoats were not the social instruments which eighteenth-century philanthropists had intended. Honorary physicians were no longer the estimable agents of charity. In a large town like Manchester by the 1820s, benefactors had little if any social contact with a Dispensary's patients or its doctors. Most recommendations for medical charities were obtained from a few sources which acted as ticket offices. Sometimes these would be clergymen; in the case of Ancoats, some tavern keepers were involved. For most patients and most subscribers there was no one-to-one contact. The giving and the getting of recommendations was routinised and no gratitude was generated.

Nor were patients grateful to the Dispensary physicians. Because it was widely known that medical men competed for office in public charities, it was difficult to convince patients that doctors were doing them a favour; many of those visited thought the service a right rather than a boon. As a Dispensary physician went around Ancoats he met very few people who could ever employ him in private practice. Rarely would any account of his treatment of patients reach those who could help his career. The handful of clergymen and businessmen who administered the Dispensary might be impressed and the majority of subscribers might know the physician's name, but his work would rarely come to their attention. Even in the case of employers who subscribed to cover attendance to injured workmen, the service was impersonal. The recommendation would probably be obtained from a manager and no representative of the employer would visit the workman as he recovered at home.

Kay wanted manufacturers to employ their own surgeons, and not just because that meant paid rather than honorary service. A factory surgeon had the authority of the employer; a Dispensary doctor did not. In a society where relationship between classes had been reduced to cash payments for work, Dispensaries were increasingly anomalous.

It is difficult to see whether Kay's critique had much effect on the medical charities of Manchester. The Infirmary certainly felt obliged to defend itself. The Annual Report for 1834 pointed out that hospitals were not included within the increasingly common criticisms of charity. In 1835 the Lying-in Charity, as its finances deteriorated, introduced a payment of two shillings per case. Those patients claiming poverty were referred to the District Provident Society, who checked them out. This change halved the number of patients; about half of those who remained paid the charge. The numbers attended at all three general Dispensaries fell in the mid-thirties but they had already begun to fall when Kay wrote, probably because of the improvement in the economy.[16]

The Dispensaries continued much as before; they provided well-qualified medical men with experience and the start of a public career, factory owners with cheap medical care for workers, local leaders and clergymen with opportunities for display. Generally they enabled the Manchester middle class to claim that medical attention was not beyond the reach of the poor. But, those who supported Dispensaries now had to argue against the 'avaricious philosophy' of the economic liberals. In 1845, the Annual Report of the Ancoats Dispensary claimed that the condition of the Institution was 'an index to the feeling with regard to the poor which has been of late years fashionable in this country'. Population, wealth and luxury had all increased: subscriptions to the Dispensary had decreased. 'With the imperfect philosophy which would repress promiscuous almsgiving, and which has dictated a false policy with regard to the poor, we have nothing to do. It is not adapted to a civilised, far less to a Christian community.' By then the 'imperfect philosophy' had for ten years been embodied in the working of the New Poor Law.

The New Poor Law and medical services
The legislation of 1834 was primarily intended to reduce the expenditure of poor rates on subsidies to able-bodied but under-employed agricultural labourers. As such it was not designed for northern industrial communities where destitution, except for hand-loom weavers, tended to be cyclical and total rather than chronic and partial. The principle of the New Law, that the able-bodied would only be given relief within a workhouse, was therefore inappropriate. Out-door relief did in fact continue in most northern Unions, because during trade depressions there was no feasible alternative. But the intention to abolish out-relief was itself a major reason for the unpopularity of the new regime.[17]

The workhouses envisaged by the Poor Law advocates were to be large institutions in which different classes of paupers could be kept apart and where those physically incapable of work need not be exposed to the spartan rigours designed to deter the able-bodied from accepting relief. But large new workhouses, planned or constructed, were usually seen as Bastilles, or prisons for the poor, and were a major source of popular resentment.

To facilitate the efficient, utilitarian management of the poor, the Poor Law advocates amalgamated the parishes into large Unions. In Lancashire each usually consisted of a major town plus its hinterland – much the same districts as now used for hospital planning. Each Union had a Board of Guardians, which was responsible to the Poor Law Commissioners in London. The imposition of this administrative machinery and especially the loss of local autonomy to central government was a third source of resentment, especially among the local ruling groups who traditionally had arranged poor relief in their own parishes. In the smaller towns brought within a large Union, the potential loss of independence was considerable. The previously powerful authorities of larger towns resented the Poor Law Commission, especially when, like the Manchester Select Vestry, they had already introduced most of the management techniques which were supposed to justify the new structure.

For all these reasons, the introduction of the New Poor Law into the north-west was very contentious and incomplete. The south of England was incorporated first and little was done about the north until 1837. But by then the mid-1830s boom was over and the need for relief was again rising, so the resistance was even greater than it might otherwise have been. The politics of this resistance varied considerably between towns, in a pattern not unlike that which we discovered in discussing the relative successes of medical charities.[18]

In Stockport and in Chorlton on Medlock, areas dominated by large manufacturers with Manchester connections, liberals who favoured the New Poor Law dominated the newly elected Board of Guardians. For the Poor Law Commissioners and for the *Manchester Guardian*, Chorlton was a model Union.[19]

In the western part of the region, where the towns were well spaced and country interests were strongly represented, the new Unions tended to be dominated by Tory anti-Poor Law Guardians, even though those elected by the towns were mainly liberal and in favour of the Law. In Preston, the radicals opposed to the Law won a majority of the places on the Board but were squeezed out of power in 1838 by the magistrate who assumed chairmanship of the Board. Generally in these western areas, there was minimal co-operation with the Poor Law Commissioners; Boards tended to operate as federations of townships, which, as far as possible, continued to give relief as they had before 1834.

The strongest resistance to the New Poor Law came in the towns to the north and east of Manchester, where working-class and some middle-class radicals were strongly opposed to the implementation of the Law. In these areas Boards of Guardians were not introduced as anything more than Registration authorities until the 1840s (Bury 1846, Rochdale and Ashton 1845, Oldham 1846). Until then, the overseers continued to be responsible for poor relief, and in Oldham at least, the overseers were radical.

In Manchester and Salford, the New Poor Law was resisted by the existing Poor Law authorities, and in Salford there was an attempted boycott, which broke down after the Guardians' election of 1838. The Manchester situation was complicated by the continuing resistance of the churchwardens to the Corporation formed in 1838. Not until 1841 was the New Law introduced, but then was easily implemented. The parties agreed on a slate of candidates for the Board of Guardians, and the regime they instituted was little different from the previous one.

In broad terms then, the Poor Law was least popular where charities had been unsuccessful – where class-consciousness and radical independence were pronounced. In Stockport and Manchester, where charities were established but increasingly routinised, the Poor Law appealed to those wealthy employers who sought a more scientific way of dealing with the poor. In the western districts, the same traditionalism which had maintained charity, helped maintain a suspicion of the 'Whig engine' for 'oppressing the poor of England'.

Even in areas where the New Poor Law was introduced, the Guardians strongly resisted the Commissioners' plans for large, segregated workhouses in each Union. For more than a decade, in most of the Lancashire towns, it would have been electoral suicide for Guardians to build a 'bastille'. In some Unions, the Guardians closed some of the smaller township workhouses, but generally they were maintained as 'co-operative establishments', where each class of pauper assisted the others 'on a family system'.[20] Only in the Unions of Chorlton and Stockport and Manchester and Macclesfield did new premises follow the introduction of the New Law.

In 1840 Chorlton Guardians built a new workhouse in Hulme. The next year, immediately to the south, came the Stockport workhouse later used as St Thomas' Hospital. The Macclesfield Guardians were forced to build a new workhouse because their old one, which dated from about 1700, was dilapidated as well as overcrowded. The new building was opened in 1845 on the site of what is now West Park Hospital. As a 'well-regulated establishment', it contained separate wards for the sick. No Lancashire town, except Manchester, built a segregated workhouse until after 1850.[21]

Manchester's huge workhouse on New Bridge Street was already divided into various sections. In 1841 it housed 1,261 paupers, though the accommodation was only properly sufficient for 1,100. There were 335 men, 490 women, 242 boys and 194 girls, including 268 in sick wards and ten lunatics.[22] The workhouse had a resident surgeon whose surgery was also accessible to out-patients; drugs were supplied by the churchwardens and the medical administration was supervised by an honorary surgeon and an honorary physician.

The new Guardians, when they bought the workhouse from the churchwardens, set up a committee to recommend any necessary changes and its report showed the influence of the central Poor Law administration. They wanted more careful calculation of the food consumed by each pauper, and they recommended that the medicines be supplied at the expense of the surgeon, who should no longer be resident. His salary was consequently

Table 2 *The wards for the sick in the Manchester Workhouse (1841)*

Male wards	No. of patients at time of inspection
Surgical ward, 2 rooms & kitchen, for 24	23
Medical ward, 2 rooms & kitchen, for 30	28
Old mens hospital, consisting of 3 dry comfortable cellars and kitchen, adapted for 54	16
Itch ward, 1 room, will hold 12	2
Boys itch ward, 1 room adapted for 12	4

Female wards	
Surgical ward, 2 rooms & kitchen, adapted for 24	23
Medical ward, 3 rooms, kitchen, nurses room, servants room and bath room, adapted for 40	38
Old womens hospital, 6 dry comfortable cellars, to the front, to which there is not any day room attached, but the inmates have the use of the general yard, adapted for 48	11
Womens and girls itch ward, 2 rooms, adapted for 30	21
Old women sick wards, 4 rooms and kitchen, adapted for 30	28
Lying-in ward, two rooms, adapted for 8	6
Boys & girls sore head ward, 2 sleeping rooms, 1 day room & yard, adapted for 80	53
Children's sick ward, 1 room adapted for 18	13

There are other sick patients in the *general wards*.

Lunatic wards – 3 day rooms, kitchen, 26 sleeping rooms and yard; they are convenient and more than sufficient. There are only 10 patients in them.

Medical department – Surgery is commodious and conveniently situated, so that out-patients may have access to it. There is a resident surgeon, and there are also an honorary consulting physician and surgeon.

Source: Poor Law Commissioners, Annual Report, 1841, Appendix B, 135–7.

increased to £250 *per annum*. They wanted probationary wards where paupers could be inspected by the surgeon, and they recommended separate accommodation for children as had been provided in some London Unions. The Guardians borrowed £11,000 to extend the central workhouse. They initially proposed to put the children in the small workhouses they had inherited in Blackley and Prestwich townships, but in 1844 they opened the Manchester Poor Law Schools at Swinton. This large and expensive accommodation was much praised by the Poor Law Commissioners and many later commentators.[23]

The Guardians made relatively few changes in Manchester, because the previous system met most of the New Poor Law requirements. The medical service for paupers in the workhouse was already well developed and was overseen by notable local professionals, usually honorary staff at the Infirmary. Most out-door paupers in the Manchester township continued to seek aid from the medical charities. Here, as elsewhere, the impact of the New Poor Law on medical services was limited and gradual.

The proponents of the New Poor Law, in their eagerness to regulate the idle overlooked the problem of sickness and debility, though there is no doubt that physical ailments were the major cause of destitution. Because there were no special provisions for medical care in the Act of 1834, the development of a medical service was largely determined by precedent and by administrative orders. In the north of England before 1837 relatively few parishes employed surgeons to attend sick paupers, other than in the workhouse. In most of the Lancashire towns which had a Dispensary, the overseers made a payment which was intended to cover the treatment of those on parish relief.

Otherwise there was little expenditure explicitly on medicine. In the townships of south Manchester for example, less than £100 *per annum* was spent on medical attention for paupers, though the population exceeded 60,000.[24] There, as in most towns without Dispensaries, the occasional medical expenditures were incurred as payments to local practitioners to whom paupers had been sent with an order for medical relief. Such medical orders were rare, often the overseer would give general relief and expect the pauper to call in a doctor if he needed one badly enough.[25] In Oldham and Ashton, which in 1841 were still outside the jurisdiction of the New Poor Law, the cost of medical relief was similarly low, even though there were no Dispensaries. In each the public medical expenditure was about a farthing (0.1p) per head of population.[26]

The Poor Law Commissioners were generally in favour of payment per case, but in almost all the north-western Unions, the introduction of the new arrangements was followed by the appointment of Poor Law surgeons on salaries.[27] In many cases the jobs were put out to tender and the doctor who offered the cheapest services was accepted. This system, as it developed in the south, had already proved unpopular with doctors. In 1836, before the introduction of the New Poor Law to the north, a meeting in Manchester of the Provincial Medical & Surgical Association pressed for salaries to be adjudicated by a third party and for sick paupers to have direct access to medical men, without a prior visit to the relieving officer.[28] These demands were to be repeated throughout most of the century.

The salaries in the north were low by southern standards – £50 was common even in populous districts – but they may have corresponded to a smaller amount of work, partly because Dispensaries, at least initially, took a higher proportion of cases, and partly because the northern poor were not in the habit of asking for medical relief, certainly if they were not already 'on the parish'. But these patterns changed, albeit slowly. The medical officer appointed to the Ancoats district of Manchester, which by 1843 had a population of 35,000, found that his work grew rapidly over the first two years as paupers discovered that it was simpler to obtain a medical relief order from the relieving officer than to get a recommendation to the charity Dispensary.

In 1843 the Poor Law surgeons of Manchester applied unsuccessfully for a rise. In that year, Mr Ker of Ancoats had about 1,000 cases, so the payment per head was about 1 shilling. From his salary he was expected to provide medicines; on William Farr's evidence that charge alone should have been twice the average payment. To the doctors these terms seemed oppressive: they now had to 'give away' the medicines which previously they had sold. When aked why he continued in post, Ker referred to the tradition of medical men aiding the poor. He also discussed his work as a vaccinator, for which he was paid 1*s* 6*d* per case; the number of children vaccinated fluctuated from year to year but was usually about 800 – 1,000.[29]

The medical officers in other north-western Unions were also poorly paid. In Burnley the salaries were 'scandalously low'.[30] In 1842, after several years of consultation, the Poor Law Commissioners issued the General Medical Order, intended to improve the medical service and the remuneration of doctors, but it had relatively little effect in the North West. In general, it limited the areas to be served by one doctor to 15,000 acres or to a population of 15,000, whichever was less. This did cause some division of medical relief districts. Bolton, for example, was divided into two but even the resulting districts were often above the maximum. The Commissioners allowed these anomalies whenever it could be claimed that Dispensaries, or benefit societies, or factory surgeons, diminished the work of the Poor Law surgeon. These exemptions applied to most of the urban districts we have considered. In Manchester, the density of the population and the large amount of charity care meant that the districts remained huge.[31]

The 1842 Order gave medical officers separate payment for cases of midwifery and surgical operation. Here again, Lancashire was little affected. In Manchester itself such cases were treated by the hospitals; in the mill towns pregnant paupers were usually sent to female midwives, who were cheaper than doctors, and many of the cases requiring operation were dealt with by factory surgeons paid for by the mill and colliery owners. Factory surgeons rarely dealt with cases other than serious accident, so they did not substantially reduce the work of the Poor Law surgeon; they merely prevented him receiving an occasional case-payment for surgery.[32]

By the 1840s, in areas where there was no Dispensary, the New Poor Law had probably significantly increased the amount of medical care received by those already on relief. Over the whole county of Lancashire, in 1844, medical relief averaged 1¼*d* per head of population, only half the national average, but higher than the level in areas still resisting the New Poor Law. Guardians had proved ready to appoint surgeons, in part because previous medical care had been so sparse; but the remuneration of surgeons assumed and ensured that the poor generally would not get into the southern habit of asking for the parish surgeon *before* they needed general relief.[33]

In areas where medical charities already existed, the New Poor Law shifted some of the load. The effects varied according to the size of the town and the rootedness of the charity. In Manchester, the Poor Law had little effect on charities; in 1844 the ratio of Poor Law to charity cases was about 6:1.[34] The Infirmary and Dispensaries did not generally exclude paupers but there is evidence that the alternative provision had led ratepayers as well as overseers to reduce their subscriptions.

In 1842–3, the Manchester overseers withdrew their subscription of £200 *per annum* to the Infirmary though the number of Dispensary patients was increasing.[35] As Poor Law medicine became more established the pay of medical men was increased; in 1854 the Manchester medical officers were paid 5*s* 0*d* per case, generous remuneration compared to the salaries elsewhere. Some Manchester doctors, especially John Leigh who was also the registrar for the Deansgate district, argued that a system of public Dispensaries, supported out of the poor rate, should replace the delay-ridden recommendation system of the charities. Each doctor would serve a given area and patients unable to pay for medicines would get them free from the local public Dispensary.[36]

Such a system would have again blurred the distinction between pauper and poor man, but such was not the intention of the New Poor Law. Its operation, in medicine as elsewhere, in fact sharpened the distinction, partly by undermining medical charities. In Blackburn, where the Dispensary had incorporated the previous work of the parish surgeon, the 'Charity' had continued to depend on a large payment from the overseers. When the New Poor Law was introduced in 1838, the Dispensary was closed. Blackburn went back to the parish surgeon system; there was to be no medical relief except on pain of pauperdom. Only ten years before the Blackburn leadership had still entertained hopes of building an Infirmary to serve the whole of north-east Lancashire.[37]

Elsewhere the effects on Dispensaries were less rapid, but generally, especially after the 1842 Order, the local Guardians withdrew their subscriptions and in return, the Dispensary excluded those already on general relief. In Kendal the 1840s saw the end of a once flourishing Dispensary and a profitable manufactory in the workhouse; by 1848 the Guardians were paying a surgeon, albeit minimally, and the Dispensary was failing for want of subscriptions. In 1848 the Poor Law Commissioners forced the Guardians to run their workhouse by the new rules; economical dietaries, segregation by sex and age, no manufactory. In the same year the Dispensary closed, leaving the Poor Law as the only means of medical relief in a town once noted for its generous and efficient welfare institutions. The 'fat, sleek, democratic Quakers' of Kendal had lost control.[38]

In Chorley, another small town, but more dominated by landowners, the Dispensary managed to survive the separation of Poor Law services. Like Blackburn Dispensary it had depended on the overseers to pay much of the salary of its house surgeon. When, after 1842, the Poor Law medical districts were reorganised, the house surgeon took a Poor Law appointment and the Dispensary could not afford a replacement. Instead it continued on a much smaller scale, dividing the work between its honorary staff, the local practitioners.[39]

In Preston too, the 1842 orders disrupted the Dispensary. The Commissioners were unwilling to allow the Dispensary house surgeon to act as medical officer for the area covered by the Dispensary, because this included far more than 15,000 people. They forced the appointment of district medical officers and so removed from the Dispensary both the paupers and the subsidy. As a result the work of the Dispensary was reduced to the level of the mid-1820s, 2–3,000 cases a year, compared to the 6,000 cases treated in the admittedly exceptional year of 1842. As in the towns where the Dispensary had suffered the removal of its 'pauper service', Preston Dispensary could no longer claim to be the only source of medical aid to the poor. Instead it presented itself as a barrier against pauperdom: many who were driven to the Poor Law in times of sickness became used to poor relief and lost their independence; a voluntary Dispensary could prevent this slide into dependency.[40]

The new workhouses

The resistance of many Lancashire Unions to central advocacy of large segregated workhouses lasted well past mid-century. We have already discussed how the New Poor Law policy was most readily adopted in Manchester and Stockport and how it was most strongly resisted in east Lancashire, especially in Rochdale, Ashton and Oldham. In Rochdale, Guardians were elected but the new regulations were not enforced; in Oldham and Ashton there were no Guardians.

THE INDUSTRIAL REVOLUTION

The resistance of these areas was finally broken in 1845. In Rochdale the *ex officio* Guardians (magistrates) arranged a special election after the usual boycott of the regular election. This produced enough Guardians to put the New Poor Law into effect. Similar measures were then used in Ashton and, the following year, in Oldham.[41]

Two of the authorities so produced, Oldham and Ashton, soon decided to build new workhouses. The Oldham Guardians came to power in the appalling depression of September 1847 and they inherited six township workhouses. Two were immediately condemned as 'small, dirty and altogether comfortless'. Within a month the Guardians had decided to build a new workhouse. It was built on Northmoor, the site of the present Boundary Park Hospital; it cost £13,305 and was opened in 1851. The Poor Law Board began to use Oldham as an example to other Unions; one of their most recalcitrant districts was now conforming admirably with the New Poor Law.[42]

In Ashton, the Guardians had come to power about a year earlier, in a town remarkable for its lack of statutory or charitable welfare provision, and were forced into a series of interim measures by the 1846–9 commercial crisis. The old Ashton parish workhouse was badly overcrowded, and an additional cottage was obtained to accommodate pauper lunatics. At about the same time, late 1846, the new medical officer began pressing for new fever accommodation. As the epidemic grew worse, the Guardians, in mid-1847, finally rented three houses and a cottage to serve as a 'fever hospital'. Conditions in the town became so bad that a Manorial Note was sent asking for central Government to intervene. A 'Union Hospital' was opened to take sick paupers and so relieve pressure on the workhouse, and a surgeon was assigned to it. In 1851 the new workhouse on Chamber Hills was opened; it contained fever wards and so superseded the interim 'fever hospital'.[43]

In Bury, in 1850, the Guardians were forced into building a new workhouse when Lord Derby refused to renew the leases of three township workhouses which in 1848 had housed 113 paupers. His local agent ordered the evacuation of this building, claiming that the Guardians had 'already spent as much money as would have built a Union workhouse by paying extra salaries and not having a labour test'. The Poor Law Board proposed to lend the Guardians the money to build a house for 400 able-bodied and sixty sick paupers. The new Jericho workhouse, Fairfield, was inaugurated in 1857. The Bury township workhouse on Manchester Road then became a workshop for Lord Derby.[44]

The majority of Lancashire Unions continued to resist central pressure for new workhouses. Initially, many of them had continued to operate workhouses to serve individual townships, and in these cases there was little room for segregation of inmates by sex and physical condition. During the 1840s the Commissioners had usually managed to force redistribution of paupers according to their condition rather than their place of residence. But it was difficult to compel Guardians to build new workhouses. Only when overcrowding necessitated building and permission for a loan were the central authorities able to secure compliance.

Bolton Guardians were particularly resistant to central pressure. In 1841-2 they (and Macclesfield) were singled out as having 'dangerous, insanitary and unclassifiable workhouses', but it was not until 1857 that the Guardians decided to build Fishpool workhouse.[45] In Blackburn the new workhouse was built during the Cotton Famine and opened in 1864.[46]

In Preston, the anti-Poor Law faction on the Board of Guardians held out until the 1860s against central pressure for a single large workhouse. Fever accommodation was less of a problem than in some other towns, for the Guardians rented the House of Recovery which the Vestry had built in 1827. In 1842 overcrowding compelled the Guardians to apply for permission to re-open a country workshop which they had previously discarded; the Commissioners reluctantly agreed, but forced the segregation of paupers between the seven premises then in use. Preston workhouse and the House of Recovery were to house the women and children and the sick; the able-bodied men were to use Walton le Dale and Ribchester; aged and infirm men were to be housed in Woodplumpton and Penwortham. About this time the House of Recovery had contained sixty-nine cases; there were 212 children under seven and 176 more under sixteen; 223 men and women were infirm, mostly through age; only 153 out of 967 paupers were able-bodied men. In 1842 the Guardians were forced to divide the various classes of paupers between their seven institutions, but they refused to build a central workhouse. Not until 1864 did the pro-Poor Law faction get their way after prolonged debate.[47]

In Burnley and Rochdale — areas with a continuing tradition of radicalism — the resistance was even more prolonged. The Burnley Guardians debated the issue throughout the 1860s under considerable pressure from central government, before buying land in 1870. The borough had been incorporated in 1861 and several schemes for civic improvement were afoot. The new workhouse, on Briercliffe Road, opened in 1877 the same year as the Rochdale Guardians opened Dearnley Workhouse.[48]

This prolonged resistance to the central argument of the New Poor Law was, in part, a rejection of central interference and is easily portrayed as mere parochialism; yet it had several positive aspects. The recalcitrant Guardians administered 'poorhouses' which were primarily refuges for the aged, the very young and the economically incompetent. In Preston, even in 1842, only 16 per cent of workhouse inmates were able-bodied males, 23 per cent were aged or infirm, 40 per cent were under sixteen years of age, and 20 per cent able-bodied women.[49]

They were allowed to live near their homes, in mixed communities. They were not seen as a medical problem, nor as an economic problem, and the Guardians were not interested in segregating them or building special accommodation, either to treat them better or to deter the able-bodied from accepting relief. The Poor Law Commissioners saw these poorhouses as slovenly and suspected the Guardians of pursuing the cheapest possible policy. Their remedy was regimentation and segregation; the workhouse would be a well-ordered deterrent. But because the able-bodied were, numerically, only a minor part of the workhouse population, even these better-ordered institutions came to serve largely as hospitals, and by the 1860s this function was seen as requiring special facilities.[50]

Notes and references

1. *Manchester Guardian*, 3 January 1829.
2. Edmund Lyon, 'Sketch of the medical topography & statistics of Manchester', *North of England Medical & Surgical Journal*, 1 (1830–1), 147–8.
3. John Roberton, 'General remarks on the best method of securing the speedy expulsion of the placenta', *North of England Medical & Surgical Journal*, 1 (1830–1), 333.
4. *Manchester Guardian*, 5 February 1831.
5. *Ibid.*, 9 February 1831.
6. Weekly Board, March 1834.
7. *Manchester Guardian*, 18 June 1831. This letter and another were published as a pamphlet: John Roberton, *General Remarks on the Health of English Manufacturers, and on the Need which exists for the Establishment of Convalescents' Retreats as subservient to the Medical Charities of our Large Towns*, London, 1831.
8. John Roberton, *Letters to the Trustees of the Manchester Lying-in Hospital*, Manchester, March 1831. (Manchester Medical Collection, John Rylands University Library, Manchester.)
9. The background to Kay's work is discussed in T. S. Ashton, *Economic & Social Investigations in Manchester, 1833–1933*, London, 1934, and in two very useful PhD theses: V. A. C. Gatrell, 'The commercial middle-class in Manchester *c.* 1820–57', Cambridge University, 1972; G. S. Messinger, 'Visions of Manchester: a study in the role of urban imagery in history, 1780–1878', Harvard University, 1971.
10. J. Roberton, *Christian Instruction Societies – respectfully addressed to christians of all denominations*, Manchester, 1830.
11. F. Smith, *The Life and Work of Sir James Kay-Shuttleworth*, London, 1923.
12. J. P. Kay, *Defects in the Constitution of Dispensaries, with Suggestions for their Improvement*, London & Manchester, 1834.
13. Report of the Select Committee into the operation of the Poor Law, Appendix, p. 142.
14. R. G. Hodgkinson, *The Origins of the National Health Service: Medical Services and the New Poor Law, 1834–1871*, London, 1967.
15. Roberton, *To the Trustees of the Manchester Lying-in Hospital*, 1831, postscript.
16. Annual Reports.
17. On the New Poor Law in general, and on its medical aspects see: M. E. Rose, *The Relief of Poverty*, London, 1972; Hodgkinson, *Origins*; S. E. Finer, *The Life and Times of Sir Edwin*

Chadwick, London & New York, 1952, 1970; M. W. Flinn, 'Medical services under the New Poor Law', in D. Fraser (ed.), *The New Poor Law in the Nineteenth Century*, London, 1976; M. A. Crowther, *The Workhouse System, 1834–1929*, London, 1981, 1983.
18. On the New Poor Law in Lancashire see N. C. Edsall, *The Anti-Poor Law Movement, 1833–44*, Manchester, 1971; E. C. Midwinter, *Social Administration in Lancashire, 1830–1860*, Manchester, 1969.
19. *Manchester Guardian*, 23 February 1839.
20. Rhodes Boyson, 'The New Poor Law in north-east Lancashire, 1834–1871', *Transactions of the Lancashire & Cheshire Antiquarian Society*, 70 (1960), 35–56 esp. p. 52.
21. On Chorlton and Manchester, see A. Redford, *The History of Local Government in Manchester*, 2, 1940, 95–129; Sheena Simon, *A Century of City Government, Manchester 1838–1938*, London, 1938; J. R. Wood, 'The transition from the Old to the New Poor Law in Manchester, 1833–42', BA thesis, Manchester University, 1938. On Macclesfield see Finer, *Chadwick*, 201.
22. Annual Report of Poor Law Commissioners, 1841, Appendix B, pp. 135–7.
23. Wood, thesis (1938), 94–7; Redford, *Manchester*, II, 127.
24. Henry Power in Apendix B to the Report of the Poor Law Commissioners on the Continuance of the Poor Law Commission and on some further amendments of the laws relating to the relief of the poor, 1840.
25. Third Report from the Select Committee on Medical Poor Relief, 1844, Minutes of Evidence, pp. 1–15 (evidence of G. C. Lewis).
26. *Ibid.*, p. 78.
27. *Ibid.*, p. 4.
28. Hodgkinson, *Origins*, 24, 143, 221.
29. Evidence of H. W. Ker, Select Committee, 1844, pp. 604–7.
30. Appendix, Select Committee, 1844, pp. 968–70.
31. *Ibid.*, pp. 732–41.
32. *Ibid.*, pp. 968–70.
33. Select Committee, 1844, p. 77.
34. *Ibid.*, p. 544 (evidence of H. W. Rumsey).
35. *Ibid.*, p. 968; Manchester Royal Infirmary Annual Reports.
36. Select Committee on Medical Relief, 1854, pp. 145–51 (evidence of John Leigh) and pp. 27–31.
37. Blackburn Dispensary Annual Reports, and see previous chapter.
38. Hodgkinson, *Origin*, 238; R. N. Thompson, 'The New Poor Law in Cumberland and Westmorland', PhD thesis, Newcastle University, 1971.
39. J. E. Harrison, 'The development of medical care and public health in nineteenth century Chorley', MSc thesis, UMIST, 1983.
40. Annual Reports.
41. Edsall, *Anti-Poor Law*, 253–4.
42. Oldham County Borough Council, *Oldham Centenary, A History of Local Government*, Oldham, 1949, pp. 128–30.
43. Winifred M. Bowman, *England in Ashton under Lyne*, Altrincham, 1960, pp. 337–8.
44. Jean Bannister, 'Jericho ...', *Bury Times*, 9 August 1974.
45. Reports relative to the Bolton & Macclesfield Unions, 1846 (661), XXXVI, pp. 15–16, 30–1.
46. George C. Miller, 'The old poorhouse', *Blackburn Times*, 23 October 1970 (cutting in Blackburn Library).
47. Winifred Proctor, 'Poor Law administration in Preston Union, 1838–1848', *Transactions of the Historical Society of Lancashire and Cheshire*, 117 (1965), 145–65; A. Hewitson, *History of Preston*, Wakefield, reprinted 1969, pp. 403–7; *Preston Chronicle*, 28 January 1860.
48. John Banks, 'Over a hundred years'. The story of the local hospitals in N-E Lancashire,

1876–1976', typescript, Burnley Public Libraries (thanks to the author for the loan of a copy); W. Bennett, *The History of Burnley from 1850*, Burnley, 1951, pp. 43–4; Frank Inston, *Birch Hill Hospital, 1877–1977*, (32 pp.), Rochdale, 1977 (?); Rhodes Boyson, 'North-east Lancashire'.
49. Proctor, 'Preston Union', 161.
50. Hodgkinson, *Origins*, 451–574.

SECTION B

*Voluntarism and the state
in established industrial communities*

CHAPTER 6

Civic show or healing environments: Manchester hospitals in mid-century

Introduction
Around the mid-point of the nineteenth century, the industrial society of the Manchester Region was radically changed. So too was the common conception of hospitals. The complex relations between these two shifts is the subject of this chapter.

From a decade after 1837, the cotton trade remained more or less depressed. In Manchester, the expenditure on outdoor relief of the poor, climbed from £7,000 to £19,000 between 1837 and 1842; after a small and short fall, it rose to £58,000 in 1847-8, before falling again in the early 1850s. In spite of economic distress, the population continued to rise rapidly. Manchester and Salford had numbered 233,000 in 1831, by 1851 they totalled 388,000, an increase of 67 per cent in twenty years. Many of the immigrants were Irish, especially during the potato famine: the number of Irish recipients of outdoor relief in the Manchester township rose from 2,500 to 21,000 between 1846 and 1848.[1] In the early 1840s many of the Irish in districts like Ancoats were trying to make a living from hand-loom weaving and so were many of the native population in the cotton towns to the north. By the end of the decade, hand-loom weaving had practically disappeared, as power-looms spread through the textile districts.

At the level of working-class politics the campaigns against the New Poor Law gave way to more general struggles for parliamentary representation. The economic crisis of 1842 stimulated strikes and demonstrations throughout Lancashire. The campaign for the Charter and for limiting the working day to ten hours built up during the mid-forties. But in the depression of 1846-7 the working-class initiative began to fail. In 1848 the Chartist petition was presented in London but had little effect; the impetus built up during the forties was dissipated.

The failure of Chartism contrasts with and was linked to the prior success of the middle-class Anti-Corn Law League which was based in Manchester. The repeal of the Corn Laws in 1846 established the Lancashire bourgeoisie as a major power in national politics; by lobbying and publicity on an unprecedented scale they had carried their argument for free trade. Thereafter, as the economy recovered, the constellation of middle-class politics began to change. In general, Lancashire employers moved to the right, away from the economic individualism preached by Richard Cobden and John Bright, towards paternalism at home and imperialism abroad. In Manchester in the 1850s, the religious and political divisions of the industrialists and merchants were softened as the middle-class groups drew together in support of common causes like public health and, to some extent, elementary education.[2]

The movement to paternalism was enhanced by the Cotton Famine of 1862 – 5 when the Civil War blockade prevented American cotton from reaching Lancashire. The economic consequences were disastrous for textile workers, but Poor Law relief and charity organised on a national scale helped prevent any significant political disturbances.[3] The Lancashire bourgeoisie emerged confident of their ability to control the textile communities, and ready to enhance their control by increased public display and increased philanthropy.

As we shall see in the next chapter, when considering Manchester satellite towns, hospitals were a particularly suitable form of philanthropy, especially from the 1860s when the campaigns of Florence Nightingale and others for better military hospitals, had popularised the notion of hospitals as ordered, healing environments, not only places where treatment could be given, nor mere refuges for the sick. In this chapter we are concerned with Manchester itself and with a complex series of developments which extended from 1845 to about 1875 – crossing the social and political transformations we have just outlined and encompassing the campaign for pavilion hospitals in which Nightingale was associated with the Manchester reformer John Roberton. We shall begin with the Manchester Royal Infirmary and return to it at the end of the chapter, because the Infirmary was the first of the Manchester hospitals to be restructured in mid-century, and the last of the major hospitals to come to terms with the criticisms of hospital reformers. In the middle sections of the chapter we shall consider the spread of homoeopathic dispensaries and hospitals, as evidence of discontent with orthodox medicine; we shall examine the restructuring of the Lying-in Hospital and of the Dispensary for Children as evidence of new attitudes towards medical philanthropy for mothers and infants; and we shall briefly survey the expansion of the Poor Law facilities, especially the building of the Poor Law infirmary at Withington. This infirmary was the earliest and most notable pavilion hospital in Manchester – the first fruit of the hospital reform campaign. Because the overall argument is complex and because the different kinds of institutions are described in separate sections, it is worth outlining the developments here by characterising each phase and considering the institutions together.

In the late 1840s and 1850s the Manchester Royal Infirmary was substantially rebuilt and the Guardians of both Manchester and Chorlton built new workhouses. The Infirmary development was largely the result of changes in the associated charities – the Lunatic Hospital and the House of Recovery, and much of the money required was raised by the sale of the land and buildings belonging to the House of Recovery. The whole scheme was a notable civic improvement for the Piccadilly district, which had become the centre of Manchester. It was not motivated by new ideas or new interest in the role of hospitals. Nor were the Guardians particularly interested in facilities for the sick. The Manchester Guardians did not provide a new infirmary; they kept their old building for use by the sick and they built a workhouse at Crumpsall to accommodate the able-bodied. The workhouse which the Chorlton Guardians built at Withington was intended to relieve overcrowding and to facilitate classification, but its infirmary very soon proved to be inadequate.

But we also find that in the same period there were notable shifts in attitudes towards medical institutions. One key change was the growing interest in hospital care for women and children. In part this was a result of medical specialisation; a few doctors, some of them immigrants, developed specialist practice in children's diseases or in gynaecology and obstetrics. A second factor was the concern over the high levels of child mortality revealed by registration returns and the propaganda of sanitarians. A third factor, which deserves much further study, was the increased involvement of ladies in the operations of health charities. It may well be that the middle-class sympathy and 'paternalism' which supported the voluntary hospital revival from the 1860s was first evidenced in the women's and children's charities of the 1850s.

These new interests were initially those of minorities and the results were limited and often contentious. The Lying-in Charity became St Mary's Hospital; its domiciliary midwifery service was reduced and played down; its out-patient clinics for women's diseases were expanded; its hopes for child in-patients appear to have been limited by parental reluctance as well as by lack of funds. The Dispensary for Children was restructured to include in-patients, but during the 1850s and early 1860s funds were very limited. A new children's Dispensary (which later became the Northern Hospital) found difficulty in attracting support. Moreover the 1850s were marked by disputes at both the Infirmary and St Mary's which centred on the relationship of doctors to lay governors. The balance of power still remained with the lay trustees, who resented attempts to remove their right to elect honorary medical staff. Doctors mobilised their growing organisations, national and local, in the attempt to secure more professional control over medical charities.

The 1850s also saw a marked increase in public criticism of hospitals and orthodox medicine in general, partly, no doubt, a reaction to the profession's new assertiveness. Homoeopathic medicine had increased rapidly since the early 1840s, though anathematised by the regular profession. Many sanitarians, including a number of doctors, pointed out that domiciliary medical services for the poor were rendered ineffectual by the conditions under which the poor lived. Hospitals were criticised for their admission policies and procedures, which failed to meet pressing public health problems and which discriminated against medical (as opposed to surgical) emergencies. The concern for cleanliness and ventilation which was developed in the public health movement, led to criticism of general hospitals as insanitary and unsuitable for surgical and accident cases. We shall follow these debates in Manchester.

One result of these debates and especially of Florence Nightingale's national reputation, was a new image of what a hospital ought to be. Pavilion hospitals on the European model were advocated and high quality nursing became central to work which a hospital was supposed to do. In Lancashire at least, this awareness coincided with a general increase in philanthropy, especially in the form of large donations and legacies. As a result the proponents of hospitals found their task considerably eased.

Thus the late 1860s saw the 'take-off' of several local voluntary hospitals and a new willingness of Guardians to spend money on pavilion hospitals for the sick poor. The Infirmary's Convalescent Home at Cheadle, the Children's Hospital's new building at Pendlebury, and the new Withington Poor Law infirmary all bore witness to this new image of the hospital. They were out of town, and the latter two were notable examples of the pavilion style.

The trustees of Manchester Royal Infirmary also contemplated a move away from the centre, but it was not to happen for a further half-century. By the 1870s, the old building stood officially condemned as insanitary, but by then the pressure for 'country hospitals' was receding. As we shall see in chapter nine, it was the pull of the University, not the arguments of the sanitarians, which finally moved the Infirmary from Piccadilly.

Hospitals and real estate
In 1845, the trustees of Manchester Infirmary decided to rebuild their hospital. This was the major project in a decade notably lacking in medical charity. The only new voluntary medical institutions begun in Manchester and its region between 1832 and 1850 were Homoeopathic Dispensaries and a small Homoeopathic Hospital. For the regular medical profession, who were strongly opposed to homoeopathy, these novelties were little more than an indication of considerable public scepticism about the benefits to be

derived from regular medicine. It is characteristic of the poor standing of medicine during the 1840s and the general suspicion of charity, that the rebuilding of Manchester Infirmary was stimulated less by the ever-increasing number of serious accident cases, than by the failure of its associated Lunatic Hospital to attract paying patients.

The founding of Lancaster Moor County Asylum in 1816 had gradually diminished the admissions of pauper lunatics to the Manchester Lunatic Hospital. Competition from private lunatic homes had proved more difficult to meet as the Lunatic Hospital's buildings aged and as the continued growth and pollution of the city made the hospital's site seem less and less suitable for the long-term care of the mentally ill. The new County Asylums and the successful private homes were out in the country, where the lunatics were removed from the public eye and able to benefit from the peace and fresh air.[4]

When the future of the Lunatic Hospital was debated in 1844–5, many trustees thought it should be abandoned altogether. Its functions had been taken over by other institutions and a new public asylum was about to be built for South Lancashire. To appropriate the Lunatic Hospital's assets might be an estrangement of funds left to a particular charity, but some trustees were willing to argue that the Lunatic Hospital had not been a real charity; it had always been a 'money-getting concern'. Others, including Joseph Adshead, a reformer who had recently published a graphic account of the 1842 distress, argued for the rebuilding of the Lunatic Hospital outside the town. There was still, he maintained, a demand from the middle classes too poor to pay for private asylums, too rich to commit their relatives as pauper lunatics. The legal opinion that the funds could not be appropriated appears to have ensured the continuation of the Lunatic Hospital on its new site at Cheadle. Its removal and the sale of its old building to the Infirmary trustees, provided a unique opportunity for the expansion of the Infirmary building, long since hemmed in by warehouses and other commercial buildings. Though there was much debate as to how best the Infirmary could be improved, it was generally agreed that it needed considerable renovation.[5]

In 1845 the Infirmary was admitting about 1,500 in-patients per year. The number had changed little since the early 1830s when the extra space provided in 1828 had been fully taken up. But the number of special accident cases had continued to increase as the dependent population rose. In 1845–6, almost half (48 per cent) of the in-patients were accident cases, and so were about 20 per cent of the out-patients. On average, about eleven accident patients for each day of the year were brought into the Infirmary, and about 20 per cent of them were admitted as in-patients. Around 1840, accidents to railway workers had become very conspicuous. The rise of accident cases meant that the average severity of in-patients complaints, and hence the mortality, was bound to rise. By the mid-1840s, it was 12 per cent, twice the level of the 1820s, and high enough to attract concern. Adverse publicity had to be countered by the surgeons explaining that over half of the deaths commonly occurred within twenty-four hours of admission; these fatalities were almost all the victims of serious accidents.[6]

Yet, as the surgeons knew full well, not all the deaths could be so explained; many were due to 'hospital diseases' – erysipelas and hospital gangrene – following injury or surgical operations. It is difficult to know how many died of these diseases, and how many had contracted them within the hospital, but the problem was already acute by the 1830s. By the end of that decade 'almost every operation that was performed was followed by more or less severe attacks of erysipelas and the mortality amongst these cases was very great'.[7] In 1839 the method of cleaning the wards was changed in an attempt to reduce the incidence of 'hospital diseases'; the floors were to be dry-cleaned with sand rather than mopped with water. For a few months this change seemed to be effective, but by 1843 it was clear that keeping the floors dry could not prevent infection.

The medical committee was asked to suggest ways of improving the ventilation, but it became obvious to everyone that the existing building, when full to capacity, could not be maintained in a healthy state. It contained 192 beds, but often there were more than 192 patients. In February 1845, twenty-eight of the patients were lying in fourteen double beds, 'which was extremely unproper'.[8] Medical patients, especially those from Manchester itself, were regularly refused accommodation when they needed hospital care. Preference, of necessity, was given to patients who had been brought from surrounding towns.

For two years the trustees discussed the twin problems of the half-empty Lunatic Hospital and the overcrowded Infirmary. When it was agreed that the Lunatic Hospital should move, plans were put forward for the reconstruction of the Infirmary. The committee wanted to rebuild on the same site, taking over the Lunatic Asylum, but some, including Richard Birley, wanted to sell the site, by then very valuable, and use the proceeds to build two Infirmaries, one to the north and one to the south of the town. This would be more economical and would give better service to the neighbouring towns. His proposal was defeated, partly because some thought the Infirmary had to be central, partly because the committee dreaded further delays.

Expediency also dictated the rejection of additional measures asked for by Samuel Fletcher and Alderman Potter. Both owned warehouses near the Infirmary and Fletcher had been involved with earlier schemes to widen neighbouring streets. In 1840 he and George Faulkner, a treasurer of the

House of Recovery which owned some of the land concerned, had organised the widening of Parker Street. In 1845 Fletcher wanted an Act of Parliament to allow removal of the smaller properties which surrounded the Infirmary, so as to obtain a two-acre site. The baths could be pulled down and a wide promenade created all around the hospital. This would allow more fresh air to the building, and it would 'add to the adornment and salubrity of the town'. It would also increase the value of the nearby warehouses owned by Fletcher and Potter, who were willing to contribute the increment to Infirmary funds. This scheme for civic improvement was only partially realised; some of the Lunatic Hospital's land was sold to the Corporation for street widening, and the Corporation later provided £1,000 to build a clock in a dome surmounting the new building.[9]

This link between Infirmary renovation and civic improvement was not a concern of the neighbours alone. The 1845 meeting to discuss rebuilding was chaired by the Mayor, Alderman Alexander Kay, and it followed a considerable public campaign about the public health of Manchester. John Leigh, a surgeon with strong interest in chemistry, had lectured in 1844 to the Manchester Royal Institution on the sanitary condition of Manchester. In 1845 he published a long pamphlet, 'Letter to Alexander Kay', praising his long-standing interest in raising the condition of its inhabitants. Several other Manchester doctors including P. H. Holland (of Chorlton Dispensary), Richard Howard (of Ancoats Dispensary) and John Roberton, had given evidence to the national public health enquiries of the 1840s, and Lyon Playfair had used the Infirmary books in compiling his 1844–5 report for the Royal Commission on the State of Large Towns. The local branch of the Health of Towns Association, led by P. H. Holland and Joseph Adshead, brought lecturers from London to discuss urban sanitation. R. D. Grainger, of St Thomas's Hospital, had lectured to the Manchester Athenaeum one month before the Infirmary meeting of 1845.[10]

Manchester had come in for massive criticism and the new Corporation was responding by trying to improve the ventilation of the close-packed courts and alleys and by making arrangements for better drainage and the removal of night-soil. In the summer of 1845 they were waiting for parliamentary approval of their pioneering Sanitary Improvement Act.[11] The Infirmary renovation was seen as part of these plans: 'they were now seeking to promote the recreation, amusement and increased health of the community' and hoped that 'the sick poor would not be overlooked'.[12]

When the rebuilding proposals were agreed in 1845, the leading citizens of Manchester were confident that the money could be raised. The committee responsible included practically all the commercial and religious leaders; trade looked promising, with the prospects of new markets in China;

all the major religious denominations had completed their large collections for churches and colleges; supporters of the Anti-Corn Law campaign had reached their target of £100,000 for the League's funds.[13] But these well-supported causes stood in marked contrast to the financial record of the Infirmary. Subscriptions had been higher in 1811 than they were in 1845, though the population of Manchester and Salford had tripled and the total number of patients had more than doubled.

In 1849, when the extensions were well under way, the future of the Infirmary's second affiliated charity, the House of Recovery, came under discussion. As in the case of the Lunatic Hospital, statutory provision was removing potential patients from the charity, and the Fever Hospital's central and expensive site was attracting attention from those interested in property development. It was the introduction of the New Poor Law which raised questions about the Fever Hospital's future. Previously patients had been admitted irrespective of their being on relief, but when ratepayers were supporting a Poor Law medical service, they began to hesitate over also subscribing to a charity which obviously included many paupers.

The fever epidemic of 1847 had focussed attention on the problem. The destitution was so severe and the diseases, mostly typhus, so fearful that the Board of Guardians took over temporary premises to relieve the House of Recovery. Over 6,000 patients were taken into hospital; the House of Recovery in 1846–8 admitted 2,000. There were 1,500 deaths from fever alone, and many more from the dysentery, diarrhoea and influenza which also attacked the enfeebled population. The epidemic left the House of Recovery short of funds, in spite of a collection made by George Faulkner and Samuel Fletcher. Consequently, in 1849, the committee asked the Guardians to pay for pauper cases. They agreed and made retrospective payments. They were then asked to pay two guineas per case in future, for the House of Recovery wanted to devote its funds to 'people who, though poor, are unwilling to claim the privilege of a pauper in sickness, and are yet unable to pay for medical aid themselves, and can avoid contagion by no other means than the removal of their sick to the Hospital'.[14] The Guardians decided that it would be cheaper to accommodate fevered paupers at the workhouse; they built new wards at Bridge Street and withdrew their subsidy to the House of Recovery, which was left with fewer if more respectable patients. By 1851 there were very few patients in the House of Recovery, but as its medical value to the town had declined, its real-estate value to the Infirmary trustees had increased enormously.

The House of Recovery stood on Aytoun Street, just off Portland Street, and land there was becoming very valuable, partly because the removal of the Lunatic Hospital had opened up the corner with Piccadilly, especially because Portland Street had just been extended to Oxford Street and had become a major thoroughfare. In 1851 the House of Recovery sold some of its land fronting Portland Street, and the magnificent Watts warehouse was designed in that year for a site very close to the fever wards. In 1852 an Act of Parliament was obtained allowing the Infirmary to take over the House of Recovery and sell its building. By 1855, when the House of Recovery was closed, over £30,000 had been transferred to Infirmary funds; ten years later, when the building was sold, another £21,000 was realised.[15]

The extended Infirmary had been envisaged in 1845 as accommodating 370 beds, but the new north wing completed in 1851 soon proved unhealthy and as work proceeded on renovating the central section, plans were revised to give more air-space per bed. No more than 277 could be included if a minimum of 1,000 cubic feet was allowed to each. But when fifty-seven beds in the south wing were appropriated for fever, more beds had to be packed into the rest, otherwise the medical and surgical sections would have been reduced to 220, only thirty more than before the rebuilding. Instead the staff dormitories were removed to the basement and the attics, allowing 275 beds for general purposes plus thirty-five for fever.[16]

The net effect of this complex development between 1845 and 1855 was scarcely commensurate with the wealth of Manchester's merchants, the value of the assets realised by the Infirmary, or the needs of the Manchester poor. The Lunatic Hospital, a paying proposition, had been moved to an ornate building in the countryside. The main burden of fever had been shifted on to the Guardians. A residual fever service for the respectable poor was unsuitably housed in thirty-five Infirmary beds, though £50,000 of House of Recovery assets had been transferred. The medical and surgical service had eighty-five new beds, an increase of forty-five per cent, but half these additional beds were liable to appropriation for fever cases during epidemics. All the rooms were full and the staff were housed in basement rooms which did not meet the standards of the 1848 Health Act.

This was hardly the massive expansion envisaged in 1848. It was a 'rationalisation' of medical charity, which had consolidated the financial assets and the buildings but had not greatly improved or extended the service. In 1845 the Infirmary complex had been semi-rural in design, a sprawl of eighteenth century buildings, including piggeries and airing-yards. In 1855 the Infirmary was a solid, porticoed structure; thoroughly urban like the large warehouses which surrounded it. Like them it was a showplace with an impressive exterior, a part of a major town centre development organised by the merchants of England's major industrial centre. But whereas these merchants and their architects appreciated the functions of warehouses as well as the frontages, no one in Manchester was then thinking of hospital architecture in functional terms. They wanted an impressive building and they got it. They had given some thought to increasing the space per bed, but pressure on accommodation minimised the improvement. For those who feared the spread of fever, the new Infirmary was arguably more dangerous than the old.

Nor were medical students satisfied. New honorary assistant posts – Dispensary surgeons – had been created in 1846 for the out-patient clinics, but this seems to have encouraged the senior surgeons to attend less at the Infirmary, to the detriment of teaching and patient care. In 1855 the students complained to the local press. Mid-century staff elections continued to be huge and troublesome, even for the new assistant posts, which were soon abandoned in favour of paid residents. The *Manchester Guardian* helped lead a campaign about the mode of elections and the success of mediocre but well-supported candidates. They agreed with the local doctors about the need to reduce the advantages of 'early information, patronage, connexion and favouritism', but did not want full medical control. Instead, a medical committee should make recommendations to a committee of trustees.

Neither the doctors nor the *Manchester Guardian* supporters made much headway. The trustees feared loss of subscriptions if staff elections were abandoned; they agreed only to reduce the time allowed for canvassing so as to diminish the expense and the harassment. The honorary staff could not even gain control of appointments to the resident medical and surgical posts.[17]

On this issue, as on others, the real power was held by the lay officials, especially the treasurer and his deputies. Thomas Markland had led the first stage of the mid-century expansion; his successor J.C. Harter was very influential. George Faulkner had directed the House of Recovery; Thomas Townend was treasurer of the Lunatic Hospital. All these were Tory churchmen: Townend and Harter were connected with most of the principal charities and interested in Church education. Faulkner was a business partner of John Owens and a trustee of the bequest which which established Owens College. Some leading Dissenters were also active in the Infirmary – Samuel Fletcher and Joseph Adshead were Independents; William Nield, the Quaker, was a member of the Building Committee – but the mid-century Infirmary was a solidly establishment institution. Since 1838 the Infirmary had paid a chaplain instead of relying on local clergymen; in 1845 a pew in the Collegiate Church was rented for the use of resident medical officers. (The matron and servants were to use St Paul's church.)[18]

During the 1840s there was little overlap, medical or lay, between the Infirmary leadership and the groups concerned with the moral and sanitary conditions of the urban poor. The Infirmary physicians, and especially the surgeons, concentrated on medical education and the local medical societies; only R. B. Howard (physician 1842–8), was known as an expert on the condition of the poor. Most of the medical authorities on the condition of Manchester were attached to the peripheral Dispensaries. The missions which sent bible readers into poor districts were set up largely by Dissenters, and were only weakly linked to the Infirmary through Samuel Fletcher and especially Joseph Adshead, whose informed arguments about the treatment of lunatics we have already mentioned. Adshead was an activist in many causes including public health: he helped lead the local Health of Towns Association, and supported homoeopathy. But he was an exception among Infirmary laymen. The leaders brought money, status and business acumen rather than an informed desire for social reform.

The mid-Victorian critique of medicine
If the Infirmary represented the Establishment of Manchester medicine, there was no shortage of medical 'non-conformists', many of them qualified medical men. The 1840s saw a rapid growth in the popularity of homoeopathy and an organised reaction by the local medical profession. The 1850s saw sanitarian themes developed into a critique of existing hospitals and Dispensaries.[19]

When first publicised in the 1790s by the German, Samuel Hahnemann, homoeopathy was one among many 'medical systems'. It was introduced into England during the 1830s, by the fashionable London physician, Richard Quinn. By the 1840s it represented a threat to an increasingly coherent but therapeutically powerless medical orthodoxy. Homoeopathists, most of whom were regularly qualified, discounted the powerful drugs and depletive therapies of orthodox medicine. They gave medicines in extremely small quantities and paid much attention to the constitution and mode of life of each patient. Homoeopathy appealed to the aristocracy but it also had a populist, even anti-professional, aspect.

In this Region in the early 1850s, there were several homoeopathic Dispensaries; two in the centre of Manchester, two in Hulme, and one each in Bolton, Blackburn, Preston and Wigan. Some were little more than the public front of a private homoeopathic practice; others were genuine public charities. The Manchester Homoeopathic Dispensary had existed since 1842. About 1847 the Dispensary took on a house surgeon and changed its rules so as to encourage patient subscriptions. The number of patients was then similar to that at Ancoats 'allopathic' Dispensary or at Chorlton. In 1850 a small homoeopathic hospital was opened in Bloom Street and soon had thirty beds.

For a few years, in the early 1850s, organised homoeopathy must have worried the orthodox profession. New homoeopathic institutions were opening and the Homoeopathic Hospital had attracted very influential support. At a meeting on its behalf in the Town Hall in 1852, the Mayor took the chair, and speakers included the eminent Town Clerk, Alderman Sir John Potter, and the new Principal of Owens College. Two well-known clergymen – Canon Slade of Bolton and Richard Durnford, Rector of Middleton – also gave support. The treasurer of the Hospital was Sir Elkanah Armitage, probably the richest man in Salford; its chairman was Joseph Adshead. These men thought homoeopathy effective, but did not want the Homoeopathic Hospital to displace the orthodox medical charities which some of them also supported. They argued for freedom of conscience in medicine.

The Rev. Durnford, after praising the Cathedral and the Manchester Royal Infirmary added:

> We think that our own modest building may be allowed to raise its humble front, side by side, with those proud porticoes, and to do good in its own measure and in its own way, although it be not the established way. Surely in Manchester where the right of private judgment and individual liberty is so largely claimed and so loudly asserted, the science of medicine is not to be the only exception. Surely we are not prepared to submit to a medical despotism, or endure a medical monopoly.[20]

These words have to be measured against the attitudes of orthodox professionals who had denounced homoeopathy as quackery. The Manchester Medico-Ethical Association, founded in 1847, explicitly forbade its members from associating with homoeopathic practitioners. The profession was consolidating the push for legal recognition and they were seeking legal restrictions on unqualified practice; they did not appreciate arguments about freedom of choice.[21]

The popularity of homoeopathy was to fade over the following decade, but its minimal doses of medicine, which seemed at least as effective as the larger and more expensive quantities used by 'allopaths', probably helped to reduce the orthodox professionals' faith in their 'cures'. By the 1860s we find many medical men trusting to cleanliness and regimen rather than medicines, and this outlook was very important for the future of hospitals. Some of these attitudes can be followed among the doctors concerned with public health in Manchester who, in the mid-1850s, presented various criticisms of Manchester's medical institutions, usually in papers to the Statistical Society. The key figures were John Roberton, Daniel Noble and John Leigh.[22]

All three were critical of the Poor Law service. It was used only as a last resort and the patients saw Poor Law surgeons less as doctors then an arm of the inquisitorial relief system. Roberton and Leigh wanted to see dispensaries established in every district; Roberton now favoured provident institutions, paid for by the subscriptions of the users; Leigh thought that if the medicines could be provided at public expense, without the taint of pauperism, then medical men would be content to prescribe without payment.[23] Either way medical relief would be accessible and more acceptable. Leigh was particularly keen to see more dispensaries dealing with children.

Leigh also criticised the way the Royal Infirmary worked, mainly because of the delays in attending to urgent medical cases. Accidents were admitted without recommendation, but in medical cases the friends of the sufferer had first to find a recommendation and then to deliver it to the Infirmary. There was no one there ready to visit urgent cases; the physicians' clerks would be out on their rounds. Not until the next day would one of them receive the recommendation and come to see the patient. Even then the clerks were only junior practitioners – if one of the senior physicians was called then a further delay was involved. Leigh wanted to see additional resident appointments to try and save lives in cases of medical emergency. He also wanted the recommendation system scrapped as an ineffectual waste of time – the medical officers were in a better position to judge the economic condition of the patient than were subscribers who saw neither the patients nor their homes.

Roberton went further in his critique. He was impressed with the work local government had done in improving sanitary conditions. By the mid-1850s, schemes for sewerage, nuisance removal and water supply were well under way. Roberton wanted to see local authorities more positively involved in the preservation of health. In a paper to the Statistical Society he proposed that the administration of hospitals would be improved if they were run by the municipality rather than by volunteers whose interest tended to be fitful. This suggestion was not to become common until the next century.

Daniel Noble, who had been a Poor Law surgeon, was disenchanted with the dispensary system, whether Poor Law or voluntary. He was convinced that medicines were rarely of use to the majority of the sick poor. Their complaints, as described in a previous chapter, were usually chronic and could only be relieved by better living conditions. That did not just mean the removal of dirt, for Noble was also disenchanted with the 'ultra-sanitarians'; it meant good diet, careful nursing and experienced medical attention as well as hygienic surroundings. These needs could only be met in hospitals. Yet Manchester and district, with a population of half a million, had 'but one general hospital, containing two hundred available beds. And the sick inmates of this single hospital are not, as they ought to be, patients who most require its advantages; but, for the most part, they are those whose ailments present pathological interest.'[24]

Roberton also had much more faith in healthy conditions than in medical procedures. From the 1830s, he had been interested in establishing a convalescent home, preferably at the seaside, which would allow some patients to recover their health away from the poverty, pollution and worries of the city. In the mid-1850s, after many years examining public health problems and some occasional experiences of the conditions at the Infirmary, he began to publicise the need for hospitals which would be truly healthy. He did so at the time when the public throughout Britain was impressed by Florence Nightingale's campaigns for the better treatment of soldiers injured in the Crimean War.[25]

The report on the State of the Hospital of the British Army was published in 1855; by the end of that year Florence Nightingale was established as a national heroine and there was general concern over the insanitary condition of military hospitals. The plans of a new military hospital at Netley, Southampton, were privately criticised by Miss Nightingale. When she returned to England in August 1856 she renewed that criticism and generalised her campaign to include civilian hospitals. She received help and assistance from the journal *The Builder*, and from John Roberton of Manchester who achieved a national reputation as a pioneering advocate of the pavilion system.[26]

In March 1856 Roberton read a paper to the Manchester Statistical Society on the construction and ventilation of hospitals. His arguments were not new – the founders of the Manchester House of Recovery would have recognised most of them – but Roberton was applying them to general hospitals, not just to fever hospitals. He contended that those responsible for general hospitals had confused them with dormitories for the healthy. A degree of ventilation which would serve in a dormitory was quite insufficient in a hospital, for, while all exhaled air was potentially harmful if not dissipated, the exhalations from the sick were much more dangerous. Without adequate ventilation a 'hospital atmosphere' was produced, in the wards, and if air could pass along corridors from ward to ward, then the hospital atmosphere could spread, and with it disease. The only answer was the 'ceaseless, it may be imperceptible, flow of the external air through the wards'. This was *Nature's ventilation*.[27]

Roberton, like Nightingale and other reformers, used recent French hospitals as models. Roberton had visited several, including one at Bordeaux which was particularly impressive, and of which he reproduced the plans. As an example of what to avoid he used the Manchester Infirmary, as typical of many in which foul air circulated to pollute the whole building. The results he had seen for himself in the early 1850s:

> patients ... instead of obtaining cure, grow worse; and occasionally owing to the breaking out of an infectious malady – known by the name of hospital gangrene, die rapidly in considerable numbers. But even should this scourge not show itself, and there be no very high rate of mortality, the health of the inmates will often deteriorate, so that wounds, fractures, burns, ulcers and other forms of surgical disease, are cured, if at all, only after great lingering and suffering ... We have few Hospitals in England that are not insalubrious whenever they chance to be crowded; and which, when crowded with such cases as burns, compound fractures, and extensive ulcers, are often the abodes of death, occurring in forms most humbling and mortifying to the pride of surgical science; since the surgeon, in such circumstances, is aware that the poor sufferers have been carried to a public institution to their destruction; and that had they been treated by him in their own homes, howsoever humble these might be, the chances of recovery would have been greater.[28]

Part of the answer lay in proper choice of sites for hospitals. The salubrity of the hospital must be the primary consideration. Of course it was important that the injured should receive immediate attention, but this did not necessitate the hospital being in the centre of town. It would be better to set up Accident Rooms in all districts, like those in Paris, where emergency care could be given before removal to a hospital. That a central site was convenient for medical men was a minor consideration.

> But, if any should still object, let me remind them that this is a sceptical age regarding the unaided powers of the Materia Medica; that whilst there are many persons very apt to descant on the uncertainty attaching to the results of the most skilful medical practice apart from cleanliness and pure air, there are perhaps none who would not concede that a removal of the sick poor from their own cottages and cellars into wards so airy and cheerful as those of the Bordeaux Hospital, confers, in itself alone, the most important benefits; and the medical staff too, would doubtless, in the case supposed, be the first to applaud arrangements so wisely designed to aid their efforts for the good of their patients.[29]

When Roberton returned to this theme in his Statistical Society paper of 1858, his work was nationally known.[30] George Godwin, editor of *The Builder* had given wide publicity to his views. In public discussion of the Crimea and of the proposed Netley Military Hospital, Florence Nightingale had argued for pavilion hospitals and Roberton was able to use her name and fame. She in turn considered him 'our greatest Hospital authority'.[31]

Roberton's campaign had two results. It encouraged the building of new hospitals in pavilion style, and it aroused the staff and trustees of existing hospitals to the defence of arrangements which they could not easily change. Both aspects were forcefully presented in 1860 in a third paper to the Statistical Society where he explored the treatment of accident victims:

If 'plague, pestilence and famine' used to be the evils most feared in bygone times, contusions, fractures, dislocations, burns, and other kinds of injury may well be regarded as the dread of the present; with this difference, – that whereas the plague and the pestilence were the terror of all ranks, the rich as well as the poor, the bodily injuries now so frequent are the lot mainly of the labouring classes.[32]

By 1860, as we shall see, plans were under way for new Infirmaries at Ashton under Lyne and at Blackburn. The first was the response by a local mill-owner to a tragic boiler explosion in 1855. The founders of the Blackburn Infirmary had been very much influenced by Roberton's earlier writings.[33] By emphasising accidents Roberton was strengthening the arguments for similar hospitals in the other cotton towns.

He was also attacking Manchester Royal Infirmary with criticism much more detailed and extended than in his previous papers. As a receptacle for the seriously injured, Manchester Infirmary had no equivalent. Over the five years 1855–60, almost half of the deaths which occurred in the hospital had been followed by inquests. In 1859–60 the figure was 57 per cent; over half the mortality was directly or indirectly the result of accidents. At the London Hospital, serving the docklands of the capital, the corresponding figure was one third. Manchester Infirmary's high proportion of serious accident cases was probably unique, but was it salubrious enough to handle such an awful load? In the previous five years there had been 166 fatal cases of 'surgical diseases', sixty of them following operations; in the last year, at least twelve patients seemed to have died from pyaemia, apparently a consequence of the hospital air.

For those who did not die, the period of recovery was prolonged much beyond that to be expected in a private home. Even among staff, the hospital induced disease – almost all new nurses suffered from sore throats. For Roberton, Manchester Infirmary was not the worst in the country, but it was worse than most. He wanted better first-aid for accident victims and better means of transport. He would have preferred that the Infirmary be pulled down and the site sold – with the proceeds a hospital of 450 beds could be provided in a healthy situation. Failing that, he wanted new surgical wards constructed behind the existing building. In a footnote he welcomed the plans which Joseph Adshead was then advocating, for a convalescent hospital to serve Manchester, a plan backed by Miss Nightingale herself.[34]

Women and children: specialists and the new philanthropy
The critique of hospitals developed by Roberton and others had little short-term effect on the Manchester Infirmary, and we therefore reserve those effects for a later section of this chapter. First we shall examine a group of

Manchester medical charities where the shifts in attitude between 1850 and the 1860s were most marked – those dealing with women and especially with children. It is our thesis that the renaissance in voluntary hospitals, which was to carry such hospitals into every town in the Region, began in the special charities of the city which devoted themselves to the diseases of women and children. Here we see philanthropy mobilised by doctors who sought and brought a special knowledge of children's diseases; here too we first see middle-class women beginning to direct the course of medical charity. The interactions of changing lay and medical interests were complex and require further investigation. Here we can only give a preliminary sketch, pointing out the problems, and linking the major themes to the others developed in this chapter.

In the 1840s, the Lying-in Hospital was the only Manchester medical charity specifically concerned with women. It was then, as we have seen, simply a domiciliary midwifery service, and during the 1840s it was in severe financial difficulties. Subscriptions had fallen steadily from 1837 and in 1847 they totalled about £250 per year, less than a third of their level in the 1820s. The delivery of poor women was not a cause for which the middle classes of Manchester were prepared to subscribe. The death in 1845 of H. H. Birley, treasurer since 1815, deprived the Charity of its most influential supporter, and in 1847 a fire in the South Parade premises destroyed much of the hospital's property. For several months the Charity operated from the Eye Hospital next door.[35] In 1849 the Charity was so short of money that it imposed a charge of two shillings on all home-delivery patients. Previously those who satisfied the District Provident Society that they were unable to pay had been treated *gratis*; henceforth those who could not pay were refused.[36]

The reconstruction of the Charity was largely the work of its senior medical officer, Dr Thomas Radford, and his wife, who created support amongst the ladies of the town. Since early in the century there had been a Ladies' Auxiliary Society which provided linen etc. for some of the needier cases, but it had little influence on the main Charity's policy. In 1849 a Ladies' Committee was organised to raise funds, and from then we find more evidence of female influence in the direction of the institution. Around mid-century, middle-class women were seeking public roles; medical charities for poor women and children were an obvious avenue. Furthermore, such charities, once divorced from worries about population increase, could more easily withstand general attacks upon philanthropy. Whatever fecklessness might be attributed to working men, their wives and children, as victims, had a stronger claim on public support.[37] For these reasons, charities for women and children are prominent among the new or revised philanthropic ventures of mid-century Manchester.

Radford wanted his Charity to provide a general medical service for the women and children of Manchester. He also wanted it to be a place of medical education, with in-patients as well as home- and out-patients. As an obstetrician of national fame with a long record of service to the institution, he had considerable influence over the lay trustees, but they paid close attention to financial constraints and for many years these severely restricted the use of the hospital's facilities. Furthermore, both Radford and the lay trustees were frequently opposed by the ordinary honorary surgeons who saw some of the extended services as impositions on their time and health. Here, as at the Infirmary, the 1850s were notable for contests over the control of the hospital.

After the South Parade fire, the medical committee drew up grandiose plans for a hospital, to the expense of which the lay trustees objected. Instead the new building had only twelve beds, intended for cases of dangerous labour and for those who needed treatment which could not be given at home. These wards were not completed until 1852, and never took more than forty-seven patients in a year. Meanwhile the surgeons had neglected the out-patient clinics which they were supposed to hold twice a week. In 1849 the trustees insisted on recording their attendance, and got their way after a dispute.[38]

The annual subscriptions had now been restored to about £600 *per annum*, and the midwifery charge was halved to one shilling to increase the usefulness of the Charity, but the change had little effect. Many of those approached to take out a subscription were suspicious of midwifery services and many thought the Charity delivered women in hospital, like the Lying-in hospitals in London. These were known to encourage puerperal fever and were not at all popular. The makeshift buildings on South Parade were cramped and airless and did nothing for the institution's reputation. Though the new wards had only just been opened, a campaign was begun for a new hospital. The Manchester sanitarians were no more impressed by the building of the Lying-in Hospital than they were with the contemporary renovation of the Infirmary.

In June 1852 Mrs Radford asked permission to begin collecting for a new building.[39] In November John Roberton published an anonymous pamphlet condemning the existing building as unworthy of the town; good accommodation was required for dangerous confinements, for female diseases, and for disease and congenital deformities in children over three; it would improve the teaching of midwives, monthly nurses and medical pupils.[40] Dr Radford was particularly keen that the domiciliary service be extended to cover children and women who were sick rather than pregnant. He shared John Leigh's concern over the levels of infant mortality and was later (1862) to campaign for a children's infectious disease hospital to be attached to

St Mary's.[41] He may also have been stimulated by the efforts which a new medical immigrant, Dr Louis Borchardt, was then making to improve the fortune of the Children's Dispensary, which from 1855 was known as the General Hospital and Dispensary for Sick Children.

These schemes met with limited success. In 1853 Radford gave his library, and lectures were begun for medical students. In 1854 the name of the institution was changed to become 'St Mary's Hospital and Dispensary for the Diseases peculiar to Women and also for the Diseases of Children under six years of age'. The rules were revised and a Board of Management was introduced to replace the open but badly attended Weekly Board. In September 1856, with considerable ceremony, the Countess of Wilton opened the new building on Quay Street which was planned to hold 25–30 children's beds and about sixty beds for women. It had cost £4,300.[42] From then until the mid-1860s there was a steady rise in subscriptions, to about £1,000 *per annum*; the out-patient service became a major part of the hospital's work. The midwifery service was deliberately played down and the curative aspects of the hospital's work was emphasised. This suited the ordinary honorary staff who were keen to establish reputations in obstetrics and gynaecology, then becoming a lucrative specialty. But Radford and his lay supporters were at least as interested in domiciliary work, which was much less popular among the staff.[43]

After the move to the new building, Radford and the Board of Management soon came into conflict with the ordinary honorary surgeons, who felt themselves over-regulated, under-represented and over-worked. New rules forbidding appointments in other charities or in public or club practice caused annoyance, for one of them, Dr Whitehead, was involved in the new 'Clinical Hospital for Diseases of Children'. Another surgeon was suspended for moving to a house 150 yards beyond the boundary within which surgeons were supposed to reside. The ordinary surgeons had recently lost their places on the Board of Management; as the Medical Committee they refused to ratify the credentials of a candidate to replace the suspended surgeon; when Radford obliged in their stead, four of the six surgeons resigned and publicised their grievances in the medical press, which tried to 'black' the posts. Among the grievances was the proposed home-patient service which, they claimed, would have compelled them 'to attend children of any age and in any disease, whether infectious or otherwise, at any time during day or night, and at any distance within the extreme hospital boundaries'.[44] The Board replied that when this service was planned, they had intended appointing six assistant surgeons to staff it. Opposition from the ordinary surgeons had prevented its introduction.[45]

In spite of much publicity, national and local, the five surgical vacancies were filled. One of the new staff was Charles Clay, the surgeon from Ashton-under-Lyne who had achieved national fame for pioneering the surgical removal of the ovary. His lectures gave St Mary's recognition by the national examining boards. He left after one year and was replaced by Lloyd Roberts, a gynaecologist who eventually took Radford's place as the medical leader of St Mary's.[46] A second house surgeon was appointed in 1861 to assist with home-patients, and this service gradually expanded. Lloyd Roberts' proposal for a branch dispensary in Ancoats (1859) came to nothing, but a satellite service was begun in Pendleton, Salford.

In spite of the necessity of in-patients to the medical education which Radford and others were keen to develop, the numbers remained small for a decade; not until 1868 were more than 150 patients admitted in a year. In the late 1850s there were less than 100 patients per year, rarely more than two admissions per week, so that very few of the beds were in use. Parents seem to have opposed the admission of children to hospital; in 1859 St Mary's advertised that sick children would be admitted without recommendations. In 1860 this 'free' system was extended to sick women, and patients anywhere in the country were to be eligible. Thereafter the number of patients rose to about 140 per year – a small increase but enough to raise financial worries. In 1862 recommendations again became necessary, and patients who could afford it were charged for board – 7s 6d per week for women, 3s 6d for children.[47]

The reimposition of recommendations was the more effective because of the peculiar system employed. Subscribers, most of whom gave one guinea per year, had the choice of two books of recommendations. One covered a woman or two children as in-patients; the other allowed four recommendations of pregnant home-patients, two for home-sick, and two for out-patients. Not surprisingly, nearly all the subscribers chose the second, and even those who took 'special' recommendations found difficulty in selecting cases suitable for admission to the wards.[48] Potential in-patients were considered by a meeting of the medical staff each Saturday, and those selected were usually approved by the Board on Mondays. The reimposition of recommendations seems to have prevented the doctors from choosing suitable in-patients from home- and out-patients lists.

To increase the use of the hospital, Radford, in 1864, wanted admission of out-patients without recommendation and more resources to be spent on in-patients, including the legacies and donations.[49] The Board opposed these proposals. They suggested that patients with more money might be admitted on payment; the medical staff objected, presumably fearing the erosion of private practice.

It seems that St Mary's was persistently unable to establish a claim on public interest. Lloyd Roberts developed wards for cancer patients from 1863 but Radford saw no appeal in specialist wards. He wanted St Mary's to take all diseases of women and children.[50] Various schemes were proposed to extend the charity – a merger with the Children's Hospital (1866) and with the Infirmary (1871); nothing came of either scheme.

But from about 1867 the income of the hospital, which had improved erratically since the late 1850s, began a consistent rise, largely from legacies and donations. An appeal for money to furnish wards allowed a dramatic increase in the number of in-patients, to about 400 per year, around which the yearly total fluctuated until it began to rise again in the 1880s. As the in-patient totals rose, so did the number of out-patients, and the number of non-obstetrical domiciliary cases. But the number of domiciliary deliveries fell. By the 1870s, St Mary's was dominated by non-maternity cases; a midwifery charity had become, in large measure, a hospital of women's and children's diseases; the change of name had begun a real change of function.

The same factors which transformed the Lying-in Charity into St Mary's Hospital were also responsible for the foundation or development of smaller medical charities concerned with women and especially with children. In them too we see something of the characteristic mid-century pattern we have discerned at St Mary's – new aspirations appearing about 1850, financial difficulties and power struggles in the next decade or so, and then a much steadier increase in work done and money received as medical charity became popular in the late 1860s.

When the Lying-in Hospital, after the 1847 fire, had provided some accommodation for in-patients, it had been hoped that some cases of children's diseases would be admitted. But this accommodation was little used and even after the hospital moved to Quay Street in 1857, the beds then provided for children were rarely, if ever, fully occupied. St Mary's was not successful in persuading poor mothers to allow their children into hospital, and its physicians and surgeons remained far more interested in gynaecology and obstetrics than in paediatrics. Thomas Radford, at various times, tried to develop medical care for children, but his plan for an infectious disease hospital for children failed, and St Mary's was otherwise only weakly involved in public debate about the high rate of infant mortality in Manchester.

One of the reasons for this debate during the 1850s was the immigration to Manchester of two continental physicians who introduced the special study of children and children's diseases which had developed in the medical schools and children's hospitals of Europe. Both used this knowledge and their connections with immigrant merchants to develop their medical practices in their adopted homeland. Manchester, with its cosmopolitan middle class and its high child death-rates, was fertile ground for their work.

CIVIC SHOW OR HEALING ENVIRONMENT

Dr August Schoepf Merei was a Hungarian who in 1850 established a local 'clinical school' for the study of the diseases of young children. He was assisted by James Whitehead, lecturer in obstetrics at the Royal College of Medicine, Manchester, and surgeon to the Lying-in Hospital. From the beginning the focus of the work was investigation and instruction more than medical relief. Merei wanted to establish an auxiliary medical school to attract students who wished to know more of children's diseases than was taught at the regular schools. In 1853, he and Whitehead met a group of potential benefactors called together by Salis Schwabe, one of the most influential of the German merchants in Manchester. They intended to launch a 'clinical hospital' where children's diseases could be studied and treated on out-patients and a few in-patients. The death of Schwabe delayed the foundation until 1856 when the 'Clinical Hospital for Diseases of Children' was opened in Stevenson Square, a few hundred yards north-west of the Infirmary.

Until 1867 when a twenty-five bed hospital was opened to the north of the city in Cheetham Hill, the institution functioned as a Dispensary. In the first year over five hundred children were seen and twenty medical students had registered. But teaching was not restricted to medical students; mothers were instructed, both informally and by lectures. In this way the 'Hospital' was extending the work of the Manchester & Salford Sanitary Association, begun in 1852; several of this hospital's physicians became regular lecturers for the Sanitary Association.[51]

Just before Merei and Whitehead had met with Salis Schwabe, the existing children's medical charity, the General Dispensary for Sick Children, began to attract more public interest. As we have discussed, it had been founded in 1829, but in 1850 the subscriptions amounted to only £60 and the number of children seen in the year (about a thousand) was less than it had been in the late 1830s. Even so, in 1852, the hospital's supporters, perhaps encouraged by the initiatives at the Lying-in Hospital, decided they should try to provide some in-patient accommodation. A donation of £250 from a 'theatrical entertainment' was accepted as the beginning of a 'permanent fund', and the new Bishop of Manchester put his weight behind the scheme. Manchester had been a bishopric since 1847; in the early 1850s the Church began to support public health schemes which previously had been the concern mostly of liberal Dissenters.

Establishment patronage helped, but the drive behind the refurbishing of the General Dispensary came from another continental physician, Dr Louis Borchardt. He was a Prussian who had helped organise the fight against typhus in Silesia in 1845. Like his fellow sanitarian, Rudolf Virchow, he went on to play a prominent role in the Revolution of 1848, after which he was forced to emigrate. He first settled in Bradford, among the community

VOLUNTARISM AND THE STATE

of German merchants. When one of their leaders, H. M. Steinthal, moved to Manchester in 1853, Borchardt came with him, and was quickly appointed to be physician to the General Dispensary. By 1855 there were children's hospitals in seventeen continental cities and Paris was about to open its second, so Borchardt (and Merei) were not short of models. In 1855–6, as Merei was establishing his Dispensary in Stevenson Square, Borchardt opened a six-bed hospital in St Mary's Parade, close to the building which St Mary's hospital was about to vacate.[52]

This was the 'General Hospital and Dispensary for Sick Children', and it too began to stress learning – 'the attainment and diffusion of knowledge regarding the diseases of children'. Its funds were increased by a series of petitions which stressed the economic effects of disease in children: whole families could be reduced to pauperdom, and 'no mills and warehouses can have vigorous men except from strong children'. But it is doubtful whether it was economic motives which brought children's hospitals to the fore. Doctors were interested as specialists or as sanitarians; middle-class attitudes softened as the Chartist threat declined and as novelists and Christian Socialists wrote to evoke sympathy for the urban poor. Mrs Gaskell, the wife of a Manchester minister, published *Mary Barton, A Tale of Manchester Life* in 1848; Charles Dickens' *Hard Times* (1854) caricatured the industrial bourgeois of the textile districts and argued for greater social responsibility. The new paternalism found its easiest objects in the children of the poor and in their mothers. The chief supporters of the Children's Hospital were the Heywood family, Unitarian bankers and philanthropists, and key-members of Mr Gaskell's congregation.

Income and admissions rose little over the late 1850s and in 1859 the committee was invited to consider amalgamation with St Mary's, then newly installed in Quay St and having difficulty attracting funds and in-patients. St Mary's had previously (1857) forced James Whitehead to drop his attachment to the 'Clinical Hospital', by enforcing a rule that St Mary's surgeons could only serve one charity.[53] Borchardt was against amalgamation and produced what was then the standard argument for medical specialisation – 'The progress of medical science, as of other sciences, is best promoted by a division of labour ... so does it appear most natural and wise, that hospitals for the treatment of the very different diseases of children and women, should ever be kept apart and distinct'.[54]

Around 1860, partly under a threat from the medical practitioners to cease their gratuitous attendance, subscriptions were substantially raised, to about £1,200 *per annum*, and twenty-five beds were opened in new premises in Bridge Street. The out-patients' number which had risen slowly from 800 in 1850 to 2,600 in 1860, jumped to 5,000 and by 1868 had topped 8,000.

The Cotton Famine had little effect on the hospital's income and as Borchardt noted, the effect on child health was positive. For all the privations suffered, the fact that mothers were at home and able to suckle their infants decreased the incidence of diarrhoea and convulsions and the other fatal consequences of feeding babies on bread or flour in water.[55]

After the Cotton Famine the children's medical charities began to be more successful, and a new charity was formed to the south of the city. Though the Children's Hospital had refused to mix women's and children's diseases, the Manchester Southern Hospital was for both and for maternity cases. It was only a Dispensary until 1871 when it acquired a few beds for serious cases; it was first situated in Grosvenor Street, Chorlton on Medlock. The main doctor seems to have been John Thorburn, who had taken over John Roberton's gynaecological practice, and was building it up using the new obstetrical and surgical techniques introduced by Simpson and others at Edinburgh. Presumably the Southern Hospital was of considerable assistance, not only in gaining experience, but in gaining connections among the middle-class women who supported the hospital. It would seem from the rules that the internal regulation of the hospital was largely controlled by its Ladies Committee.

Until the 1880s when it was developed as a maternity hospital by Dr W. Japp Sinclair, the Southern was a minor charity. Its in-patients never exceeded 200 per year, and it delivered about 300 women a year in their homes, and saw 400–600 as out-patients. The majority of the out-patients were children, the numbers of whom rose from about 1,000 per year in the late 1860s to 3,000 in the mid-1880s.[56] The charities specifically for children were rather more successful in establishing themselves.

In 1867 the Clinical Hospital moved from Stevenson Square to Cheetham Hill and opened a twenty-five-bed hospital. In the same year the Liberal MP R. N. Phillips proposed a far larger scheme for the Children's Hospital. Where the Clinical Hospital had one pavilion ward, and was situated in the poor district which it served, the Children's Hospital was to have three large pavilions. Most importantly, it was to be built out in the country in a healthy situation. The Children's Hospital, unlike the Infirmary, was following the Nightingale–Roberton plan. They were to build a country hospital which would be served by a city-centre dispensary.

The launching of this scheme followed the establishment of the Infirmary convalescent hospital at Cheadle, which we shall consider in a later section. It coincided with an increase in urban death-rates which worried sanitarians, and which led to the appointment of John Leigh as Manchester's first Medical Officer of Health; above all, it was a period when the Manchester middle class was extremely successful financially. The recollection of the workers' compliance in the Cotton Famine and the need to secure the co-operation of those workers enfranchised by the Second Reform Act, all made the late 1860s a particularly suitable time for philanthropic gestures. Land for a new dispensary on Gartside Street was purchased in 1868 and a large plot at Pendlebury was secured in 1871. In 1873 the new hospital was opened.

The annual number of in-patients rose from about 320 to about 550, and the expenditure was doubled by 1875 and doubled again by 1880. Nearly all the increase in income came from donations, legacies and local authority payments. The accounts of the Manchester Children's Hospital clearly showed in dramatic form, the decreased importance of subscription income as hospital expenditure rose. The move in 1860 had been funded almost entirely through increased subscriptions, that in 1873 owed very little to this source. Capital was replacing middling contributions as the mainstay of voluntary medicine.[57]

The hospital at Pendlebury, though outside the city, never became a 'district charity', like the Clinical Hospital (later the Northern) or the Southern Hospital. The Manchester Children's Hospital was socially central, and under the physician Henry Ashby it acquired a national reputation. It stood as evidence that hospitals, at least for cases other than serious accidents, did not need to be in the city centre; it was sufficient to have a dispensary there. Of course there were some objections. It was claimed that parents would not allow their children to be taken so far away, but this seems not to have been a real problem; children were not injured by the journey when a good ambulance was used. Nor was the hospital disadvantaged by its being less accessible for its honorary medical staff. Dr Borchardt in 1873 maintained that the staff all spent more than five hours per week in the children's hospital and that in no Manchester hospital was that figure exceeded.[58]

New workhouses and workhouse infirmaries in Manchester
It was in the Manchester conurbation that segregation and medicalisation were soonest and most thoroughly developed. The building schemes of the Manchester Union and of the Chorlton Union which covered the southern suburbs were on a scale new to the city; by the mid-1850s they had established very large workhouses at Crumpsall to the north and Withington to the south of the city. With the central Royal Infirmary these formed the triad of institutions which continues to be the basic skeleton of in-patient medicine in Manchester. The Guardians of Prestwich Union (north of the city, split off from the Manchester Union in 1850), played a more limited role. So did those in Salford, where parsimony and resistance to central pressures formed a pattern much more typical of the separate textile towns than of the city Unions.

The major workhouse developments were contemporary with the mid-century 'rationalisation' of the Royal Infirmary. In both cases, during the 1850s, building schemes were forced by overcrowding, or by a general policy of civic 'improvement' – there was no clear vision of a 'place of healing' until the agitation around 1860 which popularised both pavilion hospitals and nurse training. The Boards of Guardians of Manchester and especially of Chorlton, were involved in the local agitation, and the Chorlton Union hospital, begun in 1864, became a national model for architecture and organisation when workhouse infirmaries became a topic of wide public concern in the mid-1860s.

As we discussed in a previous chapter, the Guardians of Manchester inherited a workhouse for 1,000 paupers, those of Chorlton had very limited accommodation. The workhouse they built in Hulme in 1841 housed over 300 paupers, but by mid-century Chorlton workhouse, like Manchester and Salford workhouses, was considerably overcrowded. The Salford Guardians had tried to adapt their old workhouse and under pressure from their medical officer used a minor poorhouse for fever wards. But by 1850 the central Poor Law Board was forcing them to limit the inmates to 333 and the Guardians agreed to build a new workhouse for 700 paupers; the Poor Law Board had also to suggest that they included an infirmary and fever wards. The new workhouse on Eccles Road was opened in 1853.[59]

The Manchester Guardians also improvised accommodation. In the early 1850s they proposed to buy a mill in Ancoats to serve as a workhouse but the Poor Law Board objected that the scheme was as expensive as it was unsatisfactory. The Guardians were persuaded to build new accommodation and to save money on out-relief.[60]

The problem in Manchester was that the New Bridge Street Workhouse had rapidly filled with the sick and the aged as the population rose and the destitution of the potato famine rendered many destitute. In 1854 there were, on average, 500–600 aged and infirm inmates, 600 under medical treatment and 300 children, which left room for only 150 able-bodied males and fifty females. Many of the younger women were unmarried mothers who were difficult to discipline and the lack of space for the able-bodied of either sex meant that applicants for relief could not be offered the workhouse as a condition of help.[61] Nor could those admitted be given suitable manual labour. The Manchester Guardians were convinced that their bill for out-relief was unnecessarily high because the 'workhouse test' could not be applied, and the problem had been aggravated by the granting of settlement rights to large numbers of Irish immigrants: 'the excessive proportion of Irish pauperism to the population compared with that of the English rendered it more than ever necessary to discipline labour when it became chargeable, and thus induce Irishmen to take their proper place in the labour market and society.'[62]

The Guardians, in 1854, bought an estate at Crumpsall, four miles north of the city centre, mainly because it was the cheapest of the sites available. There they built a workhouse which could be a real deterrent to the indolent. It was to accommodate 1,660 inmates, including 745 able-bodied males and seventy-six women with infants. For the better discipline of the women, the laundry was deliberately not equipped with mechanical aids. Crumpsall Workhouse also included space for 250 idiots and imbeciles, a class for which accommodation had hitherto been restricted to fifty. The Guardians hoped that by keeping these unfortunates on their own premises they could reduce the number housed in expensive asylums and so decrease the cost to the ratepayers.[63]

The New Bridge Street premises remained as a hospital. When visited in 1866 during a national inquiry into workhouse infirmaries, it held 1,319 patients, nearly all of them adult, and about 60 per cent of whom were on the medical officer's books as sick. Even if we exclude the infirm from the calculation, this was perhaps the largest hospital in the country – three times larger than Manchester Infirmary if judged by bed numbers. Over 1,000 medicines, etc., were supplied each week to the inmates by the apothecary. They were of good quality and were not charged to the medical attendants. A superintendent medical officer visited daily and a junior medical officer was resident.

Though many of the buildings dated from 1792 the hospital was healthy and reasonably well ventilated. The fever wards, with ninety beds, were in a separate building. There were ten medical wards and seven surgical wards, with separate wards for syphilitic cases, for cutaneous disorders and for sick children. There were still eighteen single rooms for lunatics. Each ward had a water closet and there were both fixed and movable baths. Though there were no day rooms, convalescent rooms were provided for fever cases and for the general sick.

The lying-in room, with twenty double beds, was adjacent to the labour room. About two hours after childbirth each mother was carried through to a bed. Though, on average, there were births every day of the year, there had been only ten cases of puerperal fever in four years. The whole institution was much freer from epidemics of hospital diseases than were contemporary voluntary hospitals, including Manchester's.

The patients complained only about their food. The pudding was hard and indigestible; many inmates would not eat it, 'The rice as a meal was distasteful to many, whilst the pea-soup disagree[d] with some of the aged poor. The old women, especially, complain[ed] that their tea is not good of the kind, and that it is too weak.'[64]

The developments in Chorlton took a rather different course. When faced with massive overcrowding around mid-century, the Guardians decided to build a new workhouse out in the country at Nell Lane, Withington. The building was opened in 1855, while Crumpsall was being built, and was about the same size – 1,500 beds. But, unlike Crumpsall, Withington Workhouse was to accommodate all classes of pauper; the old workhouse in Hulme was abandoned.

The medical officer of the Chorlton workhouse was George Greaves, a local surgeon who took a considerable interest in public health and was active in the Statistical Society.[65] Initially he was pleased by the consequences of the removal. In 1859–60, when Joseph Adshead was promoting his Convalescent Hospital plan, Greaves provided data to show that the death-rate of workhouse paupers was lower in Withington Workhouse than it had been in Hulme.[66] But soon he was complaining about the deficiencies of the accommodation for the sick. The hospital section was greatly overcrowded and did not allow the separation of infectious diseases which was thought necessary by hospital reformers. Presumably the infirmary had been built as a small adjunct of a workhouse, without much thought to the proportion of inmates who were likely to be fevered or otherwise sick.

In 1861, as the American Civil War prevented imports of raw cotton, the Lancashire cotton industry came almost to a standstill and all Boards of Guardians were faced with more and more applications for relief. The problem was worse in the cotton towns than in Manchester, but even the city Unions experienced difficulties. In Chorlton, in 1862, as the general standard of health deteriorated, the leading members of the Board, stimulated by Greaves, began to suggest that a large Union hospital be built at Withington. James Heywood, the Chairman and a member of the banking family, advocated a hospital for 800, which he maintained was anticipating requirements by only five or six years. Many Guardians resisted this expenditure during a financial crisis but a contract was given to the architect, Thomas Worthington, to prepare a design.[67]

Worthington had previously planned an asylum for Cumberland and Westmorland. In 1861 he had drawn up a report on the condition of the Manchester Royal Infirmary and had thus become involved with Roberton's campaign for hospital ventilation. From Roberton's pamphlets, Nightingale's work, the pages of *The Builder*, and from his own knowledge of continental hospitals, Worthington designed a pavilion hospital for Withington.[68] It was the second pavilion design in the Region (Blackburn Infirmary was the first) and the first workhouse building to be planned in pavilion style. The Poor Law Board thought the plan extravagant and initially opposed it, but, to the delight of Florence Nightingale, the building proved to be quite cheap.[69] The 480 beds, in five three-storey pavilions, cost £23,000. When Worthington, in 1867, sent Miss Nightingale a description of the hospital, she replied:

> It is of the greatest use to us as giving details of the best and cheapest hospital that has yet been built.
>
> And in these days when so much attention, wise and unwise, is being directed to Workhouse Infirmaries (and so little is being really done) the world's gratitude is due to those who have solved a problem in a way which must be a model for the country.
>
> For the good and cheap must prevail over the dear and bad though it is by no means certain that the good and dear will.
>
> I shall make use of your invaluable example everywhere I can.[70]

Withington hospital was also remarkable for its nursing system. Paid nurses had been employed in the Withington workhouse and in the Manchester workhouse during the 1850s, as they were in Manchester Royal Infirmary, but the use of Nightingale's 'trained nurses' in workhouse infirmaries was pioneered by William Rathbone in Liverpool in 1864. This example, the contemporary promotion of a Nursing Institute for Manchester by the local Sanitary Society, and the Royal Infirmary's introduction of a London-trained nurse, were the background to the Chorlton Guardian's plan. As their new hospital was completed, a series of scandals over metropolitan workhouses, publicity by philanthropic women, and pressure from Poor Law medical officers drew attention to the need for better care of the sick poor.[71] Roberton in 1860 had praised the nursing of European religious orders (though Miss Nightingale did not approve) and from 1860 a number of Anglican nuns had been nursing in University College Hospital, London. In 1867 two of the Sisters of Charity were brought to Manchester to superintend the nursing at Withington; one of them died of typhus within two years. Some insight into the work expected of nurses in the Poor Law institution can be gained from an 1864 report from a medical officer to the Manchester Guardians in connection with the proposed Nursing Institute.

> In preparing a scheme for the provision of nurses for a pauper hospital or infirmary, the nature of the diseases to be treated should be steadily kept in view. Not more than a fourth — certainly not a third of the cases under treatment at any time are acute cases. Therefore for a pauper hospital a smaller number of highly trained nurses is required. About one to every eighty or hundred patients would be sufficient, who would be assisted by a certain number of under-nurses, the proportion on an average of one to every fifteen patients, besides night nurses who might be one to every thirty. These assistant nurses might be selected from the more intelligent inmates of either sex. They should wear a distinctive dress, should have better food than the ordinary inmates of the workhouse, and might receive a small pecuniary remuneration for their services, say one shilling a week,

which might be gradually raised to half a crown. The persons so employed would for the time being cease to be paupers; would be rather regarded as sub-officers or servants, but would in the case of misconduct be liable to instant reduction to their former position. I might say here that some of the best nurses I have ever had, have been trained in this way.[72]

In 1867 the Manchester, New Bridge Street workhouse was staffed by ten day-nurses and four night-nurses, assisted by a number of paupers, some of whom were excellent nurses. Withington in 1869 had twenty-five nurses under four superintendent sisters.[73]

Soon after Withington hospital was completed, Thomas Worthington was engaged to design a workhouse for Prestwich Union. Since their separation from Manchester Union in 1850 they had used the Prestwich parish workhouse at Rainsough, built in 1819 to house 120. Again Worthington used a pavilion system though only part of the building was for the sick. Again he was praised by Florence Nightingale. The new Prestwich workhouse was opened in 1869 on a site in Crumpsall very close to the new Manchester workhouse. At a later date the building was called Delauney's Hospital and it is now part of the North Manchester General Hospital.[74]

Not until the 1870s did Manchester Guardians follow the example of Chorlton and build a workhouse infirmary alongside their 'country' workhouse. New Bridge Street was abandoned not because it was antiquated nor because the site was central, but because the Lancashire and Yorkshire Railway Company wanted the land, for which they paid £100,000. The new infirmary at Crumpsall which replaced the 1,400 – 1,500 beds of the old workhouse was a model hospital on the pavilion system; it cost £120,000 and was opened in 1878. There was a possibility of opening an infectious disease hospital on the same site, but, in fact the Guardians used Monsall Hospital in which the Corporation was then playing a larger role. With the 1800 places in the main workhouse, the Crumpsall site could now accommodate 3,200 paupers.[75]

The Infirmary response, 1860 – 80

Workhouses and children's hospitals might move to the 'country', but the Manchester Royal Infirmary was not so easily dislodged from the centre of the city. Instead, compromises were reached; to understand them we return to consider the sanitarian attacks on the salubrity of Manchester's premier charity.

Roberton's paper of 1860 was publicised both in the local and in the medical press. The *Medical Times & Gazette* thought it would be a grievous shame to that centre of merchant princes, 'if amidst palaces of warehouses, and the application of high science in all matters of trade, they should allow their refuge for the sick to degenerate into a sort of medieval *Hotel-Dieu*'.[76]

The Infirmary medical men responded, led by an astute house surgeon who spotted a minor mistake in Roberton's figures. Roberton was accused of ignoring the improvements since 1858 and of exaggerating the deaths from hospital diseases.[77]

As the sanitary condition of the Infirmary was being debated in Manchester, a major row had developed in London over a proposal to remove St Thomas's Hospital to a country site. Florence Nightingale was strongly in favour, the opposition came from the medical staff, and especially from Dr John Simon, then Medical Officer to the Privy Council. By 1863 Simon had won, but realising that there was little evidence to refute or support the claim that country hospitals were healthier, he commissioned a report from Drs Bristowe and Holmes, who visited all the major hospitals in the country. For the first time central government surveyed the nation's voluntary hospitals.[78]

The report, as published in 1863, was partly a rebuttal of the sanitarians' case against city-centre hospitals.[79] Bristowe and Holmes found no evidence that medical or surgical patients recovered more rapidly in the country. They were suspicious of the generalisations about 'hospital atmospheres', and unwilling to use the incidence of erysipelas, etc., as evidence of a general unhealthiness. Their view of disease was more *specific*, in accordance with the general tendency of mid-century professional medical opinion. If there were cases of erysipelas in a hospital then there was a risk that other patients would be affected; the same was true of typhus. But if the hospital was properly ventilated that risk could be minimised.

For Bristowe and Holmes, Manchester Infirmary, with its many small wards, exemplified an unfortunate style of construction. The fault was generally admitted, as was the common occurrence of erisypelas.[80] The new danger was the fever wards: a surgical patient had recently caught smallpox from a case in an adjoining room; three nurses and a physician had caught typhus, and the resident medical officer had recently died of it. These facts were not, as we might expect, used to argue that fever cases should be excluded from the general hospital, for infection of staff was common in separate fever hospitals. In the opinion of Simon and his colleagues, fever cases could be treated in general hospitals as safely as anywhere else, provided ventilation was adequate and too many cases were not concentrated together; fever cases could be suitably spaced in general wards. This system had been tried in the Manchester Infirmary after the House of Recovery was closed, but it was quickly abandoned and not re-introduced. Smallpox was generally recognised as very contagious and the Infirmary sought separate accommodation.[81]

The argument about the siting of city hospitals tended to reach a compromise. Florence Nightingale had failed to move St Thomas's and Roberton never really thought he could move Manchester Infirmary. The medical staffs wanted the hospitals to remain central, not only for their own convenience but out of the genuine belief that country hospitals would be little used by those who most needed them; they would come to accommodate the same class of patient as the Infirmaries of country towns: chronic medical cases whose low mortality rates were less a reflection of their hospital salubrity than of the exclusion of acute and febrile diseases. The compromise involved rural convalescent hospitals working in conjunction with city-centre hospitals.

This was a plan already advocated by Joseph Adshead in Manchester, and one which had gained support, not only from sanitarians, but from members of the Infirmary staff. Indeed support seemed unanimous, for even those medical staff most adamant in refuting criticisms of the Infirmary, recognised that 'a change of air' was often necessary to complete a recovery and prevent a relapse. A place in the country would mean a more rapid turnover of cases in the town, without the risk of patients returning prematurely to the impure atmospheres of their crowded and ill-ventilated homes.[82]

The case for a convalescent home was strengthened by the increase of in-patient admissions during the 1860s. Just why this occurred is difficult to specify, but between 1864 and 1866 the admissions increased by about 50 per cent, and this increase was common to all classes of in-patients (medical, surgical, accident and fever). This may be connected with a public argument about the use of Infirmary beds begun in 1860 by William Royston, a local statistician, who showed that the average length of stay had increased from thirty to forty days between 1834 and 1859. Though costs and bed numbers had increased largely, the number of in-patients per year had only risen by 10 per cent.[83] The Infirmary doctors, sensitive to the accusation that more expensive medicine prolonged illness, may well have increased the turn-over of patients.

It is also possible that the earlier discharge of patients was connected with changes in nursing that were, again, a result of outside pressure, and a direct consequence of Miss Nightingale's work. In 1864 the Manchester and Salford Sanitary Association suggested that a Nursing Institute be set up in connection with the Infirmary. It could provide nurses to serve in local hospitals, to serve as district nurses for the poor and to be hired for the sick in private families. The immediate model was probably Liverpool where a similar institution had been founded by the philanthropist William Rathbone, with the advice of Miss Nightingale.[84] The Manchester Infirmary medical staff thought the proposals too ambitious, but they did agree to secure a well-trained nurse from London to reorganise their nursing, and they sent eight nurses to London to be trained at St Thomas's. The previous post of matron was suspended; the new Sister Superintendent had fewer domestic responsibilities; she had authority over all the nurses, but was answerable to the resident medical officer. The payments for nursing in private families became a significant part of the Infirmary's income.[85]

Though Adshead's convalescent hospital scheme was widely publicised, and Royston's arguments were offered in its support, nothing was done until 1865 when the Infirmary rented Cheadle Hall, six miles south of the city. The local residents objected to its use as a hospital and the scheme stalled until Mr Robert Barnes gave £10,000 for the purchase of a nearby estate on which a convalescent hospital could be built. Barnes was a local Wesleyan who had made a fortune from cotton spinning. For a while he had left Manchester to live on his estate in Hertfordshire; on his return he had devoted himself to charity. He had been Mayor in 1851, and his only son had died while preparing for the Anglican ministry. Altogether he gave £26,000 towards the 'Barnes Convalescent Home' which was opened in 1867. Humphrey Nicholls, another noted philanthropist, once clerk to the Collegiate Church, gave £10,000; he too had lost his only son.[86] These large donations for a new kind of hospital nicely represent the new attitudes to philanthropy and medicine which became established during the 1860s. These same shifts, plus the increasing involvement of Manchester Corporation can also be seen in the foundation of another peripheral hospital linked to the Infirmary – the fever hospital at Monsall.

Through the 1860s the number of patients in the fever wards of the Infirmary, though very variable, had averaged about 200 per year. The thirty-two beds set aside had been more than sufficient because so few sought recommendations; indeed, to use the beds, the Infirmary had taken Poor Law cases from the Unions of Prestwich and Chorlton, including some smallpox patients. As we have seen, smallpox was especially dangerous to staff and other patients. To minimise the risk the Infirmary took over a temporary 'cholera hospital' set up by the Manchester Guardians in a disused factory in Ancoats and later erected wooden sheds on the Infirmary grounds.[87]

In 1868, after petitions from the Sanitary Association, Manchester Corporation appointed its first Medical Officer of Health, the surgeon and chemist John Leigh, whose criticisms of the Infirmary we have already discussed. Leigh then began a campaign to increase the hospital accommodation for infectious diseases, especially for children, who previously had rarely been taken into hospital either at the Infirmary or at the workhouse. Since he had first served as a district Registrar, he had been appalled by the death-rate among Manchester children.

CIVIC SHOW OR HEALING ENVIRONMENT

Leigh analysed the registrar's and the hospital data for 1861–7, and showed that 15 per cent of Manchester deaths followed typhus, smallpox, scarlet fever, measles and whooping cough. Only a fifth of these deaths took place in institutions, mostly in the workhouse wards. This, for Leigh, clearly demonstrated that much more hospital accommodation was required.

> If a person suffering from one of these diseases is capable, by the breath, by perspiration, or by other excretions of the body, of infecting and charging the atmosphere surrounding him, so that it shall become poisonous to others about him and dangerous to their health and lives, and especially if the circumstances of his position are such as to interfere with his own chances of recovery, then it is clear, both in his own interest and for the public safety, that he should be isolated, and should, if possible, be placed under circumstances where skilled attendance, careful nursing, proper diet, ample ventilation, and such appliances as may be conducive to his recovery, may be brought to his aid.[88]

Leigh's argument was not new, even though it post-dated Pasteur's work on 'germs', but the fear of contagion was heightened and the emphasis widened from fever and smallpox to also include scarlet fever, measles and whooping cough. The scarlet fever cases previously sent to hospital had nearly all been adults, but 95 per cent of cases occurred in children under ten.

In 1868, the year of his appointment, Leigh presented a report to the Corporation suggesting more isolation hospitals, and several public meetings were held. The agitation was timely for 1868 saw a severe epidemic of scarlet fever and of typhus, plus increased deaths from diarrhoea and dysentery. Leigh prevailed on the Guardians to have infectious cases moved to the Workhouse Hospital and through his own staff in the new public health department he took direct action. The Disinfecting Officers of the Health Committee and the Nuisance Officers of the Sanitary Committee were given recommendation forms for the Infirmary. When they came across cases of 'febrile infectious diseases' they took the form to the hospital and gave all possible assistance in getting the patient there.[89]

Under this pressure the Infirmary trustees realised that their thirty-two beds were insufficient and that it would be very difficult to mobilise the seventy-five they were pledged to provide if necessary. Leigh had advised against the use of a general hospital and pleaded for a new fever hospital. The Infirmary's resident medical officer, previously employed at the London Fever Hospital, gave support and again Robert Barnes obliged. In 1870 he gave £9,000 to purchase an estate in Monsall, to the north of the city, and to build a hospital. It opened in mid-1871, with ninety-six beds in the main building and a wooden pavilion for thirty-two, after the trustees had already been forced to erect sheds in the Infirmary grounds to deal with an increase in fever and smallpox cases. The Corporation gave £1,000 for smallpox accommodation. Characteristically the new hospital was referred to as a House of Recovery and a Convalescent Home for fever patients.[90]

The opening of Monsall Hospital and Cheadle Hospital substantially increased the total number of beds available to the Infirmary staff and allowed a steady increase in the in-patient admissions. Monsall also meant that any cases of erysipelas who could stand the journey out of the city could be moved from the main Infirmary, as a precaution against the spread of infection. During 1867 – 73 the main building was healthier than it had been in the mid-sixties, but the new hospitals were not an unmixed blessing for the old Infirmary; the more convalescent patients that were removed and the more wards freed from fever cases, the more the beds filled with accident victims some of whom would otherwise have remained as out-patients. In spite of improved nursing and successive attempts to amend the building, the Infirmary remained unhealthy.

The next major outbreak of hospital disease came in 1874, when discussion about the removal of the medical school to the Owens College's new site on Oxford Road had increased pressure for the Infirmary to do likewise. After a Medical Committee report, a trustees' meeting called for the help of the Local Government Board,[91] one of whose inspectors, Mr Netten Radcliffe, visited Manchester and prepared a very thorough report on the site and the building.[92]

Radcliffe's report was damning. Within the eighteen months to mid-1876, not less than thirty-four patients had died from erisypelas contracted within the Infirmary.[93] Though aware that the disease seemed to be epidemic in the city, Radcliffe, much more than Bristowe and Holmes, saw each case contracted in hospital as a failure of administration. Like Roberton he counted the disease as an indictment of the whole hospital. The drainage system was antique and inadequate: after heavy rain, sewer air entered the basement, where the nurses slept, and irrupted through water closets throughout the building. In spite of recommendations in 1861, these toilets were still in free communication with the wards.[94] Many of the wards were very small and overcrowded, including those which were now used for erysipelas cases unfit to be moved to Monsall; from both the erysipelas wards currents of air passed into the corridors. Though the nurses in these wards did not work on the other wards, the house physician's duties covered all the medical wards, including one newly allotted to obstetrical cases. 'There can be no doubt that the fatal ending of the four instances of tapping for ascites in the last-named ward, … was due to the introduction of erysipelas into the ward from the erysipelas ward.'[95]

By 1876 the sanitarian campaign for the removal of city hospitals had lost its momentum. Radcliffe followed common medical opinion that there were no good data on the benefits to be gained from a country site, and any such benefits would be outweighed by the difficulties of access. But if Manchester Infirmary was to remain in Piccadilly it would need to be reconstructed and the bed-number halved if it was to meet contemporary standards for hospital building. Failing that, as a minimal improvement, the fifteen-year-old recommendation about ventilation and drainage would have to be implemented, the number of patients in surgical wards would have to be reduced, and a separate building, designed as an infectious disease hospital, would have to be provided for erysipelas cases.[96]

While these alterations were carried out, sheds were used to accommodate some of the patients. New accommodation was provided for the Dispensary and for nursing staff, so freeing more space in the main building. By 1880 the reconstruction was complete and all patients had been returned to the main building which now had 315 beds, an increase of about 50 per cent. From this time onwards there were no outbreaks of hospital disease, though many continued to criticise the site and buildings.

There is no single reason why the problem ended after half a century or more of persistent hospital disease. The improved ventilation and isolation of the toilets would considerably decrease the unpleasantness of the hospital, but we lack data to judge their likely effect on wounds. The careful isolation of erysipelas patients would undoubtedly be productive, but it is difficult to know when relevant practices changed. In the late 1850s, after almost twenty years work, a woman retired who had been employed to remove poultices from surgical patients. One cannot help wondering how often this faithful servant carried infection from patient to patient, though in 1857 the medical staff were urging 'the greatest cleanliness in the uses of sponges and dressings'.[97] Erysipelas was clearly seen as a specific and highly contagious disease by the early 1860s, but not until the 1870s were arrangements made for voluntary cases, as other infectious diseases were coming to be isolated.

Histories of medicine often draw a connection between the decline of erysipelas and the introduction of antiseptic surgery. The Manchester evidence is not clear-cut; some surgeons were using full antiseptic techniques before and during the outbreak of the mid-1870s, and their patients were not spared, but the spread of these techniques and especially the increased emphasis of cleanliness which they involved may well have been effective.

We should also consider more general factors, for erisypelas and related diseases did not occur only in hospitals. The Infirmary outbreaks of the mid-1870s followed a marked increase of cases in Dispensaries and Poor Law practice; in 1874 – 5 cases in public practice were twice as frequent as in the previous five years. The subsequent decrease in Infirmary cases may well have accompanied a decrease in the local incidence of the disease. Any

VOLUNTARISM AND THE STATE

general secular trend was probably the result of improving nutrition, water supply and standards of cleanliness. We should be wary of attributing to hospitals *per se* failures or successes which probably in large measure reflected changes in general standards of health and in the 'urban history' of streptococcus.[98]

Notes and references

1. W. Royston, Charts of Outdoor Poor Relief (Manchester Central Reference Library, M4/9/1 & 3).
2. V. A. C. Gatrell, 'The commercial middle class in Manchester *c*. 1820–57', PhD thesis, Cambridge University, 1972. S. E. Maltby, *Manchester and the Movement for National Elementary Education*, Manchester, 1918.
3. On hardship during the Cotton Famine see John Simon's Report as Medical Officer of the Privy Council, 1862, pp. 16–21 and Appendices.
4. On the mental hospitals in the nineteenth century see A. Scull, *Museums of Madness*, London, 1979. On Manchester, Nesta Roberts, *Cheadle Royal – A bicentenary*, Manchester, 1967.
5. Report of the Proceedings of the General Meeting of the Trustees of the Manchester Royal Infirmary, Thursday, 26 June 1845. (Bound in Infirmary Annual Reports, Manchester Central Reference Library.) And see W. Brockbank, *Portrait of a Hospital, 1752–1948*, London, 1952, and F. Renaud, *A Short History of the Rise & Progress of the Manchester Royal Infirmary from 1752–1877*, Manchester, 1898.
6. Annual Reports.
7. Infirmary Annual Reports; Netten Radcliffe, Report on the Sanitary Condition of the Royal Infirmary Manchester, Annual Report of the Medical Officer of the Local Government Board, 1876, pp. 77–110, esp. p. 79.
8. Infirmary Annual Report, 1845, p. 3.
9. Renaud, *Infirmary*; Brockbank, *Portrait*; Report of General Meeting, 1845.
10. Grainger's lecture was printed in the *Manchester Guardian*, 28 May 1845, and reprinted as a pamphlet, Manchester, 1845.
11. A. Redford, *The History of Local Government in Manchester*, London, 1939–40, II, pp. 152–5; and see the anonymous preface to Leon Faucher, *Manchester in 1844; its present condition and future prospects*, London & Manchester, 1844.
12. Report of General Meeting, 1845, p. 6.
13. *Ibid.*, p. 5.
14. F. Renaud, *A Short History of the House of Recovery or Fever Hospital in Manchester*, Manchester, 1885, p. 17.
15. *Ibid.*, pp. 14–24.
16. Brockbank, *Portrait*, 95–6; Netten Radcliffe, Manchester Infirmary (1876).
17. Brockbank, *Portrait*, 85–103; *Lancet*, 9 June 1855; *Manchester Guardian*, 28 April, 10 May 1855; Quarterly & Weekly Boards.
18. Renaud. *Infirmary*, p. 116.
19. John V. Pickstone, 'Establishment and dissent in nineteenth century medicine: an exploration of some correspondences and connections between religious and medical belief-systems in early industrial England', in W. J. Sheils, ed., *Studies in Church History*, vol. 19, Oxford, 1982.
20. Manchester Homoeopathic Hospital and Dispensary, Annual Report, 1852.
21. Annual Reports and Rules of Manchester Medico-Ethical Association.
22. The following section is based mainly on two papers given to and published by the Manchester Statistical Society: John Roberton, 'Suggestions for the improvement of municipal government in populous manufacturing towns', 1853–4; D. Noble, 'On some

of the vices of the Poor Law medical relief system', 1855–6. Also J. Leigh, *Letter to Alexander Kay*, Manchester, 1845.
23. J. Leigh, Evidence to Select Committee on Poor Law Medical Relief, 1854.
24. Noble, *Statistical Society*, 1855–6, p. 127.
25. On Roberton and hospital planning see Anthony King, 'Hospital planning: revised thoughts on the origin of the pavilion principle in England', *Medical History*, 10 (1966), 360–73.
26. On Nightingale see F. B. Smith, *Florence Nightingale: Reputation & Power*, St Martin, 1982.
27. J. Roberton, 'On the defects, with reference to the plan of construction and ventilation, of most of our hospitals for the sick and wounded, *Transactions of the Manchester Statistical Society*, 1856 (and reprinted as pamphlet).
28. *Ibid.*, p. 5.
29. *Ibid.*, p. 16.
30. J. Roberton, 'A few additional suggestions with a view to the improvement of hospitals for the sick and wounded', *Transactions of Manchester Statistical Society*, 1858 (and reprinted as pamphlet).
31. Florence Nightingale to John Roberton, 22 Nov. 1858; E. Bosdin Leech, 'Florence Nightingale to a Manchester surgeon', *Manchester Medical School Gazette*, 19 (1940), 44–5.
32. J. Roberton, 'On the need of additional as well as improved hospital accommodation for surgical patients in manufacturing and mining districts, but especially in Manchester', *Transactions of the Manchester Statistical Society*, 1860 (and reprinted as pamphlet).
33. Roberton, 'Additional suggestions' (1858).
34. J. Adshead, 'A plea for the establishment of a convalescent hospital for Manchester and its surrounding districts', *Transactions of the Manchester Statistical Society*, 1860 (and reprinted as pamphlet).
35. The development of the Lying-in Hospital is described in J. H. Young, *St. Mary's Hospitals Manchester 1790–1963*, London, 1964. This account has been checked and supplemented from Annual Reports, and occasionally from manuscript records. Also see J. W. Bride, *A Short History of St. Mary's Hospital, Manchester, 1790–1922*, Manchester, 1922.
36. Annual Report, 1851.
37. Annual Report, 1864.
38. Young, *St. Mary's*, pp. 37–8.
39. Young, *St. Mary's*, p. 40, and see *Manchester Guardian*, 11 October 1856.
40. [J. Roberton], *A Plea for the Erection of a New Building for the Manchester and Salford Lying-in Hospital*, Manchester, 1852.
41. T. Radford, *Remarks on the Former and Present Aspects of St. Mary's Hospital...*, Manchester, 1864; T. Radford, *A Plea for the Immediate Establishment of a Reception House, or Hospital for the Treatment of Zymotic or Contagious Diseases of Children*, Manchester, 1864.
42. *Manchester Guardian*, 11 October 1856.
43. Radford, *Remarks*.
44. *British Medical Journal*, 21 November 1857, p. 970.
45. *Ibid.*, 28 November 1857, pp. 991–2.
46. W. Brockbank, *The Honorary Medical Staff of the Manchester Royal Infirmary, 1830–1948*, Manchester, 1965, pp. 95–8.
47. Annual Reports.
48. Radford, *Remarks*, pp. 56–7; Young, *St. Mary's*, p. 52.
49. Radford, *Remarks*.
50. *Ibid.*
51. Annual Reports; E. W. Jones, *History of Manchester Northern Hospital*, Manchester, 1933; *Manchester Guardian*, 3 May 1866; Marjorie Cruickshank, *Children and Industry*, Manchester, 1981.

52. Annual Reports; Cruickshank, *Children*; *Manchester Guardian*, 16 November 1883 (obituary of Borchardt).
53. Young, *St. Mary's*, p. 47.
54. Annual Report, 1859.
55. Simon, Report, 1862.
56. Manchester Southern Hospital, Annual Reports.
57. Manchester Children's Hospital, Annual Reports.
58. *Ibid.*, 1873.
59. Salford Guardians minutes, 15 May 1846, 27 September 1850, 2 May 1851.
60. *Manchester Guardian*, 6 July 1855.
61. *Ibid.*
62. C. H. Rickards, *Manchester Guardian*, 6 September 1855.
63. *Manchester Guardian*, 6 July, 6 September 1855.
64. Edward Smith, Report on Existing Arrangements for the Treatment of Sick Poor in Provincial Workhouses, 1867, pp. 118–22.
65. T. Worthington, 'Some account of the pavilion hospital recently erected at the Chorlton Union workhouse, Withington, near Manchester', *Transactions of the Manchester Statistical Society*, 1866–7, pp. 17–32, esp. p. 21.
66. Adshead, 'A plea' (1860), pp. 13–14.
67. Worthington, 'Withington' (1866–7); Chorlton Board of Guardians, *Manchester Guardian*, 12 July 1862; Gerard Edwards, 'The road to Barlow Moor', typescript history of Withington hospital, 1975. (Copy at Manchester Central Library.)
68. *The Builder*, 17 June 1865.
69. Florence Nightingale to Thomas Worthington, 23 July 1865, 7 November 1867. (at John Rylands University of Manchester Library, Deansgate Branch) (I owe these references to Dr. M. E. Rose).
70. *Ibid.*, April 1867.
71. R. G. Hodgkinson, *The Origins of the National Health Service: Medical Services of the New Poor Law, 1834–71*, London, 1967; B. Abel Smith, *The Hospitals 1800–1948*, London, 1964; M. A. Crowther, *The Workhouse System 1834–1929*, London, 1981, 1983.
72. Edwards, 'Barlow Moor', p. 14.
73. *Ibid.*, p. 9.
74. E. Lawson (pseud. Kernal), *A Short History of Delauneys Hospital 1869–1969*, Manchester, 1969; Nightingale to Worthington, 7 November 1868.
75. *Manchester Guardian*, 23 November 1876, 11 May 1877, 12 September 1878.
76. *Medical Times and Gazette*, 26 January 1861.
77. *Report of the Medical Committee to the Weekly Board of the Manchester Royal Infirmary on the Sanitary Condition of the House and in reply to a pamphlet recently published by Mr. Roberton*, Manchester, 1861; *Manchester Examiner & Times*, 1 August 1862.
78. R. Lambert, *Sir John Simon 1816–1904 and English Social Administration*, London, 1963.
79. Report of the Medical Officer to the Privy Council, 1863, and Appendix 15, esp. pp. 614–16.
80. *Ibid.*, p. 500, footnote.
81. *Ibid.*, pp. 537–9.
82. Joseph Adshead, 'Hospitals and convalescents', read at the public health section of the National Association for the Promotion of Social Science, Glasgow, September 1860; 'A plea', (1860).
83. See Royston's letter to the *Manchester Guardian* and the Infirmary's reply in *Report of the Medical Committee*, 1861.
84. M. B. Simey, *Charitable Effort in Liverpool in the Nineteenth Century*, Liverpool, 1951.
85. W. Brockbank, *The History of Nursing at the MRI, 1752–1929*, Manchester, 1970, pp. 34–42.

86. W. Axon, *Annals of Manchester*, Manchester, 1886, pp. 330, 354; F. Renaud, *Infirmary*, p. 150.
87. Renaud, *Infirmary*, p. 148; F. Renaud, *Fever Hospital*, pp. 23–4; Infirmary Annual Reports 1868–9.
88. J. Leigh, *Report on Infectious Disease in Manchester*, Presented to the Health Committee (1870), Manchester, 1871, p. 10.
89. *Ibid.*, pp. 16–17.
90. Renaud, *Fever Hospital*, p. 25; Renaud, *Infirmary*, pp. 148–9; Leigh, *Infectious Disease*, p. 17; Infirmary Annual Reports.
91. Brockbank, *Portrait*, pp. 119–22.
92. Radcliffe, Report, pp. 77–110.
93. *Ibid.*, p. 89.
94. *Ibid.*, pp. 95–6.
95. *Ibid.*, p. 102.
96. *Ibid.*, pp. 103–6.
97. *Ibid.*, p. 81; W. Brockbank, *Portrait*, p. 104.
98. Radcliffe, Report, p. 89. And see D. Hamilton, 'The nineteenth century surgical revolution – antisepsis or better nutrition?', *Bulletin of the History of Medicine*, 56 (1982), 30–40.

CHAPTER 7

Paternalism and the hospitals of the cotton towns

Social structures and the new Infirmaries
In the thirty years between 1857 and 1887, new or larger voluntary hospitals were built in all the major towns of the Region. Most of the buildings are still in use today; together with the slightly later Poor Law infirmaries, they provided the bulk of non-mental hospital beds in the North West at least until the building programmes of the 1960s. They have survived longer in their original form than most of the buildings constructed at the same period; the contemporary mills are now converted, derelict or destroyed; many houses which were erected near the voluntary hospitals have since been pulled down, but the hospitals are still there. Why were they built?

The causes were largely social and economic; changes in medicine itself were not of great importance. The mid-Victorian Infirmaries, like those of the early nineteenth century, were promoted as places where the sick, especially accident victims, could find a health-giving environment – cleanliness and quiet, good air and good food, nursing and the attendance of doctors. Soon after they were built, the major functions of these hospitals began to change; they became overwhelmingly *surgical* hospitals. But this change was not foreseen at their foundation. Between 1830 and 1880 the social meaning of an urban Infirmary had changed very little.

It was the economic and social climate that had changed – from the turbulence of the mid-century marked by inter- and intra-class struggle, to the class cooperation of the mid-Victorian years; from the bitter poverty of the forties to cotton booms and rising standards of living; from the 'frontier' conditions of many early cotton towns to that municipal pride which was manifest in ornate town halls. By 1850, the major campaign of the northern industrialists had been won and the Corn Laws were abolished, but in 1857 Richard Cobden, the apostle of free trade and the most notable politician till then produced by the north, had lost his Manchester parliamentary seat. The defeat was symbolic. For the rest of the nineteenth century the capital of English radicalism was Birmingham, not Manchester.[1] The textile magnates, secure as a new aristocracy, were coming to terms with landed society. In a country pulled closer together by the spread of the railways,

PATERNALISM

Manchester and its region settled down as an industrial province, no longer a substantial threat to the values of metropolitan England.

The increased conservatism of northern manufacturers was in part a reflection of their changing economic interests; after mid-century new markets were more likely to be gained through British imperial power than through the free-trade policies advocated by Cobden and Bright.[2] But shifts in middle-class politics were also, in large measure, a response to the changing social and economic conditions of the working classes. In the early 1840s some manufacturers had used the threat of unrest to secure their own ends. After about 1847, as the economy improved and working-class radicalism declined, the major problem of class politics was to secure the loyalty of the working classes by taking over the major working-class causes. To this end, as John Foster has shown for Oldham, there were two major strategies. Some Oldham Tories began to promote factory legislation and so attracted working-class support. The Liberals stressed Non-conformist issues – disestablishment and household suffrage. The former encouraged a traditional, paternalist, collectivism; the latter an economic individualism which taught workers to seek their own advancement rather than that of their class.[3]

Both strategies were effective, and after 1868, when the franchise was extended, the voting pattern in most Lancashire towns showed workers lined-up behind the political party and the religious denomination of their particular employer. Whether the politics were Conservative or Liberal, whether the master and his workpeople attended church or chapel, the work-relation was the central fact of their social lives; much of life revolved around the work-place.[4]

In Lancashire, the Cotton Famine of 1862–4 was particularly pivotal. The workers had borne great hardship and deprivation, but unrest had been very limited. The economic cost had been carried by the workers themselves, but their plight had been alleviated somewhat by charity organised on a national scale, notably by the Lord Mayor of London in his Mansion House Fund. When the Famine was over and mill-work resumed, residual charity funds were made available to Lancashire towns willing to build voluntary hospitals. Here was a direct encouragement to the local leaders to 'reward' the responsibility of the working class. Mansion House Funds were a significant stimulus to hospital building in Wigan and Oldham, at least.

More generally, the establishment of mill-owning families as leaders in the towns or, in smaller towns, their coming to rival the local gentry, allowed and necessitated individual or collective expenditure which would serve to establish a public presence. Hence the public buildings and the new interest in charity which characterised the Lancashire towns after mid-century.

Infirmaries fitted this situation beautifully, especially where large employers predominated and the Conservative Party was strong. There paternalism could thrive, funded by spectacular donors who were content to see the workers appreciative. Where there were more small employers, who in wealth and attitudes were less distanced from their workers, then individualism was more prominent, and large public expenditures were liable to be dismissed as 'jobbery'. But even Liberal leaders needed public status and could not afford to neglect a popular cause. Further, the involvement of the working class in the support of hospitals meant that they had an aspect of self-help; they were not 'corrupting' like so much earlier charity.

Compared to the eighteenth-century or the early nineteenth-century foundations, the striking feature of the new Infirmaries was the prominence of large major capitalists and of workpeople's contributions. The middling classes were much less significant than they had been in smaller, more subtly-graded communities. New hospital buildings did not depend on a large number of medium contributions; they were usually initiated by one or two very large benefactions, supported by a series of fund-raising events aimed at the whole town; often, too, by organised contributions from the workers in the cotton mills. This social construction paralleled the industrial 'feudalism' which was more or less characteristic of textile towns in this period.[5]

Large donations were appropriate to Infirmaries as they had not been to Dispensaries, chiefly, of course, because Infirmaries were much more expensive to build and to run. There was room for capitalists to provide the buildings and also, in some cases, a substantial endowment. So secured, the new institutions could be run by the small businessmen and shopkeepers; the large contributors, memorialised in stone, did not overshadow the day to day operations of the charity nor destroy the feeling that the Infirmary was *of* as well as for the people.[6]

The founders of new Infirmaries sought the involvement of workers not just as patients but as contributors. Occasional workplace collections had been used earlier, but from the 1860s, they were used more systematically for Infirmary support. Once a building was provided, collections were often taken on a particular Saturday in the year – Hospital Saturday. In some towns, by the 1880s, workers were making regular weekly contributions through their workplace. Where the employer made the collection, he received recommendation tickets which could then be given to contributing workers in need of hospital care – a nice example of the provident principle combined with employer patronage. In some cases, workpeople's organisations made the collections; to encourage interest the Infirmary governor would sometimes allow worker's representatives to function as trustees – but not in numbers proportionate to the contributions. As we

PATERNALISM

shall see in a later chapter, schemes of this sort often evolved into full-blown provident programmes organised by a hospital: workers contributed as individuals and benefited accordingly; though the funds might be collected at the workplace, the patronage was no longer a simple extension of the subordination of employees to employer.[7]

Workpeople's Contribution Schemes of this kind were mostly developed in the early twentieth century. In the period now under discussion, we are chiefly concerned with contributions made as employees. This form of contribution underlined the centrality of the workplace and the relation to the owner. It was yet another way of organising the life around the factory, another way for workers to follow where their employers led. This following in turn encouraged the leaders, for if workers were contributing to the maintenance of a hospital then they were not being corrupted as they might be by traditional charity. Mid-Victorian Infirmaries were thus insulated from some of the criticisms raised against medical charity a generation earlier. The Infirmaries were sufficiently 'providential' to assure the local elite that their generosity was not wasted.

Thus, even though Infirmaries were much more expensive than Dispensaries, they could be founded where Dispensaries had never succeeded. In small, relatively traditional towns like Kendal, a County Infirmary could develop on a social basis not vastly different from the earlier Dispensary's.[8] In larger, rawer, newer towns like Ashton and Oldham, the defeat of radicalism opened the way to conservative paternalism, and large employers invested in hospitals. More favourable still were the towns where traditional dependencies had shaded into patterns of industrial subjection – Wigan with its large coal and iron companies provides a good example. But where there was no tradition of charity and where liberal employers held closer to the economic individualism of their less affluent fathers, even Infirmaries could be unpopular. Bolton, Bury and especially Rochdale, provide nice examples of continuing resistance to medical philanthropy.

This chapter reviews, in order of foundation, the early history of the cotton town Infirmaries, presenting them primarily as social institutions. It tries to show how Infirmaries reflected more general aspects of class structure and political culture. A voluntary hospital could become the major focus of a town's fund-raising and public celebrations. It provided common ground between religious sects and political parties; it brought together the employers and workers from different companies; it involved friendly societies and trade unions as well as local dignitaries. As social institutions, voluntary hospitals deserve more attention than historians have so far given.[9]

VOLUNTARISM AND THE STATE

Urban contexts of Infirmary promotion

We begin, however with Ashton – which was first and rather atypical. At mid-century, Ashton, with its neighbour Oldham, probably constituted the largest mass of population to be without any local medical charities. Leonard Horner, a factory inspector, in his report for 1843, had questioned whether such a dearth of provision could exist anywhere else in the civilised world save in Britain. In the following year a report on the sanitary condition of Ashton by J. R. Coulthart, had again stressed the appalling backwardness of this turbulent town. In 1845 the author of this report, and others, had made an attempt to raise funds for a Dispensary or Infirmary, but without success. Though the need could hardly have been greater, nothing was done; medical charity was not a cause for which the employers of the town were ready to combine.[10]

Need waited on circumstance and the large donor. As often happened, a local disaster provided a trigger, and a liberal churchman with no children provided the money. In 1858, after the Bardsley Colliery explosion, Mr Samuel Oldham, a textile manufacturer and a bachelor, promised to leave £5,000 for an Infirmary. Soon afterwards, on his deathbed, he raised the gift to £10,000. 'He had accumulated wealth through the toils of the workpeople, and he was resolved to expend it for their benefit, and to raise up a District Infirmary and a Public Park, two great necessities and improvements.' By judicious consultation his executors brought together the two parties in the town in furtherance of his wishes. A local judge presided and £7,000 was subscribed at the first public meeting. The workpeople of the town also subscribed.[11]

Ashton Infirmary was primarily an accident hospital; in some ways a later version of those at Salford or Bolton, though not preceded by a Dispensary. It was evidence of increasing concern over the consequences of serious accidents, and of the self-consciousness of some Ashton employers about the 'frontier-town' image of their district.

It was the next of the Region's Infirmaries which really set the pattern for imitation, for it was a pavilion hospital, incorporating the latest ideas on hospital construction as they had been popularised by Nightingale and Roberton. But for the delay caused by the Cotton Famine, the Blackburn Infirmary would have been Britain's first civilian hospital in the pavilion style. It was initiated by William Pilkington, then the Mayor, and its design was guided by John Roberton. Just before Samuel Oldham's promise of an Infirmary for Ashton, William Pilkington had determined to use his office as Mayor to provide an Infirmary for Blackburn. He was the son of a successful cotton merchant and a brother of the town's MP, but he 'subordinated his business and political life' to his philanthropic enterprises. Like Samuel Oldham he was childless.[12]

The Blackburn plan coincided with national agitation over the military hospital at Netley, Southampton, which was then under construction. Nightingale had attacked its design and the national journal *The Builder* was full of criticism. This debate was brought to the attention of Blackburn by a letter in the *Preston Guardian* of 19 September 1857, in which a surgeon, J. Lang, pointed out that hospitals were for the comfort and cure of the sick and wounded poor, not to adorn a town. Anyone who cared for the poor should build in the pavilion style and avoid the errors of recent, expensive and unhealthy hospitals. This stimulated the editor to enquire into hospital design and to publish his findings, including the views of Roberton. By June 1858 *The Builder* was commenting favourably on the plans for Blackburn Infirmary 'which is admittedly founded on John Roberton's valuable statements, and the observations in our pages'.[13]

The Infirmary scheme proved popular. The same leading families as had clubbed together in the abortive Infirmary scheme of the twenties, again gave their large donations. They were richer now, better established as leaders of an increasingly stable town, more ready to take some responsibility for their workers; all the more so when these workers were themselves ready to contribute to the new building. Blackburn did itself proud and built an Infirmary on the most modern lines, at a cost of £26,000. Undoubtedly the fresh air did keep erysipelas at a lower level than in some of the tiny, stuffy, accident hospitals, but, as the trustees soon discovered, the heating and maintenance bills were considerably in excess of other institutions. The Infirmary was built so that it could be extended; initially providing thirty-two beds, it had seventy by 1876.[14]

The building made Blackburn the hospital centre of mid-Lancashire. Subscriptions were given from Burnley and north-east Lancashire, as well as from the immediate environs of Blackburn. Preston, which still boasted a better class of doctor, was somewhat overshadowed until 1870 when the Preston Infirmary was opened for in-patients.[15] It was built by the Dispensary committee, adjoining and using the old House of Recovery that had been given up by the Guardians on the construction of the new workhouse at Fulwood. The main mover behind the voluntary Infirmary was the same man, C. R. Jacson, Esq., who had finally pushed through the workhouse scheme, overcoming the long standing resistance of the radicals. His success on the workhouse issue reflected the increased acceptance, nationally, that workhouses were primarily for the old and chronic sick, not a means of threatening the unemployed. His success with the voluntary Infirmary reflected the increasing dominance of the large employers and their commitment to philanthropy; particularly that of J. R. Bairstow who, at his death in 1868, left £20,000 for an Infirmary.

From its beginning the Preston Infirmary projected itself as a centre for medical education, as well as healing. Dr Charles Brown, one of its leading physicians, was a notable benefactor who used his gifts to keep the hospital equipment up-to-date. In 1873 a Nurses' Institute was established to train nurses for hospital work. These nurses were also available for work outside the hospital, so that the institution had its own income. In this way the hospital served the middle classes as well as the workers.[16]

In both Preston and Blackburn, the support of workers was soon enlisted in contribution schemes. Preston used the Hospital Saturday annual collection in workplaces, along with the Hospital Sunday collections in churches and chapels. Blackburn soon established a weekly collection system in some of the large mills. This support was of critical importance, especially in Blackburn, where financial stringencies greatly curtailed the work of the hospital in the late 1860s. Not until the workpeople's support was secure and growing was the Infirmary able to expand.[17]

The significance of working-class support was nowhere clearer than in Wigan, where a strong appeal to industrial workers was a major part of the fund-raising drive; in the early years of the Infirmary's work, collections in churches and workplaces amounted to 40 per cent of the income, always exceeding the total of private subscriptions.[18] This remarkable enlistment of the working class depended on the industrial structure of the town, which was dominated by a few, very large coal and iron companies who were the major subscribers to the Infirmary building fund. The miners were already accustomed to contributing to benevolent funds, their medical club already employed surgeons to attend to colliery injuries and the work of the new Infirmary was woven with care into this pattern. It was projected as being primarily for accidents, which in fact made up about one quarter of its work in the early years, and a special rule allowed colliery club surgeons to attend club members taken to the Infirmary.[19]

By the 1880s the system of annual works collections (Hospital Saturday) had been replaced, in many Wigan collieries and some mills, by a regular weekly collection, a form of Infirmary support which, in later decades, was to reinforce most other northern hospitals. In effect, the Infirmary rapidly became, for the better paid of its potential patients, a form of providential institution, where they were treated as of right.[20]

What they gained was not so much medical care, which was already available through their clubs, but nursing and healthy surroundings. It was the public stress on nursing which made an Infirmary seem necessary. Without an Infirmary there would be no nurses round Wigan, for rich or for poor, and, in the opinion of at least one Infirmary supporter, bad nursing could make the injured into paupers for life.[21]

This stress on nursing was in turn linked to increasing concern over public health. In 1848 a 'Wigan Working Classes Public Health Association' had been promoted by the middle classes in town to preach the virtues of pure air, pure food, pure water and washing. The Infirmary was to be an agent in the same moral crusade against squalor; its patients would not only be cured, they would be uplifted by the atmosphere of 'cleanliness, comfort and Christian suggestiveness'.[22]

Nor was this the limit of its usefulness. The richer inhabitants of Wigan were becoming aware that their town was a squalid disgrace; of its buildings, only the old parish church was fit to show to visitors. The leaders of the 'great firms' took the opportunity to provide a tasteful 'pile', into the ornamental tower of which a ventilator could be fitted.[23]

An institution that could mean so much to so many was bound to thrive. Wigan Infirmary illustrates, in a peculiarly striking way, the power of the late nineteenth-century medical charity to link large employers and the organised working class in quasi-feudal bonds. It was no coincidence that the largest private supporter of the Infirmary was the Earl of Crawford and Balcarres, a major colliery owner.

The development of Infirmaries in the cotton towns partially met a long-standing complaint of the supporters of Manchester Royal Infirmary: that the peripheral towns used the central hospital far more than they contributed to it. In the 1860s and 1870s Manchester Infirmary was desperately short of accommodation, as we have seen. Given the constraints on its central site, one obvious way to provide more general hospital beds was to extend the peripheral Dispensaries into hospitals. This occurred, but on a much smaller scale than might have been expected.

At mid-century the Salford Royal Infirmary was a ten-bed accident hospital. It was extended in 1866, 1871 and 1882, so that by the mid-eighties it had sixty-two beds, about the same size as the cotton-town Infirmaries. Salford had enough of civic identity to support this development; the Manchester townships generally did not.

The only significant development came in Ancoats where from mid-century the Dispensary had begun to benefit from subscriptions by the workpeople in the local factories. In 1848 the Annual Report stated that, 'A few donations have been received, and the Committee have much pleasure in stating that the operatives in the employ of Messrs. McConnell and Co., and Ireland and Co., have voluntarily subscribed to the Institution, which, as proof of their appreciation of the benefits conferred by it, is exceedingly gratifying'. These subscriptions grew over the following two decades and in 1869, for the first time, the Dispensary was free from debt. This support enabled the committee to consider larger premises and the provision of beds.

In 1872 a new Dispensary building was erected on Mill Street and soon afterwards a hospital building to house fifty beds was opened. Seven thousand pounds had been given or bequeathed by Miss Brackenbury, the daughter of a Manchester solicitor who had made his fortune in the railway boom of the 1840s. Her gift to Ancoats closely followed her gift to the University which, as we shall see, enabled them to establish a full-time professorship of physiology. The building of the Ancoats Hospital very clearly represented the union of capital and labour.

Unfortunately, though the hospital was receiving £100 *per annum* from workpeople and £500 *per annum* from the Hospital Sunday Fund, newly established to co-ordinate church collections, its subscriptions only amounted to £400 *per annum* and the total income was too small to maintain the beds provided. Not until 1879 were the first (six) beds opened for use. This improvement in finances may have been partly due to the formation of a Provident Scheme, to which workers contributed individually so as to secure the right of treatment without recommendation. Such a scheme had been recommended for Ancoats Dispensary in Kay's pamphlet of 1833; it was instituted forty-five years later as part of a nation-wide movement to restrict the use of medical charity to those who could not afford any payment.[24]

This movement in Manchester echoed the 1830s in several ways. It was organised through the District Provident Society which had been set up by Kay and his friends half a century before. Where the original District Provident Society had been, in part, a reaction against the liberality of the late 1820s, the new provident movement was a reaction against the growth of philanthropic medicine in the late 1860s and early 1870s. In Manchester, many charities were persuaded to follow the much earlier example of St Mary's in referring their patients for financial examination by inspectors of the DPS; several new Dispensaries were begun in the 1870s as provident institutions; of the existing medical charities only Ancoats hospital ran its own subscription scheme.[25]

The hospital soon became noted for surgery. As early as 1880 the annual report noted a Dr Yeats' successful operations to correct leg deformities in young people. Several notable surgeons made their reputations at Ancoats before moving on to the Infirmary. Technically it was a success, and it appears to have been a popular service; but as a hospital in a poor area it had relatively few large patrons. Ancoats hospital was unable to open all fifty beds until the late 1880s, when it began to receive some large endowments.

PATERNALISM

Urban contexts of antagonism to infirmaries
The years around 1870 saw quasi-municipal Infirmaries developed in Blackburn, Preston and Wigan, plus new hospital building in Manchester districts. It might be thought that the supply of capital and the popular concern over the public health made similar developments inevitable in all the industrial towns. That would be to mistake the medical functions of hospitals for their appeal, and to misjudge the temper of certain textile towns. The resistance to Infirmary development showed itself more clearly in those to the immediate north of Manchester, where the traditions of radical Liberalism were strongest and where medical charities had never been successful, Bolton, Bury and especially Rochdale. Though Ashton and later Oldham (1871) built Infirmaries, symbolic perhaps of the decline of their extreme radical traditions and the increased readiness of labour to follow capital, the towns of the Liberal heartland continued to resist what many of the tradespeople and small manufacturers saw as a kind of paternalism.

Bolton had possessed a tiny accident hospital since 1838. In 1863 a new storey was built on the Dispensary to accommodate a few more beds. The wards were tiny and overcrowded; within a few years of their opening they were described, in public, as unsatisfactory and unpopular. An enormous bequest for hospital purposes somehow escaped from the clutches of the Dispensary committee and went to provide the Blair (Convalescent) Hospital at Turton. When the leading local doctor, Samuel Chadwick, offered the Dispensary committee money for a children's ward, he stipulated that they must first agree to the building of a new hospital on a new site. Chadwick, though long connected with the Dispensary, had been a courageous advocate of public health measures. He had not feared to criticise the Bollings, major Dispensary supporters, over their ownership of cellar-dwellings; and he was ready to exert pressure on the Dispensary committee to force them to abandon their old premises and begin again. Not until the mid-1880s did Bolton Infirmary manage to establish itself as a modern hospital with widespread public support; until then the appeals to factory owners and to the working classes alike had been largely unproductive. Even then, the new building was more notable for its ornamental architecture than for the functional properties of its design.[26]

Bury, by 1880, had a population in the Poor Law Union of 120,000, and no hospital accommodation at all. Severe accident cases were taken to the Infirmary in Manchester, as they had been one hundred years previously when Bury was a manufacturing village. The Dispensary committee had never been popular enough to attempt the building of an Infirmary, and the possibility was not seriously raised until one of the local industrialists, Thomas Norris, died in 1873, leaving £4,000 for that purpose. Lord Derby,

VOLUNTARISM AND THE STATE

the major local landholder gave a site on Walmersley Road. Even then, though the proposal for twenty beds was scarcely extravagant, enthusiasm in the town was limited, and potential subscribers worried about the abuse of medical charity.

> Indeed to such an extent did this feeling prevail that subscriptions were witheld on the plea that if cases of ordinary sickness were admitted the medical profession would in many cases suffer owing to the fact that persons quite competent to pay for medical treatment would be admitted, and that the people to that extent would be pauperised.

It was to relieve this worry, rather than because of industrial need, that the committee decided to restrict the new hospital to surgical cases, an intention which was not maintained.

By 1880 building was underway but it was only finished when one of the early backers died and left £10,000. The hospital was opened in 1882 to a blast of faint welcome from the *Bury Times*:

> However a good work has been done, and if the cost has been great [£14,000] the sensible plan now is to make the best use possible of the building, to support it adequately but not extravagantly, and see that only the proper class of person take advantage of its benefits.

The hospital was opened by Lord Derby:

> What we are doing is good work. It is a work of humanity and of charity. It concerns the public health and the public interest. It concerns us in Bury locally, because we do not want our town to be left behind its neighbours in any of the essentials of civilisation. It concerns the progress of human knowledge of which the study of medicine and surgery is no inconsiderable part, and it concerns us socially and nationally, for a hospital is one of the most effective ways in which the richer classes can help the poorer without suspicion of jobbing or the possibility of abuse. And I need not say that in our country and in our civilisation without a cordial feeling between the richer and poorer classes not only can we look to no permanent prosperity in the future but we can feel no real security for the present.

As Lord Derby said, the moral sickness of emnity was increased if the poor died unnecessarily.[27]

Rochdale had no Lord Derby; indeed its characteristic stance was vehemently anti-aristocratic, anti every kind of establishment, including that of medicine. Rochdale boasted the first co-operative retail society and at least one radical leader strongly committed to public health reform. It had strong self-help convictions and enough municipal pride to pay for one of the finest town halls in the north, but many of its citizens saw in large Infirmaries little more than patronage, extravagance and medical jobbery – three of the cardinal sins.[28]

Rochdale Dispensary, it appears, was still, in the 1860s, identified with the Church party and Royds bank, though members of the anti-church faction were now on its committee. It was still a very small enterprise and during the Cotton Famine it lost further ground; the subscriptions fell from £262 in 1860 to £170 in 1864. But at the end of that decade, as Preston, Blackburn and Wigan opened new Infirmaries, suggestions for improvement were heard in Rochdale and when the Mayor arranged a meeting to discuss the possibility of an Infirmary, strong support was expressed by several participants. Some workpeople had promised to contribute one penny per week out of their wages and the town's doctors were nearly all in favour, for 'there was no town in Lancashire of the same population and opulence as Rochdale which had been so long without such an institution'.[29]

The usual reservations were never far from the surface – 'many people said ... that in small towns such things were turned into "jobs" and that the members of the medical profession would be constantly falling out' – but it was a rather different objection which led to the collapse of the proposal. Rochdale was a stronghold of homoeopathy, an unorthodox form of medical treatment, though promulgated by qualified doctors; it appealed, for the most part, to a middle-class clientele. Those of the town's elite who favoured the system wanted to make it available in the proposed hospital; the orthodox doctors would have nothing to do with any such proposals, and a public argument resulted.

Homoeopathy was not unknown in other Lancashire towns, but nowhere else had this issue of medical orthodoxy in public charities become so acute. In Wigan a proposal that a small homoeopathic dispensary should get a share of the Hospital Saturday and Sunday funds was brushed aside as lacking popular support. As we saw in Chapter Six, the homoeopathic dispensary in Manchester enjoyed considerable support from the elite and intelligentsia. Their aim, however, was only to supplement the existing, orthodox services. They did not demand that doctors in major public charities should permit homoeopathic treatments to be dispensed there.

In Rochdale, the capital of anti-establishment feeling, the supporters of medical dissent were not ready to accept a role subsidiary to that of the professional medical establishment. The issue was seen and presented as a matter of free choice between medical sects. Patients attending public charities and subscribers supporting them had every right to choose their preferred system of medicine, as they had every right to be attended by the chaplain of their choice. For doctors to band together to exclude homoeopaths was a blatant and deplorable example of unionism. When these general considerations were put into the balance, the anti-establishment case was strong enough to prevent a new Infirmary being built. As a result Rochdale lost its share of those Mansion House Fund monies which remained at the end of the Cotton Famine and which were made available to towns that would build hospitals. Oldham had taken advantage of this offer.

Unable to gain general support for a new Infirmary, the Dispensary committee went ahead and acquired new premises that could accommodate six beds for serious accident cases. As in Bolton, this accommodation was overcrowded with beds, poorly ventilated, difficult of access and often foul. Yet in 1875, a second campaign, by the doctors, for a better Infirmary was again unsuccessful.[30]

The politics of these disputes were complex and certainly cannot be presented as hospital progressives versus the tight-fisted or reactionary. Moreover, the issues and the protagonists changed between 1869 and 1875. In the earlier dispute, the senior Dispensary physician, Dr March, and the radical druggist, Alderman Taylor, had opposed the Liberal homoeopaths in their demand for a separate homoeopathic ward. March had advocated a small hospital 'attached to no system'. In 1875 both men sided with the Liberals against the Infirmary proposal. March was deeply suspicious of the increase in surgery; Taylor preferred cottage hospitals, a solution advocated, with more or less enthusiasm, by those who saw the Infirmary proponents (mostly Anglicans) as 'the knot of fussy officials who, to foist upon the town an extravagant and costly institution have done all in their power except provided a subsidy from Royd's bank'.[31]

By 1881 the 'Infirmary', still in its miserable premises was beginning to attract some support from the workpeople. A new building was finally provided in 1883 by the gift of Tom Watson, a self-made cotton man. It was opened by John Bright, MP, the apostle of anti-establishment and an old friend of Watson. At Bright's request there was little ceremony; after all, as he said, he had never been much interested in hospitals.

It might be argued that the proximity of Manchester Royal Infirmary to the towns of Bolton, Bury and Rochdale reduced the demand for an accident hospital and thus accounted for the delay in founding adequate local hospitals in these towns. Though, without doubt, the proximity of Manchester did restrict the later development of medical specialisation in these towns, and the range of services given in their hospitals, it is difficult to see either Manchester's facilities or Manchester's consultants as holding back the foundation of Infirmaries. The number of patients taken to Manchester was small, and they must have suffered terribly on the journey. The town general hospitals of the 1880s were staffed by general practitioners with few claims to special skills. Far away from Manchester, in Barrow-in-Furness, the toll of accidents in the foundry and ship-yards proved incapable of provoking an adequate response. In 1866 a tiny accident hospital was begun, not by industrialists, but by a high church clergyman and a radical editor.[32] Again, as in Rochdale and Bolton, proper facilities awaited the philanthropy of the very rich.

We can account for the pattern of foundations and the arguments of the founders more cogently in terms of social dynamics. Charity was unpopular in the Liberal heartland because it had no place in the preferred and dominant image of society. Charity was appropriate between higher and lower classes who accepted their relationship as a fact of nature; it was inappropriate to towns of industrious individuals who saw themselves as flanked on the upper side by those of undeserved privilege, and on the lower side by those whose *under* privilege was thoroughly deserved. In such towns, individual effort, or free association could provide all that was needful; medical care belonged to the former case. There was no place for patronage.

This attitude was overwhelmed by both social and medical developments. Changes in class formation favoured the symbiosis of the very rich and the organised workers. Changes in attitudes to health made hospitals more than asylums for the sick poor; by the 1880s, they were beginning to appear as medical facilities necessary to most of the population. They provided standards of nursing and cleanliness which were unattainable in most homes, so that when Lord Derby opened Bury Hospital, he could already point to the need for pay beds.[33] Hospitals were no longer to be only the refuge of the poor provided by the rich; they were beginning to appeal to the lower middle class. Medical science was beginning to achieve a status which would stifle dissent even in Rochdale, and the public was ready to provide the conditions which up-to-date doctors wanted.

By the mid-1880s, all the major industrial towns in the Region had gained new Infirmaries. Burnley was the last, when in 1886 Prince Albert Victor opened the Victoria Hospital. A Dispensary had opened and failed in the 1850s; no big donor had appeared to provide an Infirmary and there was not enough general support until, in the 1880s, the proposal by the vicar of St Matthews to build a cottage hospital in his parish was diverted, largely by philanthropic doctors, into an appeal to the town at large. Support came from all classes; the opening of the Victoria was the occasion for a general holiday as well as the town's first royal visit. One of the later cotton towns had arrived on the map of philanthropic England.[34]

Smaller towns and smaller hospitals

The few later voluntary Infirmaries were in smaller towns, previously covered by a larger centre. Accrington, near Blackburn, opened the Victoria Hospital in 1898; Leigh, near Wigan, opened an Infirmary in 1906. Even though it had taken twenty years to collect the money and put up the building, Leigh Infirmary became a very enterprising and successful hospital.[35]

These large town general hospitals of the sixties, seventies, and eighties formed the middle rank of voluntary hospital provision in the Region. The major developments in the two decades before the First War concerned the top rank and the bottom; large regional and/or specialist hospitals on the one hand, small cottage hospitals on the other. Though differing greatly in size the two ranks had certain common features; in both the doctors were clearly the major controlling element, and, both were becoming increasingly attractive to middle-class patients who could afford to pay for their accommodation and medical attention.

The first cottage hospital in England had been founded in 1859 by a surgeon, Mr Albert Napper, in Cranleigh, Surrey. He wanted to provide small hospitals which would look like cottages and would not frighten the farm hands and villagers who were to be the patients. In most instances the buildings were new. As far as accommodation was concerned, cottage hospitals were smaller, more intimate versions of the urban voluntary hospital.[36]

They were marked off from larger voluntary hospitals not only by their size but by the manner of payment and control. Patients were expected to pay, usually at least 2s 6d to 3s 6d per week towards their accommodation; the amount was decided by the hospital manager (often a doctor) in consultation with the patient and the subscriber who recommended the patient. Though some cottage hospitals later ran contribution schemes like the town Infirmaries, the basis of their operation was patient payment adjudicated and backed up by the subscriptions of the wealthy. In many cottage hospitals a medical superintendent controlled the admissions, though other general practitioners were allowed to treat those of their own patients who had gained admission. By so serving all the practitioners in a district, cottage hospitals, unlike many town hospitals, could not be accused of stratifying the local medical profession.

Most of the cottage hospitals in our Region were in small towns, especially in the rural/residential areas of Cheshire and the Fylde. Most of them were given by single donors; that in Lytham was provided by the Squire, Colonel Clifton in 1870, the Albert Infirmary at Winsford was presented by W. H. Verdin as a mark of Victoria's Diamond Jubilee.[37]

The increase in cottage hospitals about the turn of the century coincided with the increasing demand by general practitioners that their own patients should get hospital accommodation. The Chorley Cottage Hospital, begun in 1892, was suggested by the general practitioners who had been attending the Dispensary and they had to reassure the Catholic priest that,

PATERNALISM

in spite of the patient charges, the hospital would also be available to the poor.[38]

In industrial towns like Chorley, a cottage hospital might later become a small general hospital with visiting specialists and a full blown contribution scheme. Most of them, however, continued as general practitioner hospitals, sometimes with private wards as well as public, serving the less serious medical and surgical needs of patients drawn from a wide range of the small-town social spectrum. They fulfilled a need in housing patients close to home, and they allowed the general practitioners to maintain a high standard of care.

Notes and references

1. See Asa Briggs, *Victorian Cities*, London, 1963.
2. V. A. C. Gatrell, 'The commercial middle-class in Manchester *c.* 1820–57', PhD thesis, Cambridge University, 1972.
3. John Foster, *Class Struggle and the Industrial Revolution*, London, 1974.
4. Since this chapter was composed, the themes of work-place politics and paternalism in Lancashire (and West Yorkshire) have been greatly illuminated by Patrick Joyce, *Work, Society and Politics. The Culture of the Factory in Later Victorian England*, Brighton, 1980.
5. This is illustrated below, especially for Wigan.
6. See, for example, the *Oldham Chronicle*, 17 October 1891, which records the massive donations of the Lees family, and the hospital chairman's hopes that workpeoples' contributions will not be diminished.
7. Most of the voluntary hospitals discussed in this chapter collected from workmen for the initial and later buildings. Systematic, regular collections were organised by towns, following models in other regions. In 1858 Birmingham instituted a Hospital Sunday Fund, to regularise collections in churches and chapels. Manchester followed in 1869–70. In 1871 Liverpool instituted the first Hospital Saturday Collection in workplaces; Manchester & Salford followed suit in 1872. The Manchester & Salford Hospital Fund grew but slowly through the rest of the century. From 1895 arrangements were made for workmen to be represented on the governing body of the organisation. Weekly collections developed more rapidly when convalescent hospital benefits were arranged for subscribers. In 1928 the Manchester & Salford organisation launched a 2*d* per week individual contribution scheme which proved very popular. See the Centenary Annual Report, 1971, of the Manchester & Salford Hospital Saturday and Convalescent Homes Fund Incorporated. On the 'national' Sunday (1873) and Saturday Funds see Brian Abel-Smith, *The Hospitals, 1800–1948*, London, 1964, pp. 135–6.

    To take an example from the cotton towns: Bolton had a Working Men's Committee from 1877, raising funds for a new Infirmary. In 1881, it became the Bolton Hospital Saturday Committee. When the Infirmary was opened, in 1883, the Committee was represented on the governing body. Bolton adopted an individual contributory scheme in 1927. See *A Century of Service, 1877–1977*, Bolton & District Hospital Saturday Council.
8. Kendal Memorial Hospital was given in 1869 as a family memorial. It initially had eight beds and was supported by subscription from about fifty local worthies. About 1908 it was replaced by the Westmorland County Hospital, a larger institution with a wider geographical base.
9. Stephen Yeo's book on Reading is the only recent study which begins to place voluntary hospitals in the net of local social concerns: *Religion and Voluntary Organisations in Crisis*, London, 1976.

10. J. R. Coulthart, *A Report on the Sanitary Condition of the Town of Ashton-under-Lyne*, Ashton, 1844; Leonard Horner, *Report by the Inspector of Factories*, 1843, XXII, 309. Also see the Royal Commission on the Health of Large Towns, 1844, Appendix, 87–8.
11. H. T. Darnton, *A Historical Sketch of the Origins of the District Infirmary*, Ashton-under-Lyne, 1877.
12. The account of Blackburn Infirmary is drawn from Annual Reports; W. H. Burnett, 'The Blackburn and East Lancashire Infirmary', a series of sketches originally written for and published in the *Blackburn Standard*, Blackburn, 1869; *Infirmary for Blackburn and the Surrounding District, Report, 12 December 1862*, Blackburn, 1862 (includes plans); W. A. Abram, *A History of Blackburn, Town and Parish*, Blackburn, 1877; John Roberton, 'On the defects, with reference to the plan of construction and ventilation, of most of our hospitals for the sick and wounded', *Transactions of the Manchester Statistical Society*, 1856 (and reprinted as pamphlet).
13. *The Builder*, 19 June 1858, p. 417; *Preston Guardian*, 28 May 1858, Supplement.
14. Annual Reports, Blackburn and East Lancashire Infirmary.
15. An Infirmary had been proposed for Preston in 1845, without success: Charles Brown, *Sixty-Four Years a Doctor*, Preston, 1922, pp. 4–5.
16. Annual Reports; A. Hewitson, *History of Preston*, Wakefield, 1883; For help with Preston Dispensary and Infirmary, I am grateful to John Wilkinson of the Pathology Laboratory.
17. Preston Royal Infirmary, Annual Report for 1870, p. 31, rule 148: 'The foreman or nominee of contributors in the employment of any firm, company or society, shall have the same privileges of recommendation as individual subscribers of the same amount, provided the persons recommended are in the same establishment.'

    Ibid., 1871: 'The time has arrived, in the opinion of the Board, when the clergy and the ministers of all denominations, and the operatives employed in the mills and workshops, may fairly be expected to contribute systematically and substantially to the fund, as is done at Blackburn and other large towns.'

    Blackburn Infirmary, Annual Report, 1866, 1870, 1873: on 20 December 1873, a meeting of operative representatives decided to hold two Hospital Saturdays per year, and asked members to contribute, annually 5 per cent of their average weekly wage. Thereafter the Fund was a growing assurance for the hospital managers.
18. Wigan Infirmary Annual Reports and Minute Book, e.g. Hospital Sunday & Hospital Saturday Funds set up at an Infirmary meeting, 13 November 1872 (Wigan Record Office).
19. Wigan Infirmary Annual Report 1873–4, Rules esp. 65 and 72. Statistics in Annual Reports.
20. For example, Annual Report 1883–4; Minute Book of Wigan Hospital Sunday and Saturday Fund, esp., 25 October 1880, 9 December 1891, 8 December 1896, on 'systematic benevolence' in collieries.
21. Wigan Infirmary Committee Minute Book, 1866–73, first page, remarks of Mr Darlington.
22. The Wigan Nursing Institute was meant to suply maternity nurses to the poor, in the hope of reducing infant mortality, as well as providing hospital nurses and attendants for the middle classes, Wigan Hospital Sunday and Saturday Fund minutes, 5 October 1882. Also see Wigan Working Classes Public Health Association, *First Address from the Committee* (pamphlet), Wigan, 1848 (Wigan Public Library).
23. The architect was Thomas Worthington – see the Infirmary papers and plans in Wigan Record Office. On the need for a fine building see, Wigan Dispensary Minutes, Report of Special Adjourned Meeting, from *Wigan Observer*, 15 August 1873.
24. The statistics and chronicle of Ancoats Hospital are summarised in a recent, useful, anonymous booklet: *History of Ancoats Hospital, 1873–1900* (n.d.), Manchester.
25. See the Annual Reports of the Manchester and Salford Provident Dispensaries Association.

26. Bolton Dispensary, and Infirmary, Annual Reports; Bolton Reference Library, Biographical Clippings on Chadwick. The Bolton Workpeople's Saturday Fund, run by a pioneer of technical education, spent much of the 1870s overcoming popular prejudice against the old Infirmary; Biographical Clippings on John Berry.
27. Bury Infirmary, Annual Reports; *Bury Infirmary, An Epitome*, Bury, 1921; *Bury Times*, 25 March, 1 April 1882. Bury could not receive Mansion House Funds because it was not incorporated.
28. On Rochdale see John Vincent, *The Formation of the Liberal Party, 1857–1868*, London, 1968; William Robertson, *The Social and Political History of Rochdale*, Rochdale, 1889.
29. On Rochdale Dispensary and Infirmary: Scrapbook on the Infirmary, (Rochdale Public Library); Souvenir Programme, 1962; *Rochdale Observer*, 20 June 1887.
30. Newspaper articles in the Scrapbook.
31. *Rochdale Observer*, 13 February 1875.
32. *The North Lonsdale Hospital*, (fund raising pamphlet), London [1928]; J.D. Marshall, *Furness and the Industrial Revolution*, Barrow, 1958.
33. *Bury Times*, 25 March, 1 April 1882.
34. W. Bennett, *The History of Burnley from 1850 (Part Four)*, Burnley, 1951, pp. 197–8. My maternal grandfather, born in Burnley, October 1886, was called Albert Victor after this prince. A neighbour had suggested the name and had promised to buy his first pair of clogs.
35. Leigh Infirmary, *Souvenir*, 1927.
36. Brian Abel-Smith, *The Hospitals*, 102–4; H.C. Burdett, *Cottage Hospitals, General, Fever, and Convalescent*, London, 1896.
37. Blackpool & Fylde Hospital Management Committee, *Lytham Hospital, 1871–1971*, Blackpool, 1971; on the Albert Infirmary, see the Extract from the Annual Report of the Victoria Hospital, Northwich (Cheshire Record Office).
38. On Chorley, Annual Reports of the Dispensary and Infirmary; and the thesis of John E. Harrison, 'The development of medical care and public health in nineteenth century Chorley', MSc thesis, UMIST, 1983.

CHAPTER 8

Infectious diseases and hospitals, 1860 – 1910

The understanding of infectious diseases
Of all the buildings in the Region which by 1914 were counted as hospitals, the majority were hospitals for infectious diseases. In size and quality they ranged from large purpose-built hospitals like Monsall in Manchester, to remote cottages outside cotton towns, or even tents kept in readiness for epidemics. All these hospitals were owned by local authorities, not by the Poor Law authorities and not by charities. In 1870 none of them had existed.

This chapter, which deals with the whole Region, including Manchester, describes and to some extent explains the development of this pattern of isolation hospitals as the previous chapter explains the pattern of peripheral voluntary hospitals. Yet the organisation and the themes of the two chapters are substantially different; and not only because the present chapter has a rather later end-date.

In discussing the development of voluntary hospitals we have found little need to refer to national government, to local patterns of disease, or to changes in medical science. But none of these can be ignored in the case of isolation hospitals.

Almost all isolation hospitals were built under the provisions of Acts of Parliament. The Public Health Act of 1866 empowered sanitary authorities to build hospitals; the 1875 Act permitted compulsory isolation of infectious patients; the 1893 Isolation Hospital Act allowed County Councils formed in 1888 to force constituent authorities to build isolation hospitals; in 1901 these powers were strengthened. This framework is the essential background to local initiatives; the inspections of the Local Government Board between 1871 and 1914 put constant pressure on local government to provide the services which the Medical Department of the Board thought appropriate and which parliament had allowed.[1]

If we read through the annual reports of the medical department of the Local Government Board we find advice and directives to local authorities and very detailed enquiries into sanitary deficiencies. We also find appendices reporting laboratory studies; from about 1870 onwards many of these studies were of 'microzymes' or bacteria. From the 1850s medical men had gradually

INFECTIOUS DISEASES

become convinced that the 'seeds of disease' were specific to particular diseases and were conveyed from one patient to the next. In the 1854 cholera epidemic John Snow and others had shown that the disease was transmitted through faecal contamination of drinking water. By the next cholera epidemic, in 1866, John Simon, the Medical Officer to the Privy Council could write:

> the person who contracts cholera in this country is *ipso facto* demonstrated with almost absolute certainty to have been exposed to excremental pollution: that what gave him cholera was (mediately or immediately) cholera-contagium discharged from another's bowels ...[2]

Not everyone shared this view, even in 1866, for cholera had often been regarded as a disease *generated* by filth, not merely communicated by it. Such beliefs had motivated many of the public health reformers of mid-century, notably Edwin Chadwick; the observed association of dirt and disease was a sufficient basis for their attacks on the filthy condition of large towns; the subsequent provision of sewers and clean water had done much to reduce mortality in the towns. Even in 1866, public health specialists who were convinced that cholera was contagious could only suggest the remedies previously favoured by the anti-contagionists. Simon continued:

> Excrement-sodden earth, excrement-reeking air, excrement-tainted water, these are for us the causes of cholera. That they respectively act only in so far as excrement is cholera-excrement, and that cholera-excrement only acts in so far as it contains certain microscopical fungi, may be the truest of all true propositions; but whatever be their abstract truth, their separate application is impossible. Nowhere out of Laputa could there be serious thought of differentiating excremental performances into groups of diarrhoeal and healthy, or of using the highest powers of the microscope to identify the cylindro-taenium [the presumed infective agent] for extermination. It is excrement, indiscriminately, which must be kept from fouling us with its decay.

All the same, the gradual acceptance that cholera was transmitted and not generated by filth, helped shift the balance of thought about public health. Medical officers came to concentrate on the transmission rather than on the generation of disease, so that isolation came to be emphasised much more than in the 1850s. The recognition that the infective agents were particulate and animate, drew attention to direct or mediate physical contact as a means of transmission, and reduced the reliance on ventilation as a means of dissipating the poison of disease. These shifts were assisted by Lister's work on antiseptic surgery, which became well known during the 1870s. They were also assisted by changes in the disease pattern with which medical officers had to deal. After 1866 no general epidemic of Asiatic cholera occurred in Britain, though the ports maintained quarantine facilities. The diseases which attracted most attention thereafter were smallpox and scarlet fever and, towards the end of the century, diphtheria.[3]

Smallpox was particularly important because it was recognised as very contagious and very dangerous, largely because of the epidemic of 1870–3. Before then the disease had been declining but, for reasons unknown, it flared up and killed over 44,000 in thirty months.[4] Thereafter, though in fact the incidence and severity continued to decline, the first signs of epidemics brought emergency measures. The 1876 epidemic was notable for hastening provision of hospitals in this Region; later epidemics, in 1882, 1888 and 1893 were also persuasive. The very absence of the disease in 'normal' years may have served to heighten the threat of epidemics. During these 'normal' years most of the empty ward space was devoted to scarlet fever. After about 1890 when smallpox wards were recognised as a threat to surrounding houses and to other patients in hospital, smallpox cases were usually housed in buildings well away from the main isolation hospital. That too made wards available for other infectious diseases.[5]

Scarlet fever, like smallpox, was contagious but there was no vaccination available. Unlike cholera or typhoid it was transmitted by contact or through the air, so moderate sanitary measures failed to contain it. All that medical officers could advise was strict isolation. In 1863, scarlet fever killed 30,000 persons, mostly children; as a cause of death it was far more important than smallpox.[6]

Some scarlet fever cases had been admitted to the older fever hospitals, including the Manchester House of Recovery, but these were usually adult cases. Scarlet fever, much more than typhus, cholera or smallpox, was overwhelmingly a disease of children, and before mid-century children were rarely admitted to any kind of hospital. The concern in the 1860s about scarlet fever and the subsequent isolation of many cases, marked the emergence of children's diseases into the mainstream of public health concern. Sanitarians had sought to reduce the general death-rate by cleaning up the cities; reformers like John Leigh, horrified at the high death-rate of children, saw the better management of child diseases as the means of attacking the major component of general mortality. Children had been marginal to the early public health reforms; the accurate registration of deaths brought home the problem of child mortality to those who read statistics; the notification of infectious diseases pioneered by the Manchester & Salford Sanitary Association, and continued under local Acts or under the national Act of 1889, brought child disease clearly into focus.[7]

Scarlet fever cases came to dominate most isolation hospital beds by the end of the century, though by then the incidence and especially the fatality of the disease had declined markedly. By the Edwardian period, even some Medical Officers of Health had come to question the wisdom of sending cases to hospital. Isolation was still the only procedure which they could suggest, but after twenty or thirty years in which some towns had hospitalised almost all notified cases and others had hospitalised very few, there was no evidence that the former had fared any better than the latter. The isolation hospital was 'the keystone of the sanitary arch', but in the case of scarlet fever, the kinds of statistics by which the public health reforms generally had been supported, scarcely bore the weight of argument.[8]

But well before the end of the century, public health reformers were no longer dependent on simple correlations of disease with cause or cure. During the 1880s Robert Koch and others developed methods for cultivating the infective particles which seemed to be responsible for disease. Once these *bacteria* could be identified and cultured and could be used, species by species, in animal experiments, then a new medical science was established, and Medical Officers of Health could begin to claim a special science as the basis of their public health practice. We shall see, in Manchester, how university science became linked with the work of local authorities. It was now possible to check organic materials for infective agents; to establish diagnosis by the presence of bacteria; to identify 'carriers' who transmitted disease without showing the symptoms.

Therapeutic practices were little altered by the germ theory except in the case of diphtheria, for which an anti-toxin was developed in the early 1890s. By this time diphtheria was killing more children than scarlet fever and more and more cases were being taken into hospital. The development of swab-tests and the availability of the serum made rapid and accurate diagnosis both possible and important – bacteriology linked clinical practice, laboratory investigations and public health measures in a way which could only be dreamt of in 1870.

Beyond these specific measures, 'germ theory' provided new legitimisation for public health practitioners. The general public were impressed with these marvellous new discoveries; Medical Officers of Health, faced with careless local authorities or sceptical general practitioners, could claim a distinctive and impressive expertise of their own. By the Edwardian period, this Region had several notable Medical Officers working closely with bacteriologists at the University. Isolation hospitals provided the core of their clinical practice.

To take cognisance of these changing patterns, in legislation, disease and science, and to measure their impact in this Region, we can best follow the development of the isolation hospitals in three overlapping stages. Before 1870, the only public provision except in Preston, Lancaster and Manchester, was in the workhouses. Between 1870 and 1900, most of the major towns provided infectious disease hospitals and, in some cases, separate facilities for smallpox. From 1890 to 1914, as Medical Officers in Manchester and the bigger towns pursued public health researches based on germ theory, the smaller rural authorities were being prodded and pushed by the County Councils into providing isolation hospitals to serve several adjacent rural and urban districts.

Infectious diseases and the workhouses
Typhus, the 'fever' of the late eighteenth and early nineteenth century was the disease of destitution. It commonly occurred in populations short of food and too poor to keep themselves clean and properly clothed. Inevitably it occurred among those already in workhouses, or in families on 'out-relief'. Fever and pauperism were closely related.

In most township workhouses there was little room to segregate fever patients, but the formation of Unions under the New Poor Law, and the pressure of central authorities for the separate treatment of different kinds of pauper, meant that some separation was achieved, even before new Union workhouses were built. In Salford, the old Garden Lane Workhouse was used for fever in 1847–8 and for cholera in 1848–9. There were 460 fever cases and sixty-nine cholera cases, but the Guardians had to be reminded to include fever wards in the workhouse built on Eccles Road. Burnley in the 1860s was still sending fever paupers to a small house in Wapping, one of the most congested districts of town, but by then most Unions were using fever wards alongside their new workhouses. Macclesfield's fever wards were commended in an inspection in 1867, Bolton had good accommodation at the Fishpool Workhouse.[9]

Only in Manchester, Preston and Lancaster were there any arrangements for fever other than those provided by the Guardians. In Manchester, the House of Recovery and later Monsall Hospital, were extensions of the voluntary Infirmary. In Lancaster, the small voluntary hospital took both accident cases and fever cases; in Preston the House of Recovery had been built in the later 1820s by the Select Vestry, but it was rented by the Guardians under the New Poor Law.[10]

Because the workhouses were overloaded with sick and infirm paupers, the fever wards, between epidemics, were often used for non-infectious cases. In Salford, in 1861, there were thirty 'ordinary' sick cases in the fever wards and the medical officer was apprehensive about his ability to deal with an epidemic. In Preston, where the House of Recovery was often considered to be a town hospital, accident cases were 'pauperised' and admitted.[11]

Even where new fever wards were provided, they often proved quite insufficient during epidemics. When cholera threatened, the local sanitary authorities were empowered to erect or equip 'cholera hospitals', but the provision in 1832, 1848–9 and 1854 seems to have been strictly temporary. In Manchester, the cholera 'hospitals' were usually factory buildings, relinquished after the epidemic passed. Elsewhere, cholera patients were usually housed in a workhouse or a few rented cottages. The 1866 epidemic gave rise to more permanent accommodation, partly because the epidemic also stimulated a Public Health Act which allowed sanitary authorities to provide permanent hospitals.

In Salford, the 1866 epidemic found the Guardians considering an increase in their accommodation for infectious diseases. They were under pressure from the Manchester and Salford Sanitary Association who wanted to see more facilities for the isolation of smallpox and other diseases. In the late summer of 1865 the local cholera committee, under the Diseases Prevention Act, asked the Guardians to provide temporary accommodation but the Guardians did nothing; they could see no more than the usual seasonal increase in diarrhoea. When the cholera struck they were forced to act; they appropriated wards in the workhouse hospital and tried to rent some old houses on Liverpool Road; but they failed and instead erected a wooden shed in the workhouse garden. It was ready for use in November, when the epidemic was over. In August, September and October there had been 2204 cases of cholera with twenty-two deaths.[12]

Infectious diseases and voluntary hospitals
The agitation by sanitarians and the appointment of Medical Officers of Health around 1870 did not immediately lead the sanitary authorities to build isolation hospitals. Indeed, the first initiatives in this Region were based on voluntary hospitals, though the town councils and Guardians were involved. In a previous chapter we have briefly reviewed the foundation of Monsall Hospital as an extension of Manchester Royal Infirmary. The other, much less successful, venture was the erection of fever wards for paying patients as part of the new Infirmary in Preston.

Monsall came about largely through the efforts of John Leigh, Manchester's first Medical Officer of Health. On his appointment in 1868, the majority of fever and smallpox beds were provided by the Guardians; the New Bridge Street Workhouse hospital had ninety beds and Withington hospital sixty-seven, as against thirty-two at the Royal Infirmary and five in the Children's Hospital. Leigh argued that such provision was hopelessly inadequate, especially for children. He wanted to see scarlet fever cases isolated and he initially proposed that special children's hospitals should be set up in each district, but he also sent more and more cases to the

Infirmary fever wards, putting that institution under such pressure that the trustees decided to build a separate hospital at Monsall.[13]

The Sanitary Association argued that hospitals for infectious diseases should be provided by the municipality rather than by the charity. Even when Monsall was open they continued to press for municipal isolation hospitals, but without success. The Corporation was satisfied to send patients to Monsall and pay for their maintenance there. Monsall remained an extension of the Infirmary until 1896 when it was officially transferred to the Corporation.[14]

The residence of the Monsall estate was used for administration and to house the two medical officers and the matron. A detached block housed the kitchens and rooms for the eight nurses. A two storey pavilion provided four groups of three wards each – seventy beds in total. A wooden pavilion, previously in use at the main Infirmary site, was re-erected at Monsall.

By 1880 about a third of the patients at Monsall were children. Mothers were allowed to go into hospital with their children, but if they stayed for any length of time they were charged as patients. Otherwise there was little or no visiting. Relatives could enquire at the Infirmary in Piccadilly, which, by 1880, was 'in telephonic communication' with Monsall. Initially, it would seem, many parents were loath to have their children sent away where they could not visit them, but gradually, this resistance declined. Compulsory isolation was rarely used; Leigh relied on the families of former patients to spread the reputation of the hospital as an appropriate place for sick children.

Manchester Corporation paid the Infirmary trustees for most of the cases sent to Monsall, but they did not pass on this charge to the patients, though the 1866 Act suggested they should. They argued that since payments to the hospital came out of the rates, the inhabitants of the Borough had the right to free accommodation, especially since they were isolated as much for the benefit of the public as their own. Patients of a 'better class' who chose to go to Monsall could make their own arrangements with the trustees. They paid between one and three guineas per week and were usually accommodated in a 'cottage hospital' of six small wards, away from other patients.

The Manchester Guardians paid 25 shillings per week for pauper cases. Initially these cases were sent wearing uniforms, but the other patients complained about having to mix with paupers. Thereafter the trustees refused to take paupers unless their status was concealed. This problem occurred in several towns; when paupers were admitted with non-paupers, all signs of their condition had to be excluded; neither the patient's own ragged clothing nor the pauper uniform could be worn, and neither Poor Law doctors nor

Poor Law nurses could attend, lest the public discover that paupers were being treated in institutions provided for the working classes.

Monsall, like the House of Recovery which preceded it, was intended to serve patients from the whole district, not only from the City of Manchester; Leigh would sometimes send in cases from outside the City, if he thought they posed a threat to the health of Manchester. Most of the neighbouring authorities, both sanitary and Poor Law, made arrangements to send their people to Monsall and some of the minor urban sanitary authorities set up under the 1872 Act contributed to the maintenance of a 'Township hut', to which they could send thirty patients a year on payment of 14 shillings per week per case. Salford paid £200 per year. But few of these authorities sent many patients, and in some cases the arrangements were merely formal. Some authorities passed on the charges to the families who were therefore unwilling to consent; more generally, families greatly disliked patients being sent out of their home districts.[15]

The provision of fever wards at Preston Infirmary was in some ways a repetition of the scheme tried at Manchester from 1854, when beds in a wing of the Infirmary were set aside for fever patients above the pauper class. Even in a town the size of Manchester, the thirty-two beds were little used, except by domestic servants paid for by their masters. The Preston scheme proved even less successful. It had come about in a complex restructuring of medical institutions at the end of the Cotton Famine.

Preston had suffered badly in 1862, when typhus broke out among the half-starved operatives. Temporary fever wards were erected, at which a doctor and two nurses died. At the end of the Cotton Famine, the Poor Law Inspector pressed hard for a Union workhouse, and the Guardians, led by Canon Parr and Mr C. R. Jacson, eventually agreed to spend £30,000 on a new building at Fulwood. This project was bound up with the contemporary ambitions of the Dispensary trustees, also led by C. R. Jacson, who wished to build an Infirmary. Though they could not hope to raise the £30–40,000 which a new building would cost, the local industrialists were willing to pay for the conversion and extension of the House of Recovery which would be given up by the Guardians when they built a new workhouse. The complex scheme made but slow progress, partly because of disputes over how fever patients were to be housed during the transition. At first it was agreed that paupers suffering from infectious diseases would be housed by the Infirmary trustees, on payment from the Guardians. In 1868, when the trustees were wondering how to provide the twenty-five beds so required, they were offered some large subscriptions for the purpose. But the Guardians soon decided it would be cheaper to build their own fever hospital. Some of them went further in hopes of economy and suggested the old workhouse be retained as fever wards. In 1869, when an epidemic had filled the old workhouse, they agreed to build a small fever hospital on the Fulwood site, mainly for smallpox cases.[16]

In spite of this Poor Law provision the public interest in infectious disease accommodation for non-paupers remained. In 1873, during a national smallpox epidemic, E. R. Harris, one of the major Preston philanthropists, offered to build wards at the voluntary Infirmary of which he was a treasurer. The wards were opened in time for the smallpox epidemic of 1876; they were meant to benefit all classes above pauperdom. Charges were three shillings per day, a guinea per week – half the price of the London fever hospitals. 'There need be no loss of *status* or self-esteem in taking advantage of the provision thus offered and paid for.' The user was doing his duty by society and his isolation from home would free the rest of the family to carry on in employment. A total of thirty-two beds was provided, for smallpox, scarlet fever and typhoid.

This experiment in selling fever accommodation was not very successful. In early 1877 there were thirty-three smallpox cases for each of whom the Infirmary gained an average of £2 13s 0d, but the wards were not used in a subsequent outbreak of typhoid fever. In 1878 the prices were halved to equal those charged by the Guardians for non-pauper patients, but without effect; the Harris wards, 'fulfilling ... every requirement of modern scientific arrangement', were very little appreciated. By 1879 the wards were deteriorating from lack of use and the Infirmary Board, some of whom disliked bringing infectious diseases so near the main hospital, was trying to find other ways to use them. When in 1880 an epidemic of typhoid helped bring twenty-eight cases, most of whom could easily afford the charges, the Board restored the original price for those treated by the Infirmary medical staff. To raise more money, they decided to charge nine shillings a day for private patients who used their own medical adviser. An arrangement was made with the sanitary authority to take cases of scarlet fever, enteric fever and diphtheria, but the wards were little used except in the smallpox epidemic of 1888 when they were filled for the first time. Then a patient in the main hospital died of smallpox and the out-patient service had to be suspended.[17]

Lancaster was the only other town in the Region which had fever wards in a voluntary hospital. The building had been erected after the cholera epidemic of 1832 when a previous House of Recovery (1815) had proved inadequate, and the new hospital concentrated on accident cases and infectious diseases. In their report of 1863, Bristowe and Holmes praised Lancaster hospital for serving the major needs of its community much better than most small voluntary hospitals which tended to take non-infectious medical cases that derived little benefit from admittance. But by the 1870s, medical men were increasingly wary of admitting infectious diseases, especially smallpox, to general hospitals, and in the smallpox epidemic of 1876, Lancaster Infirmary experienced considerable difficulties. Forty-six cases of smallpox were admitted in that year and the fever wards were walled off from the rest of the hospital. Even so, many accident cases refused to become in-patients; their wisdom was confirmed when smallpox spread into the rest of the hospital, which then had to be evacuated. It was this experience which led the local sanitary authority to open a new isolation hospital in 1880.[18]

Smallpox epidemics and local authority hospitals
In Manchester and Lancaster, the local sanitary authorities were able to build on previous voluntary hospitals; in Preston, they continued to rely on the voluntary hospital; elsewhere the local authorities were often pushed to take responsibility for the isolation of infectious diseases, by Guardians who refused to accept non-paupers into the workhouses. Of course, such pressure was particularly effective during epidemics, especially of smallpox. In this Region the epidemics of 1870–3 and especially of 1876–7 were responsible for the first infectious disease hospitals to be built by sanitary authorities. Most of these hospitals were set up in great haste, and some were unfit to serve except as emergency accommodation, but some of the better ones were successfully converted for cases of scarlet fever and other diseases less threatening than smallpox.

Blackpool 'sanatorium' was an example of minimal provision, even though a rapidly growing seaside resort had considerable incentive to provide a hospital for infectious diseases. The wooden pavilion of 1876 contained two wards, each of five beds; only the administration buildings were brick-built. The toilets were 'ill-contrived and ill-ventilated'; worse still, the small site adjoined the local cemetery. It was maintained as a hospital after the epidemic, but proved unpopular. As Dr Thorne Thorne remarked in 1880, when discussing several such hospitals: 'it was found that people did not dread scarlatina enough to let their relatives and children be taken away to a tarred shed of repulsive aspect such as had sufficed for the district hospital when smallpox was in question'.[19] Blackburn sanitary authority in 1877 bought a hut which the Guardians had erected for smallpox the previous year. Soon afterwards they established a 'smallpox hospital' in premises at Finnington which they had bought for a manure depot.[20]

Oldham's Westhulme hospital, built during the same epidemics, was rather more substantial and proved more suitable for other diseases. The site was larger and there were three ward-pavilions, each with eight beds, plus three private wards for single patients. The initial buildings were wooden, but around 1880 it was decided to replace them with more permanent structures. In this same year, under a local Act, notification of infectious diseases was made compulsory, so that the isolation hospital could be more effective. The hospital gained a good reputation after initial suspicion; the new building was opened to the public and 13,000 visitors inspected it; from 1880 mothers were allowed to go in with their children. Some members of 'tradesmen's' families chose to enter as private patients, when they could be attended by their own doctor. Paupers were also admitted. Over two-thirds of the cases in 1878–80 were suffering from scarlet fever and about 60 per cent were children under ten.[21]

In some cases, sanitary authorities took over existing houses instead of building huts. In 1872 Wigan Urban Sanitary Authority leased an old villa to serve as a smallpox hospital. It was closed when smallpox subsided, but on the advice of a Local Government Board Inspector it was re-opened in 1874. It was little used; the officers of the sanitary authority rarely knew of the existence of infectious diseases until it was too late; when they did know, parents were unwilling to have their children admitted.[22] In Burnley the sanitary authority bought a row of four cottages, with twelve beds; in Colne and Marsden (later Nelson) a former poorhouse was rented from the overseers. Burnley's cottages were used very occasionally for diseases other than smallpox; Colne's were not.[23]

In Salford the choice between huts and an old house was the subject of lively debate, and the case is worth following in detail, as an example of how a local Council and the local Board of Guardians shared responsibility, and how the threat of epidemic disease helped provide not only an isolation hospital but also a Poor Law Infirmary for non-infectious cases.

In 1868 Salford, like Manchester, appointed a Medical Officer of Health, and the consequent emphasis on the need for isolation of infectious cases led the Guardians to advise that all cases referred to relieving officers should be removed to the workhouse, where they were hoping to build new fever wards.[24] But by 1870 these wards had not been built and a temporary shed was erected for smallpox. During the smallpox epidemic of 1870–3, Salford's provision for infectious diseases was two wooden sheds at the workhouse, with one nurse assigned to each.

Soon afterwards the Guardians began to object to non-pauper cases being sent to the workhouse. They and the Poor Law Board urged the Borough Council to provide an infectious diseases hospital of their own and the Council began to look for a site in 1874, but owners of land made purchase difficult because they were worried about the effects of a fever hospital on the value of adjacent properties. Towards the end of 1875 the Guardians gave an ultimatum that they would not take non-pauper cases. In a reply to the Warrington Medical Officer the Local Government Board had clarified the respective roles of the Poor Law and Sanitary Authorities. If an infectious patient was destitute the Guardians were responsible for taking him into the workhouse. But if he was being removed simply to isolate him, then the responsibility lay with the Sanitary Authority. Guardians who removed children of parents able to provide medical attention were acting beyond their powers; they certainly were unable to compel removal. By taking infectious cases they were also exposing the workhouse residents to the risk of infection, and as workhouses grew bigger and their sites more crowded, this risk was increasing.[25]

This ultimatum from the Guardians and the onset of the 1876 epidemic forced the local authority to act. Some councillors wanted to erect a temporary hospital and to send other patients to Monsall, but plans to purchase land for temporary buildings met with local opposition. Others, led by Alderman Walmsley, thought it would be cheaper to find a large building which could be adapted for permanent use. They eventually chose Wilton House and three adjacent houses which stood on Cross Lane. This scheme was vigorously opposed, not only by local residents and town meetings but by most of the local medical profession, who maintained that the buildings and the site were quite unsuitable. They would not allow proper segregation of different diseases, the buildings were too close to the streets, there was no room for expansion. The gas works, foundry and railway lines nearby were not the environment which authorities on hospital construction were currently recommending. Henry Knowles, a local surgeon, damned the scheme by systematically comparing the planned hospital with the recommendation of Nightingale and other reformers. A local newspaper asked Alderman Walmsley whether he would choose to send a child he valued to Wilton House or to the new Children's Hospital at Pendlebury – a very recent building in pavilion style. They argued that Salford should have followed the example of Leeds and Birmingham by erecting temporary sheds on the edge of town.[26]

The Local Government Board sent Mr Netten Radcliffe to inspect the site, a task he performed just before he studied Manchester Royal Infirmary. He, of course, condemned Wilton House as unsuitable for a permanent hospital, but he did agree to its temporary use, providing the adjacent houses were kept separate so that they could be used for different classes of disease. The Council were loaned £5,000; half of their request. His agreement undercut some of the resistance to the plan and the buildings were opened in October 1876 under the care of the Medical Officer of Health. It proved an inconvenient and expensive building, but it was intensively used.[27]

Even before the Council purchased Wilton House the Guardians had asked them to collaborate in providing a single isolation hospital. These overtures were rebuffed and the Guardians therefore decided to find a site where they could house infectious paupers and so free the main workhouse population from a preventible risk. They purchased an estate at Hope, several miles west of town.[28] When Wilton House opened and the Guardians again approached the Council they would only agree to house pauper cases at the minimum charge of 10s 6d per week, so the Guardians went ahead with their own plan and built accommodation for eighty cases at Hope. By April 1877 the smallpox epidemic had declined, there were only seven patients and some Guardians were already regretting the expenditure. The land was later used for Hope Hospital, a large workhouse infirmary.

In May 1877 the Council finally agreed to take pauper patients for a trial period of three months. Then they agreed to use a single hospital and settled on Wilton House, for the Council had powers to take pauper patients, whilst the Guardians could not legally provide for non-paupers. The agreement, supervised by the Local Government Board, meant that Wilton House needed to be enlarged. A scheme for 200 beds was put forward in 1877–8, using the house for typhus and enteric fever and new pavilions for smallpox and scarlet fever. The Local Government Board insisted that the proper isolation of the extensions required the purchase of adjacent cottages, and these were bought in 1880.[29]

During the five years 1876–80, Wilton House accommodated 1,432 patients: 231 smallpox, 517 scarlet fever, 234 enteric fever, 107 typhus, 176 measles and 167 'other active diseases'. It acquired a good reputation among the wage-earning classes and even attracted a handful of patients from the trading and professional classes. About 40 per cent of the patients were paupers; as at Monsall, distinctive uniforms or ragged clothing were removed and the paupers were clothed in suits belonging to the hospital.[30] The hospital's fifty beds were reckoned to provide about 550 places per year, and from 1880 arrangements with Monsall secured another 120 places. Even so there appears to have been considerable overcrowding at Wilton House. In the years 1884–6 annual totals of patients were: 713, 507, and 967. Yet the arrangements about overcrowding seem only to have surfaced from 1887, when the Lancashire and North Western Railway decided to build sidings very near the hospital and proved ready to pay £21,000 for the site.[31]

Once more the choice of a new site proved contentious. A site on Eccles New Road proved impossible because of covenants on the adjacent land.[32] A site was purchased at Ladywell, not far from the Poor Law hospital at Hope. Again there was a campaign to have patients sent to Monsall, which was no further than Ladywell from the main fever districts of Salford. Evidence was produced that the costs at Monsall were half those at Wilton House, and that the future costs would be lower because the local authorities who

[168]

contracted with Monsall were not burdened with the capital costs of the building. But the Public Health Committee was determined to have its own hospital:

> They were not building a pauper establishment, or a workhouse, but a place where he would be proud to send members of his own family, where they would probably get better treatment than if they remained in their own homes and subjected the remainder to the risk from contagion ... The hospital which they were now erecting was not one of charity, but one of which the ratepayers of Salford would be proud possessors, and one which would be maintained out of the rates. There was nothing nobler in the minds of men than this provision (to a certain extent) to alleviate humans suffering 'human misery'.[33]

Some councillors saw here 'extravagant officialdom' – even with the parenthesis; others saw a mistaken sense of priorities – the money would be better spent on improving insanitary housing: 'they were committing in the low part of Salford slow murder and they were building palaces outside for the poor people to die in.'[34]

The Ladywell Hospital opened in June 1892 with accommodation for about 180 patients. The number of disease cases notified increased rapidly in the late 1880s and Salford Council could now hope to isolate a higher proportion of them. The new hospital did not take smallpox cases, for which the Local Government Board now demanded much higher standards of isolation. During the epidemic of 1893 Wilton House was re-opened as an emergency measure, but as it filled up and public fears increased, land was bought at Weaste, between the cemetery and the sewage works, and sheds were erected (Mode Wheel Hospital).[35]

Philanthropy and economy: Bolton and the smallpox outbreaks of 1883 and 1893

Several other towns built isolation hospitals in the aftermath of the 1876 epidemic. Bury and Stockport opened hospitals in 1881, both had 50–60 beds, but the pattern of use was rather different, at least in the early 1890s. Bury hospital was little used except during occasional epidemics of scarlet fever and smallpox; there were only thirty-eight patients from 1888–92; in Stockport there were over 400, more than half of them scarlet fever cases. Kendal opened its isolation hospital in the following year, but several larger towns continued to rely on the workhouse or on a rented house or two. Some of the rural sanitary authorities also rented cottages; some, in cases of emergency, made arrangements with other authorities, but for the most part the minor authorities were not concerned with diseases other than smallpox and that was so occasional that permanent provision rarely seemed worthwhile.[36]

VOLUNTARISM AND THE STATE

Among the County Boroughs extensive use of isolation often resulted from the initiative of a full-time Medical Officer of Health. Manchester and Salford had appointed Medical Officers in 1868, before such appointments were made compulsory in 1872. John Leigh and J. F. W. Tatham were widely known as public health reformers: Tatham was a skilled statistician who eventually joined the office of the Registrar General. Oldham had appointed Dr John Sutton in 1873 after a Local Government Board report on a scarlatina epidemic. Bolton's first full-time Medical Officer, Dr Livy, was appointed in the same year, but was soon followed by Dr Edward Sergeant, who later became the Medical Officer to the County. Such men were able to wield considerable influence in persuading their Councils to adopt an active programme of isolating infectious disease in children.[37]

As we have noted in passing, one important accessory measure was the notification of cases of the major infectious diseases. Without such measures, only cases in Poor Law practice came to official attention. Not until 1899 was notification compulsory under national legislation, and even permissive national legislation was not introduced until 1889. But several authorities in this Region had introduced earlier schemes under local Acts. Bolton was the first in 1877; Oldham's Act of 1880 has already been noted; in Manchester notification became compulsory in 1881, although it had long been advocated by the Manchester and Salford Sanitary Association, who had collected statistics of 'public practice', i.e. Poor Law and Charity services. Compulsory notification met with opposition from local general practitioners who disliked this 'official interference' with private practice, but they enabled Medical Officers to present clearly the extent of the problem. Once scarlet fever was notified, the pressure on isolation hospitals increased markedly.[38]

A keen Medical Officer and effective notification could dramatise the need for isolation accommodation, and central pressures could reinforce the message; but only local authorities could spend the money required and provision was minimal where the authorities were dominated by 'ratepayers'' representatives who put economy first.[39] The politics of sanitary authorities and of Boards of Guardians frequently reduced to this conflict over spending. Some civic leaders, often owners of the large factories in the town, were as ready to exercise paternalism through these local authorities as they were through local charities; smaller businessmen, shopkeepers and farmers resisted 'grandiose' schemes and the designs of 'extravagant officialdom'. These issues became particularly tangled when responsibilities were shared between several authorities, with different outlooks.

We can see something of this conflict in Bolton during the 1880s, as the Guardians, the Borough Council and the Rural Sanitary Authority discussed the need for isolation hospitals. As in all rural areas, the Rural Sanitary

Authority, under the 1872 Act, was the Board of Guardians of the Union, minus the representatives of the County Borough and any other parts of the Union which had their own Local Boards. Thus, for Bolton, both the Guardians and the Rural Sanitary Authority were led by the Haslam family – liberal, nonconformist millowners who were prominent among the philanthropists of the town.[40] 'Philanthropists' seem to have been less evident on the Borough Council; they were never apparent in the smaller towns of the Union, like Farnworth, which had their own Local Boards for sanitary purposes. The Rural Sanitary Authority was quite ready to take responsibility for fever cases away from the Guardians; but the Local Boards resented the Local Government Board forcing this move, because it meant they would have to pay for isolation hospitals.

From about 1880 the Bolton Borough Council came under pressure to build an isolation hospital. Dr Sergeant had arranged compulsory notification and argued that the next step to consider was the means of isolation. The Guardians were complaining that the Borough should not continue to rely on the use of the workhouse fever hospital. The Sanitary Committee of the Borough visited several towns provided with fever hospitals and recommended that Bolton provide twenty-eight beds in two pavilion blocks. Work began in 1882 on a site at Rumworth.[41] The pressure was increased during a smallpox epidemic in 1882 when the Guardians were taking smallpox cases from the Borough, at a charge of seven shillings a week which they reckoned to be much below the real cost. In July 1882 they decided that once the epidemic was ended they would take no more non-pauper cases.[42]

When Rumworth hospital was opened in 1884, arrangements were made to take cases from outside the Borough at a charge of one guinea per week, which the Rural Sanitary Authority thought excessive. Led by J. P. Haslam they began to consider providing a fever hospital of their own. Their Medical Officer recommended that houses be taken in various parts of the district where whole families could be isolated and which could serve for various different diseases if the need arose.[43] Such schemes, though suggested by the Local Government Board in the early 1870s, were not favoured by the mid-1880s because it was difficult to arrange proper segregation and very difficult to supply adequate nursing and medical supervision. The Rural Sanitary Authority then tried to arrange for joint use of Rumworth, but the Borough were not willing to commit any beds for rural patients. Plans to act jointly with the Local Boards also failed.[44]

Once Rumworth was operational, the workhouse fever hospital was little used and various alternative uses were mooted. The Local Government Board wanted it used as a general hospital and for imbeciles; but in 1888 it had to be used to accommodate a family with typhoid who could not be admitted to Rumworth because it was full of scarlet fever patients. Haslam and some other Guardians severely criticised the Borough. The family in question had been pauperised because the Council could not accommodate them, and because compulsory notification meant that the father could not work. He had been forced to contact the relieving officer; the Poor Law doctor and the family's own doctor had persuaded the family to enter the workhouse.[45]

The use of the workhouse fever wards continued to be contentious because in 1888 there was smallpox in Preston and the various authorities in Bolton feared an outbreak in their district. Some of the Guardians wanted the fever wards made available because otherwise the Local Boards in towns like Farnworth would have to provide their own accommodation. Haslam and the Local Government Board Inspector maintained that it was not the Guardians' job to provide for non-paupers. Haslam wanted the fever wards made over to the Rural Sanitary Authority, a move allowed under an Act of 1879, but the Clerk to the Guardians maintained that the workhouse could not afford to lose the accommodation for diseases which arose among resident paupers. Instead the Rural Authority planned its own hospital. The Local Government Board refused to lend money for an iron shed, and a permanent building for ten patients was then planned for a site adjoining the Borough's hospital at Rumworth.[46]

This plan met with opposition from the Borough Council who were hoping to extend the Borough boundaries and wanted the Rural isolation hospital deferred. Haslam and his friends resented this 'meddling' and went ahead with their proposal, spurred on by the occurrence of smallpox, cases of which had to be accommodated at the workhouse.[47] The hospital, opened in 1890, had twelve beds and twelve more were planned, it was generously staffed with a resident matron and resident man, plus three nurses. The Medical Officer of the Rural Sanitary Authority was given an extra £50 per year for its medical supervision.[48] In spite of overtures from the Rural Authority, the Borough refused to arrange for the two adjacent hospitals to be jointly staffed; they intended to 'boss their own show'. In 1898, when Bolton's boundaries were extended, the 'eastern' hospital came into the possession of the Borough.

Among minor authorities Bolton Rural Sanitary Authority was unusual in providing a well-appointed isolation hospital. They did so because they were led by affluent members interested in philanthropy. The opening ceremony for the hospital was lavish, as befitted a building in 'a combination of Renaissance and Queen Anne'. Many of those present were ladies and a special place of honour was given to Miss Wardle, daughter of the chairman and widely known for her work among the poor. The Authority took pride in being progressive, and looked down on the Borough Council for providing an isolation hospital which was late and too small.[49]

When smallpox reappeared in 1892 it was recognised that the disease could not safely be admitted to the existing hospitals. The Rural Sanitary Authority again took the lead in urging the Borough to collaborate in providing extra accommodation. They also contacted all the Local Boards within the Bolton Union. This time there was more interest than there had been in 1885 when the Rural Authority had first suggested collaboration for smallpox, but little came of the scheme. For as long as the neighbouring small towns could rely on using Rumworth they had little incentive to collaborate, and some of them, especially Farnworth, claimed that they were trying to make provision for themselves, but that no one would let property to house smallpox cases. The Rural Authority went ahead on its own and added a smallpox hut to their hospital.[50]

This addition also helped relieve pressure on the Bolton Guardians who had been forced to accept a case from Farnworth, and very much resented having to house smallpox patients even when paupers. They were a danger to all the residents and unless they could be excluded the Guardians would need more segregated accommodation for fevers. As in the case of Salford, ten years before, this concern over infectious cases initiated a discussion that eventually led to a large workhouse infirmary on a newly purchased site (Townleys Hospital).[51]

Completing the coverage: isolation hospitals 1890–1914
Before 1888, as we have seen, there were several kinds of health authorities in the Region. In corporate towns, the Urban Sanitary Authority was often a Local Board established under the 1848 Act. In the remaining areas the Rural Sanitary Authority was composed of Poor Law Guardians for the rural parts of each Union. The Local Government Act of 1888 divided the country into County Boroughs (major towns) and administrative Counties which were responsible for the area of each county outside the County Boroughs. In 1894, in the administrative Counties, Urban District Councils and Rural District Councils were established which respectively took over the functions of the Local Boards and the Rural Sanitary Authorities. These local councils were responsible for most public health functions; but the new County Councils had some powers of coercion over them.

This clarification was important for hospital provision chiefly because, after 1893, when asked by twenty ratepayers or by constituent authorities, the County Councils could force Urban and Rural District Councils to federate and provide isolation hospitals under Joint Hospital Boards. The power of federation had existed since 1875 but had been little used; in the period from 1893–1914 the new powers were used more, so that by the end of the period, patients in almost the whole of our Region had access to some kind of isolation hospital. The coercive powers of the County Council did not extend to the County Boroughs, indeed, special permission had to be obtained for a County Borough to join a Joint Hospital Board. The urban–rural division thus institutionalised was unfortunate; if rural districts and small towns did not wish to collaborate with the neighbouring Borough, or vice versa, there was no way of compelling them; the County Council could only federate County areas. Many of these, individually, rarely experienced serious epidemics, and so were generally unwilling to make provision. Moreover, any hospital they paid for under a Joint Board was likely to be smaller and generally less accessible than the hospital of the nearest large town. It would be used less regularly and would be more difficult and expensive to staff.[52]

In 1888, of the major Boroughs in the Region, only Manchester, Salford, Oldham and Bolton had isolation hospitals which counted their patients in hundreds annually. The numbers isolated annually in Stockport and Rochdale were usually between fifty and a hundred; no more than in the smaller towns of Kendal and Lancaster. In Barrow, Blackpool, Burnley, Wigan, Bury and Ashton, the isolation 'hospitals' were little used except during smallpox outbreaks. Preston had no facilities except the Harris Wards at the voluntary Infirmary. Over the next twenty years, pressures similar to those which we have detailed for Salford and Bolton, led to new or better hospitals in this second series of Boroughs. Wigan, in 1889, opened Whelley Hospital with sixty beds (seventy-eight in 1912); Blackpool opened the Devonshire Road Hospital in 1891 providing twenty extra beds, and in the same year Lancaster rebuilt its hospital; Blackburn's Park Lee Hospital (1894) provided eighty-seven beds by 1912. In 1899 Burnley built the Marsden Road Hospital which had seventy-four beds by 1912. Bury Borough built the Florence Nightingale Hospital, which was opened in 1903.[53]

Preston was the last major town to provide an isolation hospital; the Council, who were not notable for sanitary improvement, had relied on the voluntary provision at the Preston Infirmary. They were forced into action at the end of the century because the town found itself without any accommodation for infectious diseases other than smallpox or cholera. The Guardians were refusing to take infectious cases, even among the destitute and throughout the 1890s they complained of the corporation shirking its duty. The Harris Wards were unavailable; some of the beds had been permanently appropriated for children's wards and the others were out of action in 1900 because of renovation. This extension of the Infirmary brought the Harris wards within the main hospital structure, when the admittance of infectious cases to general hospitals was being criticised by leading medical authorities. Thus, around 1900 the Preston Medical Officer of Health had occasionally resorted to supplying nursing to infectious patients kept at home, but the great difficulty of effectively isolating patients in most working-class homes meant that this was an ineffective as well as an expensive expedient.[54]

By 1900 an infectious disease hospital was regarded as part of the equipment of all progressive County Boroughs, but in Preston discussion continued for over five years, even when there were no alternative facilities. When a plan was agreed in 1901 it was publicly opposed by local medical men who claimed that isolation hospitals were wasteful and ineffective. Between epidemics they were useless and expensive, during epidemics they could not take enough cases. To isolate a sufferer without isolating family and contacts did nothing to remove the source of infection. It was better to leave the patient at home and isolate the whole family. That Preston could manage without such a hospital had been proved over many years.[55] This opposition, added to the usual complaints about rate increases, delayed the project even longer. Not until 1907 was the hospital opened on Deepdale Road, Holme Slack. It cost £20,000 and had room for fifty-four patients. In 1909 the Corporation agreed to take cases chargeable to the Union, on payment of £2 per week.[56]

Macclesfield opened West Heath Hospital at about the same time. By then, of the large industrial towns, only Barrow and Ashton were relying on tiny hospitals built for smallpox. Barrow's new Devonshire Road Hospital was built just after the war. The Beaumont Hospital in Lancaster was the only other general isolation hospital to be built in the interwar years.[57]

Some of these isolation hospitals built in major towns in the 1890s also served adjacent rural areas. Blackburn hospital was shared with Blackburn Rural District; the Burnley hospital was administered by a Joint Board which included Nelson and Colne; the Bury hospital was also under a Joint Board. But most of the rural areas had minimal if any facilities for isolation. Some made arrangements for use of beds in adjacent boroughs; some in the 1890s rented isolated cottages. Most gained facilities only after the Isolation Hospitals Act of 1893 provided for the newly formed County Councils to federate adjacent districts for the maintenance of hospitals.[58] We can gain some idea of how these regulations worked in practice by considering the provision of hospitals in the districts around Preston.

In 1898 the Joint Hospital Committee of Preston Rural District, Longridge and Fulwood applied to the County Council for a loan to build an isolation hospital. The site initially purchased looked as if it would be expensive to build on; it was sold and a new site at Fulwood was purchased.

There were objections from local residents and the officers of Fulwood barracks, and a Local Government Board Inspector held an inquiry. The local objections were overruled and so were complaints from Fulwood and Longridge Urban District Councils who now wanted to withdraw from the scheme because it was going to cost £16,000. This latter objection was then put by the Joint Committee to the County Council, who refused to amend the scheme except to bring Walton-le-Dale Urban District into the Joint Board. An attempt to include the town of Preston failed, for the County Council had no powers over County Boroughs. The Fulwood Hospital was opened about 1904 with twenty-six beds. The neighbouring Joint Board for the Chorley District had opened Heath Charnock Isolation Hospital in 1901 and this had served as a model.[59]

Most of the isolation hospitals built after 1890 were not expected to take smallpox cases, which were recognised as requiring stricter isolation. The Royal Commission on Metropolitan Smallpox and Fever Hospitals, 1882, had condemned the practice of placing smallpox patients near other patients or near centres of population, and in this Region the message was underlined by a series of cases in which smallpox had spread from smallpox hospitals. In 1888 there was evidence that the people in Chadderton had become infected by 'aerial diffusion' from Oldham's hospital at Westhulme. Dr James Niven, the Oldham Medical Officer of Health, produced evidence against the complaint, but in the 1892–3 outbreak he agreed that such diffusion was probably responsible for some of the new cases. When Niven was appointed to Manchester in 1894 he concluded that smallpox cases in Monsall Hospital had infected some of the neighbouring districts.[60]

These authorities, like Manchester, which had smallpox pavilions in general isolation hospitals sought additional and remote accommodation. Manchester used old factory premises in Clayton Vale.[61] Some authorities continued to use their hospitals for smallpox when they built new isolation hospitals for other diseases. Others rented or bought isolated cottages or farms, or erected huts or even, as in the case of Accrington, bought a tent.

Some of the Boroughs and Joint Hospital Boards who had recently built isolation hospitals also set up separate smallpox hospitals of reasonable quality. Burnley's Crown Point Hospital (1901) was built on the summit of a hill; overlooking the town to the north and the open moors to the south. Ainsworth Hospital in Bury (1906) comprised a large isolated house for the staff and a new building alongside for the patients. In the Fylde the Joint Hospital Board built a smallpox hospital at Elswick, near Kirkham (1915). These were among the few smallpox facilities which by the inter-war period were fit to be called hospitals. They were also, by then, practically unused, for smallpox had all but disappeared, after a few outbreaks in 1900–6.

Crown Point was later used for sickly children. Elswick, on opening, was leased to the County as a tuberculosis sanatorium, on the understanding that it would be vacated if smallpox broke out. Ainsworth was also used for tuberculosis patients from 1913 to 1921 when the Local Government Board insisted that it be kept free for smallpox, because the disease, albeit in a mild form, was beginning to reappear in the cotton towns.[62]

In some cases Joint Boards were so reluctant to provide a smallpox hospital that the County Council eventually despaired. In 1902 they brought together representatives from all the local authorities within the Wigan and Chorley Unions. The proposed joint hospital was supported by the largest authority, the Borough of Wigan, which had made no provision of its own and thought a shared hospital would be very economical; most of the rural authorities were willing to go along with the majority or with the decisions of the Joint Hospital Boards of which they were part; four or five of the twenty authorities were opposed. In the absence of agreement the Council held a local enquiry for a modified scheme; Wigan Borough was excluded as outside the County's jurisdiction and so were the Chorley districts, which had recently arranged to use ten beds at the Finnington Smallpox Hospital owned by Blackburn Borough. The objections to the scheme for the districts around Wigan were maintained at a County Council Inquiry in November 1903: Wigan Rural District had rented an isolated cottage for over fourteen years; only once had it been needed for a smallpox case; Standish Urban District had kept its cottage for ten years; the Urban District of Aspull, where half of the rates were paid by the Wigan Coal and Iron Company objected to the expense of the scheme; under a lease from the Earl of Crawford and Balcarres to Wigan Corporation they had the right to send smallpox cases to hospital in Wigan. The County Medical Officer of Health, backed by his counterpart in Wigan Borough, argued that these arrangements were inadequate: the Standish 'hospital' was 'totally unfitted for its purpose'; Wigan Rural District's was insufficient, and Wigan Corporation could not erect a permanent smallpox hospital on the land it leased because the site did not meet Local Government Board Regulations. Eventually, in 1913 the Joint Board agreed to purchase land and the County Council wanted to lease most of the proposed building for tuberculosis. The Local Government Board, having passed a similar plan for Elswick, thought one such scheme was enough; and the whole project faltered. In 1914, after thirteen years of wasted effort, the County Council disbanded the Joint Hospital Board.[63]

The importance of isolation hospitals

The development of isolation hospitals in our Region can plausibly be analysed as a resultant of two forces. On the one hand the public health campaigns of the mid-nineteenth century, expressed through national legislation and through local associations, built up a sub-profession of public health doctors during the last third of the century. These doctors saw the isolation of infectious disease as one of their major weapons; in the major cities, in *some* of the larger towns, and occasionally in suburban areas, they were able to win local support. In Manchester, that support came first through charitable donations prompted by a prestigious and highly skilled public health lobby. On the other hand there was the fear of smallpox. From the 1870s to about 1890, most of the isolation hospitals provided in the Region were emergency measures called forth by the smallpox epidemics. The contagiousness and high case-fatality of the disease, persuaded almost all major authorities to provide some isolated accommodation, once the Board of Guardians began to exclude such cases from their workhouses. The 1866 Sanitary Act gave local authorities the necessary powers, and the self-interest of Guardians as custodians of large pauper communities usually meant that they wanted to transfer the responsibility. Where Guardians as local ratepayers thought it was cheaper to house cases in the workhouse, the Local Government Board was usually able to force them to exclude non-paupers.

Local authorities with active Medical Officers of Health usually built smallpox accommodation of a reasonable standard; this was then used for other infectious diseases, notably scarlet fever, especially where a local Act had made notification compulsory. Smallpox provided the initial opportunity on which an active Medical Officer of Health might capitalise. The threat of smallpox in the 1870s and 1880s was greater because the huge epidemic of 1870–3 surprised the majority of observers who thought the disease was declining. By the 1890s, after a series of much smaller epidemics the prospects were less fearsome, and the recognition that smallpox hospitals ought to be well away from all other buildings meant that the problem of smallpox was dissociated from the problem of other infectious diseases which were filling the isolation hospitals. Thenceforth new smallpox accommodation was rudimentary, except for a few Joint Board hospitals stimulated by the County Council in the Edwardian period. Those which were finished after 1910 when smallpox seemed to have disappeared were largely used as sanatoria.

Isolation hospitals provided after about 1895 were not built to get smallpox patients out of the way of the general population; they were intended chiefly as hospitals for children. By then there were more Medical Officers of Health who were 'properly' trained and committed to a career in public health. The development of bacteriology had given a more 'scientific' basis to their practice and to their propaganda. By then, as we shall see in the next chapter the voluntary and Poor Law hospitals were established, in the towns as well as in the cities, as institutions which could offer better medical and nursing care than a general practitioner and an average home. A 'modern isolation hospital' was then 'not only a receptive institution but a curative one'.[64] We can see how the better isolation hospitals were presented by their medical staff if we briefly examine the reports of Monsall Hospital at the beginning of the new century.

Monsall, then owned by the Manchester Corporation, had separate accommodation for scarlet fever, diphtheria, enteric fever, erysipelas, puerperal fever, plus isolation wards for doubtful cases and for measles. It had a laboratory and an operating theatre for dealing with surgical complications. Convalescent wards and recreational facilities were provided for patients as they recovered. There was a medical superintendent, a senior assistant and two junior medical assistants. The nursing staff of one hundred had accommodation on the site. Each large ward was staffed by a sister, a staff nurse and two probationers during the day, and by night, a nurse assisted by a probationer.

In 1904, 2,397 patients were admitted; 1,660 had scarlet fever, 251 diphtheria, 205 enteric fever, fifty-nine erysipelas, sixteen puerperal fever, ten measles and 196 had other diseases. All but 102 of the scarlet fever patients were under fifteen years of age; about half of the rest were between five and ten. The ages of distribution of diphtheria was similar. Most of the enteric fever cases were young adults; erysipelas was fairly evenly distributed across the age ranges. In total, about 80 per cent of the patients were under fifteen. Scarlet fever cases spent an average of eight weeks in hospital, diphtheria five weeks. The average number of patients in the hospital was 308, the overall death rate was 6 per cent, for scarlet fever 3 per cent and for enteric fever 14 per cent.

The keynote of treatment and hospital regimen was 'surgical cleanliness'. Nurses working in the wards did not wear sleeves below the elbow; the wards were mopped, never swept. Treatment was increasingly active; the throats of scarlet fever patients were regularly douched with weak antiseptic using sterilised nozzles for each patient; in 1904 a bactericidal serum was proving successful; surgical operations were carried out to cure the ear discharges which were a common complication of scarlet fever. If there was a nasal discharge it was tested for diphtheria bacilli. Diphtheria cases were also douched and in the acute stages the anti-toxin was given. When the larynx was obstructed tracheotomies were performed.[65]

This emphasis on investigation and treatment provided a means of justifying the hospitals when, around 1902, the value of taking scarlet fever cases into hospital was publicly questioned. By then the disease was far milder than it had been in 1870, when beds were first provided for infected children. But this decrease in case fatality was very general, there was no evidence that towns which sent a high proportion of cases to hospitals had fared any better than those in which practically all the cases had been treated at home. In our Region, during the 1890s, Manchester, Salford, Oldham, Bolton, Rochdale, Wigan and Lancaster had used isolation hospitals for about 30 – 70 per cent of cases; Preston, Burnley, Ashton had not, but there was no obvious difference in the case-fatality rates. Nor was there any evidence that the attack rates (cases/population) were any different. A Medical Officer of Health from the Midlands argued that any advantages of hospitals were offset by the transfer of infectious complications and by cross-infection between different strains of the disease. 'Return cases' were used as evidence of this latter effect – patients leaving hospitals appeared to infect members of the households to which they returned.

The debate was embarrassing to the Medical Officers who had long been committed to the value of isolation hospitals. Some of them produced statistics of a different kind to show that more members of a household contracted the disease when the first case remained at home than when the first case was removed to hospital, but no one could produce any evidence that the introduction of isolation hospitals had lowered the incidence or fatality rates in the town concerned, when they were compared with more backward towns. Perhaps there is room here for a sophisticated piece of research in historical epidemiology. At present we can only consider the response of Medical Officers committed to using hospitals.[66]

Most of them argued that large scale statistics were misleading; the attack rates and case fatalities varied between towns for reasons which were not understood. Others, like the Superintendent of Monsall, tried to shift the terms of the debate. He preferred to speak of 'hospital treatment' of scarlet fever rather than 'hospital isolation'. 'In the heat of the discussions in the medical press a tendency has been evident to minimise the importance of the curative side of the work of the hospital and to treat the subject entirely from the statistical point of view.'[67]

The shift is of general interest. Public health campaigns from the 1840s onward had neglected curative medicine and concentrated on 'the statistical point of view'. In 1882, the Medical Officer to the Local Government Board, in an introduction to Thorne Thorne's report on the 'Use and Influence of Hospitals for Infectious Diseases', had anticipated that longer experience would enable the value of the hospital to the community to be judged by statistics. In 1902 – 4, medical superintendents of isolation hospitals were little more interested in general statistics than were doctors in any other kind of hospital. They had a method of treatment based on modern medical science and which seemed to be effective; it could not easily be administered unless the patients were brought into hospital. Parents, after decades of persuasion, were ready to act on the doctors' advice; and leading laymen were generally convinced that a spotlessly clean, well-staffed isolation hospital was a monument to the progressive spirit in the community. Hospitals for smallpox were precautions against emergencies and a remote shed would suffice. General isolation hospitals, like other special hospitals, were an esential part of modern medicine, because modern medicine was increasingly based on specialisation and on hospital treatment.

Notes and references

1. On the general history of public health in England and Wales see John Simon, *English Sanitary Institutions*, London, 1890; W. M. Frazer, *A History of English Public Health*, London, 1950; and the recent book, which I have not used, by Anthony S. Wohl, *Endangered Lives, Public Health in Victorian Britain*, London, 1983.
2. Annual Report of the Medical Officer to the Privy Council, 1866, p. 33.
3. On cholera and its apparent causes see, Margaret Pelling, *Cholera, Fever and English Medicine 1825–1865*, Oxford, 1978; R. J. Morris, *Cholera 1832*, London, 1976; M. Durey, *The Return of the Plague: British Society and the Cholera 1831–2*, Dublin, 1979.
4. Annual Report of the Medical Officer of the Privy Council and Local Government Board, 1874, p. 54.
5. On responses in London see G. M. Ayers, *England's First State Hospitals and the Metropolitan Asylums Board, 1867–1930*, London, 1971.
6. A. H. Gale, *Epidemic Diseases*, London, 1959.
7. See the discussion of children's Dispensaries and Hospitals in Chapter 6.
8. Isolation for scarlet fever was discussed in *Public Health*, 1901 and 1902; see, especially, C. Killick Millard, 'The influence of hospital isolation in scarlet fever', *Public Health*, 13 (1901), 462–503.
9. Salford Board of Guardians, minutes, 2 May 1851, 8 February 1861 (Salford Record Office); W. Bennett, *History of Burnley from 1850 (Part 4)*, Burnley, 1951, p. 14; MH 12, 981 (Public Record Office).
10. Winifred Proctor, 'Poor Law administration in Preston Union 1838–1848', *Transactions of the Historical Society of Lancashire & Cheshire*, 117 (1965), 156.
11. Salford Board of Guardians, minutes, 15 March 1861. Preston Board of Guardians, *Preston Pilot*, 18 January 1865.
12. Salford Board of Guardians, 11 May, 20, 27 July, 16 November 1866.
13. Sheena Simon, *A Century of City Government, Manchester 1838–1938*, London, 1938.
14. A. Redford, *The History of Local Government in Manchester*, 3 vols, London, 1939–40, II, pp. 409–10.
15. Annual reports of the Manchester MOH and, especially, the (national) Report by Dr R. Thorne Thorne on 'the use and influence of hospitals for infectious diseases', C 3290, XXX, pt. II, 1882.
16. See the Board of Guardians' meetings in the newspapers, especially *Preston Pilot*: 7 May, 13 August, 22, 29 October – 12 November 1864; *Preston Guardian*, 18 January 1865, January–December 1869.
17. Preston Infirmary Annual Reports, 1873, 1876–81, 1888.
18. Lancaster Dispensary Annual Reports, and see Ch. 6, n. 79.

19. Richard Thorne Thorne, *op. cit.* (n. 15), p. 413.
20. Blackburn Council Committee Minutes, January, February, June 1877. (I owe these references to Mr J. E. Harrison).
21. Thorne, *op. cit.* (n. 15), p. 214; *Oldham Centenary, a History of Local Government*, Oldham County Borough Council, 1949, p. 35.
22. Thorne, *op. cit.* (n. 15), p. 286.
23. Returns relating to Sanitary Districts (Accommodation for Infectious Diseases), House of Commons Sessional Paper, 28, 1895.
24. Salford Board of Guardians, minutes, 4 December 1868.
25. Salford General Health Committee, minutes, September 1874 – September 1875, especially 1 September 1875 (reported in *Salford Weekly News*).
26. Salford Guardians minutes and General Health Committee minutes; Knowles letter dated 3 March 1876 reproduced from the *Salford Chronicle*; MH 12/6236 (1876) (Public Record Office).
27. *Salford Weekly News*, 1, 8 April, 4 November 1876.
28. *Salford Weekly News*, 25 April 1877.
29. Thorne, *op. cit.* (n. 15), p. 228.
30. *Pendleton & Salford Reporter*, 20 January 1883.
31. Salford Council Proceedings, 2 March 1877.
32. *Ibid.*, 3 October 1888.
33. Speech of Alderman Dickens, *Salford Reporter*, 24 May 1890.
34. Alderman Hall, Council Proceedings, *Salford Reporter*, 8 February 1890.
35. Salford Council Proceedings, 1 February 1893, 4 April 1894.
36. Returns Relating to Sanitary Districts (Accommodation for Infectious Diseases), House of Commons Sessional Paper, 28, 1895.
37. See, for example, the minutes of the North Western Association of Medical Officers of Health (c/o Manchester Medical Society).
38. J. Niven, *Observations on the History of the Public Health Effort in Manchester*, Manchester, 1923; Brand, *Doctors*, 117; Annual Reports, Bolton Medical Officer of Health, 1877, 1881; E. Sergeant, *Compulsory Notification of Infectious Diseases*, Bolton, 1878; *Health Journal*, 1886 (NW Association of Medical Officers of Health visit to Salford).
39. Norman McCord, 'Ratepayers and social policy', in P. Thane (ed.), *The Origins of British Social Policy*, London, 1978.
40. This and other similar families are discussed in Patrick Joyce, *Work, Society and Politics. The Culture of the Factory in later Victorian England*, Brighton, 1980.
41. Annual Reports of the Medical Officer of Health for Bolton, 1881 and 1882. Proceedings of the Bolton Guardians, August 1880.
42. Bolton Guardians, May – August 1882.
43. Proceedings of the Bolton Rural Sanitary Authority, 12 December 1884, 22 January, 24 March 1885.
44. *Ibid.*, December 1885, January 1886.
45. Bolton Guardians, 2 February 1888.
46. Bolton Guardians, 20 June, 4 July 1888; Bolton Rural Sanitary Authority, 26 June 1888.
47. Bolton Rural Sanitary Authority, 1 August 1889.
48. *Bolton Chronicle*, 13 September 1890.
49. *Ibid.*
50. Bolton Rural Sanitary Authority, 8, 22 November, 15, 20 December 1892; 11, 26 January 1893.
51. Bolton Guardians, 17, 31 May, 28 June, 20 September, 15, 29 November 1893.
52. For statutes on notification and isolation hospitals see the Twentieth Annual Report of the Ministry of Health, 1938 – 9, Cmd 6089, 1939.
53. The statistics are derived from the Return on Sanitary Districts (Accommodation for

Infectious Diseases), House of Commons Sessional Paper 28, 1895; H.C. Burdett's *Hospital Year Book*, 1914.
54. Annual Reports of the Medical Officer of Health for Preston, 1899–1901; *Preston Herald*, 13 December 1902.
55. *Preston Pilot*, 28 September, 2 November 1901.
56. Annual Report, Preston MOH, 1905, 1906; Preston Sanitary Committee, minutes, 20 October 1908, 18 May 1909.
57. H.C. Burdett's *Hospital Year Books*.
58. Sanitary Districts (n. 53), p. 27.
59. Proceedings of the Lancashire County Council, May 1901, February 1902, and of its Public Health Committee, January 1898, July 1900, August 1902; Annual Reports of Medical Officer of Health for Lancashire County, 1901.
60. Niven, *Observations*, 76–7; E. Sergeant, 'On hospital accommodation for smallpox in Lancashire', *Public Health*, 5 (1892–3).
61. Niven, *Observations*, 78–80.
62. Burdett (1914); Annual Reports of Medical Officer of Health for Burnley; *Bury & Rossendale Hospital Group*, (Report, 1974, by the Hospital Management Committee); Lancashire County Council Proceedings 7 August 1913 (on Elswick).
63. Lancashire County Council Proceedings, November 1902, 4 February 1904, 4 November 1915; Public Health Committee; August 1902; Medical Officer of Health Report, August 1903.
64. Annual Report of the Medical Superintendent of Monsall Hospital, Manchester, 1904, p. 1.
65. *Ibid.*, 1902 and 1904.
66. See the discussion in *Public Health*, *13* and *14*, 1901 and 1902.
67. Monsall report, 1904, p. 11.

CHAPTER 9

Sciences, specialists and capital: the modernisation of Manchester hospitals

Introduction
The revival of voluntary hospitals after 1860 and the associated development of Poor Law infirmaries was not, we have argued, a response to specifically medical developments. The new hospitals provided hygienic conditions, nursing and medical supervision; they did not provide novel methods of treatment. In smaller voluntary hospitals the staff were nearly all general practitioners; in city hospitals like the Manchester Royal Infirmary, they were general consultants – physicians or surgeons; the division of labour was the traditional one between internal ailments and external or traumatic lesions. The consultants were also clinical teachers, but generally this was a minor part of their work.

Both medicine and surgery became considerably more technical from the 1860s. After the Medical Reform Act of 1858, the medical schools gradually extended their curricula and introduced more and more medical science, much of it developed in the German universities. The growth of pathological anatomy and histology and later of clinical physiology, brought laboratory investigation closer to clinical medicine, so that a physician, to be recognised as a professional leader, needed more than a wide experience of diseases – he needed to be a medical scientist; many younger physicians developed particular fields of expertise on which they published papers and so advertised themselves as authorities.

Hospital practice became more technical in the 1870s and 1880s as those who had passed through medical school after the 1858 Medical Registration Act came to hold honorary posts. Their education had included much more medical science than had been usual before and many of the surgeons, as well as the physicians, held university medical degrees. The increased number of resident appointments in teaching hospitals meant that such people could often establish a reputation and a very solid clinical background before they entered private practice. Their resident appointments provided a springboard to consultant practice and they could hope for early appointment to honorary posts, probably first in minor hospitals, then perhaps in the outpatients department of the Infirmary, then a full Infirmary post.[1]

The development of these new professional patterns was neither inevitable nor uncontentious. The medical scientists and some of the specialists tended to see hospital practice as an extension of the laboratory; they favoured division of medical labour – the medical school and the associated hospitals would form a complex corporation, comparable to the largest and most modern businesses. Other medical men adhered to an older model of general skills and individual practice, of experience rather than expertise, of civic standing rather than professional reputation.

Historians have begun to explore some of these changes and contrasts within American medicine. There the shift was often dramatic – from a medical *laissez-faire* of minimal scientific content, to medical schools and teaching hospitals like those in Baltimore, modelled on German universities, rapidly becoming the incubators of medical discoveries. The 'scientisation' of American medical schools was expensive; at Baltimore it depended on the legacy of a local industrialist, Johns Hopkins. Later developments were often funded by Rockefeller or Carnegie capital. So the major capitalists of the late nineteenth century paid to help create a scientific profession of medicine, part of the increasingly professional society built after the Civil War.[2]

No historian has looked for similar patterns in Britain. Yet, in Manchester at least, they are easily revealed. The success, albeit partial, of the scientists-specialists in creating a new kind of teaching hospital, depended largely on their access to major industrial capital. In this chapter we show how and why in early twentieth-century Manchester there developed a string of teaching hospitals extending southwards from the University.

Medical vs. lay control and the question of the Infirmary site
In the 1840s when the question of moving the Infirmary was first seriously raised, the arguments were largely economic. The city centre site was crowded and dirty but very valuable; this asset could be realised if one or more new hospitals were to be built outside the town. During the 1850s and 1860s this argument was overlain by the sanitarian campaign which concentrated on the need for pure air. In the early 1870s yet another argument was added when the medical school joined Owens College on its new site in Rusholme, a mile or so to the south of the centre. The twists and turns of the debate, which continued until the removal to Rusholme in 1908, are not without general interest, for they illustrate nicely what the various groups involved expected from a city Infirmary. The course of the debate depended on the relative strengths of these groups and their degree of control over the

Infirmary. Towards the end of the century, some of the medical staff became more powerful as they became more closely integrated into a national medical and academic community.

At the time of the student protest in 1855, there had been two proprietary medical schools which sought their clinical instruction in Manchester Infirmary. Thomas Turner's Pine Street School had flourished since 1824; it had killed off Jordan's old school in 1834 and weathered the rivalry of a school which ran in Marsden Street from 1829 to 1839. The Chatham Street School begun in 1850 by the surgeon George Southam and his friends proved a more successful rival. It was better equipped and began to attract more students than Turner. In 1856, after Turner had retired from the Infirmary and Southam had been appointed a full surgeon, the two schools amalgamated in the Chatham Street premises. Southam, a local man, was the son-in-law of Sir Elkanah Armitage, Salford's richest industrialist.[3]

Since the revival of English higher education with the foundation of University College London in 1826 medical men in several cities had tried to develop colleges which, like University College London, would include medical education. It was an obvious way for provincial practitioners to associate themselves with the learned professions and with the growing cachet of the natural sciences.

When Owens College was founded in 1851, with money left by the merchant John Owens, it was run by many of the same men who had planned and financed the mid-century reconstruction of the Infirmary. In 1856, after the amalgamation of the proprietary schools, Turner and Southam approached the Owens trustees to suggest a merger. They wanted accommodation in the College and expected eventually to receive salaries from it, but they also wanted to retain substantial authority for the medical section. The College refused, partly because its staff feared that their liberal arts students would be swamped by the larger number of socially inferior medical students.[4]

But by 1870 both Owens College and the medical students had changed considerably. Owens College was developing science departments where research was carried out on the model of German universities. Its moving spirit, the chemist Henry Roscoe, was keen to incorporate professional education. Moreover, since the 1858 Medical Registration Act had provided the first official recognition of the unity of the profession, medical schools were subject to a General Medical Council, through which representatives from the various licensing bodies could agree to raise standards of entry and education without fear of being undercut in the competition for students.

As a result of these changes, in 1872, the Manchester Royal School of Medicine was incorporated as the Medical Faculty of Owens College. In

1881 Owens became the first college of the Victoria University. From 1873 the Medical Faculty was housed in a new building on the Rusholme site, which included an excellent laboratory. The physiologist, Arthur Gamgee, was appointed as a full-time professor, linking the part-time teachers of medicine to the full-time academics of the Faculty of Science.[5]

At the time of the merger, several of the Infirmary honorary staff were men who had some experience of the 'scientific medicine' which had been developed in London and Edinburgh following French and German models. Most notable was the physician William Roberts who, after a brilliant career as a student at University College London, had built up one of the biggest medical practices in the North and still found time for notable scientific investigations in his private laboratory. His surgical colleague, Edward Lund, though older and less well educated, had been a devoted teacher of anatomy, and had introduced Lister's methods to the Infirmary. Others, like Southam and the physician J. E. Morgan, were keen teachers who devoted much time and effort to the development of the Manchester Medical School.[6]

At University College and at Kings College, hospitals had been built in the 1830s as necessary parts of the medical school. By mid-century, the older London hospitals had incorporated private schools or developed their own pre-clinical schools, so that all metropolitan medical education was closely bound up with teaching hospitals. In the provinces, that integration had not been so thorough, especially where rival proprietary schools had competed. But by 1870 many of the medical staff of the Infirmary who were also involved with pre-clinical education wanted to see a closer integration. When the medical school merged with Owens, they campaigned for a new hospital to be built alongside the College, and some wanted to see a merger of the Infirmary and St Mary's Hospital, the descendant of the Lying-in Charity.[7]

The medical staff and many laymen also wanted an end to the method of election of honorary staff – in 1866 the voting for an honorary physician had been 473:411, after a canvass of 1,200 subscribers.[8] This was a long-standing problem and so was the question of out-patient treatment, after the abandonment of the posts of dispensary surgeon. In the early 1870s there was growing criticism of 'hospital abuse'. Some institutions, notably the Southern Hospital for Women and Children, begun by John Thorburn, abandoned recommendations and tried to rely on medical officers rejecting the undeserving. In 1875, in connection with the establishment of Provident Dispensaries, the Infirmary and most of the other major medical charities adopted a scheme long used by St Mary's; they arranged for the District Provident Society to vet their patients and exclude those ineligible for free treatment (weekly income: single 12s 0d, couple 18s 0d, children 1s 6d each).[9]

This scheme followed the earlier initiative of the Charity Organisation Society in London. The metropolitan hospitals also served as a model for the medical staffing of the Infirmary's out-patient department. This was the starting point of a Committee set up in 1872, three of whose five members had negotiated the amalgamation of the medical school with Owens. They asked for out-patients to be treated by (honorary) assistant surgeons and assistant physicians (as in London) rather than by the physicians' clerks; to compensate for this move and to allow at least two special departments (ophthalmic surgery and maternity) they would reduce the number of senior honorary surgeons and of physicians. They also wanted appointment to the honorary staff to be made by the treasurer and deputy treasurer directly, or after nomination by a committee representing the trustees, the medical staff and Owens College.[10]

They got part of what they wanted. The special departments were agreed to and so were the assistant physician and assistant surgeon posts. The imminence of seven elections was then used as an argument for reforming the system of appointments. Against strong public opposition from trustees who resented the transfer of power from the public to the medical staff, a special meeting of trustees agreed to form a committee of thirty to appoint honorary staff. This committee was to be drawn from and elected by the trustees; four of the existing medical staff would act as advisers; Owens College would not be represented.[11]

The campaign for the removal to Rusholme was renewed in 1876 when a committee was appointed to examine the sanitary state of the hospital and the financial implication of a move. It was this committee, led by Hugh Birley and Oliver Heywood which brought in Netten Radcliffe whose report on the sanitary condition of the Infirmary we have already discussed. They then argued that the renovations he suggested would be prohibitively expensive; by selling the site they could raise £500,000, twice as much as would be required for a new building. The committee therefore recommended a new building for 400 patients on a new site plus a central building with fifty beds.[12]

The report prompted considerable opposition. Thomas Radford, the senior obstetrician at St Mary's Hospital, denounced the removal plan as arising from the 'personal interest' of those who wanted the hospital linked to Owens College. The Infirmary was not insanitary – 'no opinion of the loaded and foul condition of the sewers was ever thought of until Mr. Ratcliffe caused them to be opened'[13] – and even this difficulty was less a fault of the building than of mismanagement. Leo Grindon, a well-known local botanist who disliked the professionalisation of science, thought the Infirmary should be moved, but preferred a site in Whalley Range. Rusholme was not suitable, the area was cold and badly drained.[14]

SCIENCES, SPECIALISTS AND CAPITAL

At a special meeting of trustees, on 4 December 1876, the move to Rusholme was proposed and defeated, by 115 votes to 104. A substantial body of trustees had rejected the advice of the medical men and the lay leaders, mainly because they felt

> that in its present position the Management is subjected to the wholesome supervision and control of a large and intelligent body of Trustees from which it is already silently, yet surely, escaping and from which it will be practically emancipated if the scheme proposed were carried out.[15]

An attempt was made to secure a poll of the 1,400 trustees, but this was blocked. Those in favour of the move then tried to change the rules so that policy would be determined by a Board of Management rather than by the trustees generally. This they secured, but the Building Committee went ahead with plans for reconstructing the Infirmary at a cost of £23,000 taken out of capital. The construction of the nurses' home cost another £5,000.[16]

The whole dispute is a nice example of conflict between two views of the hospital. Most of the medical staff and many of Manchester's largest employers saw the Infirmary as a technical service requiring good management. They wanted a small board of directors to work in conjunction with the medical staff – shareholders' meetings were a nuisance. They upgraded the post of secretary to provide better general management and they downgraded the post of resident medical officer who had been, in effect, medical superintendent of the Infirmary and its branches. They divided his work between the resident medical and surgical officers at the main building, and the resident officers at Monsall and Cheadle.[17]

This alliance of civic leaders and medical men found themselves opposed by a group of trustees who individually had much less influence. Such an opposition was characteristic of later nineteenth century local politics, for the leaders of Manchester business were then withdrawing from local democracy, leaving their Council places to shopkeepers and small businessmen.[18] Instead the civic leaders exercised power through national politics or through voluntary associations which they could easily dominate. These associations were projected as superior to the cumbersome and disputatious proceedings of local government, and they often involved the collaboration of professionals who could give technical guidance. The Manchester & Salford Sanitary Association was one such body – an alliance of medical men, chemists, clergymen, business leaders and establishment figures.[19]

The Infirmary was poised between these two styles of politics. It was the town's major charity and attracted attention from the civic leaders; it represented the pinnacle of the local medical profession which was becoming more bureaucratised through the medical faculty; but it had a long tradition of public participation in elections. Many middling men valued their opportunity to look in on the Infirmary, and exert patronage in elections. In the mid-1870s the issues were compromised – the management structure was tightened to reduce public participation, but the Infirmary remained in the centre of town, physically distanced from the increasing influence of the medical school.

Scientists and specialists
The compromise of 1876 held for a decade or so, during which the 'Owens' men became more influential. Daniel Leech and Julius Dreschfeld had both been appointed as assistant physicians in 1873. Leech was locally educated and had been in general practice, but he rapidly developed his scientific interests and built up a department of pharmacy and experimental pharmacology within Owens College. Julius Dreschfeld had also studied in Manchester, but had returned to his German homeland to complete his medical education at Würzburg, then a major world-centre for pathology. Back in Manchester, Dreschfeld grew into the place which William Roberts had relinquished – the city's leading physician and medical scientist. But where Roberts' science had been, in large measure, an acquisition and an exercise of 'leisure' hours, that of Dreschfeld and Leech was part of an increasingly technical medical school.

Some of the new physicians continued to rise through general practice – James Ross (assistant physician 1880) was a humble-born Scot who had practised in the Rossendale valley; he became well known as a neurologist and writer on general biological questions. He had spent four years as pathological registrar, learning from Dreschfeld. Other careers were more hospital-based. Graham Steel had become interested in cardiology as a house physician in Edinburgh. He then spent several years as resident medical officer in fever hospitals, before appointment to that post in Manchester Royal Infirmary. After five years he was appointed assistant physician, later progressing to full physician and to the chair of clinical medicine in the medical school. His private practice grew slowly but he was eventually recognised as one of the north's leading consultants.

Thomas Harris rose more rapidly. He studied at Owens College in the 1870s, and took a gold medal in the London MB. After appointments as house physician to the Infirmary and as resident medical officer to Monsall Hospital he spent most of a year in Würzburg, presumably on the recommendation of Dreschfeld who had taught him pathology at Owens. After a resident post in Oxford he returned to Manchester as pathologist to the Infirmary, and as Lecturer in pathology under Dreschfeld who now held a chair. He soon became an assistant physician and by the age of thirty-two he held a full honorary appointment.[20]

[190]

SCIENCES, SPECIALISTS AND CAPITAL

Resident posts had become an essential part of the training of a future consultant, but they were usually poorly paid. Most of the men who became consultants were from well-to-do families who could afford the extended education and the rarely remunerative first years of practice. London degrees which involved appreciable research began to outnumber Scottish medical degrees, but most of the consultants had family or educational links with Manchester before they began to practise here. By the 1890s all the Infirmary physicians – Leech, Dreschfeld, Ross, Steel, Harris and Judson Bury – were clinical investigators as well as fashionable practitioners; all had their areas of special interest though none of them practised as specialists.

The transformation of surgical practice was similar in some ways, but also much more dramatic. Few surgeons in the early nineteenth century could boast a medical degree; they had the basic training, usually an MRCS and the best of them had served under a leading surgeon as an apprentice; many of them were general practitioners, with a leaning towards surgery, who worked their way to the Infirmary through service to the minor Dispensaries in which they acquired some experience of surgical operations and the treatment of serious accidents. Some of the surgeons appointed in the 1870s and 1880s had this kind of background – Bradley and Whitehead (assistant surgeons 1873) were both local men with no claims to superior education; Hardie (assistant surgeon 1876), a Scot, was also a general practitioner who had acquired a reputation for operative work. But among their colleagues were men of very different backgrounds: Tom Jones (1879) had been a brilliant student at Guy's Hospital, came to Manchester as house surgeon, and was then pathological registrar at the Infirmary for three years before establishing his reputation as an honorary surgeon at the Children's Hospital.

Frederick Southam had studied at Rugby and Oxford before learning medicine at Owens; G. A. Wright was from Marlborough and Oxford; like Southam he took a first class degree in Natural Sciences, but Wright studied medicine and held his resident appointment at Guy's before coming to Manchester as resident surgical officer to the Infirmary.

By the 1870s there was then little difference between the career paths of physicians and surgeons; young men with financial backing, in either case, had a private or public school education, followed by a university course, perhaps in science as well as medicine. They then held resident appointments, during which the physicians often took the London MD and the surgeons took the FRCS, so establishing their credentials for consultant practice. On that basis they took minor honorary appointments and began in private consultant practice. Their period as resident would have advertised their abilities to the local medical professors.[21]

Surgery had become comparable with internal medicine as a means of extending a sound general medical education into a basis for consultant practice; but in the 1870s and especially the 1880s, surgery offered more exciting career prospects, because the range of surgical operations was developing so quickly. In Manchester Infirmary, the annual total of operations performed rose from 408 in 1879, to 709 in 1884, to 1335 in 1889; in 1902 the figure was about 2,800.[22] Such was the demand for surgery that a general practitioner with flair could build up a surgical practice in a cottage hospital, as Whitehead did in Mansfield, Notts., in the 1860s. The general standard of the Infirmary surgeons around 1870 was not high, and young men who had learnt the new techniques, especially those like Jones with a good education in 'scientific surgery', had an asset which was very valuable.

During the 1880s, nursing homes began to appear in which surgeons could operate on wealthy patients – there was one near Owens College on Oxford Road, and if a surgeon could not immediately gain entry to the Infirmary staff, he could extend and display his talents by developing surgery in one of the minor hospitals. The Childrens' Hospital at Pendlebury was particularly important. Before 1874 it was dominated by physicians and did little surgical work, but Tom Jones developed a notable surgical department there, and after he gained an Infirmary appointment, G. A. Wright found an opportunity to pioneer children's surgery. Together with the hospital's leading physician, Henry Ashby, he wrote a textbook, *The Diseases of Children* (1889), probably the best available work on paediatrics.

The treatment of children did not become a recognised medical or surgical specialty until after the First World War, but the development of clinical methods and especially of surgery from the 1860s helped consolidate the existing specialties and established some others. Ophthalmic surgery had been officially recognised in Manchester in 1873 when Thomas Windsor of the Eye Hospital was appointed to the Infirmary and to Owens College. He was followed in 1878 by David Little. Obstetrics and gynaecology had been 'recognised' by the promotion of John Thorburn, from the Southern Hospital which he was largely responsible for founding. His successor at the Infirmary (1885) was David Lloyd Roberts, at Owens, C. J. Cullingworth; both had established themselves as specialists at St Mary's. Cullingworth was a notable clinician who had been resident medical officer at the Infirmary before becoming first a surgeon and then a physician to St Mary's. He was a close associate of Dreschfeld, Leech and Ross in the advancement of clinical medicine. Thorburn's major successor at the Southern, and Cullingworth's successor (1888) at Owens, was William Japp Sinclair, who had studied in Vienna and was one of the pioneers of Caesarean section. In the twenty years from 1866, when Thorburn had established the Southern Hospital to practise more modern obstetrics than St Mary's, at least three other major gynaecologists had become established in Manchester. It could be a rewarding specialty; indeed, it was defined by Lloyd Roberts as 'anything curable or lucrative'![23]

The Manchester Ear Hospital had existed since 1855 but until 1892 only out-patients were treated and methods were rudimentary – syringe and ear drops. It had been founded by W. C. Williamson, a general practitioner and the Professor of Natural History at Owens College, who had sought advice in Paris when he had suffered from an inflammation of the ear. In 1890 a Scot new to Manchester, William Milligan, was appointed an assistant surgeon and he rapidly developed the surgery of the ear, nose and throat as a special field. Milligan was enormously accomplished, a natural leader in his specialty and a notable local politician.[24]

The treatment of skin diseases was a special interest of the surgeon Walter Whitehead and of Daniel Leech, the Infirmary physician who became Professor of Therapeutics in 1881. Leech organised a clinic at the Infirmary and in 1884 he helped set up a skin clinic as part of Manchester and Salford Lock and Skin Hospital. Four years later the institution was divided to form a separate Hospital for Skin Diseases, which initially was confined to out-patients.[25]

In these ways, through minor hospitals and through university teaching, specialists built up their own expertise and their own practices. By the 1880s medicine and surgery was far more technical than at mid-century, and its claims to be a progressive, scientific activity were far more robust. But these claims had to be translated into politically effective means, if the scientist-specialists were to gain the teaching hospitals they wanted. Their eventual success depended on industrial capital which was available to Owens College and its supporters. Science meant progress; it attracted industrialists and merchants.[26] The governors of local science and medicine were seen as skilled executors, able to properly disburse the huge legacies of Lancashire capitalists.

Science and capital

In 1887 the engineer, Sir Joseph Whitworth, died, leaving £300,000 to be allocated to educational and charitable purposes at the direction of his executors: Lady Whitworth, Richard Copley Christie and Robert Dukinfield Darbishire. Both Christie and Darbishire had close links with Owens College. Darbishire, a Unitarian solicitor, was a member of the College Council, a graduate of University College, London, and a life-long supporter of higher education. Christie had been Professor of History and Political Economy at Owens; his wife took an interest in philanthropy and was particularly concerned about the plight of cancer patients.[27]

The executors offered to buy a site and to pay for Owens College to build a hospital which would provide teaching facilities, plus special facilities for skin diseases and cancer. The scheme shows the influence of Daniel Leech, who had long wanted teaching facilities under the control of the College, and who supported the Skin Hospital, then without beds for in-patients. The scheme was meant to supplement the Infirmary, which would be responsible for the management and maintenance of the additional hospital; but the Infirmary were not prepared to support the proposal and Owens College felt unable to proceed without the Infirmary's participation. The Infirmary Board of Management wanted the money spent on an extension of the Infirmary site; this the College would not countenance. The executors went ahead and bought an estate of twelve and a half acres to the south of the College, to whom they gave it, allowing the College to maintain it until part of it could be devoted to hospital provision. The College now had a considerable asset on which it could hope to develop medical institutions that complemented and supported its teaching.[28]

In January 1891 the first steps were taken towards using the 'Owens College Estate'. Darbishire called together a group of business men and doctors including Leech and Whitehead from the Infirmary, and Sinclair of the Southern Hospital for Women. Christie asked them to give their support to a proposed Cancer Hospital. These were the men behind the initial Whitworth Legacy proposal; they obtained additional support from the Legacy and from the executors of another local businessman; they decided to convert the largest of the existing houses on the estate as a Cancer Home and Pavilion, and this was agreed by Owens College. Subscriptions and additional donations were raised, and honorary medical staff were appointed. The physicians were to be Leech, Sinclair and Dreschfeld – all professors at Owens; the surgeons were to be Whitehead and Arthur Hare, who had been Professor of Surgery since 1888. In 1892 the hospital, which later became known as the Christie Hospital, was opened by the Mayor, Alderman Bosdin T. Leech, the brother of Professor Daniel Leech.[29]

This group of doctors and laymen, committed to the development of a teaching hospital, were very well connected in local business and political circles. Their next success was with the Southern Hospital, then occupying a few houses on Upper Brook Street. In 1893, the Southern took a site on Oxford Road to provide facilities for clinical teaching in obstetrics and gynaecology. This was not surprising for the hospital was effectively controlled by William Sinclair who was then Professor of Obstetrics. St Mary's Hospital had been trying to find a new site for some years, but it was much more interested in trying to collaborate with the Infirmary, where one of its leading obstetricians now held an honorary appointment, than it was with

SCIENCES, SPECIALISTS AND CAPITAL

Owens. Sinclair had been publicly scornful of St Mary's and its plans. He maintained that St Mary's was backward in not having more lying-in beds; fears of puerperal fever were out of date.[30]

The financial influence of the Owens College lobby was also applied to St Mary's Hospital, where, again, it met considerable and initially successful opposition. In 1890 St Mary's Board of Management refused to take up the offer of land on the College Hospital Estate. They thought the influential friends of the College were activated more by their desire for clinical teaching than for their consideration of the sick poor. By then the Hospital had collected £30,000 towards a new building and they bought a site on Gloucester Street (now Whitworth Street), at its junction with Oxford Street. Plans for a sixty-bed hospital, with room for expansion to 100 beds, were delayed for several months when the Corporation changed its mind about the building lines.

In 1893, when building had not yet begun, the St Mary's Board approached the trustees of the David Lewis Estate to try to raise more funds. Lewis had been a businessman with major interests in Manchester and Liverpool. He had died in 1881 and left a fortune to be distributed to charity. For this purpose, committees had been set up in Manchester and Liverpool. The chairman of the Manchester Committee, W. H. Houldsworth, was one of the businessmen who supported the Owens College Estate scheme. St Mary's therefore received a reply which offered £50,000 for a new hospital, provided it was a joint venture between St Mary's and Southern Hospital. Southern Hospital, led by Professor Sinclair, had already agreed to build on the Owens College Estate and to give Owens College access to the beds for teaching.

St Mary's was unwilling to give up its own land and the two hospitals decided to amalgamate but to build on both sites – eighty womens' beds plus twenty for children at Stanley Grove, forty lying-in beds at Gloucester Street; out-patients and home-patients departments would be at Gloucester Street. The David Lewis Trustees, however, refused to allow sufficient money to build two hospitals, and in 1896 demanded that all the in-patient accommodation be at Stanley Grove. The St Mary's Board and medical staff wanted the hospital to be in town, they claimed that Stanley Grove would be inconvenient for patients, even though tramways, telephones and electric ambulances on pneumatic tyres had reduced the need for a hospital to be central. The real objection was to the merger with Southern Hospital and to the powers which Owens College would have over the new institutions. One of the few public supporters of the St Mary's Board was the Infirmary surgeon James Hardie, who was trying to keep the Infirmary at Piccadilly, and who opposed 'the irresponsible arrogance of the wire-pullers of Owens College'![31]

When in 1903 the Infirmary decided to move to the Owens College Estate, they bought the land which had previously been given to Southern Hospital, which then acquired the next site to the south. It was now ten years since the Southern had taken land, and Owens College arranged for the new site and most of the proceeds of the old one to revert to the College if the new hospital was not completed within three years. Under this pressure, attempts were renewed to amalgamate Southern and St Mary's. The new St Mary's Hospital at Whitworth Street could quite quickly provide the facilities which Owens College needed; the decision to move the Infirmary had ended any hopes that the two major hospitals could continue substantially independent of the medical school.

Soon after the decision to amalgamate, the trustees of yet another legacy gave £48,000 for the Southern Hospital's new building. It was completed in 1910, when it became the gynaecology and children's department of St Mary's Hospital, the Whitworth Street building being used for maternity cases.[32]

Though Owens College found an alternative to St Mary's there was no existing alternative to the Infirmary as the main locus of clinical teaching. In 1890, after the rejection of the initial approach of the Whitworth legatees, the Infirmary Medical Board pressed for the Infirmary to be rebuilt and enlarged while remaining on the Piccadilly site. Instead it was agreed to build an extension of 120 beds, but before this was announced, Owens College, on receiving the 'College Hospital Estate' approached the Infirmary offering a site for a 500–600-bed hospital, which would be accompanied by a cancer hospital and a hospital for women. When this proposal failed and the Infirmary had announced its intention to build an extension, the College then suggested that the addition might be made at Stanley Grove, in such a way as to allow more beds to be provided in the future.

Neither scheme was acceptable to the Infirmary Board or to the majority of the doctors. The arguments about the unhealthiness of the old building were no longer relevant; the Infirmary was too small and inconvenient but it was no longer subject to outbreaks of erysipelas. Many laymen and most of the doctors wanted it to remain in town, where it was convenient for patients and also for doctors busy in private practice rather than teaching or laboratory work. But the major objection to either move was the feeling among most of the doctors that the Infirmary was in danger of coming under the heel of the medical school.

This fear had been sharpened in 1888 when, for the first time, Owens College had appointed a clinical professor from outside the local medical community. They had brought in Arthur Hare, a young man who showed considerable promise but who lacked the FRCS. Several local surgeons were upset by this decision; they strongly resisted moves to gain beds for Hare's use at the Infirmary. This was easy, for the FRCS was a required qualification for appointments to the Infirmary staff. Hare had to make do with beds at Ancoats Hospital. It seems that the Infirmary then applied to the Whitworth legatees for funds to begin their own medical school. They were refused, and money, as we have seen, was arranged to provide a hospital for Owens College.[33]

These issues of professional control were much to the fore in 1891. The Infirmary was willing to allow Owens College some say in the appointment of Infirmary staff, so as to facilitate teaching; but the College refused to commit itself to appoint its professors from the staff of the Infirmary. The College was a national institution, the Infirmary was local. Of the medical staff Ross, Hardie and G. A. Wright were clearly afraid that the College would come to control the Infirmary staff and that, if an extension was built on Stanley Grove, the rest of the Infirmary would soon follow. Dreschfeld, Steel and especially Leech, gave strong support to the College's scheme; they wanted a modern hospital which would make the medical school more attractive to students. The majority of the Infirmary staff supported the Board of Management in refusing College offers.

The Board then tried to proceed with their plans for an extension at Piccadilly, but they met considerable opposition and were defeated in several special meetings. Leech and others continued to argue that an extension would better be built on another site, and many major businessmen agreed. Some, no doubt, were allies of Owens College, others disapproved of the Infirmary taking more land and further congesting the centre of the city. The City Corporation was interested in the Piccadilly site, partly to allow more space for the tramways, partly to build an art gallery and reference library. The dispute continued for ten years until 1902 when a movement led by Judge Parry and Joseph Bell, forced a poll of the 12,000 trustees of the Infirmary in July 1902, when the proposal to rebuild on the Piccadilly site was heavily defeated and the Board of Management resigned. Throughout, the majority of the medical staff had opposed moving the hospital, even though they had agreed that Owens professors could have access to Infirmary beds.

The deciding factor was probably the value of the site. It was sold to the Corporation for £400,000. That money would not have been available for rebuilding at Piccadilly, though at one stage there was a plan for selling part of the site and building a hospital on the rest. Hospitals, it was argued, did not have to use the pavilion system; new methods of ventilation meant that they could be more economical in land. The Corporation and the patrons of Owens College were together a formidable lobby, and they saw no reason why patients and doctors could not travel out to cheaper land at Stanley Grove.

After the move, in 1908, only a casualty station remained in the centre; a plan to add an emergency hospital was abandoned.[34] But at Rusholme the opening of the St Mary's branch in 1911 completed the project which the Whitworth legatees had begun twenty years previously. To the south of the University there stretched a row of new voluntary hospitals – the Eye Hospital, the Infirmary and part of St Mary's. The Cancer Pavilion stood behind the Infirmary at the end of Lorne Street. There was no longer any doubt that the Medical School was the centre of Manchester medicine. It was led by the most scientific of the professionals and backed by the most influential of the industrialists, and those who controlled the disposal of large estates. This combination of corporate medicine and corporate capital overrode the claims of a more traditional medical practice and a more democratic lay control.

X-rays and radium

In seeking the support of big business, the advocates of medical science, in laboratories and hospitals, could point to the discovery of germs and the spectacular advance of surgery. After the turn of the century they could point to x-rays and to radium – discoveries which were dramatic in their sudden usefulness, which drew diagnostic and therapeutic power from those mysterious properties of matter which only advanced physicists could really understand. The history of these techniques, in and around Manchester, is a nice study in the relations between physicists and medical scientists, medical practitioners and lay supporters.

W.C. Roentgen, a German physicist, published his discovery of x-rays in December 1895, and sent copies of his paper to two English physicists – Lord Kelvin in Glasgow and Arthur Schuster, Professor of Physics at Owens College. The discovery was an immediate popular sensation; most of the daily papers contained accounts of this new kind of radiation which could penetrate flesh and so produce shadow pictures of human bones. Schuster's assistant described Roentgen's results to a meeting of the Manchester Literary and Philosophical Society on 7 January 1896, and Schuster himself announced the discovery in the *Manchester Guardian*. The medical potential was immediately obvious, particularly for doctors who wanted to locate metal, e.g. needles or bullets, lodged in flesh. Like several other physicists who were in a position to reproduce Roentgen's apparatus, Schuster was soon besieged by a series of doctors and patients anxious to have the benefit of the new tool.

In Liverpool, the first diagnostic picture was taken by Oliver Lodge, the

Professor of Physics, who was asked by Robert Jones, the pioneer of orthopaedics, to locate a bullet in the hand of a small boy. Soon afterwards Jones bought one of the sets of equipment which had been rapidly developed by commercial companies, and arranged for his assistant, Dr Thurston Holland, to provide a radiographic service for surgeons at the Liverpool Infirmary.

In Manchester, Schuster used apparatus at Owens College, and by mid March he was dealing with four or five patients a day, a load which seriously interfered with his own research work. In a lecture to the Manchester Medical Society, 18 March 1896, he suggested that, within a year, all hospitals would need facilities for taking x-ray pictures, but that, as a temporary measure, rooms should be taken close to the Infirmary, where a technician could be employed to provide an x-ray service for Manchester. None of the Manchester doctors were particularly interested in developing this diagnostic tool, and the initiative was taken by a firm of pharmacists who built up a large private practice, taking x-radiographs for Manchester practitioners.

When the Infirmary obtained an apparatus, about 1900, it was housed in a gallery of the Chapel, and operated each morning by Mr Doran who worked for the chemists and did their private work in the afternoons. His Infirmary work was supervised by the Director of the Clinical Laboratory, a post created in 1899 for W. E. Fothergill. This was a junior position for a young man who could prepare microscopical sections and advance his career by helping his seniors to write and illustrate their papers. The failure of the Manchester Infirmary staff to recognise the potential of the new method, contrasts with the readiness of the Skin Hospital to use the new radiations.

X-rays were hailed as a therapeutic as well as a diagnostic tool. The value of sunlight in the treatment of pulmonary tuberculosis was recognised by the end of the nineteenth century and during the 1890s a young Danish physician, N. R. Finsen, had explored the effects of artificial ultra-violet light on diseases of the skin. Such light was known to kill bacteria and Finsen demonstrated its therapeutic powers over tuberculosis of the skin. The Finsen lamp became a popular treatment as the effects of x-rays were being explored. In Manchester, the Skin Hospital acquired a lamp in 1901, soon after the London Hospital had pioneered its use in Britain. Because of the ultra-violet and x-ray treatments the Skin Hospital's out-patient department became enormously popular. In 1902 about half of the 58,000 out-patients attendances were for x-ray treatments.

X-ray treatments were also tried at the Cancer Hospital. Three patients from there were treated in Schuster's laboratory and the results seemed to justify the purchase of an apparatus. Between 1901 and 1905, six to fourteen patients were treated each year, most of them for skin cancers, but the apparatus was difficult to maintain and to use and seemed hardly worthwhile for so few cases. The Christie Hospital abandoned its experiment, and sent suitable patients to the Skin Hospital, to whom they donated the apparatus in 1910. After 1908 they also sent patients to the Infirmary to be treated by Dr A. E. Barclay who had established himself as Manchester's first specialist in the diagnostic and therapeutic uses of x-rays.

Barclay had grown up in Manchester, but had studied medicine at the London Hospital where he graduated in 1904. He was interested in scientific gadgets and was 'good with his hands'; the London Hospital had pioneered the use of Finsen lamps and had a well-developed electro-medical department. Barclay acted as its radiologist before returning home in 1906 to exploit his new knowledge. By then the Liverpool and Glasgow Infirmaries had established departments; Manchester Infirmary relied on the chemist's assistant.

Barclay's practice was shared with another young doctor, then an anaesthetist at the Infirmary. His first hospital appointment was at Ancoats, where he established Manchester's first x-ray department. A benefactor had given an x-ray machine to the hospital and they needed someone to operate it. That post was honorary but after the new Infirmary opened in 1908, Barclay was asked to organise an x-ray, electrical and massage service, and was paid £50 *per annum* for attending each morning. He was given a space in the basement which had been previously earmarked for 'mud-baths'. He had already begun studies of gastro-intestinal radiology, using barium meals, and he soon achieved a national reputation in his specialty. The First World War emphasised his skills and their uses; in 1918 he became a member of the honorary staff.

When Barclay was establishing himself in the new Infirmary, yet another form of radiation was being hailed as a wonder-cure. The discovery of radioactivity in 1896 had been followed by the isolation of radium by Marie Curie in 1898. Among the many physicists examining radioactivity in the early years of the new century, Ernest Rutherford was probably the most important. In 1906 he succeeded Schuster as Professor of Physics in Manchester. For a few years before he retired, Schuster had been examining the properties of a small sample of radium which had been bought in 1903 with the proceeds of a series of public lectures.

Because of the successes of ultra-violet and x-radiation in therapy, the emissions were soon tested for medical properties. A Paris dermatologist, Dr Henri Danlos, established in 1904 that radium was therapeutic in cases of skin tuberculosis, and for skin cancer, which was also believed to be caused by bacteria. The Laboratoire Biologique du Radium, founded in 1906, sponsored research on its medical uses, including the treatment of deep-seated cancer, and in 1909 the Paris Radium Institute was founded to further develop the collaboration of medical scientists and physicists. Radium, as a cancer cure, was promising but dangerous; numerous commercial 'radium' remedies appeared, most of them useless. In London, Lord Iveagh (of the Guinness family) and Sir Ernest Cassel (a noted banker) funded a Radium Institute under royal patronage. It opened in August 1911.

In Manchester, Schuster had lent and then sold a few milligrammes of radium to the Cancer Hospital. The medical superintendent, Wild, tried it out as he was losing faith in x-rays. The results were rather similar. Radium was so expensive that they could treat only localised skin tumours, and very few patients benefited. Though the Hospital could have afforded to buy more, and though it was very easy to raise funds for a 'miracle cure', they preferred to await a fall in the price of radium and more substantial reports of its successful use elsewhere. This cautious attitude probably reflected the fact that the Cancer Hospital was not the creation of an ambitious medical specialist. It had been set up, like earlier special hospitals, to care for patients neglected by the general medical charities. Nor was the Manchester Royal Infirmary interested in experimenting with radium. In 1911 it decided against buying some because of the expense.

The specialist who took the initiative in developing radium therapy in Manchester was William Milligan, who had earlier developed auro-laryngology as a Manchester specialty. He was hoping to use radium instead of surgery in cases of cancer of the larynx. In 1914 he wrote to the *Manchester Guardian* suggesting a combined effort by Manchester hospitals to buy a supply of radium for the city. Milligan was by then very influential, as a national leader of his specialty, and as a local leader in philanthropy, culture and politics. Edinburgh and Liverpool Infirmaries already had supplies, so local pride was also at stake. Sir Edward Holt, a local brewer, promised £4,000 and the Lord Mayor of Manchester launched a public appeal. The committee of businessmen, doctors and physicists, wanted £25,000 to purchase 500 milligrammes but they raised only £10,000 by the end of June 1914. Then, as Europe prepared for war, a mass appeal was launched by Edward Hutton through his newspapers, the *Daily Dispatch* and the *Manchester Evening Chronicle*. This was the first time that the power of the popular press had been used, in Manchester, to raise funds for medical charities. Local 'radium days' were arranged and collections made in factories, shops, clubs, public houses and churches. All donations were individually recorded in the newspapers and in a special seventy-four-page booklet. A total of £31,000 was raised.

The Manchester and District Radium Fund initially operated as a department of the Infirmary, with its own medical officer and physicist. They treated Infirmary patients and some in other hospitals, as well as private patients sent by their doctors. The scheme was intended to be self-supporting rather than a charity in itself. Private patients paid according to a scale of fees borrowed from the London Radium Institute; hospital patients were asked to pay what they could. If there was a shortfall, the hospitals who took part in the scheme were asked to make up the difference. This was the first common service for the major Manchester hospitals. In 1915, Bury and Stockport Infirmaries joined the scheme.

After the war, in 1920, the Radium Committee removed the service to a former nursing home on Nelson Street. Repeated efforts to gain control of some beds at the Infirmary had failed, and a scheme of Milligan's to provide a new building for both the x-ray and the radium departments had also failed. The Manchester and District Radium Institute was opened in 1921. Though it had fourteen beds, the patients remained formally in the care of the hospital or private practitioner which sent them. The radiologist, like the physicist, was paid, not honorary, though he could carry on private practice outside working hours. The first radiologist, Arthur Burrows had trained as a dermatologist. In 1929 he set up in private practice as a radiotherapist, retaining an honorary connection with the Institute. In 1932, after some years of negotiation, the Radium Institute, then named after Sir Edward Holt, was merged with the Cancer Hospital, named after R.C. Christie. A new site in Withington was bought for the new joint institution. By then the service extended to hospitals well beyond Manchester, as we shall briefly describe in the next chapter.[35]

The Edwardian Medical School
The Manchester Medical School grew rapidly in the 1870s and 1880s until there were about 350 students. Thereafter the student numbers showed little overall change until the war. The University enlarged the Medical Faculty buildings in 1894. By the Edwardian period, the medical schools in provincial cities were firmly established as university faculties; Manchester's was the most senior school and one of the largest. The University of Manchester was then an international centre of research in chemistry and physics, engineering and history; in the sciences it was rivalled only by Cambridge and London.[36] But the medical faculty was hardly of corresponding status. Neither its clinicians nor its medical scientists had the reputation to draw students from outside the Manchester region.

The preclinical subjects, especially physiology, had been developed chiefly at Cambridge, London, Oxford, and Edinburgh universities. Gamgee had failed to establish a research school in Manchester and his successor, William Stirling, though he too was appointed on his record in research, had concentrated on teaching and administration. It was not until after the war, when A. V. Hill was appointed to the Manchester chair, that physiological research began to be established here. Hill had trained at Cambridge and University College London, and he returned south after a few years. This career pattern was then common in provincial universities – scientists trained in Oxbridge or London, were appointed to Manchester chairs, and after a few years returned to metropolitan laboratories.[37]

The same pattern can be seen in pathology, which, as a scientific discipline in Britain, substantially developed out of physiology. Dreschfeld had pioneered pathology in Manchester on the basis of his German experience, and his successor in pathology, Sheridan Delépine, had been trained in Switzerland. But in 1910, when Delépine's teaching was divided to allow him to concentrate on bacteriology, the new Professor of Pathology, Lorrain Smith, was a product neither of Europe nor of Manchester. He had entered research through the physiology laboratory at Oxford. His period in the Manchester chair, 1904–12, was successful chiefly because he was ready to link pathology to clinical medicine. When Smith returned to his first university, Edinburgh, he was succeeded by A. E. Boycott, trained at Oxford and Guy's Hospital. Boycott did not feel obliged to apply pathology to clinical medicine, even as honorary pathologist to the Infirmary, and his clinical colleagues here were unready to recognise the discipline's claims to autonomy.[38]

Perhaps the most successful of the medical scientists in Edwardian Manchester was the anatomist Grafton Elliot Smith who was here from 1909 to 1919. His powerful and many-sided intellect attracted a number of medical students to do research as an alternative or a complement to clinical training. Much of Smith's work was on the anatomy of the nervous system, and so strengthened the local tradition in neurology which had been established by Dreschfeld, Ross and Williamson. The Professor of Surgery, William Thorburn, had strong interests in neurosurgery, to which he made notable contributions, but to maintain a high income he had to remain a general surgeon; there was not enough neurosurgical work around Manchester to provide a remunerative practice for a specialist.[39]

Nor had the other leading Manchester surgeons the national reputation of Berkeley Moynihan at Leeds. They were able men, successful enough in private practice to live like major industrialists on country estates, but they were not 'surgeon princes' in the national league. Some of the specialists, especially Milligan in auro-laryngology, were nationally more significant, but such subjects were traditionally peripheral to the medical school.

The physicians were mostly disciples of Dreschfeld but none had his intellectual stature. His successor in the chair of medicine, G. R. Murray, was not locally trained; he had done research on endocrine physiology in London and had held a chair of pathology at Newcastle. His introduction to Manchester in 1908 was doubly illuminating. Firstly because he was not a Manchester practitioner, and the allotment of Infirmary beds to him was resented by the other Infirmary physicians, though they could no longer prevent it. Secondly because of the hopes entertained that he would continue his investigations, though his post, like all the clinical professorships, was only part-time. Murray was an effective teacher and a very successful consultant, but he did little more research.[40]

The Manchester Medical School and the Infirmary continued to be dominated by local men. About two-thirds of the students came from Manchester or the surrounding counties; almost as many of the Infirmary honorary staff had been educated at Manchester University; about 40 per cent of them had grown up in the district. Since about the 1860s, nascent consultants had tended to take London medical degrees, rather than Scottish MDs or Royal Colleges' diplomas. The London degree, unlike most Scottish degrees did not require a period of residence at the awarding University; Manchester students did not have to leave home. After 1883, Manchester University offered its own medical degree, and by the Edwardian period even aspirant consultants rarely took any other. Manchester was by then a self-contained school. Like the city, the medical school around 1900 was probably more 'native-born' and more class-stratified than it was before 1870 or has been since 1914.[41]

This Edwardian medical school trained the men who came to dominate Manchester medicine after the First War, and who presided over the local development of the National Health Service following the Second World War. The key figures, near contemporaries, were J. S. B. Stopford, Harry Platt and Geoffrey Jefferson. Their careers were closely linked for over fifty years, and they demonstrate many of the formative influences on Manchester medicine during that period. Stopford became Professor of Anatomy, Dean of Medicine, Vice-Chancellor, and first Chairman of the Manchester Regional Hospital Board. Harry Platt developed orthopaedics as a surgical specialty in this Region, and Geoffrey Jefferson did the same for neurosurgery. All three were figures of national importance.

After graduation all three were attached to the anatomy department which Elliot Smith had made one of the intellectual centres of the University. Stopford remained in the department, where he succeeded to the chair in 1919. By 1923, at the age of thirty-five, he was already Dean of Medicine. Jefferson and Platt looked to careers as consultants and after residencies in Manchester, both sought further training in London. Jefferson served as a house surgeon to distinguished consultants at the Victoria Hospital for

Children and at the London Cancer Hospital. Platt became resident orthopaedic officer at the Royal National Orthopaedic Hospital, then the only special hospital for orthopaedics. His attraction to this specialty dated from his childhood, when he had been a patient of Robert Jones, the Liverpool surgeon.

Both Jefferson and Platt went to North America towards the end of 1913, though for rather different reasons. Jefferson had married a Canadian doctor, a protegée of Sir William Osler, and saw no future in Manchester medicine which would enable him to live at the standard married doctors expected. He emigrated to British Columbia. Platt visited the Massachusetts General Hospital in Boston which was a major international centre of the emergent specialty. By this time the Johns Hopkins Hospital in Baltimore, had established departments in which physicians and surgeons could give their full time to research and teaching. This system had been imported to Boston in 1910 when a new hospital was opened next to Harvard Medical School, using the funds from the estate of a local trader. This was the pattern which the Owens College had tried, with only limited success, to introduce into Manchester.

On his return to England, just before the war, Harry Platt was appointed an honorary surgeon at Ancoats Hospital, where in 1914 he began a 'fracture clinic' which was probably the first in the country. Ancoats was the hospital in which Dr A. E. Barclay had set up Manchester's first radiology department, and that was continued by his colleague when Barclay moved to the new Infirmary. Since the 1870s it had been common for new consultants to establish themselves in minor general hospitals or in specialist hospitals; during the early twentieth century, they tended to use minor general hospitals to develop new specialties.

The First World War substantially advanced the specialties in which Platt and Jefferson were interested. Platt spent the war in England, working with Robert Jones in developing centres for the care and rehabilitation of the wounded. Jefferson returned to Europe to serve under Sir Herbert Waterhouse in a surgical unit in Russia. After the Russian collapse he was moved to France and given charge of a surgical department responsible for gunshot wounds of the head.[42]

Manchester medicine and the First World War
At the beginning of the war, it was thought that 50,000 beds would meet the needs of the military services. Most voluntary hospitals set aside some of their beds, some public institutions were taken over, and a vast assortment of country houses and other premises collected together as an auxiliary hospital service. For the most part, the beds were staffed by general

practitioners. In the hospitals directly controlled by the War Office, the staff, including the former honorary consultants, were given military rank and a salary. As was traditional in all voluntary hospitals, each doctor retained sole responsibility over a certain number of beds.

Towards the end of 1914 trainloads of casualties began to arrive from France. By the end of the year, 73,000 wounded men had been brought back to England, forcing a scramble for additional hospital accommodation, and putting all medical services under extreme pressure. At great hardship to the civilian sick, many more public institutions were taken over. By the end of 1914, 90,000 beds were reserved for military use and by August 1917 the figure had reached 300,000. Thus when the war ended, England and Wales must have contained about 500,000 'hospital' beds if we include both military and civilian beds. Over the course of the war the total had more than doubled.[43]

Manchester was well placed to deal with wounded soldiers, and over 200,000 were brought to the city during the course of the war. They came from the railway station to the Second Western General Hospital, a collection of three school and college buildings converted to house over 800 beds. Some patients were sent directly to one or other of the city hospitals which had set aside a similar total of beds. The central hospitals were supported by hospitals in the surrounding towns and by a large number of small auxiliary hospitals run by the Red Cross. By the end of the war the total complement of associated beds was about 25,000.[44]

Most of the older consultants who staffed the 'Territorial Hospital' found that they could cope with the extra work because their private practice had declined somewhat and their 'ordinary' hospital work was reduced by the allotment of beds to the military. The major problem was the shortage of junior, resident doctors, most of whom had been called up. St Mary's Hospital was forced to rely on senior students as house surgeons, and at one stage expected to close down the High Street branch. The shortages of nursing staff was also severe and many domestic workers left to work in munitions factories.[45]

Both in the European battle-ground and in Britain, the war posed massive challenges to surgeons. New methods of operation and management had to be devised when the contamination of wounds nullified the strict antiseptic techniques which had been developed for civilian work. The rudimentary methods for the treatment of fractures meant that more and more soldiers were being discharged from military hospitals as semi-cripples. Initially the Army medical surgeons were dominated by general surgeons and physicians, sceptical of surgical specialists. But desperate needs allowed the promotion to high position of Robert Jones and others, who had for years taught and practised a much more physiological approach to injury, and who saw their task as the restoration of the locomotor system. Jones had learned his technique from his uncle, who in turn was the son of a well-known family of bone-setters. Orthopaedics in Liverpool passed from craft to modern surgical specialty in three generations of one family who had worked with the injured from dockland. Jones had run the casualty service for the digging of the Manchester Ship Canal; in the war, as Inspector of Orthopaedics, he organised a series of special casualty centres where specialist attention could be given to bone and nerve injury.[46]

The war also brought to Europe a number of first-class American surgical units. The orthopaedic surgeons and the neurosurgeons from Boston and other cities who ran surgical hospitals in France allowed Jones to bring some of his own disciples back to the army medical services in England.

The emergency services of greatest consequence for post-war medicine were the special units. In 1916 Jones established orthopaedic hospitals in workhouse infirmaries at Shepherds Bush, London and Alder Hey, Liverpool. They were short of equipment, much of which had previously been available only in Liverpool, and their work was opposed by many general surgeons. The staff were forced to spend time on new recruits with club feet, bunions or flat feet, trying to make them fit for service, instead of dealing with injured men recovering as cripples. Many such men had been operated on crudely at the 'Territorial Hospitals' and then sent to 'auxiliary hospitals' to recover. When their wounds had 'flared' they had returned to the central hospital where another surgeon would attempt a remedy; there was no continuity and no rehabilitation. Those who suffered from loss of reflex function were frequently accused of malingering. Jones's units stressed continuity, physiotherapy and moral support.[47]

Additional centres were soon established to deal with injuries to the head. One was at Grangethorpe in Manchester, a large house in Rusholme which was bought by the East Lancashire branch of the Red Cross Society in 1916 and handed over to the War Office the following year. In that same year, the orthopaedic section of the Second Western was moved to Grangethorpe from the school in which it had been established. Platt ran this section, and Stopford was associated with the work. When the war ended, Grangethorpe was taken over by the Ministry of Pensions who were responsible for the injured veterans; Jefferson joined the staff in 1920.

At centres like Grangethorpe, young specialists were able to demonstrate conclusively that their techniques could restore soldiers who would otherwise have died or lived in pain and disability. Such units were also centres of research. Platt and Stopford studied nerve injuries; Jefferson, at the end of the war, had received funds from the Royal College of Surgeons and the newly formed Medical Research Council, to continue his studies of the wounded.[48]

The lessons taught by the war to young surgeons and their superiors, facilitated the development of specialties in civilian medicine. By 1921, Platt had established a fracture unit in Ancoats; with the agreement of his fellow honorary surgeons he took all the fracture cases. The last of the general practitioners had left the honorary staff in 1914 and the hospital was gaining a reputation for progressive teachers. F. Craven Moore taught there before the war and from the mid-1920s, Norman Kletz had a large following among medical students. Platt and others gave postgraduate surgical classes at Ancoats and so achieved a reputation among Manchester practitioners.

Before the war, most of the Manchester orthopaedic practice had gone to Liverpool. After the war Platt shared it with Robert Ollerenshaw, a wealthy young surgeon whose experience at Grangethorpe had persuaded him to specialise. Platt was particularly successful in building up a unit. He was joined by E. S. Brentnall who had enough money to serve as an assistant in hospital and private practice. He later obtained a hospital appointment at Stockport. One of Platt's house surgeons, Poston, gained appointments at Oldham and Altrincham, and made up his income with medico-legal work on industrial injury compensation, etc. Thus hospitals in the satellite towns were colonised by recruits to a new surgical specialty. In 1932 Platt was appointed the first orthopaedic surgeon to the Infirmary.[49]

By that time Jefferson already had a small neurosurgical unit at the Infirmary, to which he had been appointed in 1926, against considerable opposition. He had developed his specialist interest at the Infirmary's second 'satellite', Salford Royal Hospital, where several of his colleagues were also trying to set up in specialist practice and were happy to pass their neurological and neurosurgical cases to Jefferson. From 1920 he had lectured in Stopford's department on applied anatomy and developed a reputation as a remarkably original investigator, if not an outstanding surgical technician. He was intent on developing neurosurgery as Harvey Cushing had developed it at Baltimore and Boston. He got consistent support from Stopford, from 1923 the Dean of Medicine. But the six beds of his neurosurgical unit at the Infirmary were resented by some of the other general surgeons.[50]

In 1939 the Medical School created chairs for both Jefferson and Platt. Like all the clinical professorships these were part-time appointments. Stopford had been appointed Vice-Chancellor of the University in 1934 and he was a supporter of the American system of full-time appointments in clinical units. The system had been imported to London after the First War, backed by Rockefeller funds. But not until 1945 did Manchester University Medical School appoint its first full-time clinical professor.

SCIENCES, SPECIALISTS AND CAPITAL

Notes and references

1. On the development of the British medical profession in this period, the best source is now M. Jeanne Peterson, *The Medical Profession in Mid-Victorian London*, Berkeley, 1978. Also see Brian Abel-Smith, *The Hospitals 1800–1948*, London, 1964.
2. On American medicine see Simon Flexner and J. T. Flexner, *William Henry Welch and the Heroic Age of American Medicine*, New York, 1941, reprinted 1966; E. R. Brown, *Rockefeller Medical Men: Medicine & Capitalism in America*, Berkeley, 1979. Like all recent historians of medicine, I have also benefited from the work of Charles Rosenberg, particularly from the paper on 'The shaping of the American hospital, 1880–1914' (1978) unpublished and his 'And heal the sick: the hospital and patient in nineteenth century America', *J. Social History*, *10* (1977), 428–47. Rosenberg is preparing a general history of American medical care.
3. The most authoritative account of medical education in early nineteenth-century Manchester is the forthcoming PhD by Katherine Webb (History of Science, UMIST) on medical practitioners in Manchester 1780–1860. Also see E. M. Brockbank, *The Foundation of Provincial Medical Education in England and of the Manchester School in particular*, Manchester, 1936.
4. H. B. Charlton, *Portrait of a University, 1851–1951: to Commemorate the Centenary of Manchester University*, Manchester, 1952.
5. On later nineteenth century medical education, especially in Manchester, see S. V. F. Butler, 'Science and the education of physicians in the nineteenth century: a study of British medical education with particular reference to the development and uses of physiology', PhD thesis, UMIST, 1982.
6. William Brockbank, *The Honorary Medical Staff of the Manchester Royal Infirmary*, Manchester, 1965; D. J. Leech, 'Life and works of Sir William Roberts', *Medical Chronicle* (Manchester), 3rd ser., *1* (1899), 157–89.
7. J. H. Young, *St. Mary's Hospitals Manchester, 1790–1963*, Edinburgh, 1964; Infirmary Annual Report, 1870–1.
8. W. Brockbank, *Medical Staff*, 53.
9. The economics of hospitals requires more investigation than I have so far provided. Clearly the period around 1870 was crucial, though the issue of 'abuse' flared up again at the end of the century. The Manchester debate of the early 1870s may have been stimulated by the foundation of a Provident Dispensary in Altrincham, with which Dr Arthur Ransome was associated; the University economist, Stanley Jevons was a notable critic of medical charity, as were John Thorburn and Dr Alexander Stewart, a local activist in the Provident Dispensary movement. W. Stanley Jevons, 'On the work of the Society in connection with the questions of the day' (November 1869), *Transactions of the Manchester Statistical Society* (1869–70), 1–14; John Thorburn, *Remarks on the Mode of Admission to our Medical Charities*, Manchester, 1870 (a pamphlet based on a letter addressed to the Committee of the Manchester and Salford Hospital Sunday Fund, November 1870); William O'Hanlon, 'Our medical charities and their abuses; with some suggestions for their reform', *Transactions of the Manchester Statistical Society* (1872–3), 41–69; Annual Reports of the Manchester & Salford Provident Dispensaries Association, especially (1890), 'The existing organisation of medical relief in Manchester and Salford', paper read by Mr Smith at the Charity Organisation Conference held at Oxford, 2 October 1890. Also see the enquiry made for *The Lancet*, 2, 9, 23 January 1897, pp. 70–2, 136–9, 276–8.
10. Infirmary Weekly Board, 20 May 1872.
11. Infirmary Special Board, 10 June and 21 October 1872.
12. Infirmary Site Dispute Scrapbook (Manchester Medical Collection), Report of the General Committee, including the Reports of the Sanitary and Finance Committees 1876; W. Brockbank, *Portrait of a Hospital, 1752–1948*, London, 1952, pp. 127–30.

13. *Manchester Courier*, 18 December 1876 (Scrapbook).
14. Grindon, Letter to Trustees, December 1876 (Scrapbook); W. Brockbank, *Portrait*, 127–30.
15. W. Brockbank, *Portrait*, 129.
16. Infirmary Weekly Boards and Quarterly Boards, December 1876 – July 1877, and the Special Report from the Board of Management, October 1881.
17. W. Brockbank, *Medical Staff*, 130–1; Infirmary House Committee Minutes, 14 January 1878.
18. S. Simon, *A Century of City Government, Manchester 1838–1938*, London, 1938, pp. 400–1.
19. P. A. Ryan, 'Public health and voluntary effort in nineteenth century Manchester, with particular reference to the Manchester and Salford Sanitary Association', MA Dissertation, Manchester University, 1974.
20. W. Brockbank, *Medical Staff*; Samuel Oleesky, 'Julius Dreschfeld and late nineteenth century medicine in Manchester', *Manchester Medical Gazette*, *51* (1971–2), 14–17, 58–60, 96–9.
21. See Butler, PhD thesis; most of the information about the Manchester Royal Infirmary is derived from analysing the biographies in W. Brockbank, *Medical Staff*.
22. Annual Reports.
23. W. Brockbank, *Medical Staff*.
24. On the Ear Hospital: *Manchester City News*, 6 August 1892 (letter by W. C. Williamson), and 9 January 1909; Victor Lambert, 'Manchester otolaryngology – its heritage and future', presidential address, Manchester Medical Society, 9 October 1963.
25. On the Skin Hospital, T. J. Wyke, 'The Manchester & Salford Lock Hospital', *Medical History*, *19* (1975), 73–86, and a typescript history by Mr W. A. B. Hargreaves, the Administrator (1975).
26. R. H. Kargon, *Science in Victorian Manchester, Enterprise & Expertise*, Manchester, 1972, surveys industrial backing for university chemistry and engineering. He does not discuss 'scientific medicine' except for 'public health'.
27. Edward Fiddes, *Chapters in the History of Owens College & of Manchester University 1851–1914*, Manchester, 1937, pp. 125–8.
28. Scrapbook on the Infirmary Site Question (Manchester Medical Collection) especially report of conference of 17 February 1891.
29. Cancer Pavilion & Home Committee Minutes; Theresa P. Macdonald, 'Christie Hospital and Holt Radium Institute: foundation, development & achievements 1892–1962', MSc thesis, UMIST, 1977.
30. Young, *St. Mary's*, 72–3.
31. *Ibid.*, p. 78.
32. *Ibid.*, pp. 68–88.
33. Scrapbook, especially pp. 33–48 (an exchange of opinions between the surgeon G. A. Wright and the obstetrician W. J. Sinclair), and pp. 91–5 (the Dean of Medicine discussing the Hare case). Also see W. Brockbank, *Portrait*.
34. *Ibid*.
35. See Macdonald, MSc thesis (1977); P. J. Davies, 'Sir Arthur Schuster, FRS, 1851–1934', PhD thesis, UMIST, 1983; A. E. Barclay, 'Early days of radiology in Manchester', *Manchester University Medical School Gazette*, *27* (1948), 115–21; Nora Schuster, 'Early days of Roentgen photography in Britain,' *British Medical Journal*, *2* (1962), 1164–6.
36. Kargon, *Science in Victorian Manchester*.
37. Butler, PhD thesis.
38. W. Brockbank, *Medical Staff*.
39. Warren R. Dawson, ed., *Grafton Elliot Smith*, London, 1938; Geoffrey Jefferson, 'James Ross, Sir William Thorburn, R. T. Williamson – Pioneers in Neurology', *The Manchester University Medical School Gazette* (1948).
40. W. Brockbank, *Medical Staff*.

41. Butler, PhD thesis.
42. W. E. Le Gros Clark and W. Mansfield Cooper, 'John Sebastian Bach Stopford, 1888–1961', *Biographical Memoirs of Fellows of the Royal Society*, 7 (1961), 271–9. On Jefferson, there is a useful, if critical, obituary in *British Journal of Surgery*, 48 (1961), 586–8; see also *Biographical Memoirs of Fellows of the Royal Society*, 7 (1961), 127–31. On Platt, the information is gathered from several, informal, biographical pieces and from interviews. A handlist of Sir Harry's papers is being prepared by Dr S. V. F. Butler and will be available at Manchester University Library.
43. For general accounts of wartime hospitals see B. Abel Smith, *The Hospitals*, and the volumes edited by W. G. Macpherson, *et al.*, on *Medical Services* in the *History of the Great War*, especially *Surgery of the War* (1922). The following chapters are particularly useful: C. J. Bond, 'Wound treatment in hospitals in the United Kingdom', vol. 1, Ch. 14; G. Murray Levick, 'Organisation for orthopaedic treatment of war injuries', vol. 2, Ch. 12.
44. William Thorburn, 'The Second Western General Hospital', *British Journal of Surgery*, 2 (1915), 491–509, and see n. 47.
45. Young, *St. Mary's*, 89.
46. Frederick Watson, *The Life of Sir Robert Jones*, London, 1934.
47. Levick (n. 43).
48. Patricia Gray, 'Grangethorpe Hospital Rusholme 1917–1929', *Transactions of the Lancashire and Cheshire Antiquarian Society*, 78 (1975), 51–64.
49. Interviews with Sir Harry Platt, e.g. 21 September 1977 (interviewed by author), 6 November 1981 (interviewed by Stella Butler).
50. See n. 42.

CHAPTER 10

Hospitals and welfare: paupers, consumptives, mothers and children

Introduction
The last chapter was concerned with the progressive enclosure of the major city hospitals within the growing sphere of specialists and medical scientists. These hospitals were becoming teaching hospitals; patients were admitted because they were interesting as cases; the laymen who helped run the hospitals saw their role as facilitating the development of hospital medicine and education. At the level of patients, lay governors and medical staff, technical criteria were increasingly dominant over social ones; the hospital was increasingly a world of its own, distanced from the homes of its patients, the intercourse of its lay supporters and the everyday practice of medicine.

But there is another side to medicine, even hospital medicine, and that forms the major theme of this chapter. We shall be dealing, largely, with topics which histories of public health group as the 'personal health services'; those in which individuals are treated, not as specimens of particular pathological types, but as parts of a socio-medical problem. We shall concentrate on the tuberculous, on mothers and children and on the chronic sick.

In chapter eight we discussed the development of infectious disease hospitals, in which patients, especially children, were isolated chiefly to reduce epidemics. In the present chapter we shall see how hospitals were developed as part of the equipment brought to bear on tuberculosis – a communicable disease, but recognised as depending less on exposure to infection than on general features of health and environment which controlled susceptibility. Tuberculosis became a recognised 'problem' only at the end of the nineteenth century, though its incidence had declined over the century.

The other contemporary 'problem' was the means of increasing the size and health of the population. As we have seen, the level of infant mortality had worried many doctors and philanthropists in the mid-nineteenth century, but only at the end of the century, when Britain needed soldiers and colonisers, was the weight of the state put behind efforts to conserve infant life. As those efforts met with some success, the focus shifted toward maternal

HOSPITALS AND WELFARE

mortality, which became one of the major health topics of the inter-war years. We shall explore the complex interaction of voluntary and municipal provision for children, infants and mothers, as local government and national government came to dominate these services.

The hospitals for tuberculosis and for maternal and child welfare, were mostly owned by local government, or, in some cases, paid for by local government on a for-service basis. By the end of the 1920s most County Boroughs in the Region had some sanatorium beds and some beds in a maternity home. Patients using them after 1911 were often covered by national insurance benefits which helped offset the charge on the rates. The sanatoria and maternity homes, like the earlier isolation hospitals, were intended for all the population – patients' payments could depend on income, admittance to a maternity hospital might depend on inadequate home facilities, but in general, these municipal hospitals were intended to serve all classes.

Yet until the Act of 1929 which abolished most of the Poor Law, these municipal facilities were limited and specialised compared with those provided by the Guardians, initially for the very poor. In the first part of this chapter we consider how the workhouses outside Manchester developed hospital facilities comparable to those which had developed in the city in the 1860s and 1870s. The key here was nursing, which, even more than resident medical staffing, converted a refuge into a hospital. Initially, of course, the work of the Guardians was defined by the economic status of its recipients. But as medical men led the population to put more faith in hospitals, and as voluntary hospitals became increasingly surgical, so workhouse hospitals began to fill with medical cases which earlier might have found room in a voluntary hospital, or would have remained at home. A hospital service which had been provided for paupers became generally desirable when other accommodation was so limited. By the 1920s, in many towns, the Poor Law hospital had become a general hospital for those excluded from the local voluntary hospital because they were not connected through workpeoples' funds, or because their disease was not amenable to surgery or a rapid course of medicine.

Poor Law medicine was the general background against which the more specific medical services were developed. Even in 1920, the local Guardians usually had more tuberculosis and more maternity beds than the local authority. Many progressive Guardians, proud of the services which some Poor Law hospitals offered, resented the increasing responsibility of the local authorities for specific socio-medical problems, just as they resented the higher status of voluntary hospitals. We too tend to forget the sheer size of Poor Law facilities as we concentrate on novel developments in welfare or the development of clinical medicine.

Poor Law hospitals seemed uninteresting except where they resembled other kinds of hospitals. Where there were consultants visiting then it could be claimed that the hospital was as good as the voluntary ones. Where there were tuberculosis wards then the Poor Law hospital was involved with public health and domiciliary services. But for the most part, Poor Law hospital inmates were simply the poor and bed-ridden.

After 1930 the 'clinical' and the 'public health' view of hospitals both became increasingly influential as the Poor Law hospitals were developed as municipal general hospitals. But that remains to be discussed in the next chapter. In this chapter we are concerned with the development of the 'public health' view against the background of the Poor Law hospitals.

The Poor Law infirmaries

The pattern of development of Poor Law infirmaries was, of course, determined by the pattern of workhouse building. Generally, the city Unions which had built or inherited large workhouses in the 1840s, added infirmaries in the 1860s and 1870s. We have seen that Chorlton Guardians built Withington infirmary as an extension of a new workhouse; Manchester Guardians added an infirmary to Crumpsall workhouse when their old premises in central Manchester were taken over by a railway company. When these infirmaries were being built many of the cotton towns had only recently agreed to build central workhouses. These late institutions often contained some separate accommodation for the sick, or at least, there was land around the workhouse on which separate sick wards could be added relatively easily. We shall consider Burnley and Blackburn as examples of this pattern.

But there were two other patterns to be seen among the Region's towns. One was simple: in small towns like Kendal or the market towns of Cheshire, no separate infirmary was ever built. The other pattern is found in the larger towns which built central workhouses in the 1850s, before the revival of interest in hospitals. These buildings rarely contained separate accommodation for the sick and in some cases the sites were soon so restricted as to preclude the building of additional wings. In these cases, of which Salford, Bolton and Wigan provide examples, little could be done until the Guardians wanted or were forced to acquire a new site. As we have already suggested in a previous chapter, the problems of infectious diseases among the workhouse population, was sometimes a reason for finding a new site. This was certainly the case in Salford. But there and in other towns the workhouse development was mainly stimulated by the growth of population, and especially the growth of the older age-groups within which chronic sickness was most common. When Manchester workhouse, in the 1850s, had become overcrowded with chronic sick, the Guardians had built a new workhouse and left the old building as an infirmary. By the end of the century, the growth in popularity of voluntary hospitals, and the reformist pressures from Poor Law doctors and nurses, ensured that it was the sick who received the new buildings. Middle-class women and working-class men, who after 1894 were eligible for election to the Boards of Guardians, rarely saw the Poor Law primarily as a deterrent for the idle. Able-bodied males who were permanently or frequently out of work, were now a special problem: the general problem was the adequate maintenance of destitute children, of the old and of the chronic sick. Some Guardians, at least, whether as philanthropists or out of fellow-feeling, could see themselves as Guardians of the poor. Others, of course, were Guardians of the rates. It was on the balance between the two attitudes that the timing and scale of infirmary provision depended. To survey the pattern we return to the mid-century.

If Guardians built separate hospital blocks in the 1850s and 1860s, they were usually for infectious cases. Once facilities for such cases were provided by local sanitary authorities, then these workhouse fever hospitals might be put to other uses. Discussion over such uses led, in several Unions, to the erection of new hospital blocks for non-infectious cases. The process can be seen in two Unions which built relatively early Poor Law hospitals – Macclesfield and Salford.

In Macclesfield the Union workhouse was opened in 1845. During the 1850s, under instructions from the Poor Law Board, a good quality fever hospital was added. The accommodation was regarded as satisfactory until July 1867 when, rather suddenly, the Poor Law inspector began to complain about the condition of the sick wards. As national awareness focussed on the sick paupers, double beds, previously unremarked, became objects for complaint.[1]

The Local Government Board renewed the complaints in 1874, and began to suggest that the fever hospital be used for the non-infectious patients; a smaller isolation hospital could be built to serve in epidemics. The Local Government Board then tried to persuade the local urban and rural sanitary authorities to jointly provide an isolation hospital which the Guardians could use. When, after two years of fruitless debate, the Guardians renewed the proposal to build their own isolation hospital, the Local Government Board came up with a new suggestion. By 1876 their aim was to shift responsibility for epidemics from the Poor Law onto the Public Health authorities. By then too, they were pressing, generally, for better Poor Law hospitals. For Macclesfield they suggested that the existing fever hospital be retained as such, and a new sixty-bed hospital block be built for the more serious non-infectious cases. This was done, though there is evidence that what the inspectors described as a new building was, in fact, a converted shed.

It was opened in 1879, and we have a description of its occupants in the mid-1880s.

> For the most part the inmates of these two wards are old people, who, as might be expected, are as easily upset or laid on one side as the merest infant. Above the clean white coverlet some little old faces peep, and but for the motion of the eyelids the visitor would believe he was looking on rows of corpses laid out for burial.[2]

This kind of infirmary block was provided in new workhouses built during the 1870s, as at Rochdale and Burnley. The Salford Guardians, serving a much bigger population built Hope Hospital in 1882 to accommodate 880 beds. It was meant as a general hospital; it was officially called a hospital – a word then used for voluntary rather than Poor Law facilities; it was comparable in size to Withington; but it never attained a comparable reputation as a model public hospital. Like most facilities in Salford, it was bigger than those in cotton towns but worse than those in Manchester.

The ambiguity was there from the beginning. The Hope site, as we have described, was bought in 1876 when the Guardians expected to build a new hospital of their own for fever and smallpox. Some Guardians obviously had more general uses in mind, but others had been assured that no hospital was intended other than an infectious disease hospital. When the Guardians made arrangements to use the Borough's isolation hospital, they were left wondering what to do with the land at Hope. Some Guardians wanted to put sheds there and use them for a children's hospital. Several long-term or interim schemes were discussed to reduce the crowding of the main workhouse, but it was eventually decided that permanent buildings would be erected at Hope to take over 800 patients. The Local Government Board agreed though they were worried about the problems of managing so large a hospital.

Though Hope Hospital was big and cost about £60,000, it was built of cheap brick and was not well designed. It remained, very largely, a hospital for the chronic sick. In 1907, when some larger Poor Law hospitals were doing considerable surgical work, Hope Hospital had only a primitive operating theatre and very few operations were done there. Over a third of the patients were over sixty years of age and about a third were suffering from lung diseases, mostly bronchitis. The cases of fracture were mostly patients who had been transferred from voluntary hospitals. Just before the war, the hospital was bitterly criticised by Sir Henry Burdett, the national authority on hospitals. Children with infectious opthalmia were being treated in damp sheds. The matron alone was praised, for her long battle against the penny-pinching Guardians.[3]

Of the cotton town Unions, Blackburn and Oldham took the lead in developing workhouse hospitals with good medical and nursing care. Oldham workhouse had been opened in 1851; a smallpox and fever block was added in the 1870s; sick wards were built from 1877 onwards. By about 1890 the hospital section consisted of three pavilion blocks each of two storeys and each holding about ninety beds. When the hospital was surveyed in 1894 there was no resident medical officer but the nursing staff was professional. A nursing superintendent had charge of the hospital; during the day each block had a charge nurse and two probationers; at night there was but one nurse and two probationers for all three blocks. The children's hospital was a separate block and could accommodate about sixty patients.

By 1890, the nursing system, even more than the design of the building, was the key by which Poor Law infirmaries were judged. Building separate ward blocks for the poor helped to ensure that the sick were thought of as hospital patients rather than workhouse inmates, but the break was not complete if the workhouse matron retained control or if paupers were employed as nurses. In 1895 Oldham had recently promoted a nurse to be nursing superintendent; they were still open to criticism for employing pauper attendants at night in the children's ward.[4]

In Blackburn the new workhouse, opened in 1864, had plenty of room for enlargement. A separate block for lunatics was added in 1881 and in 1888 hospital wards were built for 160 patients. The nursing, by the mid-1890s, was fully professional and probationers were being trained. But not all the sick paupers were accommodated in the new hospital. The 'foul' cases – those with itch (scabies) or venereal disease – were in the body of the workhouse, and so were the chronically infirm. The male venereal cases were under the care of the workhouse taskmaster, the attendant on the female venereal patients was untrained. Such arrangements were common – patients who in fact required careful and intensive nursing were excluded from the 'hospital section'. The condition of these patients at Blackburn was the subject of an investigation by the Local Government Board, which revealed 'maggoty beds' and 'bed sores the size of dinner plates'.[5]

In the Burnley Union, the first central workhouse had been opened in 1877, to house up to 350 paupers. Though it was considerably better equipped than the old township workhouse and though there was a separate infirmary block with eighty beds, it was soon found defective, especially by the doctors and middle-class ladies who had begun to take an interest in Poor Law affairs. One local practitioner, Dr Brumwell, was particularly concerned about the child death-rate. Another, Dr John Brown, was married to a lady who undertook a great deal of social work and who became nationally known as a temperance reformer and a member of the Women's Co-operative

Guild. Mary Brown was persuaded to stand for election to the Board of Guardians in 1894, as soon as women became eligible. Her canvassers were working class and she headed the poll.

During the 1880s reformers like Brumwell and Mary Brown brought about a series of additions to the workhouse. Several cottage homes were provided for the children and in 1885 the Guardians agreed to enlarge the site and to build a new hospital for 200 adults and twenty-five children. The proposal was heavily criticised as extravagant, and the new building was not opened until 1895. There were four main wards of thirty-four beds each; four trained nurses were appointed to staff them.[6]

During the 1890s there was a sustained campaign, both national and regional, to persuade Boards of Guardians to build separate hospitals and to staff them with trained nurses. The *British Medical Journal* ran a series of reports on Poor Law facilities which used 'model' hospitals such as Withington to highlight the defects in other Unions. In our Region, Stockport Guardians were severely criticised for maintaining sick paupers in wards which were 'little better than barns'. In one

> There was a woman with typhoid fever, with cases of paralysis, rheumatism, bad legs, phthisis, old age; the 'dirty' cases being mixed up with the other patients in the wards. There was practically no classification: we saw here two children in one bed with opthalmia. This ward was overcrowded, the beds being close together.[7]

The male patients were better accommodated in a more recent building, but, for the BMJ Commissioner there was 'only one possible course to recommend: the building of a new infirmary'. The Local Government Board was urging this course, but were meeting local opposition.

This national pressure, official and unofficial, was supplemented by regional associations of medical and lay reformers. Progressive Guardians gained mutual support through the North Western Poor Law Conference, where reformers could publicise the practices in the better hospitals in the hope of encouraging emulation. Among Lancashire Guardians, the most active was Dr J. M. Rhodes, who from his election to the Chorlton Board in 1882, gained a national reputation as an authority on diet and nursing, and especially on the proper care of children and epileptics. He became chairman of the Northern Workhouse Nursing Association, which sought to place trained nurses in workhouses. In this respect, Rhodes' own Poor Law hospital was a resource as well as a model. Training schemes at Withington were intended to supply nurses who could carry the best standards to smaller workhouses. The probationers were paid and given good accommodation; by the 1890s they were middle-class people, 'Even merchants' daughters go in for nursing now'.[8]

These campaigns for better nursing received official backing in 1897 when the Local Government Board prohibited the use of paupers as nurses. This step considerably raised the status of Poor Law nurses, and trained nurses gradually penetrated those Unions which did not have separate hospitals. But there were many problems. Unless there was a resident medical officer, the infirmary could not be recognised as a suitable training school for future superintendent-nurses, and so the quality of recruits was low. Furthermore, in the absence of a resident medical officer, the superintendent of nursing often had difficulty in resisting control by the workhouse matron, who was responsible for the domestic arrangements of the whole institution. This problem was especially acute because in most cases the matron was the wife of the workhouse master, the chief administrative officer.

But in some cases, this husband and wife arrangement could be an advantage. Mrs Hull, a trained nurse who was married to the master of Stockport workhouse, considerably improved the nursing standards, even while the patients remained in the buildings so severely criticised in 1894. Just before that time, over 300 patients had been nursed by a man and his wife, plus three assistants, two of whom worked nights. Mr and Mrs Hull came in 1893 and began to increase the nursing staff, of necessity taking inexperienced people and training them as best they could. In 1896 Mrs Hull convinced the Guardians that they would get better nurses if they could train probationers. By 1902 she had trained twenty nurses.

The benefit to Stockport workhouse was chiefly through the employment of probationers on the wards; by 1902 only one of those who had completed the three years training had been appointed to the permanent staff, but of the twenty-five nurses available in 1902, nearly twenty were probationers. The male hospital's eighty-eight beds, which in 1892 had been staffed by one trained nurse and two assistants, now had a sister, a staff nurse, and six probationers. At the end of their training, the probationers were examined by the honorary physicians of Stockport (voluntary) Infirmary. Of the sixteen trainees who had qualified and remained unmarried, eight had gone, directly or indirectly, into other Poor Law hospitals or workhouses.[9]

At Stockport, because the master's wife was a trained nurse, the strictly domestic duties had been subordinated to nursing, even before a new hospital was built and a resident medical officer appointed. But such arrangements placed a huge responsibility upon the superintendent nurse, whose regular duties were frequently interrupted by the need to take charge of urgent midwifery cases or the difficult behaviour of the mentally defective. Generally, the adoption of hospital rather than workhouse routines depended on the provision of new hospital accommodation under medical supervision. This was particularly difficult where, as in Stockport and Bolton, there was no room for expansion on the existing workhouse site.

In Bolton, the workhouse at Fishpool had been opened in 1861. By 1883 the Local Government Board inspector was complaining of a shortage of hospital accommodation. Ten years later, when the Townleys estate adjoining the workhouse site became available, the Guardians, after much hesitation purchased it; even then, it took another five years to secure a majority for the erection of a new hospital. For fifteen years, the Guardians had prevaricated by putting forward minor schemes, hoping to avoid the expense of a major project.

Initially they relied on the fact that their fever hospital was quite large. Indeed, once the Borough Council had provided an infectious disease hospital at Rumworth, the workhouse fever hospital seemed too large for its likely load. In 1887 the Local Government Board inspector suggested it be used as a general hospital, and that a smaller building be built for such infectious cases as occurred among paupers. Nothing was done, partly for reasons discussed in an earlier chapter: some Guardians were loathe to reduce infectious disease accommodation at the workhouse for fear of having to provide accommodation through the public health authorities of which they were also members.

In 1890 there was another Local Government Board report, which found the sick wards overcrowded, underventilated and quite insufficient for the needs of the Union. The medical officer wanted more nurses, and to use the fever hospital for sick children. The fever hospital began to be used on a temporary basis, but nothing else had been decided when the Local Government Board enquired again in 1891. By 1893, the Guardians could rely on the Rural Sanitary Authority taking their typhus and smallpox cases, and were more ready to free their own fever hospital by building a small infectious disease block for which the Local Government Board authorised a loan of £2,500. But at the end of 1893, the central authority, prompted by the report of the workhouse medical officer, was still asking how more hospital accommodation could be provided. It was the committee then appointed which recommended the purchase of the Townley's estate; they also recommended that the nursing system be reorganised with probationers under a lady superintendent. By May 1895 this sub-committee was recommending a hospital of 240 beds – the existing, converted fever hospital had forty. By this time the persistent complaints of the medical officer and the accession of some vigorous women to the Board had created a lobby in favour of substantial improvements, but they did not have a majority for a scheme which would cost over £30,000.

Alternative plans were proposed. The cheapest would have left the

Townleys site untouched, so as not to interfere with the revenue from the farmland. The proposal which gained acceptance used the new land, but only for two half-blocks to cost £10,000, to house 120 patients. This was opposed by 'economists' who feared it would be the first instalment of the larger plan, but they were outflanked by collusion between the Local Government Board and several local Guardians, notably the Haslam family (including Mrs Haslam), who were becoming embarrassed about gross overcrowding in the workhouse. In December 1895 John Haslam warned that if numbers rose as usual during the winter, able-bodied men would be sleeping two in a bed. 'Every sensible person would recognise that such a state of things should not be permitted to obtain, as it would lay the way open for terrible abuses, as the people who went to the workhouse were frequently not of the best class.'[10]

The Local Government Board gave support to this plan as the first instalment. By 1898 the progressive lobby was pressing for a new nurses' home and an administrative block. The proposal was supported by the chairman, a magistrate and a graduate, by the three women members, by Councillor Haslam, and by both clergymen Guardians as well as by two other Guardians. It was opposed by twenty-eight Guardians, including a doctor, who objected to the expense and denied that it was a hardship for nurses to walk the 500–600 yards along a dark lane to reach their quarters at the end of their shifts. By this time the polarisation was very obvious – the reformers wanted facilities of which they would not be ashamed, some of their opponents resented the presence of professional nurses as provoking expenditure.

A few months after this debate, in March 1899, the Townleys hospital was officially opened, by Guardians who had opposed its being built. Even they recognised the change which had occurred nationally since the 1880s. The workhouse infirmaries were taking more and more chronic cases and these had come to be recognised as requiring trained nurses and medical supervision. Though pauperism, overall, might be decreasing, the growing popularity of hospital treatment, meant that more of those who came into Poor Law institutions did so not from destitution, but because they were unable to otherwise obtain the treatment which they and the Poor Law doctors thought they needed.[11]

In some Unions the campaign for a hospital took even longer than in Bolton. Rochdale Guardians did not build a new hospital block (Birch Hill) until 1902; before then they had used infirmary wards in a relatively new (1877) workhouse. The workhouses in Wigan, Bury and Ashton were older and less satisfactory, but few Guardians wanted hospital facilities. Ashton's hospital block (Lake hospital) was opened in 1905–6 alongside the workhouse; Bury gained a 126 bed hospital in 1905; Wigan's hospital (Billinge) was opened about 1907. In Stockport, the Union hospital (Stepping Hill) was opened in 1905 though the Local Government Board had been discussing hospital plans since 1892, if not before.[12]

Thus, the Edwardian Guardians completed in the less progressive towns, the shift to hospital care which had begun forty years before in the cities and thirty years before in the more progressive Unions. There seems no easy correlation between the advance of voluntary hospitals and that of Poor Law hospitals across the range of towns around Manchester. Some towns, especially Bury and Rochdale were late-comers in both respects; in some, especially Stockport, Preston and Wigan, voluntary hospitals were founded long before there were hospital facilities under the Poor Law. In a third group of towns, especially Blackburn and Oldham, that interval was shorter and the Poor Law hospital was less overshadowed by the development of the voluntary hospital. These patterns will only be explained when we have more comparative studies of local political history, which consider philanthropy, policy for the poor and local interest in public health. We might expect that a local Council unusually interested in public health, would be associated with a 'progressive' Board of Guardians, both because of the overlap of personnel and because the use of a Borough isolation hospital by the Guardians might raise medical standards as it freed 'hospital' accommodation in the workhouse. Oldham seems to have shown such a positive link; Ashton, Wigan and Preston were probably examples of inactivity in both spheres.

During the Edwardian years, as workhouse hospitals were completed in the more backward cotton towns, the future of the Poor Law was the subject of considerable national debate, and medical relief was one of the key issues. As we have seen, the Poor Law as revised in 1834 intended medical relief for those who were paupers first and patients second. It was opposed by those who knew the majority of paupers to be victims not parasites; the victims of parental waywardness, of economic slump and, especially, of disease and infirmity. The experience of the Law's working, the outlook of Poor Law medical officers and nurses, and the growing political influence of the working classes, caused some of those responsible to recognise the fact that most of the inmates of workhouses were there because they were sick. The vast majority of the population lived close to poverty; if a breadwinner was ill or had to act as nurse for more than a few days, the family was liable to be pauperised. Whether they gained medical relief as working families or as paupers depended on their ability and readiness to find relief quickly. While their money lasted, the patient could be admitted to a voluntary hospital; once the family was destitute, they had no alternative except to seek aid from the Poor Law. In terms of the real causes of poverty, and in terms of public health, the criteria of the Poor Law were arbitrary.

This lesson was emphasised by the development of hospital services. The revival of voluntary hospitals, and especially the increased technicality of late nineteenth century medicine, sharpened the distinction between medical care and general relief, between assistance to cure specific lesions and a more general nursing support. Doctors in voluntary hospitals, because they were interested in specific diseases, wanted to treat those patients who showed them, irrespective of their financial status. The increasingly medical admission criteria in voluntary hospitals, contrasted with the financial definition of Poor Law hospitals, and this contrast was greatest where, as in Manchester, the Poor Law hospitals had facilities for the most up-to-date surgical operations. Why should these be restricted to those patients who had been branded as paupers? The more elaborate methods of treatment, especially surgery, also meant that an ever higher proportion of the population was 'destitute' when that meant 'unable to pay for appropriate treatment'. Patients at the upper end of the increased range tended to enter voluntary hospitals, now that recommendations were no longer required. The class which had previously attended voluntary hospitals was increasingly forced into Poor Law hospitals. An increasing proportion of Poor Law patients, though unable to pay for expensive treatment, were not, normally destitute.

That sick paupers were primarily patients had been partially recognised in 1885, when the receipt of medical relief alone ceased to be grounds for disenfranchising the recipient.[13] But those who wanted medical relief still had to gain the permission of the receiving officers. They could not directly approach the Poor law medical officer. Many reformers thought that this separation of function was essential. The sick poor ought to be provided with public dispensaries where they could be diagnosed and treated by salaried medical men. The question of payment for medicine should be made a secondary question.[14]

These points had been argued since mid-century, especially by medical critics of the Poor Law, but by 1900 they were exemplified in the operation of municipal public health services. We have seen how the markers between the paupers' sphere and that of other citizens had to be hidden when paupers were treated in municipal isolation hospitals. There they did not wear uniforms, they were treated like anyone else because they had a disease dangerous to themselves and others. Patients were not charged for their accommodation, partly because they were isolated for the public good, partly so as not to discourage isolation, partly because the hospitals were felt to belong to the citizens of the town who had paid for them, directly or indirectly, through the rates.[15]

But if smallpox and scarlet fever could be dealt with on that basis, why not other diseases, especially those like tuberculosis which were known to be contagious? Even in the case of non-contagious diseases, delay in treatment was likely to increase the economic loss to the family concerned and to the community. Why was all sickness not dealt with in the same way as infectious diseases? Why did medical criteria continue to be subordinated to economic and social criteria in the assessment of need? For reformers such as Sidney and Beatrice Webb the time had come to establish a national medical service, quite separate from the unemployment service, and from poor relief. They argued the case with the many witnesses called before the Poor Law Commission of 1905–9, but they failed to convince the majority of their fellow members and their opinions were consigned to a Minority Report.[16]

We can gain some idea of the balance of arguments by considering the evidence to the Commission from in and around the Region. The strongest plan for reform came from Dr Nathan Raw, visiting medical superintendent of Mill Road Infirmary in Liverpool, who stressed the anomalies and the inequities which separated voluntary hospital treatment from that under the Poor Law. The first was usually free and did not interfere with sick-club benefits; the second involved stigma, and benefit payments were suspended. Raw argued that the voluntary hospitals were taking an ever higher class of patient, because recommendations were no longer required. The 'ordinary poor' were being forced into Poor Law hospitals, which were comparable medically, but which imposed social and economic penalties. Such a system was at best anomalous; usually it was unfair to the sick poor for whom hospitals had been intended. Raw wanted a national medical service where, in all hospitals, patients would pay according to their ability. Under questioning he agreed that payment might better be made through the rates – such a scheme was impracticable only because medical men would object.[17]

Most medical men probably wanted to see patients charged both in voluntary and in Poor Law hospitals. Dr Lea of Manchester argued for municipal or state hospitals in which, as in Germany, all patients above destitution would pay something for their accommodation, and the middle class would also pay fees to their doctors.[18] Other local witnesses were more cautious in their suggestions. Mr Skevington, of the Chorlton Guardians, wanted the Poor Law hospitals separated from the workhouses. It was too easy for Relief Committees to send chronic or convalescent patients to the workhouse, too easy for Guardians to employ paupers in hospitals. Skevington was proud of Withington hospital, which was far bigger than any of the voluntary hospitals. Why should patients there be stigmatised when they all contributed, via rents or rates, to its upkeep? It ought to be seen as a citizens' hospital.[19]

Mr Cooper of Bolton Guardians also welcomed the medical development of the Poor Law hospital at Bolton. Better services meant quicker recoveries; and the Poor Law hospital had come to be viewed, not as an appendage of the workhouse, but as the town's second hospital. It should, he thought, be administered separately from the workhouse, but to retain control over the class of admissions, the hospital should remain under the Poor Law.[20] The Medical Officer of Manchester, Dr James Niven, also favoured this separation, at least in principle – but how could Poor Law hospitals be transferred to sanitary authorities when they were nearly all physically bound up with workhouses?[21] Mr McDougall, chairman of the committee for Monsall Hospital, was afraid that any such transfer would overload the local authority.[22]

The strongest arguments for realigning the work of public health and Poor Law authorities was the overlapping of their duties. The Medical Officer for Stockport gave a list of local authority functions in what could be the work of the Poor Law:

> Sterilised milk depots
> Municipal creches
> Municipal wash-houses and lodging houses
> Supply of spectacles to school-children
> Supply of diarrhoea mixture in summer and autumn
> Supply of diphtheria antitoxin
> Free isolation of cases of infectious disease, even (in Manchester) of puerperal fever
> Erection and maintenance of phthisis sanatoria
> Free vaccination and compensation in smallpox epidemics
> Payment of medical men under the Midwives Act
> Contribution to (voluntary) infirmary funds[23]

Yet for all these points of overlap, and for all the masses of evidence collected by the Commission, very little was changed. Not until 1929 were the Poor Law hospitals transferred to the municipalities. It was only after Lloyd George introduced National Insurance, in 1911, that the Poor Law machinery began to seem dispensible. It required the steady further expansion of local authority health services to demonstrate that the Poor Law hospitals could be managed in the same way. In the next sections we shall review two of these critical areas of local authority services – tuberculosis sanatoria and maternity hospitals.

The hospital services for tuberculosis patients
Tuberculosis, especially pulmonary tuberculosis or phthisis, was the major single cause of death in Victorian England. In the 1850s, phthisis accounted for about 12 per cent of the deaths in the Manchester conurbation. But it

was not a prominent disease in the records of the voluntary general hospitals. Few phthisis patients were admitted to the wards, because little could be done for them and the progress of the disease was so slow. Over the period 1850–1900 the Manchester Royal Infirmary usually admitted between fifty and 100 phthisis in-patients each year, about 2 per cent of the total. Among home-patients the ratio was much higher: 17 per cent in 1861, about 11 per cent in 1871 and 1881. Taking both classes of patient together (and assuming that there was no overlap), the Infirmary was treating about 300 cases per year.[24] If we multiply that figure by two or three to include other medical charities, the total is small in comparison to the total number of sufferers, for in the 1870s about 2,000 people a year *died* of phthisis in the Manchester conurbation.[25] A high proportion of these cases must have been treated by Poor Law medical officers as they became destitute. Some of them were housed in Poor Law institutions. Around 1900 there were about 330 beds for phthisis patients in the Manchester and Chorlton Poor Law hospitals.[26]

The first voluntary hospital in the Region which specialised in phthisis was the Manchester Hospital for Consumption and Diseases of the Throat. It had been founded in 1875 by Dr Shepherd Fletcher and Dr Alexander Hodgkinson. It initially occupied a home in St John Street with accommodation for eight in-patients. In 1881 there were only forty-seven in-patients and sixty-one out-patients, but in the 1880s support for the hospital grew as tuberculosis began to attract more public attention.[27]

The bacillus of tuberculosis was isolated and identified by Robert Koch in 1882, who, around 1890 introduced tuberculin as a supposed cure. That proved unsuccessful but the possibility of using bacteriological diagnosis to detect early cases of tuberculosis was a considerable help to physicians interested in treating the disease. The possibility of recognising the bacteria in the environment, especially in the dust of infected houses, helped confirm the previous statistical association between tuberculosis and dark, unventilated homes. The discovery that sunlight killed bacteria helped explain the value of open-air sanatoria, a system of treatment which had been extensively developed in Germany, where the mortality from tuberculosis was even higher than in England.

Several of the British initiatives in the study and treatment of tuberculosis came from the Manchester district. From the mid-1880s and especially in the Edwardian period there was considerable collaboration between University medical scientists, Medical Officers of Health and the clinicians working in the Manchester Hospital for Consumption. Sheridan Delépine, Professor of Pathology (later of Bacteriology) at Manchester's medical school, was one of the country's leading bacteriologists and he was largely responsible for demonstrating the transmission of tuberculosis to man via the milk of infected cows. J. F. W. Tatham, Medical Officer of Health in Salford (1873 – 88) and Manchester (1888 – 93), demonstrated the need for better housing to combat tuberculosis; his successor in Manchester, James Niven, had already conducted investigations of the homes of phthisis sufferers in Oldham, and had almost persuaded Oldham Council to make tuberculosis a notifiable infectious disease. That plan, for which Niven had won the approval of Oldham practitioners, would have been the first such scheme in Britain. In 1890, Niven, as Oldham's Medical Officer, had visited Berlin to report on latest German practice.

Niven and others used the North Western Association of Medical Officers of Health to extend their campaign for notification. They were supported by the Manchester & Salford Sanitary Association. In 1899 Manchester Council agreed to the scheme, and Niven was able to draw up a comprehensive plan which combined education, disinfection of homes, and hospital treatment in the hope of reducing the incidence and mortality of the disease. Manchester was second only to Brighton in introducing notification. Niven's plan was only partially realised, but it was an important step towards larger schemes which became possible in Manchester and elsewhere after the 1911 Insurance Act introduced benefit payments for the domiciliary and sanatorium care of tuberculosis patients.

In his 1899 plan, Niven wanted the Corporation to build a 200 bed hospital, but all he got, in the short-term, was the use of Clayton Vale, a former factory and detached mansion which the Corporation had acquired as a smallpox hospital. Because smallpox was in decline, the thirty-two beds were allotted, between smallpox epidemics, for the care of tuberculosis, mostly advanced cases. The only other beds available to the scheme were twenty at the Crossley Sanatorium, Delamere, which opened in 1905, as part of the Manchester Hospital for Consumption.[28]

The Hospital for Consumption had grown rapidly from the mid-1880s. In 1884 they bought a large house at Bowdon, a popular residential area for affluent merchants, ten miles south of the city. The following year when fifteen beds were equipped at Bowdon, the city centre hospital was replaced with a clinic on Hardman St, which served as the out-patients department. The accommodation at Bowdon was expanded to fifty beds by the end of the century, at the expense of W. J. Crossley, the chairman of the hospital and one of the Crossley Brothers, a very successful engineering firm founded in 1867. W. J. Crossley became a noted local philanthropist, and in 1906 was elected as MP for Altrincham, the constituency which included the Bowdon hospital. His wife shared his interest in tuberculosis patients, and her name was given to the Home of Peace, a large house which they provided in an industrial district of Manchester, as a refuge for advanced cases of phthisis.

By 1902, partly as a result of the notification scheme, the Hospital for Consumption was dealing with over 11,000 cases a year, the vast majority of them out-patients seen at the clinic in town. About 400 patients a year passed through Bowdon, which by this time was equipped with verandahs and liegehallen (rest-halls), so that a systematic outdoor treatment could be used. The diet of patients had also been improved, and when patients went home they were visited and the poorer ones were sometimes given a daily supply of milk, eggs and rice. Tuberculosis, it was recognised, preyed on the undernourished; it was for this disease that doctors and philanthropists first attempted to ensure that patients were well nourished. They did so when deaths from tuberculosis had already declined to half their rate for 1850; the Manchester Hospital for Consumption, with 11,000 out-patients, had £120 per year for after-care.

The possibility of treating Manchester patients in hospital was considerably extended when W.J. Crossley spent £70,000 to build a sanatorium at Delamere. It stood on a hill in open countryside, about ten miles east of Chester, open to breezes from the Irish Sea. The Liverpool sanatorium was close by. The Manchester sanatorium had ninety beds in large, airy wards, the windows of which faced south and opened to allow beds to be placed on verandahs. The patients spent much of their time resting on these verandahs, or in special shelters, but the poorer patients were encouraged, where possible, to do light work around the hospital. This eased the transition from hospital to their normal working lives and was meant to ensure that they did not degenerate into chronic invalids or 'loafers'. The poorer patients were confined to the grounds, which were surrounded by an unclimbable fence; the paying patients were allowed to take exercise outside. Patients could be visited once a month.

All patients who were not confined to bed were supplied each week with a removable pouch in which they kept a printed card of their assigned routine, a thermometer to measure their own temperature several times daily, and a small vessel into which they spat. Covered mugs were provided at each bed for the collection of night sputum. These mugs were sterilized each day and the sputum was regularly examined for the presence of bacteria. For most patients rest, fresh air, bathing, and good diet was the only treatment, but there was an elaborate operating theatre in which surgical treatments could be carried out. The basement contained an x-ray machine.

At any time, thirty-six of the ninety beds were reserved for patients paying two to three guineas a week. The remaining fifty-four beds were occupied by 'free' patients sent from the Hardman Street clinic in Manchester, twenty of them referred to the clinic and paid for by Manchester Corporation. The Hospital liked to send the curable cases to Delamere, using Bowdon for more advanced cases; those referred to Delamere by the Corporation were often more severe. Each patient cost about £1 13s. per week (around 1906), of which almost 11s. 0d. was spent on food. At this period, many working men earned about £1 per week, on which they were expected to feed, clothe and house a wife and several children.[29]

The hospital at Bowdon and the sanatorium at Delamere took a few hundred poor patients per year. The total number of beds available in voluntary and local authority hospitals was only 111, compared to 545 in Union hospitals, so that the majority of institutional care was still given under the Poor Law. But the responsibility was shifting and the more progressive Guardians wanted to speed that shift. In 1912 the Chorlton Guardians urged the Corporation to provide a two hundred bed hospital to take tuberculosis patients out of the Union hospitals. They offered, in return, to provide aid to the families of hospital patients.

Niven had for some years been urging the Corporation to start such a fund for assisting families. He wanted to prevent the disease spreading among family members and knew that a high standard of nutrition increased resistance. He argued the case before the Poor Law Commission of 1905–9, producing evidence as to how much subsidy would be required. The scheme was controversial because it so thoroughly reversed the old Poor Law philosophy; Niven was proposing, where necessary, to supplement wages over long periods of time, to raise family incomes to the level required for health rather than subsistence. Some public health authorities had helped subsidise families who were isolated in their homes because of smallpox, and similar measures had sometimes been used in cholera epidemics. Tuberculosis, the communicable but chronic disease, seemed to require the extension of this emergency support on a long-term basis. Niven argued that such schemes would be economically beneficial; tuberculosis, he calculated in about 1911 cost Manchester about £500,000 in lost wages, poor relief, etc.

The problem of tuberculosis, as presented by campaigners like Niven, was answered in 1911, not by transferring responsibility from Poor Law to public health authorities, or by merging the two, but through the National Insurance Act. Under this Act, most working men were registered through the many existing Friendly Societies and insurance companies; the government, from taxes, supplemented these payments. Those covered could then obtain unemployment benefit, plus medical aid from doctors who were registered with local panels. For present purposes, the significance of the Act was the 1s 3d per head per year which was allowed for tuberculosis – 6d to be paid to medical practitioners and 9d as 'sanatorium benefit'. In addition £1½ million was provided for the building of sanatoria. In Manchester, the sanatorium benefit was paid by the approved societies to the local authority, towards the costs of a revised tuberculosis scheme. Niven regretted the emphasis on treatment; in his opinion the preventive work was ultimately more useful, but he was able to build on the existing arrangements with the voluntary Hospital for Consumption, by appointing one of its physicians, Dr Sutherland, to be responsible for the treatment side of the city scheme. The clinic on Hardman Street was adopted as the city's tuberculosis dispensary, and Dr Sutherland's considerable clinical reputation facilitated arrangements with local practitioners. In 1914, Sutherland took over responsibility for the public health work also, so that he was then responsible for a service which integrated education and preventive measures, out-patient treatment and tuberculosis hospitals other than those under the Poor Law. At about the same time the Corporation finally agreed to give support to affected families and assigned £2,000. This was additional to the meagre £500 per year which had been obtained from National Insurance funds for assisting patients discharged from sanatoria.

The National Insurance monies enabled the Corporation to develop two additional hospital facilities, one at Baguley, about six miles south of the city, and one at Abergele in North Wales. The nucleus of the Baguley scheme was a fever hospital which had been opened in 1902 by the Withington Urban District Council, two years before Withington was absorbed into Manchester City. In 1910 the Corporation had considered adapting it as a sanatorium – but nothing was done until after the 1911 Act. The nucleus at Abergele was a sanatorium for about fifty patients which had been developed by the Chorlton Board of Guardians.[30] In 1914 it was taken over by Manchester Corporation because it was Government policy that the care of the tuberculous should rest with public health authorities rather than the Poor Law, except in the case of the uninsured.

The change in use of Baguley hospital meant that 100 beds for infectious diseases had to be built elsewhere. An addition was made to Monsall Hospital – an example of rationalisation which had the usual socio-geographical consequence: a large area, in this case south Manchester, was left without isolation facilities, for Monsall was on the northern edge of the city.[31] Nor was the adaptation of Baguley particularly successful. There were persistent problems with the sewers, building work caused prolonged disruption, and nurses were hard to find, both during the war and afterwards. By the 1920s there were over 300 beds there. A scheme to build a working colony failed because of an argument about the site.

The patients at Baguley were mostly insured working people, and many of them did not take kindly to the hospital regime. They were not paupers, nor infected children, nor recipients of charity, as most hospital patients had been during the nineteenth century; they had paid for the service they got.

Dr Niven found that they had 'an undue sense of their rights'; they evidently disturbed his professional paternalism.

The plan for Abergele was even larger. During the 1920s the City intended to provide over 500 beds, mostly for children. But, under Treasury pressure the Ministry of Health refused to give grants for this large scheme and by 1939 only 207 had been provided.[32] The sanatorium was one among several schemes to remove city children to the health-giving countryside. It was contemporary with the holiday schools developed by Education Committees, for slum children to experience the seaside and the open fields. All such institutions manifested the common faith of the turn of the century in the healing powers of sun and air. Lewis Mumford, the historian of technology, contrasted this faith in 'neo-technics', with the grimy, coal-based industry he dubbed palaeotechnics. Though in the towns of our Region, the workday air continued to be thick with smoke, it was to neo-technics that men looked to remedy the diseases which towns engendered. Surgical cleanliness, sunlight, rooms heated without smoke and lit by electricity, these were the conditions which would help phthisis.

For earlier advocates, convalescent homes were the antithesis of industry; a means of escaping the pressures and pollution of city life. In the 1860s, many health reformers had seen the then orthodox medicine as ineffective or superfluous: nature would cure. By the end of the century, the status of medicine had been so raised, and its connection with physical science so emphasised, that sanatoria could be seen as a new and superior form of technology, as development rather than repudiation.

Outside the Manchester conurbation there was little special provision for tuberculosis until after the 1911 Act. The only sanatorium in the Region which was at all comparable to Delamere was the Westmorland Sanatorium, at Meathop near Morecambe Bay. It was opened in 1900 by two doctors, Rushton Parker and Paget-Tomlinson who had begun a charity to convert a former convalescent home into a sanatorium for sixteen consumptive patients. The institution was supported by a variety of local authorities and voluntary organisations in Westmorland. It also took a few private patients. By 1906 it had forty-four beds, thirty-five of which were maintained by local authorities or other associations. Bolton Corporation and Bolton Guardians supported four and two beds respectively.[33]

Bolton Corporation was notable among cotton town authorities for its concern with tuberculosis. The interest had been stimulated in 1901 when representatives had visited the International Congress on tuberculosis. In 1902 the Corporation, guided by its Medical Officer, Dr J. Gould, had adopted a scheme of voluntary notification which was made compulsory in 1905. From that year, the Corporation paid for free sputum examinations.

In 1906 the beds at Meathop were hired; four more were added in 1908. This enthusiasm spread to the Bolton Guardians, and also to local philanthropists. In 1907, Mr Thomas Wilkinson gave his house, seven acres of land and an endowment of £50,000 to found the voluntary Wilkinson Sanatorium, intended for the accommodation of poor consumptives.[34]

The Wilkinson Sanatorium had twenty-five beds but the Council felt the need for more. In 1909 they proposed a twenty-four-bed tuberculosis pavilion on the site of the Borough isolation hospital. This was meant to accommodate cases waiting for transfer to sanatoria, cases for observation, and cases in the early stage of disease who needed to be taught the correct regimen for minimising the risk to themselves and others. The building of the pavilion did not begin until 1913, by which time the scheme had qualified for a government grant of £2,160 towards the cost of £5,606.

The example of Thomas Wilkinson in Bolton may well have prompted the provision of the Aitken Sanatorium near Bury. This too was a private house, given by its former residents – a relatively new form of philanthropy linked to the increasing difficulty of running large households, and to the flight of Lancashire capitalists from the towns out of which they had grown rich. Aitken was also symptomatic of the increasingly close interweaving of voluntary and local authority provision, especially for tuberculosis. The house was given, not to a charitable trust, but to the Bury & District Joint Hospital Board, a consortium of local authorities which ran the Florence Nightingale isolation hospital and the Ainsworth (smallpox) hospital. All the local authorities concerned, except Bury Corporation, were constituent parts of Lancashire County, from whom they obtained a grant. After 1915, the beds were allotted to the two major authorities: Bury Corporation paid for twenty, Lancashire County Council for fifty. In that same year, Mrs Aitken, who had maintained a close interest, bequeathed £10,000 to the sanatorium.

In the other towns of Lancashire and Cheshire, there appears to have been no such voluntary or 'mixed' initiatives, and very little action by local authorities. Only Oldham appears to have provided accommodation for consumptives before 1913. As in Manchester, and like several cases in the inter-war years, this provision was made in a smallpox hospital. In 1908, part of Strinesdale Hospital was fitted up as a sanatorium of eighteen beds. It stood on the moors above the town – pleasant in summer, but very bleak in winter. Only early cases were admitted, in case the hospital had to be evacuated for a smallpox epidemic. Some more serious cases were taken (from 1910) into Westhulme Isolation Hospital. They were kept there only to be trained and to allow their homes to be disinfected. Both facilities were expanded in 1913, as Oldham, like other towns, adopted a tuberculosis scheme under the Act of that year.

HOSPITALS AND WELFARE

After 1913, as we have seen in studying Manchester, the responsibility for combatting tuberculosis lay clearly with local authorities, and some central government money was available as grants. The Lancashire Boroughs provided very little accommodation beyond that available in 1913. Most of the less active Boroughs merely assigned some beds in their isolation hospitals: Barrow provided sixteen such beds, Blackpool twelve, Blackburn thirty-two, Salford seventy-two. Stockport had fifty beds in the former Poor Law hospital (Stepping Hill). Most such accommodation was poor quality and far from sufficient in quantity. A few Boroughs provided sanatoria: Preston opened Ribbleton Sanatorium (thirty beds) in 1919; Salford opened a 120-bed sanatorium in 1922, at Nab Top, near Marple – it was a long way from Salford and especially in winter patients were reluctant to go there. In Rochdale, a large house was converted as Springfield Sanatorium in 1934. Again, Oldham was one of the better authorities; they rebuilt Strinesdale Sanatorium after the First War and continued to develop it during the 1930s. Burnley never did provide a Borough sanatorium.[35]

The major post-war initiative in the Region was taken by the County Councils, especially that of Lancashire. Like Manchester, Lancashire County was a large and powerful authority which could afford to assign a full-time medical officer to tuberculosis. Its scheme is important as the first hospital programme in this Region to be coordinated over a wide geographical area, and because it acquired a national reputation for good organisation. Like Dr Sutherland in Manchester, Lancashire's chief tuberculosis officer, Dr Lissant Cox, was a clinician as well as an administrator. He had trained in Liverpool and was regarded as a major authority on the disease.[36]

The scheme eventually involved eight 'Dispensary areas': five of them had large urban populations, served by a chief dispensary and two or more branch dispensaries, plus a sanatorium-hospital of up to seventy beds, treating patients near their homes. Each of these large areas was supervised by a consultant tuberculosis officer with one or more assistants and a team of five to seven health visitors. In addition there were three small dispensary areas each centred on a major facility which served a larger part of the County; these were the sanatoria at High Carley near Ulverston, at Elswick on the Fylde, and the hospital for non-pulmonary tuberculosis at Wrightington near Wigan.

This was the scheme as it existed in 1939, but it had taken a long time to develop. Many of the buildings had been delayed by central government refusing financial aid during the national economy measures of the early 1920s, especially between 1922 and 1925. Even before then some members of the Lancashire County Council had objected to building schemes because of the high costs and wage-rates currently in force.

VOLUNTARISM AND THE STATE

The first residential facilities were attached to isolation hospitals. In 1913 the County Council got government permission to lease the newly-built smallpox hospital at Elswick as a sanatorium for forty patients. In 1915 they tried to get a similar arrangement for a proposed smallpox hospital at Orrell near Wigan, but were refused – partly because the site was unsuitable. A tuberculosis sanatorium was added to the isolation hospital at High Carley, and a children's sanatorium (Oubas House) was built close by during the 1920s. Before the First War, Elswick and High Carley were the only sanatoria owned by the County, and County patients had to be sent to a range of voluntary and County Borough institutions. After the war, waiting lists lengthened, partly because of the discharge of tuberculous servicemen, and the County was hard-pressed to provide more accommodation. For the area around Oldham and Rochdale they leased a former smallpox hospital at Chadderton, and built the Wolstenholme Pulmonary Hospital within Rochdale Borough. This latter hospital came to be used for male cases, from the Borough as well as the County district: the Borough Sanatorium took the females. The Withnell Pulmonary Hospital was opened about 1927; it served the districts around Blackburn and Burnley.

If the early 1920s were difficult years in which to gain government grants and expensive years in which to build, they were good years for buying estates cheaply. The 'servant problem' and the state of the national economy forced many rich families to give up their mansions; the collapse of the Lancashire cotton industry was the occasion for many local capitalists to move out of the Region. The houses they left behind were sometimes converted into hospitals. By 1920 Lancashire County had plans for sanatoria at Peel Hall near Bolton, Rufford Hall near Ormskirk, and Wrightington Hall near Chorley. The Peel Hall hospital was opened in 1921, and eventually had fifty-seven beds. Rufford and Wrightington were both delayed by reductions in government expenditure, and in both cases, the first plans were considerably scaled down as Lancashire County tried to get the schemes under way. Rufford was opened in 1926; it came to take fifty-six female cases, males going to Peel Hall. Wrightington, which in 1920 had been projected as a 480 bed hospital was opened in 1931 with 226 beds, including 146 for children with non-pulmonary tuberculosis.[37] By 1939 there were 352 beds. Many of the children who were sent to Wrightington would otherwise have gone to the voluntary orthopaedic hospitals. The hospital at Oswestry in Shropshire begun by Agnes Hunt and Sir Robert Jones, the orthopaedic surgeon, was the best known. Similar rural hospitals had been opened at Leasowe in Cheshire (the Liverpool Open-Air Hospital for Children) and in the Lake District (the Ethel Hedley Hospital). There was also a children's orthopaedic hospital at Marple, near Manchester.[38] They specialised in bone deformities caused by rickets and especially by tuberculosis, and they enjoyed the services of the Region's best orthopaedic surgeons. The support which the Ministry of Health gave to the Wrightington project derived, in large part, from the County's intention to provide a similar highly professional service, which would free the voluntary homes to take more cases from the County Boroughs who had no specialised facilities for these children. Sir Robert Jones was appointed honorary consulting surgeon to Wrightington: his protégés in Liverpool and Manchester, T. Porter McMurray and Harry Platt, were appointed as consultant surgeons. Another well known surgeon, Mr Morriston Davies (of Liverpool), was engaged by the County for thoracic surgery, which was performed at High Carley.

The main lines of the Lancashire scheme were thus established by 1931. Later additions included a pavilion at the Heath Charnock Isolation Hospital, Chorley and one at the new isolation hospital near Lancaster (1934). By 1939 the service supplied one bed for pulmonary tuberculosis for each 2,351 of the population, or ninety-six beds for each 100 pulmonary tuberculosis deaths. The corresponding figures for non-pulmonary beds were one per 7,696 or 121 per 100 deaths.[39]

The Lancashire County service came to be generally recognised as first-class, much better than that provided by the County Boroughs other than Liverpool and Manchester. But by 1939 only Rochdale had made arrangements so that County and Borough accommodation could be shared. In Cheshire, a much smaller county, the County Boroughs and the County Council had formed a Joint Sanatorium Committee in 1912, to collaborate in meeting the requirements of the Act of that year. The Sanatorium they planned was delayed by the war. It was built at Market Drayton in Shropshire, and by 1939 provided 245 beds, much fewer than required. The Boroughs had little additional accommodation so the whole area was chronically short of beds and relied heavily on voluntary institutions.[40]

Hospitals and homes for the citizens of the future
Tuberculosis was one of the two major foci in Edwardian discussions of the nation's health; the other was the mortality and morbidity among children. From the end of the nineteenth century until the 1930s, public attention was repeatedly drawn to evidence that high infant and child mortality and poor domestic environments were producing a citizenry which was inadequate both in numbers and in quality. The supposed degeneracy of England's poorer classes worried the rulers of the Empire, as it worried those more concerned with order in the cities of the motherland. Many doctors, philanthropists and local politicians shared these concerns. And as central government legislated for better medical services, especially for the

inspection of schoolchildren, so more evidence became available to support the case.[41]

Worries about the degeneracy of the urban poor were not new in Lancashire. As we have seen, moral education was the usual prescription in the 1830s. By the 1860s some of the early liberal capitalists were disillusioned and began to suggest that degeneracy was inherited. But for most commentators, better sanitation and, especially, elementary education, would reduce the problem of the urban poor. As experienced public health officials knew, that expectation was fulfilled – the decline in adult mortality rates after mid-century was evidence of a better standard of life. But by the late 1890s the problem of the urban poor had taken on a new guise. The standard of judgement was no longer historical; the lower classes of cities like Manchester were being judged as potential combatants for British imperial power. By that standard, the flat-footed, narrow-chested men from Manchester were grossly inadequate. In 1899, of 11,000 who volunteered for service in the Boer War, only 3,000 were passed as fit to fight, and of them, only 1,000 were thought fit for the line regiments.[42]

> There is no doubt of the degeneracy and deterioration of the masses of our town-bred population. It is saddening to see the pallid, stunted, ill-set up lads and girls, many of them married, streaming out from the factory gates at closing time, and still more saddening to see the puny infants, of perhaps a few months old, with emaciated faces and the weary careworn look of old age, who are brought by their ill-developed mothers to the out-patient rooms of our hospitals. Apart from the pity of it, the prospect of a large proportion of the next generation born of such a stock and living under the conditions at present prevailing in our large towns is a serious one for the nation.[43]

The evidence from recruitment offices was the recurrent reference point among campaigners for a more robust population. One prescription was eugenics, the selective elimination of the unfit by restricting their breeding. As we shall see in the volume on mental health services, such negative eugenics was a popular solution to the problem of the feeble-minded. The Lancashire and Cheshire Association for the Permanent Care of the Feeble-Minded, sought sheltered, separate environments for their charges – partly to protect them, partly to prevent their reproduction.[44]

Very few Lancashire doctors campaigned publicly for eugenics as a general remedy for urban degeneracy. Among those who knew most, the Medical Officers of Health, such remedies were especially suspect, though at least one member of the North Western Association was a keen eugenist. Dr A. W. Martin, from the Manchester township of Gorton, proposed to his colleagues that the sterilising magic of x-rays could be used to prevent the reproduction of degenerates.[45]

HOSPITALS AND WELFARE

James Niven, and most of his fellows took the view that 'degeneracy' was an old problem which would continue to decrease as wage levels rose and the public health effort was extended and diversified. The health of infants and children required attention because the mortality rate at lower ages had remained high whilst that at higher ages fell; indeed the infant mortality rate had risen during the 1890s. General sanitary measures were no longer enough: the remaining problems required special remedies. The reduction of infant mortality, like the suppression of tuberculosis, required doctors and health visitors to visit the homes of the vulnerable, to educate and perhaps to subsidise.

As in the case of tuberculosis, the maternity and child welfare campaign depended more on domiciliary and clinic care than on residential hospitals. But so prominent were these campaigns and so productive of legislation and local authority action, that they substantially affected hospital provision and hospital-based services. In surveying the development of institutional facilities for children and mothers, we shall again be looking at the complex interaction of voluntary, Poor Law and local authority services, and at the growing role of the public health committees in overseeing the health of their districts.

In 1901, the Local Government Board inspector, surveyed the Boards of Guardians asking about their facilities for groups who needed special care away from the main body of the workhouse. Did they have separate accommodation for imbeciles and epileptics; could they offer comfortable accommodation to the aged and deserving; where were the children housed? The Manchester Guardians, since the 1840s, had used their Swinton Schools to house and educate pauper children. The buildings had been models in their day, but by 1900 they were seen as 'barracks schools' and contrasted unfavourably with cottage homes in which an approximation to family life could be created. Such homes had been provided by the Chorlton Guardians, who had built a colony at Styal, to the south of the city. Salford Guardians were about to follow this pattern at Culcheth. Few of the cotton town Unions had rural residential homes, but many had provided cottage homes in the grounds of the workhouse.[46]

Cases of sickness among the pauper children were mostly housed in the wards of Union hospitals, but during the first decade of the new century, the number of indoor paupers rose very rapidly over most of the country and led to severe overcrowding. In South Manchester in 1910 the Withington children's wards were overcrowded as were the wards for tubercular patients. The Guardians were pressing Manchester Corporation to take more consumptives into sanatoria; the workhouse committee wanted to build a 300-bed children's hospital. This latter scheme was referred back, probably because the Guardians were still looking for the merger of the Manchester and South Manchester (Chorlton) Unions which had first been proposed before 1900.[47]

It was in their capacity as education authorities that local councils first began to provide accommodation for children suffering from diseases other than infectious ones. Manchester Education Committee took over Swinton House in 1903 to provide a residential school for children crippled by paralysis, rickets or surgical tuberculosis. The sixty-five beds were medically supervised by the staff of the (voluntary) Royal Manchester Children's Hospital, and some hospital patients were sent to Swinton House to convalesce. But this hospital-school was too small for the demand; by 1919 the Education Committee were complaining to the Ministry that facilities were inadequate for the proper treatment of surgical tuberculosis. The Corporation replied that they were going to build more accommodation at Abergele. By the 1930s this plan had been realised and Swinton House was being used for the treatment of the mysterious pandemic of 'sleepy sickness', encephalitis lethargica.[48]

Similar developments took place in the more progressive cotton towns. Oldham Council opened Castleshaw Residential Sanatorium School in 1916. After the war Oldham developed an orthopaedic clinic, which was visited fortnightly by a specialist, and mainly for children with rickets and surgical tuberculosis. An open-air school was begun in 1936.[49] The main hospital accommodation for non-infectious children's diseases was developed between the wars at Boundary Park hospital. Rochdale too built a children's block (1934) in the municipal hospital.[50]

The major development in hospital provision for Manchester children came after the merger of the Manchester, South Manchester and Prestwich Unions in 1915. The amalgamation was intended to spread costs more equitably and ease relationships between Poor Law and local government by securing common boundaries. It also enabled the Guardians to advance their system of 'classification'.

Prestwich Guardians had built a new infirmary at Booth Hall in 1908. From the beginning of the war it had been used as a military hospital, and in 1915, after amalgamation, it was handed over completely to the War Office, civilian sick cases having been transferred to the workhouse. But in 1916 it was decided to house the soldiers at Withington, and Booth Hall was converted into a children's hospital for the whole Union – the largest children's hospital in the north of England.[51]

Booth Hall Hospital had about 430 beds until a two-storey block of cubicle wards was added in 1927. Most of the patients were medical rather than surgical. In 1920, out of 1775 cases, 366 were tuberculosis, and 131 bronchitis and bronchopneumonia. Next in order of frequency were the infectious diseases, measles 135, chicken pox fifty-six, whooping cough sixty-five, scabies 108, ringworm seventy-nine; eye disease, seventy-five, was probably mostly infectious opthalmia. Over 100 cases of marasmus (extreme emaciation) were admitted, fifty-three of enteritis, forty-one of infantile dyspepsia, and ten of debility. The surgical cases were mostly tuberculosis. Accident cases were not common, in 1920 there were about thirty; most accident cases were taken to general voluntary hospitals. Though Booth Hall was one of the largest children's hospitals in the country, its reputation was poor, at least until it became a municipal hospital in the 1930s. As a Poor Law hospital its patients were the children of the very poor, suffering, largely, from the consequences of their poverty. The average length of stay was long, over ten weeks; 13 per cent of the patients died, and only a third of those discharged were counted as cured rather than relieved.[52]

By contrast, the Royal Manchester Children's Hospital at Pendlebury took far more surgical cases and had a much faster turnover. With only a third of the number of beds at Booth Hall, it took 25 per cent more cases in the year; the average stay was only twenty-four days. Pendlebury did not admit infectious diseases. Booth Hall was left to make a virtue of its plentiful beds. When Pendlebury was performing over 6,000 tonsil and adenoid operations each year, and treating the vast majority of the children as outpatients, Booth Hall was offering tonsillectomy with three days accommodation at an inclusive fee of one guinea. This enabled the child to avoid exposure to infection on a homeward journey an hour or two after surgery. 'This pernicious custom of operating on a child for tonsils and adenoids, and discharging the child an hour or two later, is still in force in some hospitals, and here, certainly, the rate-supported hospitals lead the way in humane and more enlightened methods.'[53]

Of the sanitary indicators most assiduously followed by Edwardian Medical Officers, infant mortality rates were paramount. Nationally they remained persistently high until the war; many towns in Lancashire had rates consistently above the national averages. Manchester and Salford, and towns like Ashton, Preston and Burnley were notorious for the 'annual slaughter of innocents', the summertime deaths of babies. Many possible causes were suggested and investigated. Pail closets, still common in Manchester, seemed to be a feature of many of the areas where infant mortality was highest. Contaminated milk was blamed. But the majority of the Manchester research, carried out under Niven and Delépine, concentrated on the role of house flies as carriers of infection. They were able to show a close correlation in time between epidemic diarrhoea and the number of house flies.[54]

The remedies were threefold; clean milk supplies, better systems for the removal of human and animal manure and, especially, instruction of mothers in the hygienic care of the baby. In Manchester, the Ladies Health Society had long employed working-class women to visit the poor and teach them about hygiene. From 1890, six of the fourteen visitors were paid by the Corporation and Tatham, the Medical Officer, began to supervise the work. In 1905, as concern over infant mortality increased, Miss Eleanor Greg was appointed, under Niven, to superintend the visitors and in 1907, the Council set up an Infant Life Protection Sub-committee which took over the payment and supervision of the whole staff of visitors.

These visitors were sent to tuberculosis cases and also to the mothers of new babies. From 1902 all midwives had to be registered with the local authority and Manchester employed a woman doctor, Dr Margaret Merry Smith, to supervise them, so it was relatively easy to get the names of most of the mothers attended by midwives. Under the 1907 Notification of Births Act, notification of all births could be made compulsory, but this was only enforced in Manchester after 1912.[55]

The voluntary effort was renewed in 1908 when the first local School for Mothers was opened in Ancoats. This, like the associated Mothers' Guild, was a venture begun by the Ladies Health Society; the School for Mothers was modelled on earlier ventures in London and aimed 'to check the high rate of infant mortality by providing meals at low charge to expectant nursing mothers, by general instructions in the care of and feeding of infants, in general hygiene and by other means'. They were now 'helping the child to come into the world healthy and to keep it healthy'. For the most experienced of the women reformers, poverty, not intemperance or thriftlessness was the great difficulty.[56]

The involvement of lady philanthropists and of lady doctors led soon afterwards to a second voluntary initiative – the Duchess of York Hospital for Babies begun in 1914. The medical women of the Manchester region had become more vocal and organised a series of campaigns against their exclusion from hospital posts. In 1910 the Manchester Royal Infirmary Board had refused to admit women to resident posts, and one of the leaders of the campaign was Dr Margaret Merry Smith, the supervisor of Manchester midwives (another was the wife of John Stopford). It was these women doctors who took the initiative to found a hospital for babies, to concentrate on the treatment of diarrhoea, poor nutrition and alimentary disorders. The major financial support came from Miss Margaret Ashton, the chairman of the Maternity and Child Welfare Committee. One of the honorary physicians was Dr Catherine Chisholm, the first woman to have been a medical student in Manchester. By 1919 the hospital committee had raised £10,000 towards the building of a new hospital, but as an interim measure they purchased Cringle Hall, a large family house which would allow a small increase in the bed number – they proposed to put ten cots in the greenhouse for the open-air treatment of rickets. The new Ministry of Health, which had taken over the functions of the Local Government Board, had begun to make money available, to voluntary bodies as well as to local authorities, for maternity and child welfare schemes. When the Babies' Hospital applied for help in adapting Cringle Hall, the Ministry sent doctors to examine the building and the plans. They thought the scheme expensive and refused to put money into a temporary building. As a result, the plans were revised so that Cringle Hall could serve for at least fifteen years. The Ministry then paid half the costs and the interest on the loan. The building fund, now at £15,000 was to be lent as required to the general hospital account.

The Babies' Hospital, in 1930, was heavily dependent on local as well as central authorities. Manchester Corporation maintained thirty of the eighty beds and cots. Various 'Schools for Mothers', some voluntary, others with local authority support, paid for babies to be admitted. The hospital is a good example of the very close relationship between voluntary and statutory bodies which, though it had Victorian precedents, was particularly characteristic of Edwardian reforms.[57]

There were few similar developments outside the city. The most notable was at Burnley, then at the height of its prosperity as a weaving town, but suffering a very high infant mortality rate. From 1893–6 Lady O'Hagan, a member of the major local gentry family, had privately supported the work of two trained midwives. In 1896 that service was taken over by a newly-formed Burnley Obstetrical Society, a group which during the Edwardian period became involved with child welfare clinics. It was this voluntary body which urged the founding of a milk depot and a hospital for mothers and for babies, and in 1916 the Corporation bought Bank Hall, the former home of another gentry family, the Thursbys, which was then in use as a war hospital. In 1919 it was opened as a Maternity and Children's Home. The maternity ward had seven beds, the children's ward twenty-four, and there was a clinic attached. The children admitted were usually in need of care and attention more than medical aid. The only similar local authority hospital seems to have been a maternity home cum babies' hospital on Seedley Terrace which Salford Corporation opened in 1925. Other towns concentrated not on babies' homes but on maternity homes.[58]

Maternity hospitals
The first legislation to involve local authorities in the supervision of childbirth was the Midwives Act of 1902. At this time, the vast majority of confinements were accomplished in the home, as they had always been. Only in cases where the woman had no home or where there were medical grounds

to expect a very difficult birth, was there any likelihood of birth taking place in an institution or hospital.

In most towns in the Region, the only non-domiciliary births took place in Poor Law institutions; many of the mothers were unmarried or deserted. In Edwardian Salford about eighty women per year gave birth in the workhouse. That these were admitted for social rather than medical reasons is underlined by their being dealt with at the workhouse rather than the separate Poor Law hospital (Hope). There was no doctor resident at the workhouse; the births were supervised by midwives. Facilities were limited but clean, and there was little or no puerperal fever. Disreputable though the workhouse was, its labour wards had a good reputation; very occasionally a working man's wife would declare herself deserted in order to gain admission. Where homes were poor and very overcrowded, the chance of a few days' rest, even in the workhouse, must have been attractive.[59]

In Manchester there were Poor Law maternity wards at Crumpsall and Withington hospitals, but because many of the cases were venereal, there was an additional stigma to deter poor women from using these facilities.[60]

General voluntary hospitals took very few maternity cases, and only in Manchester were there hospitals which specialised in obstetrics and gynaecology. The Northern Hospital took a few obstetrical cases, but the main maternity provision was in the St Mary's and Southern Hospitals which amalgamated in 1905, soon after St Mary's had opened its new building on Whitworth Street. Initially this building had forty maternity beds, but this was reduced to twenty, so as to accommodate more gynaecological cases. Only when the High Street hospital (the present St Mary's) was added in 1911 were the maternity facilities expanded to fifty beds. Not until the 1930s did St Mary's have money to provide over a hundred beds. During the Edwardian period, the annual number of maternity in-patients in the amalgamated hospitals did not exceed 700 and was usually less than 500.[61]

For the vast majority of women, childbirth took place in the home and was attended by a midwife. Some paid their general practitioner to attend, some were visited by Poor Law medical officers. In the city, a proportion of mothers were home-patients of St Mary's Hospital. From 1900 to 1910 the number of home-patient deliveries rose from 2,500 to 4,000, a large number compared to the totals of under 1,500 recorded in the mid-1870s, but fewer than were attended in the far smaller city of the 1830s. Following a pattern by then over a century old, St Mary's home-patients were attended only by midwives unless the delivery was difficult, when a doctor was called. In the Edwardian period the doctor on call was a paid, resident obstetrical officer.[62]

The Midwives Act made relatively little difference to this balance of provision. Its chief purpose was to ensure that only the properly trained could qualify as midwives, but unqualified practitioners already in business were allowed to register. In Oldham, of seventy-nine midwives admitted to the register only eighteen were fully trained and twelve or fifteen were entirely illiterate.[63] The Act gave some professional standing to midwives but it also brought them under medical control. It was a contentious Act and Manchester was a major centre of struggle. Some local doctors, organised by the Medical Guild, wanted midwives only as assistants; some local midwives, organised through the Manchester Midwives Association, resented any subjugation of midwifery to medicine. The struggle was bitter here because general practitioners were less secure than London consultants, and because Manchester midwives were more independent than their London leaders.[64]

The Act called for local authority supervision of midwives and also allowed Councils to pay doctors called on to assist the midwives in difficult cases. In most of the towns the midwives were supervised by the Medical Officer of Health; in Manchester the work required a separate officer and this was the appointment of Dr Margaret Merry Smith, whose role in the women-doctors movement and the Manchester Babies' Hospital has already been discussed. Manchester and such Boroughs as Oldham were quick to reinforce the midwifery service by paying doctors for attendance. Indeed Manchester went further and made extra payments for cases of puerperal fever for which a special ward was provided at Monsall isolation hospital.

Though midwives were licensed and supervised by local authorities they continued to be paid by their patients, except when working for the Poor Law or a hospital like St Mary's. Thus childbirth continued to be a major financial burden to all such families as sought qualified attendance. Even at St Mary's patients were expected to make a contribution.[65]

The burden was eased by the 1911 National Insurance Act under which maternity benefits were available for the payment of a midwife or a general practitioner. St Mary's then further reduced its home-patient service, by contracting the boundaries of the district served. It ceased to employ midwives registered by the local authority and closed a hostel for midwives which it had maintained in one of the poorer parts of town. Instead it made all its patients into 'doctors' cases', which in practice meant that they were dealt with by medical students and pupil midwives, more or less under the supervision of the house surgeons. Those who were insured under the National Insurance Act were invited to contribute to hospital funds. In the 1920s the hospital was admitting most of the first-pregnancies as in-patients, and the number of home-patients was little over 1,000 *per annum*. By 1938 home deliveries, at 807, were only a quarter of the total midwifery cases; in 1904 they had been over 90 per cent.[66]

The major reason for this increasing proportion of hospital births was the contemporary preoccupation with the size and quality of the population. When homes were poor, hospital deliveries promised safety, especially for the baby. The Maternity and Child Welfare Act of 1918 increased the supply of beds by making government money available in support of voluntary and local authority schemes for the welfare of mothers and children. By 1938 almost every town in the Region had provided a municipal maternity home or had upgraded the maternity wards in the former Poor Law hospitals.

During the Great War and during the depression which Lancashire experienced so soon afterwards, the easiest way for a town to provide a maternity home was to take over one of the large houses built by the local gentry or industrialists. Many such had been converted to temporary hospitals during the war and there was little demand for them afterwards as the cotton trade began to collapse and the families of philanthropists left the towns they had dominated for decades or more. We have seen that Bank Hall in Burnley, the home of a Tory family which had grown rich on coal, was bought as a maternity home as well as for babies. During the 1930s the children's beds were moved into the ex-Poor Law hospital and Bank Hall became entirely a maternity home. Fern Lea in nearby Nelson was a large family home used as a nurses' residence. In 1919 the local council arranged with its owners and the nursing association to use part of it as a maternity home. The experiment was successful and later the whole house was converted to take ten maternity beds.[67] Similar accommodation was provided at Bolton in 1920 when the Haslam family gave one of their homes to the Borough. Crewe gained Linden Grange in 1921; Blackburn, Springfield in 1923; Accrington, Rough Lea in 1928; Oldham, Green Acres in 1928; Barrow, Risedale in 1930; Wigan, The Firs in 1931, and Ashton, Aspland in 1932.[68]

Maternity homes were also provided by the conversion of other kinds of hospitals. In Colne, the local council took over the voluntary cottage hospital as a maternity home when a rich native of the town, the jam manufacturer William Hartley, provided a new general hospital. The maternity home was named after his daughter Christiana.[69] In Radcliffe, near Bury, a large house given by the Bealey family as a convalescent home for the district was converted after the trustees ran into financial difficulties. It was opened as a maternity home in 1926, the Council justifying their expenditure as a means of reducing the infant mortality rate.[70]

The municipal maternity homes were the major provision in many of the smaller towns and in some of the larger ones. They enabled local authorities to claim that they were active in an important cause, and they enabled many poor women to escape from difficult domestic circumstances for a brief but critical time. Most of them also admitted paying patients under the care of their own general practitioners. This increased their popularity with local doctors and also meant that the hospitals appeared as serving the whole community, at least below the level of those who could pay higher fees for private nursing homes. They were rarely *hospitals*, if that implies a highly technical service; they were maternity *homes*, run by midwives under the supervision of the Medical Officers of Health. They provided an alternative environment for childbirth.

The other method of providing this service was to upgrade Poor Law facilities. In the cities this process was well under way in the 1920s. In the towns, it took place in the 1930s after the Poor Law hospitals had been transferred to municipal control.

In Manchester, the Guardians developed their services considerably following the merger of the three Unions in 1915. After 1921 Withington and Crumpsall, as well as Booth Hall, acquired a list of distinguished visiting specialists as well as the resident medical staff. Both Crumpsall and Withington admitted paying patients treated by their general practitioners, and they were keen to take other patients who were able to pay at least part of their maintenance costs. Some of each group were maternity patients; at Withington they were housed in the same wards as 'assisted cases', at Crumpsall there was a separate maternity ward for private patients, in which six of the sixteen beds were paid for by the Corporation. Patients intending to use this ward were invited to attend ante-natal clinics conducted by the resident medical officer.[71]

In Salford, Hope Hospital had become greatly overcrowded during the 1920s and the Guardians had agreed in 1928 to build a large extension, though they shelved proposals for a separate 200-bed children's hospital. Part of the problem was the rapid increase in the number of maternity cases: in 1926 there were 366 births in Poor Law institutions, over four times the number in 1907. The 250-bed extension was completed in 1931, soon after the hospital was taken over by Salford Corporation. Because of the economic depression the extensions were not opened until 1936, after the hospital had been transferred from the Public Assistance Committee to the Public Health Committee, and the maternity wards were integrated with the local authority midwifery service. This move ended years of overcrowding at Hope, and a decade where the Public Health Committee's only maternity provision was ten beds in Seedley. Hope hospital now had sixty-eight maternity beds, and the Babies' and Maternity Home at Seedley was closed.[72]

The other major developments in municipal general hospitals came at Rochdale and Oldham. In Rochdale a good maternity block with fifty beds was opened at Birch Hill in 1934. In Oldham a similar block was provided in 1940 at Boundary Park Hospital; it had eighty beds and replaced the Greenacres Maternity Home.[73]

By the end of the 1930s, the local authorities were involved in all aspects of maternal and child welfare. After 1937 they could employ midwives as well as supervise them. For mothers who chose to use local authority services the best authorities provided ante-natal and post-natal clinics, domiciliary or hospital midwifery, health visitors and child welfare clinics. But even by the end of the 1930s facilities were very uneven. In Preston, municipal maternity wards (in Sharoe Green) were poor and those who could sought entry to the voluntary hospital. In Bolton there were a hundred beds at Townleys hospital but they were insufficient; the Haslam home was regarded as superior, and further large houses were converted during the war. The municipal homes in Wigan and Ashton, which had not been opened until the 1930s, were much too small to meet the demand. East Manchester was dreadfully short of maternity accommodation. Even in Oldham, where the excellent maternity block in the municipal hospital had eighty beds, this was found insufficient, and twenty-three beds in the main hospital were used for mothers in the second week after childbirth. By this standard, all the Lancashire towns needed more maternity beds.[74]

The growth of maternity institutions was one of the major features of the interwar hospitals. As we have explained, this growth was stimulated and sustained by national concern over population, the focus of which gradually shifted from infant mortality to maternal mortality. This campaign was supported by obstetricians as a means of advancing their specialty, and the voluntary hospitals in which they worked. Consultant obstetricians were less happy about the growing involvement of local authorities who dominated the service outside the city centres. General practitioners, who were generally suspicious of municipal medicine, were ready to support maternity homes because they continued to have access to the patients in them.

But the campaign was not simply a matter of national government or professional interests; it was a popular campaign supported by many women's organisations, especially by the Women's Co-operative Guilds and the women's sections of local Labour parties. In Manchester, as we shall discuss in a later chapter, there was an active Maternal Mortality Committee which brought together women's representatives and local politicians. One of their recurrent demands was for a new maternity hospital in East Manchester.[75]

Yet popular though maternity hospitals were, we should not assume that they were an effective answer to the problem of maternal mortality, nor that this problem, as officially construed, really reflected the difficulties faced by mothers during the interwar depression. The national maternal mortality figures did not decline significantly until the advent of sulphonamide drugs which reduced the fatality of puerperal fever. One of the most effective means of reducing maternal mortality was the better education of general practitioners who had often received very little training in midwifery. It was Dr Andrew Topping, the Medical Officer of Health of Rochdale, who demonstrated between 1930 and 1934 how much the mortality rates could be lowered by systematically educating the doctors along with midwives and mothers-to-be. But his example was rarely followed inside or outside the Region.[76]

'National mortality' was a technical, statistical way of representing a diffuse socio-economic problem. The death of mothers and of babies was, of course, in part preventible by improved obstetrical techniques and by the provision of a clean, warm environment. But much depended on the general health of the mother which depended to a large degree on the income of the family and the number of children she had borne. While the state, through local authorities, was providing maternity homes, it had excluded married women from the medical coverage of the National Insurance Act, and in 1932 the unemployment benefit paid to married women was reduced. In the homes of Lancashire, as generally in working-class homes, the mother took what was left when the husband and children had eaten. It is not surprising that in many towns, notably Preston, the maternal mortality rate was much higher in the 1930s than it had been at the end of the war.

State attention to 'maternal mortality' offered little relief to working-class mothers, but it did affect attitudes to childbirth. As Elizabeth Roberts had noted in her studies of Barrow and Preston, mothers grew less fatalistic about childbirth; 'Both husband and wives in the 1920s and 1930s (unlike their parents' generation) regarded confinements rather less as an inevitable, frequent and natural occurrence to be borne stoically, and rather more as a time of crisis for which all possible help needed to be sought.'[77]

One way to minimise the risk was to reduce the number of pregnancies, but, except in very exceptional circumstances, neither the state nor the medical profession had any interest in teaching women how to limit the size of their families. The women who campaigned to reduce maternal mortality avoided discussion of birth control, and local authority clinics did not give advice on family planning. The Salford Birth Control Clinic, set up in 1926 – the first in the Region, attracted much hostile publicity, and confined itself to advising mothers whose physical health would be severely threatened by pregnancy. About eight years earlier Mr H. V. Roe, who was later to marry Marie Stopes, had offered to fund a birth control clinic at St Mary's Hospital; the offer had been refused.[78]

VOLUNTARISM AND THE STATE

Notes and references

1. The widespread interest in sick paupers was aroused by philanthropic London ladies and by Poor Law doctors. It constituted part of a general re-evaluation of hospitals as public spaces for the restoration of health. See B. Abel-Smith, *The Hospitals, 1800–1948*, London, 1964; and G. M. Ayers, *England's First State Hospitals and the Metropolitan Asylums Board 1867–1930*, London, 1971. Also see the recent M. A. Crowther, *The Workhouse System, 1834–1929*, London, 1981 and 1983, Ch. 7.
2. 'The Workhouse' notes from Macclesfield written about 1886; also MH 12/981 & 982.
3. Report of Guardians' meeting, *Salford Weekly News*, 6 May 1876; Proceedings of Salford Guardians 1878–80; Report of the Royal Commission on the Poor Laws and Relief of Distress (1909), Appendix, vol. XIX, pp. 39–52, 289–94; *The Hospital*, 4, 18 December 1909, 29 January 1910; 'Hope Hospital' typescript notes from the hospital, written in the mid-1970s.
4. Oldham Directory 1895; *British Medical Journal*, 2 February 1895.
5. *British Medical Journal*, 24 November 1894, 12 January 1895.
6. W. Bennett, *The History of Burnley from 1850*, III, Burnley, 1951, pp. 43–4; Angela James and Nina Hills (eds), *Mrs John Brown, 1847–1935*, London, 1937; John Banks, 'Over a hundred years: the story of the local hospitals in North East Lancashire (1876–1976)', typescript, Burnley Library, (1976?); House of Commons Sessional Papers 365 (1891).
7. *British Medical Journal*, 6 October 1894.
8. On Rhodes, *Manchester Evening News*, 27 September 1909; On Withington, Evidence of Dr Rhodes to the Departmental Committee on Nursing of the Sick Poor in Workhouses (1902) Pt. II, 46–50 (Cmd 1366), quote, p. 49. On Poor Law nursing see C. Maggs, *The Origins of General Nursing*, London, 1982.
9. Nursing of Sick Poor in Workhouses (1902), Pt. II, pp. 84–6.
10. Reports of meetings of Bolton Guardians, *Daily Chronicle*, especially 18 December 1895 (quote), and 22 June 1898.
11. Bolton Guardians, March–August 1899, especially 2 March 1899. On LGB reports and loans see MH 12/5650–2.
12. MH 48/307, Conference notes 1892. *Hospital Survey (North Western)*, 1945.
13. The Medical Relief (Disqualification Removal) Act restored the vote in all but Poor Law elections.
14. On Poor Law medicine see R. Hodgkinson, *The Origins of the National Health Service*, London, 1967; and J. L. Brand, *Doctors and the State; The British Medical Profession and Government Action in Public Health 1870–1912*, Baltimore, 1965.
15. See Chapter 8.
16. S. and B. Webb, *English Poor Law Policy*, London (Cass Reprint), 1963.
17. Poor Law Commission (1909), Appendix IV, pp. 99–111.
18. *Ibid.*, pp. 56–62.
19. *Ibid.*, p. 38.
20. *Ibid.*, p. 54.
21. *Ibid.*, p. 121.
22. *Ibid.*, p. 45.
23. *Ibid.*, pp. 136–7.
24. Manchester Royal Infirmary Annual Reports.
25. Statistics from the Decennial Supplement of the Registrar General's Reports. I am indebted to Marilyn Pooley for data on Manchester mortality rates.
26. Evidence of J. Niven to Poor Law Commission (1909), Appendix IV, p. 128.
27. Annual Reports.
28. The tuberculosis services were described in J. Niven's *Annual Reports of the Medical Officer of Health for Manchester*; summarised in his *Observations on the History of Public Health Effort in Manchester*, Manchester, 1923.

29. Annual Reports; *British Medical Journal*, 19 July 1902; 'W.J. Gros Crossley' in *Manchester Faces & Places*, 1902–3, and obituary in *Proceedings of the Manchester Literary & Philosophical Society*, 1911–12; Report of the Medical Officer for 1905–6 on Sanatoria for Consumption ..., 35th Annual Report of the Local Government Board, 1905–6 (Cd 3105, xxxv. 1), pp. 275–7, 348–57.
30. MH 52/341.
31. MH 52/346.
32. MH 52/341.
33. Report on Sanatoria, 1905–6, pp. 490–4, 514–15.
34. MH 48/193 and Annual Reports of the Medical Officer of Health for Bolton.
35. J. T. Chalmers Keddie, 'The public health service' in *Oldham Centenary, A History of Local Government*, Oldham, 1949. *Hospital Survey (North Western)*, 1945.
36. J. D. Marshall, ed., *The History of Lancashire County Council 1889 to 1974*, London, 1977, p. 92; Annual Reports of Central Tuberculosis Officer of the Lancashire County Council, e.g. for 1927; H. F. Hughes, 'The economics and administrative arrangements of statutory and voluntary anti-tuberculosis measures at home and abroad', unpublished thesis, Manchester University, 1936.
37. MH 52/75–77 (Peel), 77–8 (Rufford), 79–81 (Wrightington).
38. *Hospital Survey, The Hospital Services of the North-Western Area*, Ministry of Health, 1945, p. 92.
39. *Ibid.*, p. 89.
40. *Ibid.*, pp. 92–3; MH 48/436.
41. Jane Lewis, *The Politics of Motherhood*, London, 1980; Anna Davin, 'Imperialism and motherhood', *History Workshop Journal*, 5 (1978).
42. G. Searle, *The Search for National Efficiency*, Oxford, 1971; *Eugenics and Politics in Britain 1900–14*, Leyden, 1976; *Lancet*, 10 May 1902, p. 1361; 24 February 1900, p. 578.
43. *Lancet*, 20 October 1900, p. 1167.
44. See Searle, *Eugenics*; our forthcoming volume on Mental Hospital Services; and the forthcoming book by David Barker (Department of Social Administration, Manchester University) on Edwardian policies for the feeble-minded.
45. A. W. Martin, 'The elimination of the unfit by the state, the evolution of a higher race and a third sex', *Public Health*, October 1907, 35–45. On Martin, see E. Sylvia Pankhurst, *The Suffragette Movement*, London, 1931, reprinted 1977, p. 129.
46. *Lancet*, 26 January 1901, p. 286; D. M. Jones, 'Local government policy towards the infant and child, with particular reference to the North West, 1890–1914', MA thesis, Manchester University, 1983.
47. *Lancet*, 10 December 1910, p. 1728; 12 November 1910, p. 1448; 2 June 1900, p. 1615.
48. Manchester Education Committee Annual Reports 1908–9; MH 52/341; Emrys L. Jones, *Manchester's Health*, Manchester Labour Party, Municipal Pamphlet no. 1, (1930?), p. 9.
49. Oldham, *Centenary History*, pp. 38–9.
50. *Hospital Survey (North Western)*, pp. 60–2.
51. Manchester Board of Guardians Annual Reports 1914–17.
52. Manchester Union, Annual Reports, esp. 1920.
53. Royal Manchester Children's Hospital Annual Reports; *Poor Law Officers Journal*, 1924, p. 7.
54. For example, the Supplement to Forty-Second Annual Report of the Local Government Board: Second Annual Report on Infant & Child Mortality (1912–13) lists the twenty-five towns in England and Wales showing the highest infant mortality rates. The first five were all in Lancashire: Stalybridge, 189 deaths per 1,000 births, Ince in Makerfield 185, Burnley 171, Farnworth and Ashton 164. Also see Niven, *Public Health Effort*, pp. 69–77.
55. See Niven, *Public Health Effort*, and Sheena Simon, *A Century of City Government, Manchester 1838–1938*, London, 1938, pp. 209–11.

56. *Lancet*, 4 June 1910, p. 1590.
57. Manchester Babies' Hospital Annual Reports 1914–1919; typescript history, 1934 (Manchester Medical Collection; MH 52/328).
58. Bennett, *History of Burnley*, *4*, p. 201; Salford Council Proceedings, 3 February 1926.
59. Dr McVail, Report on Salford Union, Appendix XVII, p. 290, Poor Law Commission (1909).
60. Manchester Board of Guardians Annual Reports, e.g. 1920.
61. St Mary's Annual Reports.
62. *Ibid.*
63. Oldham, *Centenary History*, p. 41.
64. Jean Donnison, *Midwives and Medical Men*, New York, 1977, esp. Chapter 7; *Lancet*, 13 March 1897, p. 723; The 'midwife' question was well ventilated in the *Manchester Medical Guild Quarterly*.
65. *Lancet*, 18 February 1905, p. 462; Evidence of Dr Niven to Poor Law Commission (1909), especially Appendix VI (E); Manchester Medical Officer of Health Annual Reports.
66. J. H. Young, *St. Mary's Hospitals Manchester, 1790–1963*, Edinburgh, 1964, pp. 89–95.
67. Bennett, *History of Burnley*, *4*, 201; Banks, 'Over a hundred years'.
68. Dates mostly from MOH reports.
69. Banks, 'Over a hundred years'.
70. Bury & Rossendale Hospital Management Committee, *Bury & Rossendale Hospital Group* (Report), 1974.
71. Anonymous pamphlet, 'Booth Hall, Crumpsall & Withington Hospitals', reprinted from the *Poor Law Officers Journal* (1924).
72. MH 52/360 esp. September and November 1934; Salford Board of Guardians Minutes; Hospital Sub-Committee Minutes 1930–6 esp. July 1933, December 1935, April 1936.
73. *Hospital Survey (North Western)*, pp. 60–4.
74. *Ibid.*
75. Judith Emanuel, 'The politics of maternity in Manchester (1919–1939), a study from within a continuing campaign', unpublished MSc thesis (Community Medicine), Manchester University, 1982.
76. A. Topping, 'Maternal mortality and public opinion', *Public Health*, *49* (1936), 342–9; Lewis, *Motherhood*, 152–3.
77. Elizabeth Roberts, 'Oral history investigation of disease and its management by the Lancashire working class 1890–1939', in J. V. Pickstone (ed.), *Health, Disease and Medicine in Lancashire 1750–1950*, Department of History of Science & Technology, UMIST, Manchester, 1980, pp. 33–51, esp. 43–4.
78. Young, *St. Mary's*, 90; Ruth Hall, *Marie Stopes*, London, 1978; Emanuel, MSc thesis (1982).

CHAPTER 11

The pattern of hospital services in the 1930s

Introduction
In the last three chapters we have described the formation and development of the three types of hospitals which made up the hospital service of the inter-war years: the infectious diseases hospitals, largely for children; the voluntary hospitals, increasingly dominated by specialists and surgeons; and the municipal hospitals, inherited from the Poor Law or developed under the welfare legislation of the early twentieth century. The vast majority of the hospitals which the National Health Service was to inherit in 1948 as the basis for a single hospital system, were already in place by the early 1920s. Development between the wars was limited, not least by the collapse of the cotton industry and the more general economic depression which followed.

The subject matter of these earlier chapters has already been extended, as appropriate, into the inter-war period. In this chapter we shall stress pattern more than development. We shall survey the hospitals of the Region mainly to see how they related to each other, within the city, within the towns, and to a growing extent, between the city and the towns.

The voluntary hospitals
At the end of the First World War, the Manchester voluntary hospitals had serious financial difficulties. In 1922, the only hospitals which showed an appreciable surplus on ordinary income and expenditure were the Babies' Hospital and the Hospital for Skin Diseases, both of which were largely supported by public funds. The Royal Infirmary showed a loss of about 10 per cent on its gross expenditure – the deficit would have been 20 per cent but for a grant from the Voluntary Hospital Commission. Overall, the voluntary hospitals and Dispensaries in the city showed a net deficit of £15,847 out of a gross expenditure of £289,043.[1]

For several years the deficits did not decrease in spite of warnings that without generous support the voluntary system would break down: 'If the answer is in the negative ... most surely the institutions will become either State or Municipal institutions, with all the objections to which such institutions are liable.'[2] But the system did not collapse: by 1930 the Manchester voluntary hospitals as a whole were showing a surplus on gross balance, though the ordinary accounts were still in deficit. Ordinary income rose during the late twenties to reach 94 per cent of ordinary expenditure in 1929; by 1933, economic depression had brought the figure to 81 per cent around which it stuck until the outbreak of the Second World War. Thus, though the hospitals entered the Second War, as they had left the First, in considerable financial difficulties, the relatively easy period in the late twenties had enabled the system to survive. As the traditional support through subscription and donation became inadequate, other sources of funds were increasingly exploited.

Table 3   Income of Manchester voluntary hospitals, 1922–38

	1922		1930		1938	
Total income (£ thousand)	261		447		494	
	Income	% of total	Income	% of total	Income	% of total
Investment	51	20	63	14	52	11
Donations & legacies	42	16	115	25	116	23
Annual subscriptions	55	21	72	16	77	16
Sunday Fund, Alexandra Day, etc.	12	5	16	4	10	2
Saturday Fund Workmen's Collections	9	3	27	6	47	10
Patients payments inc. approved societies	40	15	58	13	116	24
Public authorities (in respect of patients)	35	13	32	7	36	7

Source: Reports of the Local Voluntary Hospitals Committee, 1922–38.

Table 3 shows how the income of the Manchester hospitals changed over the inter-war years. While total income rose by 80 per cent, support from public funds did not increase nor did contributions from the hospital charities; donations only kept pace with rising expenditure. Most significantly, patients' contributions rose rapidly and so did the workmen's contribution schemes, organised by the Hospital Saturday Fund. By 1938, one-third of the hospital income came from the patients, in direct payment or through insurance schemes. Thus, the increased expenditure of hospitals during the thirties was financed by the patients themselves rather than by the traditional sources of charity.[3] Outside Manchester the dependence on workpeople's contributions was ever greater.

The expansion of the voluntary hospital service between the wars was, however, limited, partly because the whole Manchester Region was severely damaged by the rapid decline of the cotton industry. The textile towns were hit harder than the city; depression began in the mid-twenties, and recovery was very limited until World War II, especially in those towns like Oldham which depended on the kind of coarse spinning which was developed most rapidly by Lancashire's foreign competitors. This decline of cotton hastened the departure of many of the major textile families, a drain of capital away from Lancashire that could no longer be counteracted by the growth of smaller textile firms.[4] More than ever, the voluntary hospitals came to depend on the workpeople's contribution schemes and, to some extent, on government or local authority payments.

Only one large voluntary hospital was built in the Manchester Region between the wars. Appropriately it was, at Blackpool, the major resort and retirement centre of the Region, which had grown very rapidly in the late nineteenth century and which continued to grow in the early decades of the twentieth century, when the population in the cotton towns had stabilised. One of the few new inter-war cottage hospitals was close to Blackpool, in St Anne's (1922).

Nelson, a weaving town near Burnley, shared with Blackpool a history of very rapid growth in the late nineteenth century. The Reedyford (cottage) hospital opened there in 1920 as a war memorial and enjoyed the support of an extensive fund-raising machinery. The only other new cottage hospitals were in the suburbs of Manchester, catering to the increasing middle-class demand for hospital treatment: Stretford hospital opened in 1931.

For the rest, the history of voluntary hospitals between the wars was mostly a succession of extensions on increasingly crowded sites, new ward blocks or new facilities usually paid for by special appeals, bazaars, fund-raising concerts, etc. Few foundations could afford to build on a new site, like the Chorley hospital in 1933; but Chorley was in west Lancashire and not so dependent upon cotton as many small towns.[5]

Perhaps we can get some feel for the progress of a relatively prosperous hospital by looking at Preston Royal Infirmary, examining not only the work done, but the attitude of its major supporters.

The Chairman of the Infirmary Board from 1924 to the time of his death in 1937 was Mr Alex Foster, from the third generation of an important cotton family. His grandfather had joined with Daniel Arkwright, a relative of Sir Richard, in building the Arkwright mill. Alex Foster had joined the firm in 1888, after education at Preston Grammar School and a semi-public school at Penrith, and he had soon become a director. He was a convinced Liberal free-trader; he withdrew his interest in the party 'over Lloyd George'. Though never himself engaged in local government, he maintained close contact, partly through the annual dinner which he gave for the Mayor and the council. He was a keen supporter of the voluntary principle: maintaining that an Infirmary such as Preston's was run much more efficiently than it would be in public hands.[6]

Foster's conviction depended upon the enthusiastic support which the Infirmary received from the people of Preston. The maintenance and increase of that support was the life work of John Gibson, appointed as full-time secretary of the Infirmary in 1914, a post he retained until the introduction of the NHS, when he became Group Secretary. Gibson had scarcely turned thirty when he joined Preston Infirmary. Previously he had been secretary to the YMCA in Kendal; both jobs were 'works of practical Christianity'. By organising charitable 'efforts' and by pleading the Infirmary's cause, Gibson managed not only to maintain and enlarge the Infirmary services, but to build up a very large capital fund.[7]

We might reasonably regard Foster as a remnant of the textile plutocracy; Gibson as a semi-professional member of the Anglican middle-class, devoted to prestigious good works. Behind them, and increasingly important to the financial success of the hospital, was Councillor R.C. Handley, Mayor of Preston in 1935, long-time chairman of the Work-people's Fund.

The Fund had begun in 1919 when, at a public meeting to consider proposals for a war memorial, the question of the Infirmary's financial difficulties was raised. Considerable enthusiasm was shown for a system of mass contribution. Initially each man who entered the scheme agreed with his employer that 1*d* per week should be stopped out of his wages. In 1921, a year of very poor trade, the contribution was raised to 2*d*, which also covered the workman's family.

So far as the Infirmary work was concerned, Handley was only one of a team which 'thought Infirmary, talked Infirmary and lived Infirmary, to succeed in its efforts'. Such an attitude was not uncommon among the leaders of working-class good-causes. 'We have just lived ordinary lives, working in the interests of others. We do not want to be regarded as anything better or worse than ordinary working people.'[8] For most of the workmen who contributed their weekly 2*d*, the fund was a useful insurance. For its leaders, the fund for which they gave much of their spare time, was a moral campaign and a source of civic pride.

The work of the hospital expanded enormously between the wars. The number of in-patients per year rose from 2,000 in 1918 to 7,000 by 1938, the number of out-patients from about 5,600 to 36,500; the surgical operations on in-patients from just less than a thousand per year to 2,600 per year. With this rise in the in-patient load, and the increased separation of the technical task of the hospital from that of the general practitioner, the home-patient visiting service declined even further; the 200 home-patients per year of the First World War fell to less than twenty per year by the beginning of the Second War.[9]

The special services continued to increase in number: an electro-massage department was begun in 1922; a light department for ultra-violet radiation therapy was opened in 1926 by Professor Leonard Hill of the National Institute for Medical Research. In 1933 a radium department was begun.

Besides these special departments, the general growth of the hospital continued. New wards or blocks were opened in 1921, 1925, 1936 and 1938; large houses were acquired and turned into convalescent homes in 1922 (Lostock Hall) and 1928 (The Willows). The hospital began an orthopaedic department in 1934 and an obstetrical department when the maternity wards were opened in 1936.[10]

The increased finance came chiefly from the increase of workpeople's contributions, which more than doubled between 1921 and 1938, while the annual subscriptions and the contributions from public authorities decreased by about 50 per cent. By 1938, workpeople's contributions paid for over half of the hospital expenses; payments from non-fund patients added another one-sixth. In 1938 the Infirmary's income was 12 per cent higher than its expenditure. When most hospitals were in financial difficulties, Preston was very comfortably off, thanks largely to the Workpeople's Fund.[11]

As one might expect, many hospitals which had not developed full specialist services, had also been slow to increase their bed space. Oldham, Rochdale, Bury and Bolton all had about one voluntary bed for each thousand people in the catchment area of the hospital, well below the national average of 1.4. In Preston, the comparable figure was 2.3; 1.4 in Blackpool; 1.2 – 1.3 in Blackburn and Burnley and Salford. But the smaller towns, in the north of the Region, were also well-provided with voluntary beds: 2.3/1,000 in relatively affluent Lancaster and Kendal and, more surprisingly 2.1 in industrial Barrow. If the Barrow figure seems anomalously high, then that of Stockport is peculiarly low; in spite of Stockport Infirmary's large range of specialists, it provided only 0.6 beds per 1,000 population, by a considerable margin the lowest figure in the Region (1938).[12]

The resolution of these anomalies can probably be sought in the economics of the voluntary hospital. The ability to expand and maintain a relatively large number of beds depended in part on the wealth of the neighbourhood, (private subscribers and benefactors); in part upon the success of the workmen's contribution schemes. It is likely that in north Lancashire, away from the major concentration of specialists, the former factor predominated at Lancaster and Kendal, the latter at Barrow. In the cotton towns, a go-ahead committee was a necessary condition of large scale support from the workpeople, support which was more likely to be forthcoming if a full specialist service could be offered. However, in areas containing a relatively high proportion of remunerative patients, e.g., south Manchester and north Cheshire, specialists would be ready to attend relatively small voluntary hospitals, in order to maintain good relationships with the local populace and especially the general practitioners. Hence Stockport Infirmary attracted Manchester specialists though it had not been particularly successful in projecting itself to work-people. This explanation also accounts for the relatively high proportion of Stockport Infirmary's income which came from patients' payments: 24 per cent, twice as high as most hospitals in the Region.

The Poor Law infirmaries
At the time of the First World War most Poor Law infirmaries were filled with chronic cases and an increasing number of acute medical cases. By the beginning of the Second World War, these infirmaries were the major hospital service in several Lancashire towns, though in other towns, their role had changed very little. Two major factors determined the degree of development: the effectiveness of the voluntary hospitals in meeting the increased demand for hospital services and the enthusiasm of the town council in taking charge of and developing the former Poor Law premises.

The Manchester authorities, not surprisingly, were pace-setters in the development of public hospitals. As we have seen, they began in 1915 with the considerable advantages that accrued from the merging of the Chorlton, Prestwich and Manchester Unions. This merger gave them enormous resources and the possibility of assigning hospitals to particular purposes. As a result, all three hospitals developed specialist services and gradually took on more and more acute cases, including an increasing amount of surgery.

The hospitals were reasonably modern and spacious. Withington, in south Manchester, was made up of pavilions which occupied a large site adjoining the workhouse proper. At Crumpsall, in north Manchester, the buildings were not so well designed, though newer, but the site was good. Booth Hall, the children's hospital has been recently built (1910). Well designed for 564 beds, it had been 'rearranged' to accommodate 750 beds, a degree of overcrowding which continued to the Second World War.

In 1920, the admissions at Booth Hall Hospital totalled 1,368, with average stay of 79.5 days. By 1924 the admissions had almost doubled (2,651), the duration of stay had fallen to 52.2 days, and the average number of occupied beds had risen by about 25 per cent.

[256]

Even so, as the national debate over the Poor Law continued, the Guardians of the Manchester Union were on the defensive. A pamphlet of 1924 claimed high standards for the Manchester hospitals; Booth Hall was a mainstay of their case. So too was the high professional repute of the consultant staff, many of whom also held honorary appointments at the Royal Infirmary and the better voluntary hospitals in the city. Since the war the consultant staff had been increased by the appointment of a Union pathologist, and an oto-laryngologist also a second gynaecologist, a second radiologist, a second child specialist, additional dentists, and a third visiting surgeon.[13]

Between 1924 and 1929 specialists in orthopaedics and dermatology were added, and facilities for x-ray, electrical therapy, heliotherapy and massage were extended to all three hospitals. A report of 1929 claimed that almost 9,000 patients, i.e. about one-third of the total in-patients, were seen during the year by the various specialists. Though the range of specialists was still narrower than had been found at Ancoats hospital in 1923 – neurology, cardiology and genito-urinary surgery were not differentiated – it compared favourably with the range in voluntary hospitals outside Manchester.[14]

The difference between the public and voluntary hospitals of the city now lay more in the organisation of medical care than in the range of specialists. To follow a small voluntary hospital like Ancoats in its post-war development was to see a great deal of professional initiative directed at a small (110 beds) hospital in the middle of a packed mass of poor housing. One sees the aspiring consultants of Manchester drawing on this crush of humanity to develop their own departments; Harry Platt setting up a special fracture service is an obvious example. Platt would attend three mornings a week, as a rising consultant specialising in orthopaedics; then as the head of a two-man, then a three-man department. His registrar, E. Stanley Brentnall, took over the orthopaedics department when Platt was appointed to the Manchester Royal Infirmary. Similar patterns can be seen in the ENT department. The consultant staff was well known locally; patients were attracted from a wider area, and the resident staff was large enough to give close care to the patients of each department. In 1923, there were five resident staff under nineteen active honorary staff, for 120 beds. By 1931 six residents served under twenty-four active honorary staff, giving a resident:bed ratio of twenty.[15]

By contrast, in 1920, the three Poor Law hospitals together were paying the equivalent of ten full-time residents; by 1929 when each had about eight residents, the overall bed:resident ratio was still above 160. Unlike the Ancoats residents, these doctors resident in public hospitals were directly responsible for the patients. The visiting staff of the public hospitals, always much smaller than that of the voluntary hospitals, was there in a consultant capacity only. Primary responsibility lay with the overworked resident.

Such then was the divide between the hospitals of the city: the Manchester Royal Infirmary represented the advancing edge of medicine. Several smaller voluntary hospitals served as stepping stones to the Infirmary, linked to it by the promotion of staff. Together these hospitals were the arenas of the consultants, the aspiring specialists, the university teachers. The total number of patients treated was rising slowly, the quality of medicine rapidly.

The large public hospitals were much closer to general practice. They continued to be, primarily, a refuge for the sick poor, who, while in hospital received care from the resident staff: institutional practitioners, or recent graduates. Consultants were called in as required, as they might be by a workman's 'panel doctor'. The hospitals were much pleasanter places in 1930 than they had been in 1870. They served a wider section of the community. They might even be regarded as 'A paradise for sick old ladies'; but they were institutions of public service rather than instruments of medical treatment. There is evidence that Booth Hall was unpopular among parents.[16]

The connection with general rather than specialist medicine was underlined by the development of paying blocks within the public hospitals. After 1922 patients with the means could enter separate sections of Crumpsall or Withington, where they could be treated by their own general practitioner. These patients were not poor but they could not afford the fees for nursing homes, or to have nursing care in their own homes.[17]

The Guardians' hold on the Poor Law hospitals lasted until 1929 when the Local Government Act which was introduced by Neville Chamberlain, allowed for division of their powers between the Public Health Committees and the Public Assistance Committees of local authorities. The Manchester Public Health Committee quickly took over the Poor Law hospitals. They also took over the management of the Institutions, the workhouses proper, which were now the responsibility of the Public Assistance Committee. These Institutions at Withington and Crumpsall contained about 3,200 beds, those at Withington being used exclusively for the infirm.[18]

The Public Health Committee had become steadily more enterprising as the tired municipal politics of the late nineteenth century had been reinvigorated by the influx of labour councillors. They knew, at first hand, the continuing wastage through suffering and death which was characteristic of the poorer areas of the city.[19] The chairman of the Public Health Committee, R.G. Edwards, was a liberal, and a pharmacist by trade. He was not an orator but he was exceedingly good in committee. During the thirties he devoted an enormous amount of energy to the cause of public health.

HOSPITAL SERVICES IN THE 1930s

Dr Veitch Clark, the Medical Officer of Health, was efficient and imaginative. Under his leadership the Public Health Committee had proposed a series of improvements in health care; sunlight treatment, family planning, massage treatment, an extended scheme for tuberculosis, increases in maternity and infant welfare expenditure, further increases in public health. Though several of these schemes were designed to take advantage to Ministry grants, others had exceeded the Ministry's offers and throughout the twenties the Ministry had refused to provide extra money.[20]

The hospitals transferred to the Council in 1930 included 4,790 beds, over four times as many as the Council already possessed in its fever hospitals, and over twice as many as were available in voluntary hospitals serving Manchester. Since Withington Infirmary had been begun in the 1860s the number of hospital beds in public institutions had grown way beyond the capacity of the voluntary system. The workhouse infirmaries had come to play a very large role in the hospital services and the Manchester Guardians had been regarded as national leaders in hospital provision. Now, for the first time these hospitals were under the direct control of the City Council.

The private hospital wings continued as general practitioner units. They were developed during the thirties under encouragement from the BMA and from such professional bodies as the Association of Assistant Schoolmistresses, which were able to secure reasonably priced accommodation to serve their insurance schemes.

In April 1935 the private block of Withington Hospital was closed for modernisation. It re-opened under a new name. Despite the protests of labour councillors the 'Nell Lane Auxiliary Hospital' became the 'Hospital for Private Patients', and the Council began to wonder how the private accommodation at Crumpsall could suitably be distinguished.[21] At about the same time the town planning committee was considering the Royal Infirmary's scheme for a Private Patients Hospital. This was opened in 1937 by Lord Dawson of Penn. As charitable and public services were being constrained by private and public economies, commercial medicine was invading the hospital field.[22]

The other wards in the municipal hospitals continued for several years without radical change, but not without plans for change. The city wished to upgrade its hospitals, and that meant adopting those features of voluntary hospital practice which were prestigious and regarded as advanced. Essentially, upgrading, in terms of staff, meant the extension of specialist responsibility within these hospitals. Withington and Crumpsall were to follow the example of the Manchester Royal Infirmary, Salford Royal Infirmary, Ancoats, etc. This confluence of medical structure, spanning the diversity of funding procedures, was fundamental to hospital co-ordination in the late thirties in Manchester; as throughout the whole Region in the 1940s. It was the basis of the work of the Manchester, Salford and Stretford Joint Hospital Board, begun in 1935; that is the subject of a later chapter.

Outside Manchester itself the development of former Poor Law hospitals varied enormously from town to town. The majority of rural institutions were simply transferred to the Public Assistance Committees of Lancashire or Cheshire County Councils and remained as low-grade accommodation for the chronic sick: Public Assistance Institutions at Kendal, Northwich, and Knutsford, provide examples. Several slightly better institutions were distinguished by having small maternity units which were much in demand; Chorley Public Assistance Institution was one such, Moorlands Public Assistance Institution at Rawtenstall, another. In these small towns there were no other maternity beds.

Because the majority of institutions taken over by the County Councils were small and inadequate for the sick, few were appropriated as hospitals under the health committees. Cheshire earmarked the West Park County Hospital at Macclesfield, which had a good site, and they intended to develop it as a general hospital to serve most of east Cheshire, but little was effected before the Second War. Lancashire County Council, in spite of its huge area and large population, had only three general hospitals remotely worthy of the name: Park Hospital in Davyhulme, Manchester, Lake Hospital at Ashton-under-Lyne and the former Whiston Institution near Prescot in the Liverpool Region. Both Davyhulme and Ashton were in dense urban areas which had never been made into County Boroughs. As far as the County was concerned, Park Hospital was a fortunate, if poorly-planned inheritance. It was the Region's only Poor Law infirmary built between the wars; it had opened in 1928, just before the Boards of Guardians passed out of existence. Without this hospital the County service would have been even more dependent than it was on hospital beds in the County Boroughs. Park Hospital could be used when Boroughs were unco-operative and the local voluntary hospitals were overcrowded: during the 1930s patients from County areas outside Barrow-in-Furness were being sent eighty miles to Davyhulme to find general hospital beds. Because it had been built as a general hospital and because it was the mainstay of the County service, Park Hospital was developed with an extensive team of visiting consultants.

Of the County Boroughs in the Region, only Bury failed to inherit a Poor Law infirmary. The Jericho hospital was situated in Bury and served its citizens, but it came under the administration of Lancashire County Council, as a Public Assistance Institution. It remained an unpopular place, the overcrowded infirmary scarcely separated from the 'house'. The only evidence of upgrading was the appointment of a visiting obstetrician who took charge of thirty-eight maternity beds. The only other medical staff were two part-time general practitioners.

A similar staffing arrangement prevailed at Wigan, in spite of the fact that Wigan, not the County, came to own the Billinge hospital, and that this hospital had a good, if remote, site, well away from the former workhouse.

The Medical Officer of Health of Wigan had tried repeatedly to persuade the Council to develop Billinge as a general hospital under the Health Committee but nothing was accomplished, for the problem could not be solved without considerable expenditure. Whereas in many towns, the old workhouse was just about suitable for the accommodation of the chronic sick and mental cases, Wigan's Frog Lane Institution was quite unfit for anyone not in the best of health. Though the Wigan Guardians had once intended that all the institutional as well as hospital accommodation would be provided at Billinge, they had only erected a hospital. This accommodation could not be used for its intended purpose because it had to be used for the mental and chronic cases that no humane medical men could consign to Frog Lane. Except for a few maternity cases and occasional medical emergencies, these long-stay patients made up the work-load of the Billinge Hospital in 1932. By 1939 a tragic situation had become worse. As demands for medical beds increased, some chronic cases were displaced from Billinge; this, together with the increased demand for chronic accommodation meant that the nursing staff at Frog Lane had to be increased and those grossly unsatisfactory buildings used to accommodate the chronic sick. The voluntary Infirmary at Wigan, was by now quite unable to relieve the situation; its 180 beds were insufficient to serve even the surgical needs of a population exceeding 200,000.

Wigan was probably the worst provided of the Lancashire towns, but others were little better. Barrow, likewise maintained its Poor Law infirmary (Roose) as part of a Public Assistance Institution; again the one major improvement was the appointment of a specialist gynaecologist-obstetrician, who did gynaecological work in the Roose Infirmary as well as superintending the small municipal maternity home. In these towns; Bury, Wigan and Barrow, the public infirmaries had done little to supplement the hard-pressed voluntary hospitals.

In Preston, the municipal authorities were keen to develop Sharoe Green and to increase its acute load. The medical superintendent held a medical outpatient clinic once a week, a visiting surgeon performed some surgical work, and a specialist obstetrician supervised the maternity work. This consultant was also on the staff of Preston Royal Infirmary, the only voluntary general hospital in the Region with substantial provision for maternity cases; apparently most of the Royal Infirmary cases were County, those from

Preston Borough went to Sharoe Green. Yet in spite of this shared consultant, there was little co-operation and some friction between the two hospitals. Though the Royal Infirmary was crowded and largely outdated, its consultants had no wish to integrate with the miserable hospital overshadowed by a huge Poor Law Institution. The consultants saw PRI as providing a sub-regional service, and they wanted a whole new building on their existing site; they were not 'town-minded'. The Preston consultants with second appointments elsewhere were mostly attached to the voluntary hospital in affluent Blackpool, not the municipal hospital at Preston (Blackpool did not even possess a municipal hospital).

Outside Manchester and outside the Preston – Blackpool area, there was relatively little remunerative private practice for consultants, but the growth of public responsibilities for maternity and child health services, together with the increased load on municipal hospitals, had begun to provide the basis for specialist employment in cotton towns. A specialist there could supplement his private fees by doing work for public authorities; somewhat removed from the competitive medicine of the cities, he could develop all the opportunities in his town for the practice of his specialty. This situation may well have been the necessary precondition for the co-ordination of municipal and voluntary hospitals; councils with reasonably good hospitals which they wished to upgrade, found the voluntary hospital doctors ready to co-operate.[23]

This sharing of specialists between voluntary and municipal hospitals developed quite well in Blackburn and Burnley, also in Rochdale and somewhat later, in Oldham. Most of the consultants involved did not practise in Manchester (or Preston), though they often served a pair of cotton towns. We may illustrate the kinds of arrangement which developed in the thirties by considering Burnley.

In 1932 the Borough Council was considering the proposed adaption of Primrose Bank infirmary to be the Municipal Hospital. There was accommodation there which could be used to relieve the long waiting list at the voluntary Victoria Hospital. If 'certain difficulties' could be overcome, then the infirmary could take surgical and gynaecological cases, for which the waiting lists were particularly long. The 'difficulties', i.e., the reluctance of the public to enter Primrose Bank while it was counted a Public Assistance Institution, were overcome when the Ministry of Health approved a scheme for separating the infirmary as a hospital. The Council then had a meeting with the Board of Management of the Victoria Hospital and agreed that:

1. That ten beds in the main maternity wards of the municipal hospital should be made available to gynaecology and for surgical cases from the waiting list of the Victoria Hospital.

2. Subject to public assistance cases being first accommodated, beds for ten males and for ten females would also be made available to the surgical wards.

The two surgeons with the longest waiting lists at the Victoria were to be appointed consultant surgeons at the Municipal Hospital, without remuneration, for a trial period. The resident medical officer was to act under their instruction. For each patient who was a member of the voluntary hospital contribution scheme, the Victoria Hospital would pay to the town 32s 6d per adult, and 17s 6d per child. Out-patients were worth 2s 6d and the cost of appliances. Non-contributing in-patients would not entail payment by the Victoria Hospital; the Municipal Hospital would recover what it could by a means test – as they would have done for patients applying directly to the Municipal Hospital.

In return for this arrangement, the Council were entitled to send to the Victoria Hospital occasional municipal patients who might better be treated there. This experiment, which lasted for one year, formed the basis of further co-operation.[24] By 1938, the Burnley Municipal Hospital was carrying out 17 per cent of the total surgical operations in Burnley. In Blackburn, the comparable figure was only 7 per cent, in Bolton 10 per cent, in Stockport 17 per cent, in Oldham 20 per cent and in Rochdale 27 per cent.

The differences in the figures above 10 per cent are due less to the different loads of the municipal hospitals – all did 760–950 operations a year – than to the considerable differences between voluntary hospitals. The Rochdale proportion especially, is high because the Rochdale Infirmary (Voluntary) had remained a small, basically general practitioner hospital, and had been outstripped by Birch Hill Hospital, which had the same range of visiting specialists and considerably better facilities, including a new suite of operating theatres, a first-class ward block for children and a good maternity block. Only in Salford did the surgical load of the municipal hospitals come to approximate that of the voluntary hospitals; Hope Hospital performed about 3,000 operations in 1938, 48 per cent of the total performed in Salford.[25]

Yet even where the surgical work was best developed it formed only a small part of the total load of the municipal hospitals which carried the huge weight of medical and chronic cases; patients who were rarely 'interesting' to the specialists, but who occupied most of the Region's hospital beds. This medical and chronic load varied considerably between towns, much more so than the surgical case load. It was heaviest in and around the Manchester conurbation, lightest in prosperous towns such as Blackpool. The extent to which these huge and important differences in hospital bed occupancy reflected socio-economic conditions in the 1930s, and the extent to which they were the results of different levels of provision developing over decades, cannot be fully ascertained here, but in considering the development of hospital services under the NHS we must not forget this very considerable difference between the parts of the Region. Because of variations in medical and chronic load, the total hospital admissions per thousand population varied from about twenty-seven in Blackpool to seventy-three in Manchester. Most of the towns in Lancashire fell between these extremes; in general, those nearer to Manchester had more admissions than those farther away.[26]

A sketch of the Region's hospital services in 1938
By following the development of various kinds of hospitals we have assembled the elements of a complex pattern which can only be understood historically. At this stage, before we move on to discuss the local and national hospital planning which produced the National Health Service, it may be useful to sketch the pattern of hospital services as it appeared in the Manchester Region in 1938.[27]

Consider first the small country towns, such as those of agricultural Cheshire. Most had a voluntary cottage hospital, a Public Assistance Institution run by the County Council, and a small isolation hospital usually run by a consortium of minor local authorities. Because 'fever' was very rare by the 1930s and smallpox unknown, the majority of the cases were scarlet fever and diphtheria in children. The small separate smallpox hospitals stood empty or were used for other purposes; sometimes for tuberculosis patients, sometimes as convalescent centres.

The cases in the Public Assistance Institutions were usually aged or chronic patients who required nursing but not constant medical attention; the inmates had nowhere else to go. The patients of the cottage hospital were usually relatively mild, more or less acute cases who did not require more than minor surgery. All patients had to be recommended by their general practitioner and most made some payment towards their keep. A few poor but respectable patients were admitted on the recommendation of those charitable neighbours who subscribed to the hospital funds.

In larger towns the range of hospital services was greater. Here the Public Assistance Institutions were barrack-like buildings, lacking in amenities, still feared as a place of last resort for the old and chronic sick. There were few cottage hospitals in the towns (of say 70–250,000 population), though in some, e.g. Bury and also Barrow, the voluntary hospital was mainly staffed by general practitioners. However, like all the town-centre voluntary hospitals, these were supported very largely from work-people's weekly contributions rather than directly by patients' payments, and they were mostly filled with surgical cases. The better voluntary hospitals were largely controlled by specialists. Some, e.g. Wigan, had separate accommodation for patients who paid the full cost of their treatment.

Paralleling the town voluntary hospital was the municipal hospital. Just as the voluntary hospital might be little more than a general practitioner hospital, so the public 'hospital' might be little more than an extension of the Public Assistance Institution including provision for the municipal maternity service. Elsewhere, the municipal hospital could have a similar range of specialists, better facilities and more room than the voluntary hospital.

Within the Manchester conurbation we also find some of these same 'town' facilities, plus others characteristic of the regional capital. Cottage hospitals, not unlike those in the Cheshire market towns could be found in residential districts such as Stretford, served by local general practitioners and admitting their moderately affluent patients; there were no equivalents of the country Public Assistance Institution. In Salford, though it merged with Manchester for many voluntary hospital services, there was a range of facilities comparable to those in the cotton towns, though somewhat larger and better developed. Other districts which enjoyed no official identity such as Ancoats, had their own separate voluntary hospital; some small voluntary hospitals, e.g. the Northern for Women and Children and the Jewish Memorial Hospital served particular neighbourhoods and particular groups of patients.

For municipal hospital and for chronic sick institutional accommodation Manchester City divided more or less formally into north (Crumpsall) and south (Withington); for the more specialised aspects of the service like child health (Booth Hall) and infectious disease (Monsall) the whole city was served by single large hospitals.

This specialisation was most fully developed in the voluntary hospitals which served the whole Region, mostly those near to the city centre. Most of these were separate hospitals devoted to particular specialties (obstetrics, gynaecology, children, cancer, skin diseases, venereal disease, eye diseases, ear diseases, tuberculosis, diseases of the foot), and they drew patients from all over the Region. So too, did the specialist clinics in the Manchester Royal Infirmary, for which there were long waiting lists. Some of the smaller special hospitals took a high proportion of paying patients, referred from general practitioners. The larger hospitals – Manchester Royal Infirmary and St Mary's and the Eye Hospital – also did a great deal of more or less routine work; between them they had about 1,100 public beds which provided the clinical teaching for the medical school. The Manchester Royal Infirmary also had a hundred beds in a separate private patients' home, opened in 1937.

Such, in outline, was the pre-war pattern; roughly speaking, a pattern of hospitals which increased in size, sophistication and specialisation as one passed from rural areas to large towns and to the regional city.

In most discussions of pre-war hospital services, this general pattern is counterposed to some ideal distribution of facilities; the difference is said to demonstrate the necessity of reform; the distance from the ideal is attributed to the vagaries of charity, or the lack of system and co-ordination among the various bodies administrating hospitals. But such an attitude, by subordinating history to reform, deprives us of the opportunity to learn from that history. Thus, what we stress here is not the failure of hospital services in the North West to conform to some rational plan, but the variety of systems, formal and informal, which were more or less evident in the Region at the time of the Second World War. These different arrangements illustrate the range of potential systems of which the NHS was but one; thus they help elucidate the negotiation of the NHS. So too they help us to understand how the implementation of the NHS depended on the variety of existing arrangements.

At one extreme stands Preston – a county town in which the hospital services were dominated by the voluntary Infirmary. By 1938 the Preston Royal Infirmary was the largest specialist-staffed hospital in the Region, outside Manchester itself. It provided about 2.3 beds per 1,000 population in the district, a figure not exceeded by any voluntary hospital in the whole Region, Manchester not excepted. Significantly it possessed a large, *new* maternity block, so that Preston was the only one of the cotton towns where voluntary provision for childbirth exceeded municipal provision. Given this dominance of voluntary over municipal services, it is no surprise to find that Preston, during the war, was a stronghold of the British Hospitals Association, which argued for the preservation of voluntary hospitals by means of state aid; a hospital service which would continue to be dominated by medical consultants and the charitable middle class.[28]

If Preston hospital services were dominated by the Preston Royal Infirmary, those in Rochdale, Bolton and Oldham were increasingly dominated by the local authority hospitals. The war time surveyors wrote of Rochdale: 'The Municipal Hospital (Birch Hill) here is definitely the principal hospital, with well-developed specialist services. The voluntary hospital is small and unsatisfactory in buildings and equipment, but it has several specialists on the staff and appears to have quite a progressive outlook.'[29] By contrast with Preston, the new maternity provision in Rochdale was at the municipal hospital and the close association between the public health services, the school medical services and the hospital services of the local authority had been underlined by the building of children's wards at Birch Hill (1934).

Had Rochdale been left to itself, it seems quite likely that the development of the local authority services would have overshadowed the voluntary hospital to such an extent that the latter would have found expansion very difficult; it would probably have come to depend on servicing the local authority. Relationships between Birch Hill and the Infirmary were quite good, and common staffing would probably have developed into a more or less formal division of labour between the two institutions. As we shall see, the likely development of Rochdale services nicely exemplifies the assumptions about national developments which underlay government planning during 1941, when it was anticipated that the responsibility for providing a general hospital service would be placed on the major local authorities, who could then make contracts with voluntary hospitals for as long as the latter could maintain themselves.

Those who favoured this prospect, before and during World War II, thought in terms of a single layer of unitary health authorities, covering both hospital and public health services. They saw hospital specialists as important elements in the service, but not its dominant feature. The key medical man was the Medical Officer of Health.

Much of the complex socio-politics of hospital medicine could be illustrated by considering the nuances of the specialist – MOH relationship. In Preston, the specialists were deeply suspicious of those who saw hospital medicine as a part of local government. In Rochdale, specialists worked happily in a hospital which was under the charge of the MOH and a resident medical superintendent.

But neither of these towns, nor both together, provide for a sufficient study of the resolution of these differences in the NHS. To gain a more adequate perspective we must also consider Manchester itself: not just because any hospital service planned for a nation must solve the peculiar problems of large cities but because the problems which were more evident in Manchester than elsewhere in the Region, came to dominate the planning of the NHS. These were not the day-to-day problems of medicine or administration; they were the second-order problems of co-ordination and change – the development of new specialist services in a properly co-ordinated set of hospitals. The optimism of planners, building on paper for a post-war world in which all the old inadequate buildings would be replaced, naturally led them to emphasise these second-order problems. In this context, the role of the medical school specialists seemed very important: they were the experts who could advise on the new specialties, they had the prestige to co-ordinate doctors in both kinds of hospital.

These second-order problems were very evident in Manchester between the wars. Examination of the steps towards their resolution there will help to explain the rationale of planning during the Second World War, as studies of smaller towns alone do not. It is for this reason that the next chapter reviews in detail the creation and the work of the Manchester Joint

Hospitals Advisory Board, an evolved precursor of the Regional Hospital Board.

Notes and references

1. Local Voluntary Hospitals Committee for the City of Manchester, Accounts & Statistics for the Year 1922 (Manchester Medical Collection). The Committee was set up following the (national) Cave Commission (Final Report 1921, Cmd 1335).
2. *Ibid.*, p. 13.
3. Table and Statistics compiled from the reports of the Local Voluntary Hospitals Committee, 1922–38.
4. B. Bowker, *Lancashire Under the Hammer*, London, 1928.
5. Annual Reports of the hospitals, and the *Hospital Survey, The Hospital Services of the North-Western Area*, Ministry of Health, 1945.
6. Preston Royal Infirmary Annual Report for 1935; *Lancashire Daily Post*, 6 October 1937 (Scrapbook, Preston Royal Infirmary).
7. *Preston Guardian*, 13 April 1935 (Scrapbook).
8. *Lancashire Evening Post*, 31 March 1952 (Scrapbook); Infirmary Annual Reports.
9. Statistics in Annual Report for 1941.
10. Annual Report for 1938.
11. Annual Reports.
12. Statistics from the *Hospital Survey (North-Western)*, 1945.
13. The pamphlet from which the information in this section is drawn, was republished from an anonymous article 'Booth Hall, Crumpsall & Withington Hospitals', *Poor Law Officers Journal* (1924); Guardians Annual Report, 1920.
14. Report on the Local Government Act of 1929, Manchester Public Health Committee, 1930; Manchester Board of Guardians, *Souvenir* (1930).
15. Ancoats Hospital Annual Reports, and the *History of Ancoats Hospital, 1873–1900*, (anon., n.d., published by the hospital) and interviews with Sir Harry Platt.
16. *Poor Law Officers Journal* (1924), p. 19. On Booth Hall, notes on interview with Dr Sylvia K. Guthrie.
17. *Poor Law Officers Journal*, p. 19.
18. *Ibid.*, p. 33.
19. The Labour Group of the former Poor Law Guardians and of the City Council met with the Executive of the Manchester Labour Party and determined to overturn a recommendation of the Parliamentary Sub-Committee of the City Council, that the Council would only undertake responsibility under the Public Health Acts for the treatment of sick children, blind persons and adult sane epileptics. At a Council meeting of 28 August 1929, the Labour Group moved and supported a resolution that the Council assume responsibility for the hospital treatment of all of the sick of the City. They also resolved that district medical officers should come under the jurisdiction of the Public Health Committee. See Emrys L. Jones, *Manchester's Health*, Manchester Boro' Labour Party Pamphlet no. 1 (1930?).
20. A. Redford, *The History of Local Government in Manchester*, III, London, 1940. pp. 315–38.
21. *Manchester Guardian*, 6 April, 4 July 1935.
22. Manchester Royal Infirmary Annual Report for 1937.
23. The hospital provision during the Second War, with statistics for 1938, was admirably reviewed in the *Hospital Survey (North-Western)*, from which most of my information is taken.
24. Victoria Hospital Burnley, Annual Reports, especially 1933; *Burnley Express and Advertiser*, 2 March, 12 March, 12 April 1932.
25. Statistics from *Hospital Survey (North-Western)*. Because the operations performed on the Salford patients in Manchester voluntary hospitals are roughly balanced by the

HOSPITAL SERVICES IN THE 1930s

operations on non-Salford patients at Salford Royal Infirmary, this figure is little changed if we consider the percentage of the total operations on Salfordians, that were carried out in the municipal as opposed to voluntary hospitals.

26. *Ibid.*
27. This section relies heavily on the *Hospital Survey (North Western)*.
28. Preston Royal Infirmary Board of Management contained representatives of the Corporation of Preston. The hospital also had a large 'Ladies Maternity Committee'. For the role of the British Hospitals Association see Chapter 13.
29. *Hospital Survey (North Western)*.

SECTION C

*A regional perspective
on the construction of
the National Health Service*

CHAPTER 12

The Manchester Joint Hospitals Advisory Board

Voluntary hospitals and the municipality
The 1929 Local Government Act introduced by Neville Chamberlain finally abolished the English Poor Law and the Boards of Guardians, putting their hospitals and institutions into the hands of the major local authorities, the County and County Borough Councils.[1] In Manchester, as in other progressive Boroughs, all the Poor Law services to the sick were placed under the Public Health Committee, care of the destitute and the vagrants resting with the Public Assistance Committee.[2] Welcome though these changes were, they did little to integrate the services of voluntary hospitals and the public hospitals. Indeed, as the removal of the Poor Law taint helped to increase demand on municipal hospitals and to increase their load of acute work, so the problems of hospital co-ordination became more pressing. There was provision under the 1929 Act for local committees linking voluntary and public hospitals, but in most areas such committees either were not set up, or they did little work.

Manchester was exceptional; by the mid-thirties, a joint committee was doing a great deal of useful work. In a number of ways to be elucidated later, it served as a forerunner of the Regional Hospital Board. The reasons for its success are therefore worth examining and we may begin by looking at the voluntary hospitals.

Throughout the twenties and thirties these hospitals were more and more influenced by the health authorities. In some cases the voluntary hospitals were used to fulfil the statutory obligations of local authorities: thus St Luke's Hospital for venereal disease was very largely dependent on public funds[3] and twenty of the cots at the Hospital for Babies were supported by the City under the Infant Welfare scheme.[4] The upgrading of municipal hospitals increased the interaction: general practitioners were concerned lest the easy access to public beds led their patients to leave the waiting list of voluntary hospitals and hence their care.[5] Overcrowded voluntary hospitals, without money for expansion, began to offload cases, especially long-stay patients, into the empty beds of municipal hospitals. All these interactions inevitably raised problems.

[272]

THE JOINT HOSPITALS ADVISORY BOARD

As unemployment worsened, the workers' contributory funds, now an important source of hospital revenue, began to run into difficulties. In order to maintain the level of their payments to the hard-pressed voluntary hospitals, the funds sought and obtained an indirect subsidy from the City. They had been paying £1 per week per patient to the municipal hospitals, for up to thirteen weeks per patient. This covered only 40 per cent of the true cost. Even so the City agreed to reduce the rate to 14s 0d per week, falling to 7s 0d per week after six weeks, and continuing to ten weeks. In so doing, the City gave about £1,600 *per annum* to the voluntary hospitals.[6]

With this aid, and with increasing payment from patients, the Manchester voluntary hospitals were still in difficulties. They could not hope to effect the substantial expansion necessary to relieve overcrowding, and they were especially burdened by accident cases, which could not be refused or shunted quickly to the municipal hospitals. In 1932 the Manchester Royal Infirmary spent £1,096 on 214 persons injured on the roads, and had no prospect of recovering more than 35 per cent of that sum from patients or insurance companies. From 128 such in-patients, Salford Royal Infirmary recovered £99 out of £665 cost.[7] In response to pressures from the voluntary hospitals the government set up a Select Committee and passed the Road Traffic (Compensation for Accidents) Bill. In Manchester the Public Health Committee prepared a scheme for accident services which greatly increased the role of the municipal hospitals. In future, police and ambulance drivers were able to take accident cases to the nearest hospital whether voluntary or corporation. The place of each hospital was to be determined by geography not by the status of the hospital or the patient.[8]

The Public Health Committee hoped that the scheme would help the voluntary hospitals, but it was not an act of charity. Municipal hospitals were empowered to recover costs from patients and thus could expect to lose less per case than the voluntary hospital had done. Further, there was a strong economic argument for upgrading the standard of casualty care. In 1938 it was estimated that improved fracture services could save the nation £2.5 million in costs to industry. Already in 1921 Harry Platt had written that 'employers, insurance companies and trade-unions [were] alive to the necessity for reform'.[9]

To receive casualty cases properly the municipal hospitals needed new facilities but, characteristically, the major capital expense involved in this project, a £5,000 accident block at Withington, was deferred. Temporary accommodation was improvised while the Public Health Committee planned a larger addition. Extra staffing was also required and was long overdue.[10]

Upgrading the municipal hospitals

Manchester Public Health Committee was keen to upgrade the hospitals and services it had taken over from the Board of Guardians in 1929. The Poor Law taint was to be expunged; the services were to be the equal of those previously used by the more prosperous members of the working classes; the parish doctors were to give way to an extended system of panel practice;[11] the public hospitals were to use consultants like the voluntary hospitals. As growing unemployment threw more and more working men on to the corporation medical services, it became imperative that these services be the equal of those used by the men when at work. But the economic crisis prevented the improvements which it demanded. The Public Health Committee was not given the money for new staff, and a five-year ban on new expenditures was imposed.[12] Even though the committee had taken on massive new responsibilities, the Executive of the Council refused to provide an extra medical administrative officer. The existing staff were expected to develop a system of hospitals, while at the same time carrying out the mass of detailed work involved in medical services, public health services and slum clearance.[13]

Not surprisingly, no substantial plans for the upgrading of municipal health services appeared until 1934.[14] By then the period of extreme financial stringency seemed to be drawing to a close. The Public Health Committee, especially its Labour members, was pushing hard for a large increase in expenditure. The Medical Officer of Health was anxious that the staffing of municipal hospitals be improved, for the proportion of acute work done in these hospitals had continued to increase while the resident and consultant staffs remained very small.[15]

In April 1934 the Medical Officer of Health, Veitch Clark, proposed an increase of six in the resident medical staff of the municipal hospitals; three at Withington, two at Crumpsall and one for Booth Hall, as the first step in upgrading the municipal staffs. The increases were long overdue. At Crumpsall with five residents, the bed/resident ratio had been 309 (184 if only acute and maternity beds were considered), when the ratio at the Manchester Royal Infirmary was twenty-four. Moreover, the Royal Infirmary residents did not also have to care for the inmates of a Public Assistance Institution, nor supervise 600 mental cases, though they did do more outpatient work. Equality in these ratios was neither appropriate nor intended, but numerous complaints from over-worked staff and consultants underlined the need for substantial increases. It had been unusual to find any mature and experienced residents apart from the superintendent, but under the new plans Crumpsall and Withington would each have a deputy medical superintendent, a resident surgical officer and a resident obstetrical officer (new at

Crumpsall) as well as five other residents (one of whom, at Withington, was a tuberculosis officer). The ratios of beds to residents at Crumpsall would now be 193.[16]

Even so, it was difficult to get the City Council to agree improvements, especially where capital expenditure was involved. To gain approval for a new operating theatre at Withington Hospital the Public Health Committee had to be so candid about the existing deficiencies that the public cried out for reassurance.[17] On 1 May 1935 the *Manchester City News* published an open letter lamenting that Veitch Clark, 'Health Guardian of 800,000 souls', was constantly being frustrated by the apathy of a laggard City Council.[18]

Given this inertia, it seems likely that the innovations of 1934–5 would have been less striking without the outside pressures of 1934. As the plans for improving the municipal hospitals were germinating, the death of a patient led to a public outcry against the poor obstetrical services and the lack of hospital co-ordination. Later in that year, a Ministry report on Manchester Public Health Services lent its weight to the pressure for reform and for proper co-operation between the different hospitals.

A public inquiry

Before any of Veitch Clark's proposals could be effected, on 12 May 1934, a young Jewish mother, Mrs Molly Taylor, died in Crumpsall Hospital. She had been transferred there from the overcrowded St Mary's on the previous evening, an hour after giving birth in the out-patients room. The family, aided by several local welfare organisations, questioned the treatment and the quality of obstetrical care provided in the city. An inquiry chaired by Walter Cobbett of the Infirmary, failed to satisfy public opinion and in September a public inquiry was held in Manchester before two officers of the Ministry of Health. The audience was large and vocal, and the case attracted considerable publicity.[19]

Both inquiries agreed that death was due to delayed obstetrical shock which could not have been foreseen and which was probably not induced by the removal of the patient from St Mary's to Crumpsall. Nor was there evidence of negligence by the medical staff. None the less the public inquiry was able to point to several instances of insufficient care: no one took the trouble to see that the patient was fed before being removed, the nurse who travelled in the ambulance was inexperienced; the patient was not seen by a doctor on arrival. Most importantly, the case showed up the inadequacy of the accommodation and staff available for maternity cases. St Mary's was one of the best maternity hospitals in the country, if judged by the eminence of its staff, but neither it nor the municipal hospitals could guarantee the facilities needed by a straightforward childbirth.

Mrs Taylor had attended ante-natal clinics at St Mary's, she had paid the two pounds voluntary contribution towards the cost and she had been given a ticket to present to the hospital when the child was due. 'Come to the hospital as soon as labour commences' was the instruction, but her mother-in-law knew well enough that cases presenting with lots of time to spare were likely to be sent off to Crumpsall. Thus labour was well underway when they arrived at St Mary's at 6 p.m. The resident officer considered that delivery would occur in about four hours; the hospital was full to overflowing, because one large ward, containing a fifth of the total beds was out of action for spring-cleaning; there was time for the patient to be transferred to Crumpsall, and an ambulance was called. Soon afterwards the patient was delivered and since both mother and child appeared to be healthy they were taken to Crumpsall at 7.25 p.m.

The admission ticket for St Mary's had stated that no bed could be guaranteed; the best alternative arrangements would be made. In practice this usually meant transfer to Crumpsall, where the 114 maternity beds were rarely all full and where, because of the variety of patients, the accommodation was more elastic. Unfortunately Crumpsall had no resident obstetrical officer and was generally short of resident medical staff until the proposals of April 1934 could be put into effect. The public inquiry stressed the need for this improvement in resident staff; it further stressed the need for improving co-ordination between St Mary's and the municipal hospitals. On 21 February 1935 representatives of the Public Health Committee and St Mary's began a series of meetings where they agreed measures to increase co-operation in maternity services.[20]

This same need for co-ordination was stressed in the report of a more general survey of the public health services in Manchester, undertaken by the Ministry and communicated to the Council in November 1934. The officials praised many aspects of the Public Health Committee's work, but stressed the need for a medical administrative officer in charge of hospitals, for upgrading the municipal consultant staff, and for more closely linking the work of the Public Health Department and the Schools Health Services.[21] Many of the items had been raised by the Medical Officer of Health during 1934 or before, and by the time the Ministry report became public plans had been drawn up to deal with the deficiencies. The report helped to strengthen the case for substantial new expenditure, even though the financial restrictions had not yet been raised.

Municipal plans
In May 1935 the committee was ready with a five-year expenditure plan including a new smallpox hospital (£37,000) to replace the delapidated

building at Clayton Vale; a new fever hospital at Wythenshawe, to replace Monsall which was unsatisfactory and expensive to run; a new extension at Baguley Sanatorium which would take tuberculosis patients from Withington, thus freeing beds for general hospital use; a new nurses' home at Withington; a new seventy-five-bed orthopaedic hospital to cost £75,000; and two new maternity and child welfare clinics, at Sharston and Collyhurst, which would bring together public health and school health services as suggested in the government report. Of this impressive list, the fever hospital and orthopaedic hospital were immediately shelved, though the committee reserved the right to renew the proposals; the new smallpox hospital was never built for the committee were persistently unable to find a site which was not too expensive and no new smallpox outbreak occurred to intensify the search.[22] The problem, of course, was money. In 1936 the Finance Committee was still complaining that the cost of equipping the new operating theatre at Withington had been above estimates.[23]

The proposals which did not involve capital expenditure fared rather better, especially the scheme for extending the consultant services in the municipal hospitals. The number of beds served by each resident had long been a disgrace. So too had the time wasted by senior resident staff on domestic administration.[24] Clearly there was need for substantial reform.

The consultant services, as we have seen, were fairly extensive in 1930, but between 1930 and 1935 the acute work of municipal hospitals had increased very steeply, without any increase in consultant staff. The total number of specialist attendances at the three hospitals still was only thirty-nine: an equivalent of four full-time specialists for over 2,500 beds.

The government inquiry of 1934 recommended an increase in consultant staff, but Veitch Clark's proposal was more radical. In his opinion, for as long as the public hospitals maintained a system of staffing where residents, rather than consultants, had charge of the patients, they would not escape the slur of the Poor Law. He therefore proposed that the consultant staff be greatly increased and that they take charge of the patients. On 18 June 1935 the Public Health Committee approved the proposal. By September more detailed schemes had been drawn up, examined by the local Voluntary Hospitals Committee, and passed by the Council. They called for the number of appointments to be increased from thirty-nine to ninety-five. The salary bill would rise from £4,500 *per annum* to £12,500 *per annum*.[25]

Not surprisingly, some residents were upset by the scheme. In voluntary hospitals the residential staff were all trainees, justifiably subordinated to the consultant staff. But public hospital residents had often spent long careers becoming expert in the special demands and difficulties of their work.[26] Were these men to be subordinated to visiting consultants? The residents like their former employers, the Guardians, could not but resent their low prestige. The public and the profession looked to the techniques of the new medicine and surgery; little attention was paid to the persistent problem of the chronic sick, which was often the public hospital residents' area of expertise.

The *Manchester Guardian* had reservations of a different sort. Apparently fearing the growth of a body of consultants working for salaries, the paper suggested that 'many eminent specialists may still prefer to divide their time between remunerative private practice and free service in voluntary hospitals'. Councillor Edwards, the Liberal chairman of the Public Health Committee, was able to reassure them. He stressed that the consultants would be part-time: 'It is our intention that the consultation specialist service provided in our hospitals shall be fully of the same character as that of the voluntary hospitals. It will differ only in this respect, that our consultants will be paid for their services.'[27]

The service was not only to be similar to that provided in the voluntary hospitals, the two were to intermesh. Already some consultants held appointments in both spheres; an extension of this practice would draw the spheres together more: 'Care has been observed in the preparation of the scheme to bear in mind the desirability – indeed the necessity – of allowing for its practical development along lines which will ultimately enable the closest collaboration and possibly fusion with the work of the voluntary hospitals of the city.'[28] As Edwards explained, the new scheme was to be a real advance towards the point at which voluntary and municipal hospitals would be able to discuss, on a basis of equality, the most effective division of labour.[29] Such a discussion had already begun on an *ad hoc* basis in connection with maternity services. But the consultancy scheme discussion provided the first and primary issue with which the Joint Hospitals Advisory Board was to deal.

The birth of the Joint Board

One week after Councillor Edwards had announced the municipal plans, Walter Cobbett of the Royal Infirmary welcomed the scheme and suggested that a joint board should be set up to allocate specialists to both the municipal hospitals *and* the voluntary hospitals: 'What we hope will emerge from the negotiations which are now proceeding is some sort of staff appointments in voluntary hospitals and municipal hospitals made by a thoroughly representative body composed of representatives of the medical profession and hospital governors. Such a scheme, if well devised, will be of lasting benefit to the city.'[30] In commending this scheme, the *Manchester Guardian* emphasised the need for the voluntary section to put its house in order, to adopt a common system of contributions, as seen in Liverpool, rather than have hospitals competing with each other for donations.[31]

The paper was right to stress this need, but wrong to suggest that the co-operation of voluntary hospitals over financial support was a prerequisite for the success of a joint board. This board, unlike the Local Committee of 1922, was primarily concerned with medical services, and as the world of high prestige medicine became more independent of the political and social life of the city, so doctors could afford to distinguish between the job of finding money, and the job of practising medicine and pushing new specialist departments.

The support of Walter Cobbett was important, for many voluntary hospital leaders were jealous of the voluntary principle and wary of change. So too was the enthusiasm of those councillors who took a pride in the municipal hospitals. But the key figures in the formation of the Joint Board were not the lay leaders of the hospitals, they were the professionals: Veitch Clark, Stopford the University's medical Vice-Chancellor, and the medical school's leading specialists. They were the people most closely concerned in working out the details of the municipal consultancy scheme and they most clearly saw the need to link the two branches of hospital work. Their aspirations were reflected in the government report of 1934, which after discussing the need for extended municipal consultancy, suggested:

> Having regard to the quality of the voluntary hospitals and their staffs, it appears to the Minister that substantial benefits would ensue if steps were taken to secure such consultation [with representatives of voluntary hospitals] not only on this [consultancy] question but also on the measures of co-operation best suited to the future development of the municipal and voluntary hospitals of the city.[32]

Five years before, the Local Government Act had called for joint consultation, but nothing had been done in Manchester beyond the formation of the Statutory Committee representing voluntary hospitals and the medical profession. The Public Health Committee had not even appointed a sub-committee until August 1934, prompted, no doubt, by the Government Survey. The first joint meeting took place on 26 March 1935.[33]

Such joint consultative committees had existed longer in other cities, and had borne little fruit. But by 1935, as Veitch Clark planned the extension of municipal consultation schemes and discussed them with specialists, he could see very definite roles for a prestigious coordinating board. At the first meeting of the joint committee he proposed that it be strengthened beyond the requirements of the 1929 Act.

> It was suggested that such a body should be representative of the City Council and the Voluntary Hospitals Council and when consulted could, as a single governing body entrusted with the policy of hospital provision, both as regards quantity and type, whilst preserving the independence of the particular hospital

concerned, advise any of the constituent hospital authorities as to the proper co-ordination of hospital services or on other matters or projects which required impartial decisions in the best interests of the hospitals in the city, viewed as a whole.[34]

The proposal was favourably received.

Veitch Clark was concerned throughout the discussions of 1935 to emphasise cooperation and coordination with the voluntary hospitals. In July, speaking to the Health Congress at Bournemouth, he stressed the need for a Joint Hospitals Board. Too little attention had been paid to local authority doctors in questions of hospital organisation. In future, hospital planning would have to be a joint venture in which overlapping was prevented and rivalry restricted to the regions of professional attainment.[35]

This was a lesson learned from experience. The Molly Taylor case had attracted much publicity, and the National Unemployed Workers' Movement had attempted to arouse a similar protest over the case of a Mrs Shuffleton. Her bronchial cancer had been misdiagnosed by the local District Medical Officer and later, pregnant and dying, she had been transferred from Withington to Ancoats and back again because no bronchoscopic examination could be made at the municipal hospital.[36] These were the occasional flarings of a continuing difficulty. The Medical Officer of Health was constantly having to deal with delicate questions concerning the two sets of hospitals. Were the employees of St Luke's Venereal Diseases Hospital to receive pension benefits from the City? Officially the hospital was voluntary, in fact most of the funds were public.[37] Should the Council go on maintaining cots at the Duchess of York Hospital for Babies, or would they do better to develop similar facilities of their own at the underused Booth Hall Hospital?[38] Any attempts to upgrade the municipal sector was bound to raise a host of new problems which could only be adequately handled by a joint board.

Events were to prove that some of the smaller voluntary hospitals were touchily independent but the teaching hospitals, at least in Manchester, were closely linked to the University and maintained good relations with the City. Hence the advantage of including the University on the Joint Board. University representation would allow training to be discussed; more importantly, a 'neutral' element would be introduced between the voluntary hospitals and the municipality.

Harry Platt, the orthopaedic surgeon, was among those who took part in discussions around 1935 between Veitch Clark, Professor Stopford and various leading specialists. Platt had a particular interest in ensuring that municipal plans for orthopaedic services were coordinated with existing services to provide an efficient city-wide network.[39] Other specialists linked

THE JOINT HOSPITALS ADVISORY BOARD

with the University had parallel plans. Since about 1933 a commission of the Infirmary Medical Board had been trying to get better arrangements with the adjacent St Mary's Hospital.[40] Now wider possibilities were open.

On 18 June 1935 the Public Health Committee approved the establishment of a Joint Hospitals Advisory Board. On 8 August 1935 it was proposed that the University be represented. On 13 August the Public Health Committee agreed, appointed ten of its own members to the Joint Board, and added the Medical Officer of Health. The Voluntary Hospitals Statutory Committee was to provide six members, and the University five, including the professors of medicine, surgery and obstetrics. Professor John Stopford was invited to be chairman but in fact that post was occupied for the first few years of the Board's existence by Sir Christopher Needham, chairman of the University Council.[41]

The voluntary hospitals felt that they were under-represented. Because of the way in which places had been allotted only three laymen from voluntary hospitals had gained a seat, so they pressed for, and gained, a further place. When the three doctors from voluntary hospitals turned out all to be surgeons there was a request for a fourth place to be awarded to a physician. The voluntary hospitals also gained assurance that when the future of any particular hospital was being discussed, a representative from that hospital would be present.

The University had fewer reservations. It wanted the removal of stipulations as to which professors should be members, so that the most suitable people (rather younger specialists?) could be appointed. Meanwhile the University would comply with the Health Committee's suggestions, for the University Council was strongly in favour of the scheme.[42]

The Manchester Joint Hospitals Advisory Board met for the first time on 28 October 1935 with Sir Christopher Needham in the chair; the vice-chairman was Councillor R. G. Edwards, for many years the enthusiastic chairman of the Public Health Committee. The honorary secretaries were the Town Clerk and R. L. Newell, a leader of the local British Medical Association who was to play a prominent role in medical politics. The Council representatives included Councillor Meadowcroft and Councillor Chadwick, a socialist general practitioner, both of whom were very active; together with Edwards and Veitch Clark. The voluntary hospital section was led by Walter Cobbett of the Manchester Royal Infirmary and James Sillavan of the Duchess of York Hospital for Babies, a hospital which was heavily dependent on public funds.[43]

In addition to Needham and Stopford, the University representatives were the professors of medicine, surgery and clinical obstetrics and gynaecology: Professors Ramsbottom, Telford and Fletcher-Shaw. All three were local men of considerable distinction. Two University teachers were also included among the eight voluntary hospital representatives: John Morley, who succeeded E. D. Telford as Professor of Surgery in 1936, and Harry Platt, whose long connection with the teaching of orthopaedics in Manchester was soon (1939) to be recognised by the award of a personal chair.

One could scarcely have collected a more distinguished and appropriate team of medical professionals, including national leaders in obstetrics and gynaecology, orthopaedics, public health administration and medical education; most of them local men with strong commitments to the improvement of Manchester hospital services. When we also consider the interests, expertise and authority of the non-medical members there can be no surprise that this Advisory Board found its advice readily accepted. It was to be consulted on: (a) projected or anticipated developments of hospital work or accommodation; (b) training of medical students; (c) principles underlying the medical and surgical staffing of hospitals; (d) any other matters such as have relation to the work of the Voluntary and Municipal Hospitals controlled by the constituent bodies represented on the Joint Board.

Most of the voluntary hospitals registered their approval of the Board's aims and constitution. The most notable exceptions were the Jewish Hospital, the Manchester Ear and Eye Hospital, the Royal Eye Hospital, St Luke's Hospital and the Manchester Hospital for Consumption.

The Board wanted to maintain the initiative of the hospitals, while leading them forward in a spirit of co-operation. To this end it decided to publish quarterly and annual reports and to meet annually with all members of the constituent bodies. The Lord Mayor presided over the first such annual meeting, and Sir Christopher Needham was able to report that the Board had worked throughout the year in a spirit quite free from partisanship.[44]

During that year an executive committee had been formed (Meadowcroft, Chadwick, Edwards, Veitch Clark, Cobbett, Sillavan, Needham, Stopford and Telford); the Board had agreed to collect information on hospital waiting lists, and had begun to take control of the planning of specialist services in the Manchester hospitals.[45]

The personnel of the Board changed but little over the years except that in 1936 representatives of local doctors were added: apparently the general practitioners were worried lest the upgrading of municipal hospitals led Friendly Societies to bypass the congested voluntary hospitals and secure immediate admission of their members to public hospitals. This switch reduced the patient's loss of income, but it interfered with freedom of choice of hospital. It also reduced the time during which patients were under the care of their general practitioners.[46]

The greatest change came in 1942 when Salford and Stretford arranged to join the Board, then reconstituted as the Manchester Salford and Stretford Joint Hospitals Advisory Board. The total membership was increased from twenty-five to thirty. Salford Council had five representatives, Stretford two, against Manchester's eight; the voluntary hospitals' representation was maintained at eight, and the University representation at five. The local practitioners combined to have two representatives (one of these was Dr D'Ewart, former superintendent of Booth Hall Hospital). At the same time Stopford, recently knighted, took over as chairman from Sir Christopher Needham. Alderman Edwards continued as vice-chairman. The Board now contained three Medical Officers of Health including C. Metcalfe Brown who had recently succeeded Veitch Clark in Manchester. Overall, twelve of the thirty members were medical men.[47]

The Joint Board and the appointment of consultants
The Board's first important task was to help formulate the scheme for more municipal consultants. After discussing his plans with the medical superintendents of the hospitals and with the existing consultants, Veitch Clark presented his proposals in terms of total appointments. The distribution of the positions and the method of appointment had been left open; on these questions he wanted the advice of the Board. The power to advise on new appointments of consultants immediately made the Joint Advisory Board a real influence throughout the hospitals of the city.

In order to deal with this sensitive question the Board appointed a Medical and Surgical Subcommittee. All five university representatives were members, along with four councillors and the Medical Officer of Health. Walter Cobbett of the Manchester Royal Infirmary was chairman. Thus, effectively, the senior medical staff of the University were advising the Public Health Committee; Sir Christopher Needham and Cobbett added long civic experience and prestige.[48]

The original proposal was to appoint two medical, two surgical and two obstetrical/gynaecological consultants, who would each attend three times weekly at Crumpsall and Withington; the medical consultant would also attend Booth Hall, making a total of forty-two additional attendances. Instead the Joint Board suggested that more consultants be appointed and the number of visits be limited to two per week. Only in this way, it was argued, could one expect consultants to divide their time between municipal and voluntary hospitals and such sharing of staff, especially between neighbouring hospitals, was to be strongly encouraged.

Initially the committee considered making all appointments on a geographical basis, each municipal hospital sharing staff with the closest voluntary hospital. In this way patients could be moved when necessary. But the obvious division into north and south would have left Crumpsall and Booth Hall linked with small voluntary hospitals or special hospitals, while Withington would have been linked with the Royal Infirmary and St Mary's; the balance would have been very different in the two areas. The Royal Infirmary was not comparable to the smaller voluntary hospitals; it could not be a district hospital 'because the natural course of a medical career in Manchester drew the best and most experienced men to the Royal Infirmary, the teaching hospital'. Because any simple geographical link would have furthered the development of Withington at the expense of Crumpsall, the committee proposed to establish panels which would advise on all the consultant appointments and thus be able to co-ordinate them without zoning; to the same end, meetings were to be held between the staffs of geographically related hospitals. The new municipal vacancies were to be advertised in the medical press; individual consultants were not to be separately informed and no notices were to be placed in the local papers. The Advisory Panel of the Board was to report to the Public Health Committee.

The composition of this panel was to vary slightly according to the medical specialty under discussion; Meadowcroft and Edwards, Cobbett, Needham and Stopford would always be present; so too would Professor H. S. Raper, physiologist and Dean of the Medical School. When surgeons were being considered, Professors E. D. Telford and John Morley would advise; for medicine, Professors Ramsbottom plus Dr T. H. Oliver, who succeeded Ramsbottom to the chair of medicine in 1940; for obstetrics and gynaecology the special advisers would be Professors William Fletcher-Shaw and Daniel Dougal. In addition to Raper, Oliver and Dougal, who were not then members of the Joint Board, other advisers might also be called upon to deal with particular specialities; these co-opted members would be able to vote.[49] It is characteristic of the activities of the Board, that whenever it appointed committees and panels to examine questions of concrete detail the representation of the medical faculty increased markedly. The medical professoriate had moved into a central position.

In its first year the Advisory Panel reviewed sixty-eight applications for thirty vacancies and with very few exceptions its recommendations were accepted. On 15 July 1936 the Public Health Committee thanked the Joint Board for the services of the Advisory Panel, and suggested that it also be used for appointments in voluntary hospitals. This latter proposal was very much within the future which Veitch Clark, Stopford and Cobbett envisaged for the Board, but many years passed before it was implemented. During 1939/40 the Manchester Royal Infirmary used the Advisory Panel in filling two vacancies, but not until 1946 did the Joint Board urge all its constituent hospitals to use the services of the Panel for all appointments of consultants, other than those holding full-time teaching posts. Though by then the Board had been enlarged to cover Salford and Stretford, only one hospital (The Memorial Jewish) refused.

The work of the Advisory Panel increased rapidly after the war, because of the extended area covered by the Board and because of the termination of many temporary wartime appointments. As Bevan planned his National Health Service, the Advisory Panel of the Joint Board was demonstrating the potential of a medical school as a means of directing specialist medical services throughout the hospitals of its metropolitan area.[50]

The Joint Board and special services

During the first year of its operation the Board received a memo from Professor Telford suggesting that directors be appointed in medicine, surgery, and obstetrics, to oversee the developing services of the municipal hospitals. They should be senior consultants, acting in an honorary capacity, men of experience and contacts who could encourage links with the voluntary hospitals and the University. The Board agreed, and suggested to the Public Health Committee that they appoint three honorary directors for a two year experimental period. G.R. Murray, Professor Emeritus of Systematic Medicine, E.D. Telford, Professor of Surgery, and D. Dougal, Professor of Obstetrics and Gynaecology, were so appointed. In accepting the services of these directors the Public Health Committee expressed the hope that the voluntary hospitals would follow suit. As in the case of the advisory panels, the Board did not feel able to make such a recommendation.[51]

In 1939 the question of directors was raised again, and was considered by a sub-committee of the Board. They favoured the appointment of honorary advisers, who would collect data and supervise research, visit other hospitals when necessary, and generally help to improve the services of their specialty. The advisers were to be responsible to the Board rather than the Council or the voluntary hospitals. Any risk of factionalism between specialties could be avoided by appointing a committee of advisers. The nucleus of this advisory committee would represent medicine, surgery, obstetrics and orthopaedics; neurology and paediatrics could be added when necessary. So composed, the committee could explore the introduction of special work for neurosurgery, plastic surgery, genito-urinary surgery, rheumatology and haematology. The existing Advisory Panel for consultant appointments was to be used to choose this Committee of Advisers.

Clearly the Board wanted to be more closely involved in directing the specialist functions of the hospitals. The municipal hospitals had already shown themselves to be co-operative; the voluntary ones would hardly have accepted directors for each service, but they might be more receptive to an advisory committee impartially appointed and backed by the Board's prestige.

Even so, the hospitals were being cautious. Ancoats wanted the Advisory Committee's activities to be confined to research; the Manchester Royal Infirmary wanted a representative of every hospital on the committee; the Hospital Council and Statutory Committee (on which the specialists were well represented) approved, 'subject to the method and duties of the Committee being more clearly defined'. The Joint Board replied by stressing that the Committee of Advisers would be under the authority of the Joint Board, it would act to improve co-ordination and to develop desirable new services. Thus in September 1942, the Honorary Advisers of the Clinical Services Sub-committee was replaced, on its own recommendation, by the Medical Advisory Committee. In fact the committee was little used, though most of its members were active on the Board. It handled the enquiries into facilities for children with cerebral palsy, but most special enquiries were handled by *ad hoc* sub-committees.[52]

Nonetheless, in the difference between the two sets of proposals for honorary directors one can perhaps see the influence of the younger specialists; the emphasis had shifted from directing existing services, to creating new ones. The stress on travel, and the collection of information was characteristic of Harry Platt; the whole proposal was a generalisation of the tasks these specialists had already carried out to advance their own specialties in the voluntary hospitals. These specialists were able now to use the Joint Board to widen the area of hospital coordination and thus broaden the base for specialist services. In the rest of this chapter we shall review these developments.

Again we may first take the case of orthopaedics, probably the most rapidly developing speciality of the inter-war years. Harry Platt had been building a separate fracture service at Ancoats Hospital since the First World War and he was involved in the British Medical Association's report of 1935 which recommended the nationwide establishment of fracture clinics. In February 1935 the Ministry of Health circulated this report to local authorities requesting them to consult the voluntary hospitals in their areas. In Manchester, of course, the matter was referred to the Joint Board which set up a committee plus a working sub-committee of four surgeons and the Medical Officer of Health (Platt, Telford, Morley and Newell plus Veitch Clark). When, in July 1936, the fracture clinic of the Royal Infirmary was opened under the direction of Mr Platt, a Government Committee visited Manchester and took the opportunity to discuss the extension of fracture services in the city. Platt was able to get data from government sources and this he placed before his colleagues on the sub-committee. They worked out a scheme which was approved by the Board and most of the hospitals.

Five thousand fractures occurred each year in Manchester; 70 per cent of them in homes, 18 per cent in the street, 12 per cent in industry; 30 per cent of the cases were children. Since 1934 patients had been taken directly to the nearest hospital, but it was not practicable to provide a full fracture unit at each hospital. Instead, where possible, one unit would be provided in each zone. Thus the Manchester Royal Infirmary would serve the central area, and Withington, the southern area. In the north, Crumpsall would take the in-patients and Ancoats the out-patients; ideally these two facilities would be controlled by the same orthopaedic surgeon. But the third general hospital in north Manchester was less co-operative; their surgeon did not attend the committee meeting and the Board publicly commented. 'It is to be hoped in future that the Jewish Hospital will see the desirability of adopting the principles laid down in the reports of the BMA and the Inter-Departmental Committee respecting the segregation of fractures. With its limited in-patient accommodation, it should continue to provide a useful moderate sized out-patient service.'[53] Soon afterwards the Board welcomed the proposal by Ancoats Hospital to erect a new out-patients department, a development intimately associated with its recommended scheme for fractures.

In January 1939 a new orthopaedic block was opened at the Manchester Royal Infirmary by the Minister of Health – 'the first concrete, or rather ferro-concrete result of the co-ordination of the city's hospital services which had been taking place under the aegis of the Manchester Joint Hospitals Advisory Board during the last three years'. The Minister, Walter Eliot, referred to the Board, with appreciation, as the first of its kind in the country. It merited the most sincere congratulations on the remarkable work it had initiated and in some respects already completed.

The case for separate fracture units was a strong one which had already been demonstrated in voluntary hospitals. That few cities had followed the example of Manchester and Liverpool only strengthened the case; public pressure was beginning to mount against the failure of fracture treatment generally to advance beyond its pre-war state and the Board was able to use the British Medical Association and the Ministry of Health Reports as well as its own authority.

In concluding their report the sub-committee on fractures recommended that an honorary adviser on orthopaedic services be appointed to ensure full cooperation. In fact the Board continued to work by appointing special sub-committees even in orthopaedics. Thus when in 1945 a letter and memo from the British Orthopaedics Association recommended that soft-tissue wounds should be treated along with fractures, Platt was appointed to head a committee to examine the suggestion. In principle the Board agreed; they welcomed the development of the Birmingham Accident Hospital, which was entirely devoted to wounds of both hard and soft tissues. There, accident surgery was to establish itself after the Second World War as orthopaedic surgery had done after the First, Ruscoe Clarke playing a role similar to that of Robert Jones. In Birmingham the authorities had converted a general hospital for accident use. In Manchester there seemed to be no hospital suitable for such conversion. Instead the fracture units at each general hospital centre were to be reorganised to take all accidents; thus Withington, Manchester Royal Infirmary, and Crumpsall/Ancoats would serve the city. The Board had by this time been enlarged, so that Salford and Stretford were also to be planned: the Salford Royal Infirmary and Hope Hospital would serve Salford; Stretford could best be served by Park Hospital in Davyhulme. All the hospitals, except the Jewish Hospital, agreed in principle, but there were great practical difficulties preventing the fusion of accident services at Ancoats and Crumpsall. Salford Royal and Hope Hospital, Salford, did effect some coordination.[54]

By this time, largely because of the Second World War, neurosurgery and plastic surgery had become recognised divisions of surgery. Both would be required in each major accident unit. In addition, units for severe burns were to be provided, one in Salford and one at Withington, then developing as the regional centre for plastic surgery. The concentration of advanced services at Withington was furthered by the removal there of the Emergency Medical Services' unit for jaw and facial injuries which had been opened at Baguley military hospital during the war. The place of Withington was fully recognised when the Manchester Royal Infirmary plastic surgery unit, long neglected by its honorary director Mr T. P. Kilner, was finally closed down and Kilner was not replaced.[55]

The continuous differentiation of medical and surgical specialties before, during and after the Second World War provided a large field for innovation which the Board could direct and in some cases stimulate. In 1937–8 they decided to concentrate major thoracic surgery for tuberculosis at Withington; no tuberculosis patients were to be accepted at the Royal Infirmary; Baguley sanatorium was to handle only routine tuberculosis surgery; Withington would act as a regional centre by accepting patients from outside Manchester when the relevant local authority promised to pay. Mr Gordon Bryce was appointed as surgeon in charge of the clinics at the Manchester Royal Infirmary and Withington; anaesthesia facilities at Withington were to be strengthened; theatre and ward nurses were to be sent to Brompton Hospital in London for special training.[56]

Neurosurgery in Manchester had been pioneered by Mr Geoffrey Jefferson at Salford Royal. During the First World War he had gained considerable experience in the treatment of head wounds, and at Salford his fellow surgeons had allowed him access to all neurological cases as might benefit from surgery. Jefferson, who was extraordinarily gifted, made full use of this opportunity; he published several important papers on neurosurgery and by 1926 was recognised as an authority. In that year he was given a small neurosurgical unit at the Manchester Royal Infirmary.

At Salford he had spent much of his time in general surgery. At the Infirmary he could specialise more but the facilities open to him were very limited, and there were too few beds to allow an adequate concentration of material. From 1933 until 1939 Jefferson also operated at the National Hospital, Queens Square, London, the country's only centre for special treatment and research in nervous diseases; but in 1939 he abandoned this connection when given a personal chair in neurosurgery at the University.

In December 1942 the Manchester Royal Infirmary submitted to the Board proposals for 'a Neurological Institute to serve the Manchester Region and the wider area over which the influence of Manchester now exists or may exist in the future'. By then, the Manchester leaders, having co-ordinated city services, were hoping to set up regional centres which would take patients from outside Manchester, not as an extra, when time, space and suitable payment allowed, but as a natural consequence of the large populations required to justify the most elaborate of the developing medical specialties.

The Infirmary memo was submitted to the Manchester Medical Officer of Health, now Dr C. Metcalfe Brown, who was to enquire about suitable sites (and about financial support?). He concluded that at least part of the new Institute should be built near the Infirmary and the University. Here the special clinical and teaching work could be carried out. The long stay facilities might be placed there also, or at Withington, or at a new hospital in the country where the air was fresher than in Manchester.

The Board preferred the country hospital, but stressed that 'training and fitting experience of a new generation of specialists in neurology was a matter of urgency, that the establishment of the Institute was necessary, and that the premises should be new, extensive, and in architecture worthy of the City, the University and the vast region which it would be called upon to serve'. The report was sent to the constituent authorities. A neurological unit was finally built, in 1951. Meanwhile, in 1943–4 the Nuffield Provincial Hospitals Trust gave £5,000 to the Department of Neurology for the remuneration of staff, teaching and research.[57]

In all these cases: orthopaedics, plastic surgery, thoracic surgery, and neurosurgery, it was the university specialists who made the running, and undoubtedly the co-ordination of these advancing specialities was the major work of the Board. In one case, this meant opposing the demands of the profession. When Ancoats was refused certification as a training hospital for fellowships of the Royal College of Surgeons, because it did not have an eye department, the Board intervened successfully, arguing that the general upgrading of all the city hospitals was contrary to the demands of a rational hospital system.[58]

In the case of paediatrics, proposals submitted to the Joint Board helped establish the University chair. In 1942 the Royal Infirmary, St Mary's and the Royal Children's Hospital, Pendlebury, advocated setting up an Institute of Child Health. The following year the Children's Hospital submitted a memo to the Board which also advocated the foundation of a University chair in paediatrics. The proposal met with unanimous support at a conference held in the University on 29 June 1944 but not until 1946 was the chair advertised. The funding of the chair reflected the growing regionalism of health services: local authorities including the Lancashire and Cheshire County Councils and most of the Lancashire Boroughs had joined Manchester and Salford in providing £3,500 per year for five years; the Children's Hospital had given £500 and so had the Manchester and Salford Hospital Saturday Fund.[59] Also in 1946, the Board began to investigate the possibility of a school of speech therapy.[60]

Not all the initiative however came from the profession or the University. In several of the less glamorous specialties it was the local authorities who felt the need for action. In other cases we find national associations, founded to help particular classes of sufferers, approaching the Board with suggestions for future developments. In most of these areas the results were slight.

In 1936–7 Veitch Clark asked the Board to set up a special unit for rheumatology. Two years later the Empire Rheumatism Council requested help in setting up an East Lancashire Rheumatism Council to be centred on Manchester and to include, if possible, the large spa hospital at Buxton. But not until 1947 did the University set up a rheumatism research unit, for which beds were provided at Withington.[61]

Cancer services did not attract the attention of the Board until 1939 when the Cancer Act required each local authority to provide adequate services. In Manchester, a committee was set up on which the Joint Board was represented together with the Public Health Authority, the Royal Infirmary, and the Holt Radium Institute and Christie Hospital. Nothing was achieved during the war, and in 1946 the Lord Mayor of Manchester was requested to convene a meeting of the neighbouring local authorities to consider a joint scheme centred on the Radium Institute. Soon afterwards the Board gave its approval to this scheme.[62]

Hearing aid clinics were suggested to the Board by a circular sent in 1937–8 by the National Institute for the Deaf. Manchester University already had a pioneering unit for the education of the deaf led by Dr Ewing, who had apparently helped originate the circular. During the war, when the Board received some money from the Nuffield Provincial Hospitals Trust, it directed the funds to this department. But no hearing aid clinics were set up.[63]

Although the Royal Infirmary appointed its first psychiatrist in 1939, psychiatric care did not appear in the Board's reports until 1944 when Manchester Northern Hospital (for women and children) requested Nuffield funds for this purpose. The hospital had become 'psychiatry-minded' when the Emergency Medical Services assigned doctors to all hospitals as a precaution against the widespread psychiatric disturbances which it feared might result from bombing. The Board referred the request to Alderman Edwards and Mr R. L. Newell, advised by Dr F. R. Ferguson at the Manchester Royal Infirmary.

Edwards and Newell stressed the need for a rapid expansion of facilities and recommended a joint committee of the Board and University. The Northern Hospital received a grant of £250 (subject to review) to develop a small clinic mainly for child guidance. Their plans did not work out; the hospital's own Medical Board decided to wait for a city-wide scheme, and the money was returned to the Board. Once again the Board had found itself in difficulties over its relations with a small, non-teaching voluntary hospital, even in a field where facilities were minimal and demand enormous.

The Joint Committee report of 1945 demonstrated just how sketchy the psychiatric services were. Both Manchester and Salford Education Authorities ran small clinics for child guidance. The Royal Infirmary neurological division held five out-patient sessions per week and used electro-convulsive therapy, but the war had reduced medical staff from two part-timers to one, and the available beds from two to zero. Small clinics at the Northern Hospital and at Salford Royal worked three sessions per week between them but had no beds. The Lancashire Mental Hospital Board held out-patient sessions at Ancoats and at Hope Hospital, Salford, and certifiable cases could be sent to their large mental hospitals. Otherwise, the only mental wards available were at Crumpsall, where 670 beds were maintained in the Institution, not the hospital proper.

The Committee acknowledged the staffing difficulties and the uncertainties concerning demand, but they were quite clear that psychiatry had to become a proper specialty, with a University chair, an expanded service at the Royal Infirmary and departments in the various general hospitals. The facilities at Crumpsall were to be integrated into the hospital rather than the Institution. These recommendations accorded with progressive thinking in mental health circles, but in Manchester, as elsewhere, their implementation did not come until long after the Regional Hospital Board had replaced the Manchester, Salford and Stretford Joint Hospitals Advisory Board.[64]

The Joint Board in retrospect
The Manchester Joint Hospitals Advisory Board stood as a useful object lesson to the men who planned the National Health Service. Its history is still a useful yardstick for measuring the potential and performance of various kinds of hospital co-ordination. Like the Regional Hospital Boards after 1948, it was concerned with three major tasks: (1) the coordination of hospitals serving the same catchment areas; (2) the extension of specialist care from major voluntary hospitals to other general hospitals; (3) the development of new services on a regional basis.

We have seen how the controversies in 1934 over obstetrical services hastened the birth of the Joint Board. That no other controversies of this type appeared suggests that the arrangements to coordinate St Mary's with the municipal hospitals did at least alleviate this problem. The Board helped guide the development and rationalisation of accident services; changes in bed allocation also followed some of the major innovations, for example the development of thoracic surgery at Withington, but the Board did not attempt any redistribution of beds except in connection with new developments in medical services. That the hospitals all remained under separate management did of course limit the Board's potential for effecting redistribution; but before we can conclude that its lack of executive authority was here critical, we shall need to examine the scope for re-allocating as it was later explored, and the heavy constraints which buildings, auxiliary facilities, etc., imposed on any aspirant rationalisers.

The Board did lay the basis for the functional grouping of Manchester hospitals. For accident services and also for blood transfusion, the obvious threefold division into North, Central and South was used because the need for easy access was paramount. When links between hospitals were considered for pusposes of specialist staffing, the constraints were different. In terms of physical geography the complex of voluntary hospitals in south-central Manchester stood between the huge municipal hospitals in the north and south of the city; but in the geography of medical careers the Royal Infirmary stood above the municipal hospitals. Both considerations combined to maintain the voluntary complex as a service to the central area loosely linked with both north and south and with the regions lying beyond the city boundaries. Even so, the proximity of Withington to the Royal Infirmary, the spaciousness of its site compared to that of the Infirmary, and the quality of its buildings compared to those of Crumpsall combined to ensure that Withington was selected to provide most of those new specialist facilities in which the medical school and the municipality both had an interest.

The motive force of the Board was the desire by university-linked specialists on the Board or its advisory panels to expand both the range and depth of specialist services. Because the city shared these goals and the major voluntary hospitals cooperated, the specialists had scope for action. They were able to appoint their junior associates to consultant posts outside the traditional teaching hospitals; they were able to develop new special units within the traditional centres. The Board clearly demonstrated the importance of a vetting agency for consultant appointments in up-grading the coordinating hospitals. Its major failures concerned small voluntary hospitals in which the medical staff were independent of local authority control and not integrated into the professional hierarchy centred on the medical school.

As the major specialists were built up and plans extended to include more esoteric services such as neurosurgery, so the University became more involved in the execution of the plans; the arbitrating 'third force' on the Board itself became a major component of regional schemes. These concerned authorities outside Manchester, and even outside the conurbation. The Board itself was expanded during the war to cover most of the conurbation; further expansion over the whole region served by Manchester remained a possibility that was to exercise both the Nuffield Trust and the Ministry of Health. Certainly the Board had begun to influence the outer areas, in this respect as in several others, generalising and coordinating developments which had begun in separate specialities, e.g. radium treatment. Because the outer authorities wanted services which only the teaching hospitals could provide, there was scope for co-operation.

Notes and references

The majority of the newspaper articles used in this chapter were examined in a collection of clippings on Manchester Public Health in the Manchester Local History Library.

1. Since this chapter was written Frank Honigsbaum has published his *The Division in British Medicine*, London, 1979, by far the best available guide to medical politics in the 1930s.
2. Manchester Public Health Committee, Annual Report, 1930.
3. Manchester Public Health Committee, 12 June, 11 December 1934.
4. Manchester Public Health Committee, 1, 8 December 1936.
5. Manchester Joint Hospitals Advisory Board, Annual Report, 1937.
6. Manchester Public Health Committee, 19 December 1933.
7. *Manchester Guardian*, 15 July 1933; *Manchester Guardian, Manchester Evening News*, 11 January 1935.
8. Manchester Public Health Committee, 23 April 1934; *Manchester Guardian*, 24 April 1934.
9. Manchester Royal Infirmary, Annual Report, 1938; *Lancet*, 2 (1921), 620–1.
10. *Manchester Evening News*, 13 December 1934; *Manchester Guardian*, 11, 12 January 1935.
11. On the development plans for upgrading the Poor Law general medical practice and merging it with the panel service see Manchester Public Health Committee, 13 May

1930, 20 September 1932, 28 November 1933, 20 February 1934, 30 October 1935; Manchester City Council Minutes 1934–5, Vol. II, Appendix, pp. 1699–1732; *Manchester Guardian*, 9, 10 January, 3, 23 February 1934, 29 May 1935; *Manchester Evening News*, 5 July, 21 August 1935; *Manchester Guardian*, 3, 28 October 1935; *Manchester City News*, 28 October, 2 November 1935.
12. *Manchester Guardian*, 12 January 1935.
13. Manchester Public Health Committee, 18 January 1932, 12 June, 17 July 1934.
14. Manchester Public Health Committee, 17, 23 April, 14 August 1934; Manchester Medical Officer of Health, Annual Report, 1934.
15. On the work of public hospitals, Manchester Medical Officer of Health, Annual Report, 1937.
16. See n. 14.
17. Manchester Medical Officer of Health, Annual Report, 1933, p. 98; *Manchester City News*, 8 July 1933; Manchester Public Health Committee, 18 February 1936.
18. *Manchester City News*, 1 May 1935, 'Sir, I am a democrat, but for the sake of democracy I would make you dictator in your own sphere'.
19. Manchester Public Health Committee, 17 July, 11 December 1934.
20. Manchester Public Health Committee, 19 March 1935.
21. Manchester Public Health Committee, 13 November 1934, 15 January 1935, 18 February 1936; *Manchester Guardian*, 18, 23 January 1935; *British Medical Journal*, 2 February 1935.
22. *Manchester Evening News*, 27, 28 May 1935; *Manchester Guardian*, 29 May 1935; *Manchester City News*, 1 June 1935.
23. *Manchester City News*, 6 March 1936.
24. *Manchester Evening News*, 11 December 1936; E. D. Simon, *A City Council from Within*, London, 1926, reprinted 1944, pp. 21–2.
25. Manchester Public Health Committee, 18 June 1935; *Manchester Guardian*, 19 June 1935; *Manchester Evening News*, 24 April 1936; *British Medical Journal*, 14 September 1935, pp. 515–16.
26. Letter in *British Medical Journal*, 28 September 1935, p. 600.
27. *Manchester Guardian*, 20 June 1935.
28. *Ibid*.
29. *Manchester Guardian*, 19 June 1935.
30. *Manchester Guardian*, 27 June 1935.
31. *Manchester Guardian*, 28 June 1935.
32. For survey see Manchester Public Health Committee, 13 November 1934; *Manchester Guardian*, 23 January 1935.
33. Manchester Joint Hospitals Advisory Board, Annual Report, 1936; Manchester Public Health Committee, 11 June 1935.
34. *Ibid*.
35. *Manchester City News*, 20 July 1935.
36. Manchester Public Health Committee, 17 September 1935.
37. Manchester Public Health Committee, 11 December 1934.
38. Manchester Public Health Committee, 1, 8 December 1936.
39. Harry Platt was very active in the discussions which set up the Manchester Joint Hospitals Advisory Board – interview 18 June 1974. On the development of British orthopaedics, see his *Selected Papers* (1963) and *Lancet*, 2 (1921), 620–1.
40. Manchester Public Health Committee, 19 March 1935; *Manchester Guardian*, 4 November 1938; *British Medical Journal*, Supplement, 12 November 1934, p. 304.
41. Manchester Public Health Committee, 18 June, 8, 13 August 1935; Manchester Joint Hospitals Advisory Board, Annual Report, 1936; *Manchester Guardian*, 14 August 1935; *Lancet*, 24 August 1935.
42. Manchester Joint Hospitals Advisory Board, minutes 1935.
43. *Ibid*.

THE JOINT HOSPITALS ADVISORY BOARD

44. Manchester Joint Hospitals Advisory Board, Annual Report, 1936.
45. *Ibid.*
46. Manchester Joint Hospitals Advisory Board, Annual Report, 1937.
47. See Manchester Joint Hospitals Advisory Board, Annual Reports for membership changes.
48. The minutes of the subcommittee (one volume) and the minutes of the Board (one volume) can be found at Manchester Town Hall.
49. Manchester Joint Hospitals Advisory Board, subcommittee minutes, pp. 13–16; Manchester Joint Hospitals Advisory Board, Annual Report, 1936; *British Medical Journal*, 28 March 1936.
50. See Manchester Joint Hospitals Advisory Board, Annual Reports, for relevant years.
51. Manchester Joint Hospitals Advisory Board, Annual Report, 1936.
52. Manchester Joint Hospitals Advisory Board, Annual Reports, 1936 and 1939; minutes, p. 117; subcommitee minutes, pp. 17–18, 60–2, 82–6; *British Medical Journal*, 28 March 1936, p. 654.
53. Manchester Joint Hospitals Advisory Board, subcommittee minutes, p. 50.
54. Manchester Joint Hospitals Advisory Board, Annual Reports, 1936, 1937, 1938, 1939; minutes, p. 229, 248, 259; subcommittee minutes, pp. 42–51; *British Medical Journal*, 28 January 1939; Platt, 'The care of the injured', in his *Selected Papers* (1963).
55. Manchester Joint Hospitals Advisory Board, minutes, pp. 247, 268.
56. Manchester Joint Hospitals Advisory Board, Annual Report, 1938.
57. Obituary of Jefferson, *Bio. Mem. Fellows Roy. Soc.*, 7 (1961); Manchester Joint Hospitals Advisory Board, Annual Reports, 1943, 1944.
58. Manchester Joint Hospitals Advisory Board, Annual Report, 1938.
59. Manchester Joint Hospitals Advisory Board, Annual Reports, 1934, 1944; minutes, pp. 125–6; subcommittee minutes, pp. 110–13.
60. Manchester Joint Hospitals Advisory Board, Annual Report, 1946; subcommittee minutes, p. 220.
61. Manchester Joint Hospitals Advisory Board, Annual Reports, 1937, 1939; minutes, pp. 70–2; subcommittee minutes, p. 217.
62. Manchester Joint Hospitals Advisory Board, Annual Reports, 1939, 1946.
63. Manchester Joint Hospitals Advisory Board, Annual Report, 1939; subcommittee minutes, pp. 61–2.
64. Manchester Joint Hospitals Advisory Board, Annual Reports, 1944, 1945; minutes, pp. 160–6, 181; Manchester Royal Infirmary, Annual Report, 1939, p. 24.

CHAPTER 13

The hospital service and the Second World War: actualities and plans

The Emergency Hospital Service in Lancashire
The First World War greatly advanced a number of medical specialties and considerably changed middle-class attitudes to hospitals, but had little permanent effect on the organisation of the hospital service. Military hospitals had been improvised and filled with wounded soldiers. In the Second World War, hospital accommodation was planned in advance mainly in the expectation that it would be required for civilians wounded in air-raids. Casualties were, in fact, far less numerous than had been anticipated and as a consequence, the Emergency Hospital Service was never severely tested. Its importance in the history of British hospitals lay less in its performance than in its being the first attempt by central government to plan a national hospital system. The experience of a planned, national system during war-time stimulated considerable discussion of possible future systems. The Ministry's new responsibilities led civil servants to explore the available options. Above all the role of the Ministry of Health during the war made the subsequent adoption of a National Health Service easier to imagine and easier to accept than it would have been otherwise.[1]

The Emergency Hospital Service was administered on a regional basis; in the North West, Dr W. H. C. Patrick, of the Ministry of Health, ran the regional office in Manchester. His staff included Dr F. N. Marshall, formerly of the Manchester Public Health Department, later medical head of the Manchester Regional Hospital Board. Group Officers were appointed for each major city, usually senior medical men from the local voluntary hospitals; Mr A. Burgess, Professor Emeritus of Surgery at Manchester University, co-ordinated the medical services of Manchester (including Salford, Stretford and Stockport). The link between the Ministry and the voluntary hospitals symbolised in Burgess' appointment was further strengthened when Miss Duff Grant, matron of the Manchester Royal Infirmary, was appointed as Group Nursing Officer. The co-ordination of lay staff was supervised by Mr Cotton, seconded from Veitch Clark's staff; further links with local authorities were made in the running of first-aid centres, which were controlled by the local Medical Officers of Health.[2]

Outside Manchester and Liverpool all hospital and first-aid services came under the control of the Medical Officers of Health, co-ordinated by the regional office. Damage outside the big cities was relatively light and there was little call for co-ordination between Boroughs. The main problems came in Manchester and Liverpool, especially the latter, where there were some complaints from voluntary hospitals that the emergency service was interfering with their work.[3] Generally the system worked well, facilitating removal of patients when city hospitals, including Hope Hospital (Salford), Salford Royal and the Manchester Royal Infirmary, were hit by bombs in December 1940.

This emergency administration, like the Manchester Joint Hospitals Advisory Board, worked through the co-operation of the voluntary hospitals and the local authority services. In both cases the prestige and expertise in the teaching hospitals enabled the non-governmental sector to play a considerable role in administration of the service. In both cases the new arrangements were best developed in the cities, where expertise was concentrated, where co-ordination was most required and where the medical needs were greatest. Indeed, the Manchester Joint Hospitals Advisory Board became an important link in the war-time service; it was, for example, on their recommendation that Burgess was appointed Group Officer.[4]

The independence of cities and regions under the Emergency Hospital Service was a reflection of the exigencies of war. The whole Civil Defence service was in the hands of local authorities, under regional officers who by June 1940 had gained considerable autonomy. The devolution of power to regional level was a response to the fact that all major cities might be targets for bombing; central power was also limited lest attacks on London should destroy the headquarters. The hospital service was never as fully devolved as civil defence, partly because the Ministry felt that the supplying and equipping of new hospital units could be more effective on a national basis; partly because it might in various cases be necessary to override regional boundaries, especially in London where the 'regions' were sectoral and somewhat unnatural, more generally in the provision of specialised units serving more than one region.[5]

Some of these units were based on existing specialisms; for example the Royal Devonshire Hospital near the famous Buxton spa was used for the treatment of rheumatic servicemen. Some were appropriated for patients separated on non-medical grounds; the Bucklow Hospital, Knutsford, was taken over by the War Office as a hospital for prisoners of war. As in the First World War there were special centres for treatment of injuries;

THE CONSTRUCTION OF THE NHS

Winwick Hospital, near Liverpool, was developed for the treatment of head and spinal, orthopaedic and peripheral nerve injuries; Baguley Sanatorium, to the south of Manchester, became a major centre for chest injuries, plastic surgery and jaw injuries. This jaw and facial injuries unit continued after the war and was transferred to Withington Hospital.[6]

Thus the emergency fostered special services. It also drew attention to the relationships of city and country hospitals. Though this feature of hospital geography, already manifest in the growth of convalescent facilities outside cities, was in fact to decline in importance after the war, it was an important consideration in some war-time plans for future services. In each emergency hospital region, country hospitals were assigned, their facilities were enlarged, and some of their patients were decanted or crowded together in order to make room for possible evacuees from city hospitals.[7]

For the Manchester conurbation there were two main groupings of reserve beds. Initially about 2,000 beds in so-called 'base' hospitals had been assigned to the group, at Macclesfield, Buxton and Knutsford hospitals, at Baguley Sanatorium and at Winwick mental hospital,[8] but, as we have seen, most of these hospitals were later assigned to special functions. By August 1940 only 703 casualty beds remained in the outer-zone hospitals. Additional accommodation was later provided in new huts, each taking about 30 beds, but the major raids on Manchester had already passed before these extension and upgrading schemes could be carried out.[9]

The reserve beds on which the regional officers had counted, and on which they had to draw during the raids of December 1940, were in the large mental hospitals of the Ribble Valley. Calderstones and Whittingham each provided about 900 casualty beds, though they were never officially linked to the Manchester group.[10] Some of these beds were emptied when mental patients were moved into newly-completed accommodation at Brock Hall, others were freed by overcrowding the remaining wards and restricting the admission of new patients. The consequent conditions, especially the placing of mentally defective children in the same wards as adults, were the subject of repeated complaints. These mental patients and the sufferers from tuberculosis, overcrowded in hospitals or denied access to them, must be counted among the victims of the war. Their plight was the more galling as so many of the casualty beds remained unused.[11]

As we have noted, Salford Royal Infirmary and Manchester Royal Infirmary were damaged in the bombing; much of Hope Hospital, Salford, was destroyed. On the other hand, the Emergency Hospital Service was responsible for some upgrading of hospitals and for the provision of new beds in hutted wards. Taking twenty-six beds as the peacetime capacity of a hut, about 3,200 new places were provided in the hospitals which passed under the Manchester Regional Hospital Board, a net gain of about 1,000 beds.[12] This expansion helped vindicate central direction of the service. For those who were worried about the poor quality of many hospitals and the near bankruptcy of most voluntary hospitals, the wartime experience of a government service was encouraging.

The War and plans for the future

By forcing some regionalisation of hospital control, and bringing country hospitals into closer relation with those of the cities, the war shook the ill-co-ordinated hospitals much more than could the feeble efforts of the British Hospitals Association. No one could suppose that once peace came the hospitals would be allowed to slip back into the old disarray, if only because the finance of many voluntary hospitals would again become precarious if war-time government assistance were withdrawn. The wartime hospital surveys disabused anyone who thought Britain had an adequate set of hospitals; the faults were common knowledge and the public wanted reform. The shape of that reform remained to be decided, and the medical profession and the hospital associations entered an active debate that went some way towards laying the foundations of a reformed system. Their voluntary efforts were, in part, taken over by the government, as ministers and civil servants began to consider the likely post-war situation, but not before the voluntary schemes had demonstrated some of the potentials of reform – both real gains and real obstacles.

The establishment of the Emergency Hospital Service evoked much critical discussion as to how hospitals ought to be organised. Because the colossal air attacks anticipated in the plans happily did not materialise, many doctors, especially in London, spent much time sitting around half-evacuated hospitals, often grumbling about their conditions of service, sometimes discussing how hospitals really ought to be run, once the Ministry could be got off their backs.

The *Lancet* published a timely article in October 1939 outlining some of the present difficulties and future hopes.[13] How could one get a healthy hospital baby out of the 'eclamptic primigravida' of the emergency hospital system? (eclampsia is a disorder of pregnancy characterised by dizziness and headaches in mild cases, repeated convulsions in more severe). This 'fearless accoucheur's' method was to take the best from both pre-war and wartime arrangements: the staffing arrangements and medical control of the voluntary hospitals, rather than the bureaucracy of the public hospitals; the public financing and salaried staffs of the municipal hospitals, rather than the 'Robin Hood' consultants who were finding it harder and harder to make a good living; the central plus regional control, and the unified service of the

Emergency Hospital Service, rather than the pre-war chaos. The likelihood of other wars and aerial bombardment was used as one justification for regionalisation; it was also used to argue that large hospitals should be built outside cities, to be served by casualty stations in the city; doctors and patients could be moved between the two. Hospitals would retain as much autonomy as possible, being run by management committees, but group officers (medical), and regional officers (lay?) would continue their wartime work. Their contribution was valued, and should be retained in the delivery of a peace-time system. But how to keep them while getting rid of ministerial control? Here was a tricky problem, made worse by the real danger of all the hospitals falling into the hands of local authorities. The solution preferred by the *Lancet*'s special commissioner, was a national hospital corporation, operating, like the BBC, under a five year charter.

The *Lancet*'s commissioner focussed on the hospital group: a base hospital and supporting hospitals serving a population of about 500,000. Such a unit, which had not featured in previous plans, appears to have been a product of wartime experience, where the hospital group in a city was the key unit. The writer assumed that in each region, the communities outside the existing groups could be made into additional groups; the regional officer would only need to see that the whole area was adequately covered and the groups were co-ordinated.

By contrast, the voluntary hospital lobby wanted full regionalisation; not just hospital groups in the cities, but a fully developed system where each hospital in the country would look to a major hospital as the central hospital of its region. In November 1939, Mr W. M. Goodenough, the banker, asked Lord Nuffield, the automobile millionaire, to support efforts to achieve hospital co-ordination throughout the provinces (London already had the King Edward's Fund). Nuffield had been associated with the area scheme in Oxford and he saw the need for similar developments elsewhere: he offered one million shares in Morris motors (£1.25 M) and he wrote to the Minister of Health to announce his intention of creating a Provincial Hospitals Trust.[14]

The Board of Trustees was 'to include men and women who are actually identified with voluntary hospitals, medical organisations and local authorities in the provinces, in Scotland, in Wales and Northern Ireland'. The objects of the Trust were twofold:

(a) to encourage the organisation of Regional and Divisional Hospital Councils and, where necessary, to assist in the formation of these Councils by making contributions towards the cost of their organisation.
(b) the Trustees are also authorised to make grants and donations to hospitals through approved Regional and Divisional Hospital Councils. They will not,

ordinarily, make these grants or donations to individual hospitals otherwise than through these Regional and Divisional Councils.

Nuffield money was to fertilise the ground on which a co-ordinated voluntary system would grow in association with local authorities:

> In effect therefore the Trust has undertaken the task of assisting the development of proposals which, in their full application, will lead to the creation of a co-ordinated and fully effective National Hospital Service. In this way the Trust seeks to make a definite contribution towards national reconstruction.[15]

The Minister of Health, Mr Walter Elliott, was grateful for the help.[16]

The Trustees set up a Regionalisation Council which had thirty-nine members, four of them medically qualified, eleven from local government at some level, four from the British Hospitals Contributory Association, three from the British Hospitals Association, two from the British Medical Association, and twenty-three primarily as voluntary hospital representatives.

Its Medical Advisory Council comprised distinguished professors and senior consultants, often men with experience of hospital administration, including Professor Harry Platt of Manchester. Several members were experienced in public health, either as teachers or as Medical Officers of Health. Among this last group were Sir Frederick Menzies, recently retired from his important work as Medical Officer of Health for the London County Council, and Dr William Pickles, the general practitioner from the Yorkshire Dales who had gained international acclaim for his studies of epidemiology in country practice. Two pathologists were included, so were a number of practitioners and BMA representatives. The chairman was Sir Farquhar Buzzard, Regius Professor of Medicine at Oxford.[17]

The Medical Advisory Council provided the real muscle of the Provincial Hospitals Trust. In this respect the Trust functioned rather like the Manchester Board: it enabled the medical men to push their specialist projects, and it provided a means of shaping hospital services according to the aspirations of the consultants. Thus, in the first report of the Trust, the Medical Advisory Council outlined a scheme for unified accident services (one of the first successes of the Manchester Board had been its fractures scheme);[18] later it outlined a scheme for co-ordinating pathological laboratory services. But more important than these technical advances was the stress which the Medical Advisory Council gave to the principle that regions should be centred on teaching hospitals. This principle, though mentioned in the Sankey Report, had not been observed in the regionalisation of the Emergency Health Service, but it was crucial in the schemes of the Nuffield Medical Advisory Council. Each hospital had to be connected to a centre where special services were concentrated, and from which expertise could flow outwards.[19]

During 1940 and 1941, the Trust had a limited amount of success in setting up Regional and Divisional Councils. The Oxford Region was already organised. In the South West, a Regional Council was established to cover Devon and Cornwall. Each of these Regions had three Divisional Councils. A Yorkshire Regional Hospitals Council covered Leeds, Bradford and Hull. In addition, Divisional Councils were set up in Bristol and Surrey.[20]

It is perhaps surprising that more Divisional Councils were not formed; for the Divisions more or less corresponded to the wartime groups. Hard-pressed doctors may have felt that the wartime arrangements would serve until peace came; then there would be time for exploring new links. It is not surprising that few *Regional* Councils were formed, for there were many difficult issues to be resolved. We can illustrate the problem by considering the fate of the Nuffield proposals in the North Western Region.

The Manchester Joint Board learned of the Nuffield Trust through press notices, and immediately (11 December 1939) referred the matter to its executive committee. The secretaries of the Board were keen to establish that any new regions should be based on university medical schools, rather than, say, the geographical divisions of the British Hospitals Association, where Manchester was included in an area comprising Cumberland, Westmorland, Lancashire, Cheshire and the five northern counties of Wales. Apparently the executive committee took no action – nor do the minutes record any discussion.[21]

The question was taken up in earnest a year later, in January 1941, after the Nuffield Trust had written to the Joint Board, asking them to act as the Divisional Hospital Council for Manchester. Such Divisions were to be grouped into Regions, and the Joint Board was also asked to undertake preliminary organisation of the other Divisional Councils within the Manchester Region. The subsequent history of these proposals is strongly influenced by the fact that, at the time of this first approach of the Trust to the Manchester Board, a provisional council headed by the Vice-Chancellor of Liverpool University was already undertaking preliminary organisation in the Merseyside area. The Nuffield Trust suggested that the Manchester Board might meet with the Liverpool Committee to get a provisional agreement about the boundaries between the two regions.[22]

The Manchester Board was whole-heartedly in favour of regionalisation and had three suggestions to make. Firstly, they wanted to be recognised 'Not as the Divisional Hospitals Council for Manchester but as the body responsible as agents for the time being of the Nuffield Trust for the organisation of the Regional Hospitals Council'. It would be difficult for the Manchester Division, as such, to organise other Divisions within the Region. Secondly, the Board stressed that any rational 'Manchester Division' ought to include Salford and Stretford. Thirdly, they wanted a meeting with the Trustees to discuss the method of approach and detail of organisation. They wanted to know more about the workings of the Trust itself, and they wondered to what extent the Trust had the backing of the Ministry of Health.[23]

The Trust's reply was positive on all counts, and the Board appointed a powerful sub-committee to negotiate with the Trust and with Liverpool. The meeting with representatives from Liverpool was held on 11 March 1941, but progress was limited. The Manchester representatives felt that Liverpool was forcing the pace, for they had already called a meeting of voluntary and municipal hospital representatives from a wide area, at which they were proposing to ask for the adoption of Nuffield proposals for the constitution of a Liverpool Regional organisation. Manchester 'considered that much more time should be spent on educative and propaganda work before any constitutional steps were taken'. Manchester would in the meantime approach Salford and Stretford to increase the area of the Board's influence.[24]

It was unfortunate that the two cities never got into step over hospital co-ordination; particularly so because the area controlled by Lancashire County Council obviously included many areas dependent on Liverpool as well as a majority of areas which were dependent on Manchester. Cheshire too was so divided and the proposals of Liverpool to invite Cheshire County Council to their big meeting, may have given rise to apprehension in Manchester. Certainly there is evidence that Liverpool's haste reflected a considerable unease lest the new arrangements follow the war-time administration in subordinating Liverpool to a regional authority based on Manchester. Nonetheless, the representatives did agree on a provisional boundary, and accepted that each group would continue with regionalisation in the way it thought best.

The Manchester Sub-Committee met separately with a number of local authorities, but the multiplicity of authorities threatened confusion. Various attempts were made to get agreement on policy between Liverpool, Manchester, Lancashire, the smaller Boroughs and the voluntary hospitals, but it proved very difficult. A large meeting of those concerned on 4 September 1941 produced only a plan for a meeting on 20 March 1942 at which arrangements could be made for a survey of hospital resources.[25]

The confusion and inaction within Lancashire contrasted with, and in part resulted from, the continuing independent initiatives of the Liverpool group. They had gone ahead with their large meeting at Chester, to which representatives of Chester, Cheshire, Denbighshire, Caernarvonshire, Anglesey and Merionethshire had been invited, together with representatives of the voluntary hospitals within these counties and Flintshire. It had been agreed that these authorities should consider forming one or more Divisions of a Liverpool Region as envisaged in the proposals of the Nuffield Trust. This position was formally reported to the Manchester Committee who felt unable to discuss the situation because of lack of information.[26] The apparent distance between the Joint Board and the Trust, the impression of minimal communication, is surprising, because Walter Cobbett was a member of the Nuffield Regionalisation Council; Harry Platt of their Medical Advisory Council, and Mr R. L. Newell of both.

The progress on Merseyside and the confusion in the Manchester region which Nuffield initiatives had produced, were both superseded by government initiatives in the autumn of 1941. As we shall see, the Ministry of Health's own future planning had been speeded by the advances of the Nuffield Trust, and on 9 October 1941, the Minister, replying to a parliamentary question, promised that the government intended to produce a comprehensive, free hospital service, to be based on local authorities, but administered in bigger units; to this end a survey of hospitals would be made.[27]

The Liverpool Committee, advised by a Nuffield committee, responded by concentrating on the formation of a Divisional Council for Merseyside, leaving those local authorities away from the centre of the conurbation to be assigned according to regionalisation schemes drawn up in London.[28] This new policy was decided before all the Lancashire authorities met in Preston for a second time on 20 March 1941. Given the many uncertainties, suspicions and administrative complications which regionalisation had already raised, the authorities were happy to turn over to the Ministry all responsibility for the proposed survey of the county's hospitals.[29] This particular survey was among the first carried out, and it provided a model for surveys of other regions. We shall consider it in detail in a later section. Meanwhile we should note one of the few positive results of the Nuffield Trust's efforts, the expansion of the Manchester Joint Hospitals Advisory Board so as to include Salford and Stretford.

The Medical Planning Commission
Similar concerns were evident in the wartime plans of the organised medical profession. The British Medical Association together with the Royal Colleges and some Medical Officers of Health had set up a Commission in August 1940 'to study war-time developments and their effects on the country's medical services both present and future'. The draft report (there never was a final report) appeared in June 1942, and throughout the country doctors debated its proposals with that enthusiasm for radical planning which was

widespread during the early years of the war; several of the Commission's conclusions, welcomed then, were to be attacked when they appeared as government policy in 1944; the Commission even outlined the merits of a salaried service. Their policy on hospitals had three major elements: co-ordinating of voluntary and public hospitals under unified control, strong regional and central authority, and considerable medical representation at all levels. The keynote was sounded in their attack on local authority control: 'The rapid advance of medical science and the increasing complexity of medical practice have outstripped the ability of the average local councillor to make informed decisions concerning the provision and management of medical services, and too often policy is determined by local politics and personal factors.' Not below regional level was control by elected bodies acceptable; and since that would have required local government re-organisation, regional authorities, serving populations of half a million and upward, would probably have to be appointed. Each would comprise medical, lay and local authority representatives and be responsible to the central authority.

That central authority might be the Minister of Health, or perhaps a corporate body like the BBC. In its centralisation and appointed regional councils, the national hospital service envisaged by the BMA Commissioners in 1942 was closer to Bevan's eventual National Health Service than were any of the alternative wartime plans.

As in the case of the Nuffield Trust, the British Medical Association, by planning early, hoped to block the separate development of a local authority hospital service. They were eager to see Regional Councils established without waiting for local government reform, and made strong suggestions that such councils might take some executive responsibility for municipal hospitals – there was, apparently, no problem of 'takeover' in the voluntary sector. Even where local government areas were already large and suitable for hospital administration, medical men and non-elected laymen were to take a hand:

> It may be found in forming these hospital areas that the area of existing local authority provides a suitable region for hospital administration. Even if this be so, there should still be established for the area, a Regional Hospitals Council as described in the preceding paragraph, on which the local authority should be represented.[30]

The Ministry of Health and plans for hospital development, 1941
Even before the war, the Ministry of Health along with the BMA and many other bodies had been concerned about the poor co-ordination between voluntary and municipal hospitals.[31] But the solutions proposed in 1941 by the Nuffield Trust were received with ambivalence; few could dispute the

desirability of their objectives; many felt uneasy about their tactics and curious as to how the Trust fitted into government plans.

Such curiosity was certainly justified; the Ministry of Health was itself ambivalent. From its initiation, the Trust had courted and received government support, but as its activities extended and more Regional and Divisional committees were formed, the Ministry grew increasingly nervous; not only was the Trust playing a role which many local authorities, especially socialist authorities, thought should be reserved for central government; they were playing in an area where the Ministry was ignorant. More information and some agreed Ministry policy had to be produced quickly if the activities of the Trust were to be superseded, or even supervised. The government needed to make a policy statement, to reassure the country that any voluntary initiatives were within an agreed framework.[32]

Such a statement would have to be vague, for the information necessary for effectively re-organising hospital services was not available at the Ministry and much ground-work was required. This too could not be postponed indefinitely for whenever the war ended, the Emergency Hospital Service would have to be unscrambled. There could be no return to the pre-war set-up, because it was the war which had rescued many voluntary hospitals from bankruptcy; there had to be a better system in waiting.

Between January and September 1941, during some of the worst months of the war, the senior civil servants on the Office Committee worked out the series of proposals which lay behind Ernest Brown's announcement of 9 October 1941, that the government were considering the future of the nation's hospitals, that they were going to survey the hospitals of London, and that the national hospital service would utilise both voluntary and local authority institutions.

Behind these intentionally bland pronouncements lay a plan which had been conceived by senior officials and submitted to the confidential and critical attention of one or two trusted advisers. It represented a minimal interference with the pre-war arrangements, because it assumed that the constraints on hospital policy would remain those of pre-war days; yet it was radical, because the pre-war situation was unstable and the constraints already operating were producing significant changes in the balance between local authority, professional and middle-class interests. To accept pre-war assumptions was to accept that these changes would continue after the war.

The Office Committee on Post-war Hospital Policy produced the outlines of an agreed solution very quickly. A memorandum stamped 24 January 1941 recorded the consensus as a basis for further contributions. The following assumptions set up the problem:

1. Local government reform will not occur soon.
2. Government policy will be to ensure adequate facilities and therefore to that end a duty will be imposed on some body.
3. 'that the Government will not wish to vest the direct administration of hospitals either in a Minister of the Crown or in a body such as the Assistance Board operating under the general supervision of a Minister'.[33]

This seemed to leave only two alternatives: either the duty would have to be imposed on the existing Counties and County Boroughs, following the precedent of public health legislation, or the duty would have to be placed on *ad hoc* bodies at a regional level. While it was generally acknowledged that co-ordination and planning were required on a regional level, the committee was not convinced that such bodies could *administer* hospitals better than their existing owners – 'unless there is a strong case on merits for so radical a change it is for obvious reasons to be avoided'.[34]

Thus a Bill would have two major functions: it would impose a statutory duty on the major local authorities and it would set up regional scheme-making bodies which might or might not continue as permanent regional committees. The scheme-making body was to be predominantly representative of local authorities (two-thirds plus), the rest being made up of doctors and nurses, etc., together with representatives of voluntary hospitals. Regions were, in general, to be centred on teaching hospitals, but their areas were not to be defined in the Bill.

The major difficulty, for the committee, was the position of the voluntary hospitals. They accepted that the Government would want to keep voluntary hospitals going as long as possible; they saw that any extension of municipal provision would remove incentive for workers to contribute to hospital savings funds, but they could find no real solution, only the hope that 'if a really effective system of recovery of expenses from the patient can be introduced, the alternative of voluntary insurance by way of savings associations will retain its attractions'.[35]

Thus it was recognised that voluntary hospitals could only be preserved for as long as hospitals were not treated as a public service like education. The committee were willing to enforce cost recovery from patients to maintain a separate revenue for voluntary hospitals, but no one expected the voluntary hospitals to continue indefinitely. The important question, for the Ministry was how to organise the local authority services.

Their solution was endorsed by a number of officials who had each approached the problem from a different angle. Mr John Wrigley (Acting Deputy Secretary), for example, began his discussion paper with a plea for local democracy:

> In my own view it is more important that the general body of people should be interested in these services, and should themselves be responsible for the manner in which they are governed and in which these services are provided, than that they should be provided from above with a mechanically perfect organisation for which they have no responsibility and in which they take no interest.[36]

Ad hoc bodies would not attract the necessary interest, regional authorities would be too remote. Wrigley then discussed the whole range of public services to show that whatever the demands of the particular service, there were very few examples of voluntary combination of authorities and there was little chance of producing effective authorities at a regional level unless it was for established 'technical' services such as water supply. Health services were not established; they were more personal than technical; they required effective local interest.

It may be significant that Wrigley was one of the officials responsible for supervising the development of municipal hospitals after the 1929 Local Government Act. He looked with favour on the way in which local authorities had taken over the functions of the *ad hoc* Poor Law Guardians, but even he had to regret one feature of this change: the splitting of the Poor Law Unions between County and County Boroughs which had underlined the urban–rural split in local government, a split which was particularly unfortunate in the case of hospital services. Obviously hospital services should be organised around major urban hospitals, thus linking the Boroughs with the surrounding countryside but such a grouping was so tainted by its association with the Guardians that Wrigley felt its reintroduction to be outside the scope of practical politics.[37]

Wrigley's estimate of practicalities was probably correct, for the possibility of resurrecting town plus hinterland groupings was rarely mentioned in later planning. It would have meant removing important powers from the powerful County Councils, and for this reason, too, it was impracticable under governments which seemed to equate local interests with the interests of major local authorities. Throughout the negotiations of the war years, the viewpoint of the County Councils Association was always treated with respect; minor local authorities were regarded as irritants; local public opinion remained unknown because it could only really be brought into evidence by publishing plans for particular localities, and the Ministry was always frightened of stirring up a chain of hornets' nests right across the country.

For those who valued the tradition of local government there seemed to be little alternative except to place responsibility on existing local authorities and let them administer hospitals within a regional plan. After all, forty-three out of forty-eight of the administrative counties and forty-one out of seventy-nine of the County Boroughs had populations in excess of 100,000.

Thus, the vast majority of major authorities could support at least 700 hospital beds, sufficient base for most specialist services. The more esoteric services could be obtained by joint arrangements.

Such arrangements might be supervised in each region by a small commission which would prepare a plan, help coordination and educate authorities' staffs and the public in the requirements of a modern hospital system. Each commission should be high-powered but should operate mainly by enlisting help. It should not be allowed to become too powerful of itself; its secretary, for example, could best be provided by another authority. Possibly, if the regional health committee was successful, and if similar developments occurred in other governmental services, the regional commissions could be linked with each other and with new, elected, regional authorities. If the health commissions were not successful they could be allowed to die and some other method of co-ordination substituted.

Though the future status of regions was unclear, Wrigley saw a bright future for local authorities. Almost certainly they would soon be employing both hospital doctors and general practitioners; voluntary hospitals would gradually disappear.[38]

Wrigley's views reveal little sympathy for the organised medical profession or the voluntary hospital lobby. By contrast, Mr Arthur Rucker opened with the claim that health services might best be run by a regional authority, which might then delegate hospital management to local authorities. If general practitioners were to practise from health centres, as most medical progressives had suggested since the time of the First World War, then they too ought to come under a regional authority. But when Rucker came to consider putting such a scheme into practice, two enormous obstacles appeared. The medical profession was not likely to countenance any radical change in the system of practice, nor were any directly elected regional assemblies likely to be created within the forseeable future. As a half-way house, Rucker suggested, like Wrigley, that a duty be imposed on the local authorities; perhaps health insurance could be extended in scope and regionalised.[39]

The enthusiasm of these civil servants for a local authority service was soon tempered by one of their senior colleagues[40] who pointed out the real power of the voluntary hospital and medical lobbies: 'I feel that there is a great risk that a statutory declaration that hospital provision was the responsibility of local authorities would upset the apple-cart right at the start notwithstanding any amount of window dressing on behalf of the voluntary principle.' No doubt some socialists and some local authorities would support the proposal, certainly the London County Council would, and so might some of the more energetic Medical Officers of Health, e.g. Glasgow. But most County Councils would oppose the scheme and it would be quite unacceptable to the British Hospitals Association and the voluntary hospitals.

> On the financial side the local authorities would fear that their new responsibility would saddle them with unknown but large responsibilities in respect of the voluntary hospitals, while the voluntary folk would take fright at the prospect of local authority controls of their expenditure and everything else.

A diplomatic reticence would be safer. The Minister might express his intention of designating regions for hospital development and announce that for each hospital 'there would be a Hospital Board representative of local authorities, voluntary hospitals, etc. whose function and constitution shall be on the lines of the Manchester Joint Hospitals Board, with such additions as are found possible.' The constituent bodies would retain autonomy.

Forber was sure that such an announcement would gain approval, though even this limited initiative would require some very careful preliminary discussion, notably about the divisions of Lancashire and the London area.[41]

The exercise of preparing the scheme revealed how little the Ministry knew about hospitals. Mr Alford was set to prepare memoranda, especially on voluntary hospital finance.[42] Mr Wrigley argued for a rearrangement of functions within the Ministry so that the administration of the Emergency Hospital Service could serve as an information source and administrative base for the planning of future hospital sources.[43]

By August 1941, Sir John Maude had hurriedly composed a revised proposal which paid more attention to the demands of the voluntary hospitals. As Forber had suggested, the Regional Councils were stressed, and less attention paid to the new duties of local authorities. The Regional Councils would 'bargain' with voluntary hospitals, giving payments where voluntary hospitals fulfilled the demands of the regional scheme. Local authorities would be obliged to fulfil these demands.

It was still expected that hospital contribution schemes would continue; though the question of social security had already been referred to the committee which produced the Beveridge report, the national insurance scheme was not expected to fully cover hospitals for four reasons:

1. it would not be available in time;
2. it only covered part of population that used hospitals;
3. the requisite number of hospital beds could not be guaranteed for some years; and
4. the voluntary hospitals saw voluntary insurance as the mainstay of their independent existence.

But for all these changes of emphasis, the Ministry intention remained 'not to guarantee the continuance of the voluntary hospitals but to establish a system in which they or the best of them can continue so long as, and only so long as, their resources, buildings, endowments, contributions and savings justify their independent existence'. The more that the Ministry discovered about the state of voluntary hospital buildings and the more ambitious became the government's proposals for social insurance, the shorter the future of separate voluntary hospitals must have seemed.[44]

The question of national insurance, including hospital insurance was referred to an interdepartmental committee chaired by William Beveridge in May 1941, amidst public excitement over the prospect of universal social security,[45] but as the hospital planners debated, it was still assumed that voluntary hospital contributions would continue.

As Sir Lawrence Brock, chairman of the Board of Control, pointed out:

> At the present time, the main inducement to subscribe to the 'penny in the pound' and similar schemes is that it gives the contributor some preferential right of admission. This is, of course, not specifically admitted by the voluntary hospitals, which must, at least nominally retain their right to select their patients. But in practice, there can be little doubt that the mass contributors have a better chance of admission, and know they have, because the hospitals dare not antagonise the management of mass contribution schemes or allow it to be supposed that the mass contributor gets no advantage in return for his contributions except that he escapes the exaction of the almoner.

The voluntary hospitals savings scheme could only be saved by extending voluntary insurance to cover municipal authority hospitals; collection would then be very difficult and in any case it was iniquitous:

> If there is a duty on the local authority to provide a complete hospital system, it is not clear on what grounds a limited section of the community can fairly be asked to tax themselves to meet the cost of a service which would otherwise fall on the rates and which would be more equitably distributed if it did so fall.[46]

The most that could be expected from voluntary hospitals was that they would survive until bed provision reached acceptable levels.

At almost the same time the Ministry received a new set of proposals from the Nuffield Provincial Hospitals Trust. As we have seen the Trust had been working hard to produce a survival plan for voluntary hospitals which would be acceptable to a majority of local authorities. Any such scheme would be almost unanswerable because it would represent all the major interest groups and would thus be sure of an easy passage; the only objections would come from those who felt loyal to some philosophy of public service which was not adequately reflected in the scheme.

The Trust proposed that voluntary hospitals should be paid, not through local authorities but by Regional or Divisional Councils according to the tasks which they performed. A hospital insurance scheme would cover the same geographical areas and include both classes of hospitals. Ownership and management would remain with the existing bodies; all councils would represent a mixture of voluntary hospital and local authority interests.[47]

The strategy of the voluntary hospital lobby was clear: to gain acceptance for the notion that voluntary hospitals and local authorities would be equal partners in the hospital service of the future. This practical programme, represented a middle way between the hopes of some medical men that *all* hospitals would be run by a body similar to the University Grants Committee or the BBC, and the plan favoured by the Ministry, in which hospitals would be essentially a local authority service with some regional planning.

Of all the local authorities whose hopes were threatened by the voluntary hospital lobby, none was more endangered than the London County Council. London had developed the best municipal hospital system in the country. It also contained the most vocal and reactionary segments of the medical profession and the voluntary hospital lobby. Charles Latham, the astute socialist leader of the London County Council took to the press to publicise the threat to the public hospital system which he saw in the Nuffield proposals. On the proposed hospital councils, local authorities would be relatively powerless. Now that voluntary hospitals could no longer maintain themselves, the powerful interests behind them sought the integration of hospitals under predominantly professional control. In effect, they were trading-in part of the independence of bankrupt hospitals for a large say in the running of hospitals funded by the public authority.[48]

Latham's immediate fear was that the government would set up a special commission to plan the hospitals of the Greater London area.[49] Rather than have a Nuffield-type planning council come into existence on his doorstep he preferred that the Ministry should do the work itself. This was agreed, for the Ministry, too, was anxious to keep ahead of Nuffield – a reason which could only fuel Latham's worries. Sir Sydney Johnson of the London County Council wrote to the Ministry asking for a government statement: 'We are rather inclined to think that there is some danger of the county councils and other authorities concerned becoming too deeply committed on Nuffield lines'.[50]

Meanwhile, William Goodenough, the Chairman of the NPHT, was having a quiet word with Barrington-Ward of the *Times*. Maude had given him permission to intimate that a government statement was imminent. Goodenough had suggested that it be linked with the news of the Nuffield Trust's new proposals for a Middle-Class Medical Insurance, a scheme for which Lord Nuffield had promised £150,000.[51]

By the beginning of October, Maude had discussed the outline of the government plan with the leaders of the British Hospitals Association and the Nuffield Provincial Hospitals Trust and the King Edward Fund as well. They were, he thought, ready to accept these terms as the best that voluntary hospitals were likely to get. The Association of Municipal Corporations and the County Councils Association were in favour, though the County Councils Association were suspicious of 'regionalisation', a word avoided in the statement. The London County Council would go along with the plan, though 'there [were] undoubtedly members of the Council who would like to see the early demise of the voluntary system'.[52] Having achieved this compromise, Maude was distressed to find that 'some apprehension has been felt in the Treasury that the announcement may be thought to weight the scales somewhat against the voluntary hospitals'. He sought to reassure Sir George Chrystal that 'nothing was further from our intention'.[53] Indeed, the crucial question as to whether voluntary hospitals would be funded through local authorities, had not been finally resolved. The Ministry had wanted to exclude direct funding, except for teaching hospitals,[54] but the issue was left open in the government announcement.

The anouncement of 9 October drew sharp criticism from some Labour members, including Aneurin Bevan, who objected to the support of independent 'charity' hospitals from public funds. It brought a note from A. V. Hill, MP, eminent physiologist and member of the University Grants Committee: Could not the Minister consider setting up a body like the UGC 'to guide the distribution of hospitals' and 'to act as a buffer between them and the state on one hand and the special interests of the medical profession on the other'?[55]

The government statement had the desired effect, in as much as the County Councils Association called a halt to its co-operation with the Nuffield Provincial Hospitals Trust except in forming Divisional Councils. The Nuffield Provincial Hospitals Trust agreed to drop schemes at a regional level and concentrate on Divisions, which could help collect information for the hospital surveys. Under pressure from the County Councils Association, the Nuffield Provincial Hospitals Trust agreed that Divisions would normally be co-terminous with Counties. Apprehensive that County Boroughs might disappear as potential hospital authorities if Counties became Divisions, the Association of Municipal Corporations representative found himself increasingly out of sympathy with Nuffield proposals.[56]

For the first half of 1942, the Ministry's activities were largely confined to the setting up the hospital surveys. It was difficult to find suitable personnel to undertake the work, difficult to resist the Nuffield Provincial Hospitals Trust offers of help, but important that the Ministry should maintain control over such parts of the work as might appear to be recommending a future scheme. It was particularly important that the London and Lancashire surveys, obviously hugely problematical, should come under direct Ministry control. But equally, the scheme could only be successful if all concerned were keen to collaborate. Hence the Ministry's eagerness to be invited to do the Lancashire survey.

Notes and references

1. See the excellent history of wartime welfare services in R. M. Titmuss, *Problems of Social Policy*, London, 1950. Also the volumes of the official war histories by C. L. Dunn, *The Emergency Medical Services*, 2 vols, London, 1952–3; and the volume edited by A. S. MacNalty on *The Civilian Health and Medical Services*, 2 vols, London, 1953–5. For an excellent account of the context of the wartime planning see Paul Addison, *The Road to 1945*, London, 1975. Since this chapter was written, the details of the health service negotiation have been set out in J. E. Pater, *The Making of the National Health Service*, King's Fund, London, 1981.
2. Dunn, *Emergency*, II, p. 344.
3. *Ibid.*, II, p. 327.
4. Manchester Joint Hospitals Advisory Board, Annual Report, 1939.
5. Full details of the administrative arrangements and their development can be found in Titmuss and Dunn.
6. Dunn, *Emergency*, II, pp. 343–4.
7. On 'The price paid', see Titmuss, Ch. 24.
8. Dunn, *Emergency*, II, pp. 343–4.
9. *Ibid.*
10. *Ibid.*
11. Report of Mental Deficiency Accommodation Committee 1940 in their minutes (LCRO); *Daily Dispatch* and *Daily Telegraph*, 27 November 1946. Also *Lancashire Daily Post*, July 1944, quoting R. Constantine, Accrington representative on the Lancashire Mental Hospitals Board (cuttings, HBV 1 in LCRO).
12. Ernest Rock Carling and T. S. McIntosh, *Hospital Survey, The Hospital Services of the North-Western Area*, Ministry of Health, 1945, pp. 117–9.
13. 'A plan for British hospitals', *The Lancet*, 28 October 1939.
14. *A National Hospital Service. A Memorandum on the Co-ordination of Hospital Services*, published by the Nuffield Provincial Hospitals Trust, Oxford, 1941, pp. 8–9.
15. *Ibid.*, pp. 9–10.
16. *Ibid.*, p. 9.
17. *Ibid.*, pp. 5–7.
18. *Ibid.*, pp. 19–21.
19. *Ibid.*, pp. 16–19; *Report of the Voluntary Hospitals Commission* (1937).
20. *Ibid.*, pp. 12–14. The British Hospitals Association tried to persuade its former regions to approach local authorities under the auspices of the Trust, so as to set up Divisions. The former BHA *Regions* were to be known as *Areas*: British Hospitals Association, *Memorandum of Policy on Regionalisation of Hospital Services*, London, November 1941.
21. Manchester Joint Hospitals Advisory Board, Annual Report, 1939, minutes, 11 December 1939.
22. Manchester Joint Hospitals Advisory Board, Annual Report, 1940–1, sub-committee minutes, 27 January 1941.
23. Manchester Joint Hospitals Advisory Board, Annual Report, 1940–1.

24. *Ibid.*
25. *Ibid.*
26. Manchester Joint Hospitals Advisory Board, sub-committee minutes, pp. 87–104.
27. The background to this announcement can be followed in MH 77–25.
28. *Ibid.*
29. See correspondence about the survey in MH 77–5.
30. *British Medical Journal*, 20 June 1942, pp. 743–53.
31. As an example of the difficulties faced: the following paragraph appeared in a letter from the Chairman of Charing Cross Hospital to Neville Chamberlain, Minister of Health (29 December 1927): 'Instead of trying to harass me, instead of trying to co-ordinate our Voluntary Hospitals with your comfortless Infirmaries and Rate-aided places, why can't you do the work which ought to have been done years ago, cleanse the slums which here in the centre of London are a disgrace, but even so cannot compete with the disgusting dwellings in your own former constituency of Ladywood in Birmingham' (MH 512). Also, memo by Sir Frederick Menzies to the Ministry, August–October 1941, MH 77–25.
32. For example, Sir John Maude to Sir Laurence Brock, 25 August 1941, MH 77–25: 'The Nuffield Trust are rather forcing our hand with a propaganda campaign which is causing a certain amount of suspicion among local authorities, and unless we are prepared to take the lead fairly soon in discussions, there is a danger of the matter getting out of hand.'
33. Memo of 24 January 1941, MH 77–25.
34. *Ibid.*
35. *Ibid.*
36. Note by Mr Wrigley for the Office Committee on Post-war Hospital Policy, MH 77–25.
37. *Ibid.*
38. *Ibid.*
39. Notes by Mr Rucker, 6 February 1941, MH 77–25.
40. Sir Edward Forber (1878–1960), Deputy Secretary at the Ministry of Health 1925–30.
41. Forber to the Ministry, 9 February 1941, MH 77–25.
42. Alford memo, 31 March 1941, MH 77–25. The fact that about half the insured population had insured themselves and their dependents through hospital contribution schemes was 'a clear indication that medical protection or benefit in some form has a strong hold on the working-class mind'.
43. Wrigley memo, 23 January 1941, MH 77–25.
44. Paper by Sir John Maude, August 1941, MH 77–25.
45. For the impact of Beveridge and references, see the following chapter.
46. Brock to the Ministry, 29 August 1941, MH 77–25.
47. National Provincial Hospitals Trust draft, to Ministry, September 1941, MH 77–25.
48. Article by Latham in *The Star*, 12 August 1941.
49. See notes by Dr Daley (Medical Officer of Health, London County Council), 29 August 1941; and the letter and memo from Sir Frederick Menzies to the Ministry, 27 October 1941, both in MH 77–25. Also memo by Mr Neville, 2 September 1941, which mentions the friction within the London Emergency Hospital Service sectors, MH 77–25 and CAB 117/211.
50. Johnson to Maude, 23 September 1941, MH 77–25.
51. Goodenough to Jameson, 25 September 1941, MH 77–25.
52. Maude to Sir George Chrystal, 4 October 1941, CAB 117–211. The records of the discussions with interested parties are in MH 77–25.
53. *Ibid.*
54. Letter from Ministry to Sir Alan Barlow, Treasury, 23 September 1941; memo by J. E. Pater on Voluntary Hospitals, 12 December 1941, MH 77–25.
55. *Hansard* for 9 October 1941; letter from Hill to Ministry, MH 77–25.
56. Minutes of a meeting of 27 November 1941 between Nuffield Provincial Hospitals Trust, County Councils Association and Association of Metropolitan Councils, MH 77–25.

CHAPTER 14

Ministry surveys and plans, 1942 – 5

Introduction
The report of the British Medical Association Commission, in June 1942, coincided with the resumption of planning by the Ministry of Health, and with the official survey of the North West's hospitals. All three stressed the virtues of large administrative units. We have already considered the medical case; in this chapter we shall examine the results of the North West Survey and consider the evolution of government policy up to the plan of February 1943, the most radical of all the official wartime proposals. We shall then examine the responses to that draft, the compromises in the 1944 White Paper and the further dilution of the coalition government's policy which occurred up to the general election of 1945. Throughout, we shall of course, be concentrating on the meaning of these schemes for the Manchester Region.

The North West (1942) Survey and its impact
The invitation to the Minister to conduct a survey of hospitals in the North West was the inevitable result of the troublesome rivalry between Liverpool and Manchester and the County authorities at Preston; it was the immediate result of contacts between the Ministry and Sir George Etherton, the Clerk of the Lancashire County, who encouraged the suggestion of a Ministry survey and saw it accepted by a meeting of the authorities concerned in March 1942. Given the complexity and the sensitivity of the issues, Ministry 'arbitration' was essential.[1]

The Ministry was soon to find out how sensitive the issues were. The Liverpool representatives at the March meeting had been markedly defensive, obviously afraid that a North West Region would be centred on Manchester. Soon afterwards they asked the Minister for two surveys, one to be centred on Liverpool and one on Manchester; powerful deputations from Liverpool University went to pressure the Minister to give Liverpool autonomy under the Emergency Medical Service; they objected to their Group officer coming under the control of the Regional officer in Manchester.[2] There were also stirrings among the Preston doctors, belatedly formulating demands for a survey of their own.

On the advice of Etherton, the Ministry dropped its proposal to appoint Veitch Clark of Manchester as one of the surveyors. Wisely they decided to appoint 'outsiders', E. Rock Carling, a London consulting surgeon and T. S. McIntosh, a Medical Officer of the Ministry, who headed the wartime service in the Leeds region.[3] The survey was announced on 21 April 1942; it would cover Lancashire, Cheshire, North Wales and other neighbouring areas which looked to these counties for hospital treatment.

Rock Carling was a well known London surgeon, interested in 'scientific' medicine, especially radiology, and very acceptable in medical circles. McIntosh was particularly welcome to the Liverpool group because of the survey he had done of Liverpool voluntary hospitals before the war. He had also helped the British Hospitals Association with the survey which led to the separation of three British Hospitals Association districts – Manchester, Merseyside and the residual North West Region.[4] McIntosh's experience and strong opinions were perhaps the major determinant of the form taken by the survey.

Then there was the third man whose participation greatly increased the significance of the survey. This was Niven McNicol, the Ministry officer designated to facilitate the survey by handling data collection, visiting arrangements, etc. He accompanied McIntosh on many of the key visits (for some of which Rock Carling was not present); he drew from the survey those general principles which might serve to guide Ministry policy; he linked this survey with the ones begun later under the auspices of Nuffield, and thereby, with varying degrees of success, tried to ensure that all the surveys pointed in the direction first established by the North West Survey. Indeed, at one time he proposed that Carling and McIntosh should do *all* the surveys themselves.[5]

At various times, during and after the surveys, it was politic for the Ministry to claim that they were merely collecting information, but this was a more or less conscious piece of positivistic bluff. The Lancashire surveyors were very much aware that they were exploring possibilities of new administrative arrangements and their findings were significant in changing the emphasis of government plans.[6]

The surveyors visited Lancashire in June 1942, testing their general notions of hospital organisation against the different arrangements in various parts of the county, and especially against the already existing schemes of co-ordination. They visited almost all the hospitals in the Region and their report, as published in 1945, largely comprised descriptions of the hospital services in and around each of the major Lancashire towns. The more the surveyors looked at these hospital districts the more certain common features emerged. Almost always the central town had a voluntary hospital on an overcrowded site, short of funds, in need of renewal and extension. The municipal hospitals often had larger sites but most had very poor buildings. The voluntary hospitals were almost entirely surgical hospitals: the municipal hospitals took most of the medical cases. Here, already, was division of labour, but one that was often inefficient and inequitable. It was, in fact, unrealistic to speak of two hospital systems, in most of the towns there was only one. Somehow this *de facto* organisation had to be adapted so that each town had a single district general hospital, responsible for both kinds of patient. For a while, both sets of old buildings would have to be used, but before long, almost every major town in the North West would need a new general hospital. Immediate amalgamation of staffs would provide a basis for a complete merger in the future.[7]

What then of their staffing arrangements? McIntosh was sure that these ought to be approximated, for both systems had good and bad features, and a new intermediate pattern was needed. The voluntary hospital system, where each doctor had charge of a number of beds, was widely praised by doctors as an admirable example of effective co-partnership. In as much as the people in charge were specialists, the system did indeed allow considerable freedom for innovation, and it brought top specialists to hospitals used by the working class. Several municipal hospitals had rapidly increased their specialist services during the thirties and some had allocated beds to specialist units. Both McIntosh and Rock Carling welcomed these developments; the orthopaedic and maternity units in some of the local authority hospitals were among the best in the region and their success indicated a considerable demand for the extension of such facilities. 'But', added McIntosh, 'I doubt if the interests of the patients are best served by placing them under the care of physicians and surgeons who earn their living wholly or mainly outside the hospital and visit the hospital for a few hours daily, or perhaps not every day'.[8]

McIntosh sounded a note even more rarely heard, when he engaged in a defence of medical superintendents. Voluntary hospitals lacked any presiding medical authority 'whose business it [was] to see that the machine [ran] well as a whole and that a proper balance [was] maintained between its various parts. For want of such an officer even such important matters as the spread of infection [received] surprisingly insufficient attention.'[9]

The opposite side of the argument can be presented from Rock Carling's notes. While accepting the medical superintendent, he wished to ensure that they merely co-ordinated, rather than supervised, the activities of consultants. In the best of municipal hospitals, doctors were treated as colleagues not subordinates and if this pattern could be established in all public hospitals, then eminent medical men would be happy to serve. Such developments seemed likely, because all the medical superintendents seen on the survey visits had been able, fair-minded and keen.[10]

If the different hospital buildings of a town were to be used in a co-ordinated way, then the problem of medical superintendence would arise at the level of the town:

> To get the best out of the hospitals in any area the chief Medical Officer of the area must have power to exercise a co-ordinating control over them. He should have the power to require hospitals to play their proper part to meet the needs of the area, not in accordance with a rigid classification of hospitals, but in accordance with the needs of the moment.[11]

McIntosh's vision corresponded to the war-time realities of the Lancashire towns, where the co-ordination of hospital services was secured by the local Medical Officer of Health, by and large successfully. Certainly, he did well to point to the need for flexibility. Far too often it was assumed that the allocation of duties to hospitals could be done on a more or less permanent basis.

The surveyors had to assume that hospitals would remain under their existing owners, yet so much of the existing system, from the dilapidated buildings to the shortage of specialists, seemed to urge the creation of a single new service. The surveyors could but hope that the arrangements would permit common staffing on a new basis; that any future developments, if not existing services, would come under the auspices of authorities which would represent the best in both the local authority and in voluntary traditions.

As they travelled around the region they were impressed by the opportunity for radical change. Opinions were in a state of flux; many men within the different traditions of public service were genuinely open to innovations.[12] It remained to be seen whether or not the Ministry could devise a plan which would reflect the aspirations of the hospital services and the realities of the existing hospital groups.

This conviction, that only a new and powerful system of hospital administration could effect the required renewal of services, led the surveyors to favour large administrative units. The Ministry officials also came to favour large joint authorities because as they began to work out the implications of relying on local authorities, the discrepancies between local government areas and the catchment areas of hospitals became more and more obvious. In June 1942 the revised draft of the hospital plan gave the Government power to force the formation of joint authorities where necessary: in general, County Boroughs would be linked with the surrounding County.[13] When the officials attempted to draw out the new service in detail, then two features became clear: (1) very few local authorities would *not* be in joint authorities, (2) London and Lancashire especially posed enormous problems.[14] It is worth examining the Lancashire problem in detail, both in the North West Survey and in the Ministry's own proposals.

Whatever the problems of arranging joint authorities in the county, Lancashire afforded a very strong argument against doing without them. To have left the hospital services in the hands of County Boroughs might have been satisfactory, but to have left the County as an administrative unit would have been folly. Lancashire County Council had very little hospital accommodation, except for tuberculosis. It controlled three ex-workhouse infirmaries, at Prescot, Davyhulme and Ashton-under-Lyne. These were inherited from the Guardians in Unions based on large urban areas that had not achieved County Borough status. Away from these centres, the County possessed little but poor quality rural workhouses. The majority of County residents, when they attended rate-supported hospitals, used those of their neighbouring County Borough. When this was impossible, for example in Furness where the municipal hospital at Barrow took only County Borough residents, the patient might be faced with a long and difficult journey to a County hospital. Occasional patients from Furness travelled to Davyhulme, a suburb of Manchester.[15]

This situation was hardly the fault of the County authorities; only since 1930 had they been responsible for hospitals. Whatever the merits of the 1929 Act, it had produced a geographical folly in Lancashire. Any rational scheme of hospital organisation would have to reunite the hinterlands of towns with those towns.

In simpler counties, this could be done by merging the County and the Boroughs. To do it properly in Lancashire would have meant destroying the County as a hospital authority, not a large task in fact, because the County was already subdivided into town-based districts, but one which looked forbidding to a Ministry facing the County Councils Association. The County Councils Association wanted to preserve all-county units, and the Ministry also favoured this policy initially. In February 1943 the Ministry was suggesting a 'joint authority' for Lancashire that would have included one County Council and seventeen County Borough Councils, overseeing five million people and two medical schools.[16] This unit of 'local government' would have been almost twice as big as any of the regions proposed by the voluntary hospital lobbies and rejected as too large. It was being advocated at the same time as the Ministry was suggesting that Joint Authorities would in general serve populations of 200,000.

This 'whole county' solution was one of three plans discussed with local government associations in April 1943.[17] The second involved removing

Manchester (and Salford) and Liverpool (and Bootle), leaving the rest of the County, including the smaller County Boroughs. This might have appeased the Association of Municipal Corporations by preserving the independence of the big cities, but any such plan raised huge problems for the hospital service. The remainder of the County, population 3.2 million, would have been very difficult to subdivide, especially around the cities, and it would have been very short of hospital beds and specialists.[18]

The third scheme for Joint Authorities involved splitting the County administration. Some variant of it was favoured in mid-1943:[19]

North Lancashire – Barrow, Blackpool, Preston, Blackburn, Burnley + part of Lancashire County Council area (population 1,118,000).

South East Lancashire – Bolton, Bury, Rochdale, Oldham, Salford, Manchester + part of Lancashire County Council area (population 2,208,000).

South West Lancashire – Wigan, Warrington, St Helens, Southport, Bootle, Liverpool + part of Lancashire County Council area (population 1,688,000).

As far as Lancashire was concerned, this was more or less the scheme which finally came to be suggested under Bevan's Bill of 1946, that would have given north Lancashire some degree of independence from Manchester and Liverpool. Of course, the adherence to county boundaries would have raised considerable problems in Westmorland and Cheshire, whose populations to some extent depended on Manchester and Liverpool.

It is curious that the scheme eventually published by the surveyors was not mentioned in 1943, even though McNicol, who had co-ordinated the survey, was involved in the discussions and had consulted McIntosh about the division of Lancashire.[20] In any case, the surveyors' scheme is worth considering, as an example of the approaches which led to the Joint Authority proposals, and because the reasoning given in the published reports can be supplemented from the surveyors' own notes.

The region offered one example of 'voluntary hospital planning'. The North West branch of the British Hospitals Association had been formed by the division of the old North West branch into three parts; Manchester area, Liverpool area and the rest. The new North West branch was centred on Preston, and had campaigned, belatedly, for the government survey to follow the boundaries of the British Hospitals Association regions. It was now campaigning for its area to be treated as a full hospital region centred on the Infirmaries of Preston and Blackpool. But it did not have the support of the Lancashire County Council (who had wanted the survey to follow county boundaries) or of the County Boroughs of Blackburn and Burnley, which were included in this North Lancashire region but who appeared suspicious of the British Hospitals Association plan.[21]

The surveyors had little time for the scheme: the region was not a natural grouping, for Carlisle and others of the northern-most towns looked more to Scotland or Newcastle than to Preston; the proposal appeared to be promoted by consultants in Preston and Blackpool who did not want to come under the influence of Manchester or Liverpool. In any good hospital scheme, a centre of specialist medical skills would have to be present, both as a resource for the area and as a nucleus from which specialists could be dispersed. Preston already served a large geographical area, and with the affluent resort of Blackpool it could support private specialists, but it did not have a medical school, and medical schools were the obvious basis for hospital regionalisation.[22]

The potential of medical schools within an organised hospital system could be seen more clearly in Lancashire than in most of the country. The surveyors found the universities of Liverpool and Manchester ready to take an active interest in hospital development. Immediate developments might include university representation on the bodies responsible for the selection or nomination of hospital specialist staff and more involvement of peripheral hospitals in the work of the medical school. The university might send temporary assistants to hospitals, which would be in line with developments in the other areas of university concern, e.g. education and engineering. If the university sent students, it would have to inspect facilities. There was great potential here for upgrading and co-ordinating hospitals.[23]

The importance of the medical schools to the future shape of the hospital services may not have emerged into public consciousness until the Goodenough Committee on Medical Education reported in 1944; but for those, like Stopford, who looked at hospital planning from the vantage point of the medical school, the potential was obvious. Rock Carling, when he reported to the surveyors of other regions about the problems of the North West, saw clearly how an expansion of the teaching base would, almost automatically, result in upgrading and regional co-ordination.[24]

The pre-war experiments seemed to show that university based co-ordinating bodies were welcome and their advice on consultant staffing acceptable. The arrangements in Manchester had been successful though there had been some conflict in Liverpool.

> From Liverpool and other municipalities there may come opposition to proposals that would interfere with the authority of the municipalities in the election and appointment of their staffs. But the county clerk of Lancashire (Sir George Etherton) citing the inefficiency (and (?) nepotism) of the joint board for lunacy in the region is strongly in favour of appointment by other than an elected body

and sees in the machinery created by Manchester the lines of a solution to the problem. Opposition would probably wither before a reasonable statement of the case for at least a sifting by an independent and expert body and the successful example of Manchester is bound to have a big effect.[25]

As we have already seen, the Manchester Board had done more than advise on staff appointments. It had also advised on hospital extensions and provision of specialist services. Some such body would have to exist in each area to co-ordinate the activities of those hospitals whose catchment areas overlapped, but should there be similar separate bodies in each of the large towns, or in each group of large towns, or should the Manchester Board be extended to cover the whole area over which Manchester consultants were active?

There was no doubt about the potential of the Board for the area of the Manchester conurbation itself:

> The representatives of the University, of the voluntary hospitals and of the Corporation say that this machinery of the joint advisory board is capable of tackling successfully any problem (e.g. the provision on a big scale of any additional hospital facilities) that is likely to emerge. They consider that they have found the machinery for co-operating for Manchester. The question of extending the work of this machine to Salford and other towns in the immediate neighbourhood is being discussed (Salford has been invited by the Joint Board to come in), but there is a less confident note about extending the Joint Board to cover the whole sphere of influence of Manchester.[26]

The Liverpool Board were moving in the same direction, but in the smaller centres there was less co-ordination. Often there had been little co-operation before the war came, little more than the use of a few voluntary hospital clinics to satisfy the local authorities' duties under the venereal disease and tuberculosis regulations. Yet the apparent suspicion between the Corporations and the voluntary hospitals did not necessarily prevent them finding ways to cooperate. The local Labour councillors might dislike the voluntary hospital system but they could usually see clearly enough when co-operation with their own particular voluntary hospital might be of benefit to the town.[27]

If the co-ordination at the level of the towns could be improved, and if expert services could be provided by association with medical schools, was there really a need for a regional authority? McNicol thought not. His memorandum, like the final report, favoured the creation of new, city-sized groupings outside the conurbations:

> And if hospital re-organisation, as is likely, precedes the reform of general medical practice and a recasting of local government, there would probably be an advantage in not setting upon elaborate regional organisation for one branch of public service in advance of a more general reform. In the absence of an

outside regional organisation, the Ministry would have to give a positive lead on and take an active part in shaping of policies for the regions. On this point it is worth noticing how often one encounters a remark in the vein of 'The state should say what it wants and see that it gets it'. This from rather combative members of local authorities may be significant.[28]

A second reason for opposing over-elaboration of regional authorities emerges from a memorandum by McIntosh, written for the other surveying teams. Apprehension about 'regionalisation' usually centred on the fear that the periphery of the region might lose such autonomy as it possessed and in return gain only a regularisation of the arrangements under which it was serviced from the centre. 'If my conception of our aim is correct, I think the surveyors may be able to do something to allay this apprehension. I take it that one of our objects is to secure a greater dispersion rather than a greater concentration of specialist staff.'[29] The likelihood of Preston's not being a regional centre ought not to mean that it would lose its present specialists. The inclusion of Burnley in the Manchester region ought to *increase* the number of specialists who were resident thereabouts.[30] One way to do this was to make the peripheral authorities strong enough to support a full range of specialists; not just one of each kind, but enough to avoid the problems of professional isolation. This meant that the Boroughs of northern and central Lancashire would have to be grouped to form areas of population comparable to Liverpool and Manchester.

How then were hospitals to be administered? In their published report the surveyors favoured federations of local authorities. Though the bulk of the report had dealt with the 'hospital districts' centred on moderate size towns, and with regional capitals, the chapter on administration broke with that existing pattern of service in favour of professional arguments for large administrative units:

> Hospital Districts are merely the areas that seem to be convenient and natural gathering grounds for the general hospitals, having regard to geography, communications and the social and commercial habits of the people. They are not intended to be Administrative Areas in the sense of being separate Hospital Authorities, for which they are not suitable.[31]

The reasons for much larger administrative authorities were as follows:

1. special services provision, e.g. tuberculosis and orthopaedics;
2. flexibility in bed allocation – pooling by groups of adjacent authorities rarely works;
3. ease of experiment;
4. employment of several specialists in each of the major specialisms so that

no specialist suffered from professional isolation, and so that there would be specialist cover during holidays, etc.;
5. mobility of nursing resources;
6. specialist technical staff.[32]

These remarks of the surveyors show an important accord with those of the Medical Planning Commission's draft report and the actual arrangements of the war-time service, where the significant groupings were at city level, rather than region or town. When the surveyors' report finally appeared, they suggested the following groupings:[33]

North Lancashire Unit: Lancaster & Kendal, Furness, Blackpool & Fylde, Preston, Blackburn, Burnley (population 1,163,000).
East Lancashire Unit: Bolton, Bury, Rochdale (population 707,000).
Manchester Unit: Manchester, Salford, Oldham, Stockport (population 2,036,000). And perhaps also East Cheshire (extra population 186,000).
Liverpool Unit: Liverpool, Southport & West Lancashire, Wirral (population 1,471,000). And perhaps also Cheshire & District (extra population 171,000).
Central Unit: Wigan, St Helens, Warrington (population 563,000).

This scheme nicely demonstrated a key feature of one-tier plans: the separation of the peripheral parts of conurbations into units formally comparable to that at the centre of the conurbation. It demonstrated, too, the obvious difficulty of implementing such schemes when previous development has concentrated facilities in the centre of conurbations. Bolton, Bury and Rochdale would, necessarily have remained heavily dependent on Manchester until many new specialists had been appointed and new facilities provided, yet in as much as this difficulty posed a proper challenge to improve underprivileged peripheral areas it deserved to be accepted.

A second additional difficulty was more formidable. The peripheral units, initially short of facilities and specialists were also so artificial that they were unlikely to enjoy the advantages of vigorous local government. The towns of east and central Lancashire were better connected to Manchester and Liverpool than to each other. Federation of such towns was unlikely to produce administrative units coherent enough to overcome the handicap of technical dependency.

The surveyors had decided to begin their grouping of services from the bottom. First districts, then groups of districts. They had refused to begin by dividing the North West into a Manchester zone and a Liverpool zone, and when they returned to the question, they found themselves in a quandary:

We come now to something more intangible, namely, the Spheres of Influence of the universities and hospitals of Liverpool and Manchester. It is questionable if they could or should be precisely delimited. They are the areas which look to one or other of the universities as their centre of inspiration and leadership, and which depend on the hospitals of the university towns for certain highly specialised services, and for the highest degree of medical skill and authority. According to that definition it is only to be expected that the two spheres will somewhat overlap, and there seems to be no reason why they should not. It does seem, however, to be necessary for the central hospital of each Hospital District to be definitely and formally associated with one or other university and this may lead to a fairly precise definition of the two university territories.[34]

Here then was a scheme which fully recognised the need for a comprehensive set of specialists within each administrative area but which paid as little attention to the existing distribution of medical expertise, or centres of prestige, as it did to the claims of local authorities.

These recommendations were probably written at a time when government policy favoured large joint authorities of this type. They appear in the Report as a separate chapter, hardly linked with the main body of findings. Yet it would be a mistake to see them as mere reflections of central policy. It is clear from the preliminary notes of the surveyors, that the idea of largely self-contained hospital districts was one which appealed to the surveyors themselves and which may have been instrumental in shaping government policy.

The high level civil servants more familiar with local government than with hospital services had wanted local authority control. As surveying and planning continued, the proposed administrative units grew larger. Wartime experience was used to emphasise the case for large units and Ministry officials, like McIntosh, could see the potentialities of these self-contained city groups. Medical leaders, like Rock Carling, saw large authorities as a necessary condition for successful specialist staffing. Ministry planners, like McNicol, increasingly confident of the Ministry's ability to run the hospital service, were happy to take on the additional work which a one-tier system of health authorities would impose on the central body.

As it became obvious that almost all local authorities would in any case be working through Joint Boards, so the need for a regional authority seemed to decrease. Maude's plan of June still included regional authorities, appointed by the Minister and responsible for (i) preventing overlap; (ii) co-ordinating arrangements as to boundaries; (iii) overseeing arrangements with the key hospital; and (iv) securing the proper liaison between the key hospital and the hospital authorities in the matter of consultants and appointments to medical posts in the hospitals.[35] But by February 1943, the Ministry proposals stressed Joint Authorities to such an extent that only regional advisory committees were required between the Joint Authorities and the Ministry.[36]

As detailed consideration of Lancashire shows, Joint Authorities would probably not have worked well; either the units would have been very large and remote, or they would have been awkward and very unevenly equipped. The scheme had become popular because it appeared to preserve local authority control while meeting professional claims that very large units were required for specialist services. This last argument, though not always presumed, especially by those who argued from precedent, was never fully opposed: it fitted too well with the technocratic optimism of the period; planners looked to a brand new service. Thus the local authority case became compromised and weakened. The case was further handicapped because no wartime discussion had brought out the real functional connections between local authority hospitals and the rest of the health service.

Because it was always assumed that some hospitals would remain in local authority hands, there was no need to emphasise the integration of hospital work with domiciliary, clinic and especially welfare facilities. Curative facilities and scientific medicine demanded a new hospital service, who was going to worry about liaison between wards for the chronic sick and homes for old people? Not until Bevan removed all hospitals from local authorities, in the interests of scale and specialist services, did anyone seriously consider these real functional links. Though the Joint Authority proposal of February 1943 looked like a triumph for local government, appearances were to prove deceptive.[37]

Central negotiations and compromise
The problems of setting up Joint Authorities continued to be debated during 1943 and 1944, but they were not the most controversial aspect of the 'Brown plan'.

This outline was not confined to hospital services alone. Entitled 'A comprehensive health service', it also dealt with general practitioner and clinic services, and formed the basis for a long series of discussions both in the Reconstruction Priorities Committee of the Cabinet and in meetings between the Ministry and the various interested parties. The proposal was the first fruit of a marriage between the ongoing plan for post-war hospitals and the Beveridge report on social services, which had appeared in November 1942.[38] Beveridge had assumed that a comprehensive medical service would be available to all, and funded, largely, from Exchequer payments. When the government accepted the principles of his report, the Ministry of Health was required to add general practitioner and clinic services to the hospital plan and mould the whole to fit a new financial context. Hence the

February 1943 plan.[39] All health services were to be controlled by Joint Authorities; general practice was to be based on health centres and some, at least, of the health-centre doctors would be full-time salaried staff.

The major problem with the 1943 plan, as Brown quickly discovered, was that the representatives of the medical profession loathed it. Their fears resulted largely from the plans for general practice, and so lie outside the scope of this study; it is sufficient to say that the Ministry believed that the traditional pattern of competitive one-man practice produced a low level of medical care, insufficient co-operation between doctors, and inadequate clinical facilities.[40] The continuing popularity of hospital out-patient clinics, even when waiting times were long, seemed to indicate that many patients preferred a well-equipped service, backed by consultants, to the independent endeavour of the family doctors. Some local authorities were ready to oblige.[41]

The medical profession had itself toyed with the notion of health centres, but even in the progressive climate of 1943, it could not accept the Ministry proposal. It involved too much of a leap from the known paths, and threatened the independence of the profession. Negotiations on this aspect of the 1943 scheme jerked and stalled, and broke down after about three months.[42]

Both the proposed integration of all health services and the minimal role alloted to the regional medical capitals also threatened the hopes of the voluntary hospital lobby for a major part in the future hospital service. Even while the Ministry still assumed that 'patient costs' (hotel costs and drugs) would be paid by the patients, and that hospital insurance schemes would continue, they intended such schemes to be operated by the health authorities, not by the hospitals. Contributions schemes would be rearranged so that both classes of hospital would benefit equally; the scheme could no longer be used as a way of ensuring entry to a voluntary hospital.[43]

The voluntary hospital lobby reacted violently when they met the Ministry officials at Whitehall on 30 March 1943. Where was the equal partnership which they had been promised? What had happened to the regional planning boards, long a staple item of Nuffield hospital plans? Under the Ministry scheme, voluntary hospitals would be dominated by the local authorities 'that is to say by the Medical Officer of Health'.[44]

The Ministry officials may have been disturbed but they were probably not surprised to hear such a response from Sir Bernard Docker; they accepted him as a voluntary hospital extremist. But they were disturbed to hear similar views from Sir Walter Cobbett of Manchester. Here was a man known for a generous attitude, and long accustomed to the pursuit of better cooperation with local authorities. Yet he, too, saw the proposal as subordinating voluntary hospitals to the public health committee of the local authorities, which would be able to control staff appointments and the type of patient to be treated.[45]

Cobbett's position is of particular interest because he was in close touch with the Ministry officials concerned in the North West Survey. They hoped that men like Cobbett, genuinely interested in achieving a better hospital system, would help lead the voluntary hospitals into a fruitful association with government, even if it meant opposition to the more reactionary elements of the British Hospitals Association. McNicol therefore took the next opportunity to visit Manchester and see what could be salvaged from the Whitehall meeting.

A week or so after the meeting the surveyors, McNicol, Cobbett, Mr Newell (British Medical Association man and member of the Manchester Joint Hospitals Advisory Board) and some others had dinner at Sir Walter's Manchester Club. To McNicol's evident relief, Sir Walter was very amenable. He had read over the government discussion paper on his return from London; he thought it a poor presentation, but it was not such a bad plan as Docker had made out. Reflecting on the Whitehall meeting he felt he had been tricked into an unreasonable antagonism, and now he had informed Docker and Wetenhall accordingly.[46]

McNicol was obviously pleased. He explained the Ministry position in more detail. The crucial point for Cobbett and Newall was the role of the Advisory Committee. If such Committees, local and national, could speak out and be heard, then the voluntary hospitals had no need to fear local authority domination. The Ministry should hurry to clarify the position and emphasise that the medical profession and the voluntary hospital lobby would retain a strong voice.

McNicol's satisfaction was further increased because two other senior voluntary hospital men, in London, had expressed similar views of the Whitehall meeting and the British Hospitals Association position. All these men would have preferred to see hospitals planned by a Hospital Board and administered by 'a new local machine altogether',

> but in close talk they appreciate the case against this idea and I am quite convinced are prepared to accept the broad principles for administration through the Ministry and the Local Government Organisation, subject to the safeguards of Advisory Committees with real Authority.[47]

Presumably Cobbett wished to ensure that in Manchester a body like the Joint Board would continue to exercise a dominant influence on specialist staffing and patient allocation. He may have been satisfied with McNicol's assurances, but when the Joint Board leaders next met, his previous suspicions were violently reawakened; the new Medical Officer of Manchester

City seemed to see the government plans as an assurance that the Public Health Committee would take full control. The Royal Infirmary development proposals, previously welcomed by the city, were now to be put into abeyance. The Medical Officer of Health 'could not have adopted an attitude more convincing to show that he expected shortly to not only be giving us orders as a hospital, but to intervene in regard to teaching'. Cobbett's desolate letter to Rock Carling continued:

> The attitude of the Medical Officer of Health showed to my mind a complete reversal of sentiment and I attribute it entirely to the Minister's intimation that Manchester as a major Local Authority shall have control of the Hospitals in that area.
>
> There seemed to be at the University a feeling that I was unreasonable in my attitude towards the proposals and took an extreme view of what their effect would be. I think this instance shows that I was right and I have at the moment a feeling that all we have accomplished in the way of co-operation through our Joint Board in the last 8 to 10 years has been destroyed.[48]

We have here a cameo of the government's dilemma. They did not want to see a continuation of a binary hospital system liable to stratification but they recognised the resistance which any interference with the voluntary hospitals would meet. They disallowed the combination of elitism and medical corporatism which seemed to underlie much of the British Hospitals Association rhetoric, but they allowed that the medical men and administrators associated with voluntary hospitals did have a considerable contribution to make to any future system, and that the medical profession ought to have a major part in its organisation. How could these groups be integrated?

In the 1943 plan, each local authority or joint authority was to have a Hospital & Medical Services Committee, with professional representation and representation for voluntary hospitals. There would be a separate subcommittee for each major hospital, but in all probability its numbers would be drawn from the main committee. Local sub-committees could be set up where necessary. The regional authorities of previous plans were reduced to staff appointment committees appointed by the Minister, with the added possibility of there being regional advisory bodies reporting to the Minister in the same way as the proposed Central Medical Board.[49]

The local authority organisations accepted the plan for medical advisory committees, but they were opposed to co-option of medical professionals on to the committees of the authority. Even so, they would almost certainly have accepted the compromise proposed by the Ministry, which gave the medical advisory committees the right to nominate two representatives on to the executive body – not enough representation to appreciably alter the voting patterns, enough to guarantee to the doctors that their point of view would be heard.[50] In the light of the considerable power previously exercised by medical men on joint boards and advisory committees, there is every reason to suppose that the compromise proposed was quite adequate to ensure that any health authority would have had considerable difficulty in opposing the policies of its advisory committees.

The Ministry felt its way forward along a narrow path, seeking the support of the co-operative element in the profession, the universities and the voluntary hospitals, without giving the less cooperative elements any reason to suppose that they had an independent future. The discussions in Cabinet committees reflected these negotiations. Several points were conceded to the doctors: no attempt would be made to force the change over to health centres, a modified panel system began to loom large as the likely major form of practice. The medical advisory bodies were to be strengthened, and, most importantly, a Central Medical Board was to be the employer for general practitioners, not as originally proposed, the Joint Authorities. In agreeing to this arrangement the Reconstruction Priorities Committee was adapting the English plan to the form preferred by the Scots. Indeed, throughout these discussions, the Scots had a strong influence, mainly because they were much better informed about the likely concrete results of any proposals, and therefore were better able to measure the strength of local opinion.[51]

From our point of view, the most interesting opposition to the Ministry plan came, not from the doctors, but from Labour members of the Cabinet, especially Herbert Morrison. As usual, Morrison set out to defend the interests of the major local authorities, especially the London County Council. His role in the 1943 debates resonates curiously with his performance in 1945–6, when local authority hospital services were again under attack. In 1943, to oppose Joint Boards he invoked a state service as a supplement to local authorities; in 1945 he invoked Joint Boards as a defence against Bevan's national plan. His arguments were better in 1943, though no more effective than his later efforts.

Morrison, in 1943, argued from a premise which deserves more attention than it has normally received: if services need to be upgraded and made more technical, then higher level authorities should provide the additional services required; they should not also take over the existing services. Thus, Morrison suggested, if local authorities were too small to run laboratories, employ a range of consultants and organise supplies effectively, the state should perform these functions. Those local authorities which were large enough to own hospitals were large enough to run them on a day-to-day basis. For the rest, a state service for all doctors would provide an excellent career structure and an effective means of maintaining technical standards in hospitals.[52]

The Minister, loyal to his department's proposals, opposed Morrison, as he did those who would have allowed a mixture of Joint Boards and local authorities. He also opposed Ernest Bevin when, apparently misunderstanding the meaning of a Scottish suggestion about central employment of general practitioners, the Minister of Labour suggested a state run service; Bevin's propoal, it was said, would destroy local government.[53]

Morrison, as usual, was tenacious. He lost, on 8 September 1943, partly because the Scots reported that the Hetherington Committee favoured Joint Boards, partly because the Minister was able to claim that his was a *unified* scheme, whereas Morrison had mixed state and local authority services.[54] Soon afterwards, 16 September 1943, the Minister conceded that the Joint Authorities would only run the hospitals; local authorities would retain their clinical services and general practitioners would be employed by a central board.[55] There was a lesson to be learned here on tactics in opposing 'integrated plans', but, as we shall see, Morrison did not learn it.

In November 1943, Henry Willinck, Conservative, replaced Ernest Brown, National Liberal, as Minister of Health. The Reconstruction Priorities Committee was wound up at about the same time, after spending almost a year on intensive examination of the various schemes connected with the Beveridge Report. Just before it came to an end, Clement Attlee had been appointed to it, and had objected to the watering down of the February 1943 proposals, especially those concerning general practice.[56] The Labour attack was continued in the Reconstruction Committee meetings of January 1944 where a draft of the White Paper was subjected to detailed criticism. Morrison tried again to reduce the emphasis on Joint Boards but most of the discussion concerned general practice. The Labour representatives reserved their position on full-time salaried service. Churchill, for rather different reasons, was equally unwilling to be committed by the Coalition White Paper. It was issued as a tentative compromise.[57]

But it did contain one very important advance on the Ministry proposals of February to July 1943: the new service was to be free of charge to the user. The issue had been fought in the Reconstruction Priorities Committee, where the majority favouring a free service were opposed by the Minister of Health who argued for 'hotel costs' as a protection for hospital contribution schemes. In January, the debate was taken up again in the Reconstruction Committee where, after two meetings, it became evident 'that it would be illogical to require additional payments for these purposes when what was claimed to be a comprehensive health service was being introduced'.[58] The attack on charges had been led by the Secretary of State for Scotland.

At this second meeting, 10 January 1944, the Minister of Health tried to reserve his position, and the Minister of Reconstruction, Lord Woolton, undertook to meet the voluntary hospital representatives, to gain their acquiescence. They had maintained that hospital contributions were a form of insurance against costs; he hoped to 'get the minds of the hospital people on to a somewhat higher plane'; to convince them that contributions would continue, no longer out of fear, but out of affection for the voluntary system. On 18 January 1944, he met with some success; the rather volatile Sir Bernard Docker seemed agreeable, the wiser Sir William Goodenough was not impressed.[59] Other representatives, before and after the White Paper, continued to insist that contribution schemes would be killed.

Meanwhile the White Paper was already being drafted.[60] The decision not to charge for hospital care was taken during the drafting. This is important, because, whatever Lord Woolton might have claimed, the decision fundamentally changed the whole context of the debate about voluntary hospitals. When plans for post-war hospitals had been first drawn up, in 1941, it had been assumed that voluntary hospitals would disappear as separate institutions as their funds dried up; there was no need to abolish them. Once it was decided that the new hospital service would be free, one had to *decide* the future of the voluntary hospitals. If they were to be funded from public monies, they would, presumably, continue indefinitely. Any decision not to fund them would be seen as a deliberate act of destruction.

The publication of the White Paper in February 1944, brought the debate out into the open. Most responses were predictable enough. Doctors were frightened of a salaried service being imposed, while Labour MPs complained about concessions to the doctors. Local authorities disliked losing powers to Joint Boards, especially because it divided hospitals from public health services, while voluntary hospitals were horrified at their subsidiary role. Though popular with the public, the White Paper was opposed by almost all the interested parties.[61]

We shall see later how the opposition whittled away the bulk of the 1944 scheme, but first we should consider two less predictable responses, both based on Lancashire experience, both concerned with integration of voluntary and municipal hospitals.

Sir Ernest Rock Carling wrote to Jameson as follows:

These are my first reactions to the White Paper. Unprejudiced men of goodwill would have little but praise for it, but are there any such?

My general criticism would be that it is at once too timid and too conciliatory. Too timid in failing to indicate frankly the size and comprehensiveness of the new Health Authorities, and in stating baldly and boldly the urgent need for big areas. Too conciliatory in encouraging a perpetuation of isolation of the Voluntary Hospitals from the County and Municipal. I may be misled by my intensive study of Lancashire, but I believe it absolutely essential in almost every

County Borough and surrounding hinterland to effect a fusion of resources that almost amounts to fusion of the hospitals, and I believe that the picture the Paper seems to have in mind is that of 1942, whilst in January 1944 the preliminary sketches of a very different picture are to be found in the secret drawer of every M.O.H. and Hospital Secretary. The moment this White Paper comes out those sketches will be torn up. Think of Coventry, on the brink of a combined, new, modern Hospital; the Paper will confirm the Voluntary Hospital, instantly, in their struggle to keep their independence and individuality. It might even be so in Liverpool.

Be conciliatory, but don't come to grief over trying to please everybody. At the very least, it seems to me, the Paper should say to the *Public*: 'You can keep the two systems if you insist upon it, we'll try and make them run in double harness; but there is a better way: wherever the two parties are ready to pool their assets we will give all the encouragement in our power'.

This second defect is in my judgement of far less importance for the future than the timidity with regard to plain indications of the fundamental requirement as to large *areas* for the Health Authority. At a first reading there seems to be a good deal of muddle over what shall be left to this little authority, and what shall be handed over to combinations. I believe the right idea runs through the Paper where it constantly refers to 'the general plan' and 'the Minister's approval', and so on, but it wants an initial bold, stark, statement that for *Health* there is going to be a strong, far-flung *Authority* that knows no parochial bounds. '*That* there is going to be – now get on with your plans inside its area'.[62]

It almost seems that inside Carling's view of the White Paper proposals there is a premonition of Bevan's later plans. Areas for Carling had become, more or less, the traditional Regions. Behind a local government system, he was looking for strong central direction. Again we see the tensions which lay beneath the elastic notion of Joint Authorities. The White Paper had done little to disperse the obscurity; in responding to it, some bodies assumed the number of Joint Boards might be as low as twelve; others assumed that all major towns large enough to run a proper general hospital service would be centres of Joint Authority areas.[63]

One such town was Oldham, from where the Governors of the voluntary Infirmary wrote to the Ministry about their own proposals for a 'joint authority' made up of representatives from local authorities, hospitals and the medical profession. The proposed authority would run the general hospitals, receiving money from an enlarged contribution scheme; a regional body would administer state grants, weightings, etc.[64] Such a proposal was already out of date in as much as the service was to be free and the Joint Authority areas much larger than the Oldham district. But it is worth considering none the less, for, with other such schemes, it indicates how much truth there was in Rock Carling's comments about plans for future co-operation in the towns and cities.

MINISTRY SURVEYS AND PLANS

If grants, technical services and medical staffing had been nationally or regionally organised then it might have been possible to merge voluntary and municipal hospitals under *small* Joint Authorities containing non-voting representatives of medical and charity interests as well as a majority of councillors. Once medical staffing had been dealt with separately, there was little reason why the local dignitaries who ran the voluntary hospitals locally should have refused to do so through the Council seats which many of them held.[65] Almost certainly, the opportunities in the towns for merging the hospitals, was greater than the chances of getting the corresponding national bodies to agree on any merging of interests, as the government was soon to find out.

Throughout 1944 the government negotiated with the profession, the hospital representatives and the local authority association. All were agreed on resisting change. The Ministry officials fought to preserve Joint Authorities as executive bodies, but in October, the Reconstruction Priorities Committee conceded that they should do no more than plan.[66] This was but one of many concessions.

By May 1945, Willinck was sure that his plans had the support of all the interested parties:[67] general practice would be based on an extension of the panel system; local authorities would run their own hospitals; the voluntary hospitals would continue as before, as self-governing bodies, funded, not from a health authority, but from exchequer payments and local payments, channelled through an 'area clearing house'.[68]

The voluntary hospitals had done remarkably well, for in addition to a financial arrangement parallel to that of the municipal authorities, they were to have a strong say in hospital planning. On the Health Services Councils, the vestiges of the Health Authorities, they were to have representation equal to that of the local authorities, and in addition there were medical representatives. On the Regional Advisory Councils, which were to share planning responsibility, voluntary hospital representatives would meet with 'local government experts'. The rest of the Regional Council was to be made up of specialists and university people, usually sympathetic to voluntary hospitals.

The fears of Lord Latham had almost come true, for the voluntary hospitals sector, which had entered the war with shaky finances and a limited life expectancy, looked like coming out as a permanent equal partner in a hospital service entirely supported by public funds. The voluntary hospitals had given up their freedom of policy, to conform to the regional and area plans; in return they were to receive indefinite public support and an upper hand in the making of the relevant plans.[69]

As these discussions continued, word got around that Willinck was compromising the 1944 White Paper by making too many concessions. He denied the charge and had a White Paper drafted: 'Progress with proposals for a National Health Service'. The Ministry jumped the gun and had proofs printed.[70] But by then, the 1945 election had been announced.

On 6 June 1945 the Conservative Cabinet discussed the publication of the White Paper. They did not want to be open to the charge of stalling, of having used the break up of the coalition government to delay legislation prepared under the coalition. Willinck was convinced that all the major interest groups were now satisfied, but the Tory strategists were not convinced that the people would be. Thus they suppressed Willinck's White Paper.[71] They were voted out in July 1945, and Aneurin Bevan became Minister of Health in Clement Attlee's Labour government.

Notes and references

1. Minutes of a conference at the Ministry, 28 January 1942, MH 77–26; Correspondence about Preston meeting MH 77–5.
2. Dr Henry Cohen to Jameson, 27 April 1942, MH 77–24; Professor McNair to Maude, 26 March 1942, MH 77–5.
3. Sir Wm. Ascroft (Chairman N.W. branch of BHA) to Ministry, 22 April 1942, MH 77–5.
4. Memos and correspondence of Maude with Etherton and McNair, April 1942, MH 77–5.
5. See for example, the memo on London Voluntary Hospitals, 18 December 1939, MH 77–25, where McIntosh's work for Liverpool is cited as an example of Ministry help to voluntary hospitals. Dr F. N. Marshall, who was then attached to the Manchester region of the Emergency Medical Service, had worked with McIntosh at the Ministry and had considerable respect for his abilities (interview). There was an obituary of Rock Carling in the *British Journal of Radiology*, *33* (1960), 593.
6. NW Survey correspondence MH 77–5; especially McNicol memo of 17 July 1942, MH 77–19.
7. *Hospital Survey, The Hospital Services of the North-Western Area*, Ministry of Health, 1945, pp. 15–19; Memo, 'Some miscellaneous observations' (by McIntosh), undated but used at a conference of survey officers, 5 October 1942, MH 77–5.
8. McIntosh, Memo on voluntary hospitals (staffing), MH 77–5.
9. *Ibid.*
10. Rock Carling, 'Personal impressions gained at the outset of a survey', 22 September 1942 (sent to Jameson), MH 77–19.
11. McIntosh, Memo on voluntary hospitals (staffing), MH 77–5.
12. Rock Carling, 'Personal impressions ...', MH 77–19.
13. 'A post-war hospital policy – outline of proposals and "Hospital service"', MH 77–26.
14. The London hospital arrangements were particularly contentious because the emergency hospital service divided the LCC as a hospital authority, and provided massive public subsidies to voluntary hospitals not responsible to local government. These points were raised by Aneurin Bevan in questions to Ernest Brown on 9 October 1941 when the Minister of Health made his announcement on hospital policy.
15. *Hospital Survey (North-Western)*, 1945, p. 22.
16. On 27 February 1943, Sir John Maude wrote to the Minister outlining Mr Pater's tentative grouping of authorities: 'Taking Lancashire as an example we have very carefully examined the possibility of an intermediate course by way of linking up a number of neighbouring County Boroughs with the intervening and surrounding parts

of the County. But that means in effect tearing to pieces the County administration and would in addition involve very serious technical difficulties. In short, we have been forced to the conclusion that it would not be practicable to combine *parts* of the Counties with the County Boroughs and that in every case the constituent units of combination must be a whole County or County Borough', MH 77-26.
17. On 23 March 1943 representatives of the Association of Municipal Corporations, the County Councils Association and London County Council considered the proposals. Generally they favoured maintaining county boundaries, but recognised Lancashire and the West Riding of Yorkshire as difficult cases. MH 77-26.
18. This alternative was mentioned in the paper NHS 16 submitted to a meeting of local authority representatives on 16 April 1943. The representatives refused to discuss particular schemes at that meeting, MH 77-26. Also PR (43)46 in CAB 97-13 in which Brown reported to the Cabinet that he was thinking of splitting Lancashire County Council area into three or four parts and combining them with the boroughs.
19. *Ibid.* (NHS 16).
20. For example, McNicol wrote to McIntosh, 15 January 1943: 'the main subject on which I would like to have the benefit of your wisdom is the areas of administration in Lancashire. It is a terrible problem, I confess it beats me at the moment; but you know the area well and you have your views', MH 77-5.
21. Letter from Sir Wm Ashcroft, chairman of new NW branch of BHA, 22 April 1942; and from Sir Bernard Docker national chairman BHA, 2 May 1942. Report of the informal conference between representatives of local authorities and voluntary hospitals in north and east Lancashire, held at Preston Royal Infirmary, 18 August 1941, MH 77-5.
22. 'Some points' on preliminary tour, 30 June – 3 July 1942, MH 77-5 (drafted by McNicol).
23. Rock Carling, 'Personal impressions gained at the outset of a survey', 22 September 1942, MH 77-19.
24. *Ibid.* Stopford was the vice-chairman of the Goodenough Committee. Since Goodenough was a banker and Stopford a medical vice-chancellor, we can be sure that Stopford was influential.
25. 'Some points', MH 77-5.
26. *Ibid.*
27. Rock Carling, 'Personal impressions', MH 77-19.
28. 'Some points', MH 77-5.
29. McIntosh, 'Some miscellaneous observations', MH 77-5.
30. Harry Platt discussed the question in a memorandum prepared for the Nuffield Provincial Hospitals Trust on 'The future staffing of hospitals'. He pointed to the Scandinavian countries where specialists were well distributed, and he hoped to 'check the growth in numbers of travelling consultants (more especially 'carpet-bag' surgeons) who descend at intervals on the smaller hospitals – a system which results from the over-staffing of the great hospital centres', p. 7.
31. *Hospital Survey (North-Western)*, p. 95.
32. *Ibid.*, pp. 95-6.
33. *Ibid.*, p. 97.
34. *Ibid.*, p. 97.
35. 'A post-war hospital policy – outline of proposals', MH 77-26.
36. 'A comprehensive health service' (2 February 1943), PR (43)3 in CAB 87-13, also in MH 77-26.
37. Very few voices were raised to question the assumed importance of *hospitals* in the new service. One such was the Medical Practitioners' Union, which wrote to the Ministry, 1 September 1942, enclosing a pamphlet produced in August, 'The transition to a state medical service'. The Medical Practitioners' Union argued that 'As a monument to

sentimental desires to prolong all lives, however useless and at whatever cost, the hospital is doubtless justified. As a useful health factor its activities require a considerable amount of re-orientation.'
38. On the background to the Beveridge report see Paul Addison, *The Road to 1945; British Politics and the Second World War*, London, 1975, Ch. 6.
39. The February 1942 draft, 'A comprehensive health service' assumed some 'hotel cost' payments would be made by hospital patients, but hoped for a free, comprehensive service, MH 77–26.
40. Discussion papers NHS 5 and NHS 6 (spring 1943), MH 77–26; PR (43)3, 2 February 1943 in CAB 87–13.
41. In September 1943 the Medical Officer of Health for Manchester issued a plan for fifteen large health centres, each with four subsidiary centres.
42. The BMA was particularly worried that some doctors might find themselves working for local authorities, rather than joint health authorities. Sir John Maude promised at a meeting, 15 April 1943, to give special attention to single authority areas, arguing that the move to large joint authorities had been, in part, a result of the recent inclusion of general medical services in the health service plan. Dr Dain was adamant that the profession would not work for local authorities. MH 77–26.
43. For example, discussion paper NHS 24 (1943), MH 77–26.
44. Minutes of meeting, 30 March 1943, at which NHS 10 was discussed, MH 77–26.
45. *Ibid.*
46. McNicol to Hawton, 10 April 1943; note on McNicol's visit to Manchester, MH 77–26.
47. *Ibid.*
48. Cobbett to Rock Carling, 14 April 1943, forwarded to Jameson, MH 77–24.
49. PR (43)3, 2 February 1943, CAB 87–13: 'We believe that nothing will contribute more quickly to a general improvement in the standard of the hospital services than some control over the appointment of senior medical staff. What we are seeking is that before making any appointment a hospital should be required to seek the advice of a representative committee (probably operating over a 'region') on which the teaching side of medicine would be strongly represented.'
50. NHS 17, and minutes of meeting with local authority representatives, 16 April 1943, MH 77–26.
51. Committee on Reconstruction Priorities, meetings 16–19, 24 and 29, in July–November 1943, CAB 87–12, and the associated papers in CAB 87–13.
52. PR (43) 16th meeting, 30 July 1943, and PR (43) 17th meeting, 18 August 1943, CAB 87–12; and PR (43)49, 17 August 1943, CAB 87–13.
53. PR (43) 16th meeting, 30 July 1943, CAB 87–12.
54. PR (43) 18th meeting, CAB 87–12.
55. PR (43) 19th meeting, CAB 87–12.
56. PR (43) 24th meeting, 15 October 1943, CAB 87–12.
57. R (44)2 Draft White Paper, R (44)24 and associated notes in CAB 124–244; R (44) meetings 3–5 on 10–11 January 1944, in CAB 87–5; war cabinet meetings 17, 18 and 21, on 9, 11, 15 February 1944, CAB 65–41; also drafts of White Paper in MH 77–28.
58. R (44) 3rd meeting, 10 January 1944, CAB 87–5.
59. CAB 124–244, meetings reported in MH 77–76.
60. Drafts in MH 77–28.
61. Reports of meetings at Ministry in MH 77–100 and MH 77–30B.
62. MH 77–28.
63. NHS (44)6, reporting a meeting at the Ministry with the County Councils Association and London County Council, 14 June 1944, MH 77–30B.
64. June 1944, MH 77–76.
65. An argument to this effect was developed by Dr A.C. Mowle, BMA Wiltshire, at a Regional Conference in Bristol, 13 September 1944, MH 77–76.

MINISTRY SURVEYS AND PLANS

66. R (44) 65th meeting, 2 October 1944, CAB 87–6.
67. The British Hospitals Association gave general support at an April Conference – MH 77–100; The BMA representative body meeting 3 and 4 May also approved – MH 77–119, though the profession did not wish to enter the 'political arena' just before an election – see meeting 24 May 1945, MH 77–119. A 'caretaker' Cabinet of 15 June 1945 was told that the plan was supported by all the interested groups except the London County Council, CM 9(45)1 in CAB 65–53.
68. Draft White Paper, May 1945, MH 77–30A.
69. See Chapter 13, n. 48.
70. Sir Arthur Rucker to HMSO, 15 June 1945, apologising for premature request, MH 77–20.
71. MH 77–20 and CAB 66–66, CP (45)32, 11 June 1945.

CHAPTER 15

Bevan and the new National Health Service

Profession and government – a realignment
When Aneurin Bevan, the Welsh parliamentarian and socialist, took office as Minister of Health in August 1945, he found the records of intensive discussions dating back to 1941 about how the hospital services of Britain could be re-organised. All major sources of information and opinion had by then been tapped and civil servants had pondered the results. Major politicians of both parties had been involved in prolonged deliberation about future policies and a number of solutions had been proposed: the 1941 plan, the Brown plan and the Willinck plan. Yet within about two months of taking office, Bevan was offering his Cabinet colleagues a bold and imaginative scheme very substantially different from anything the government had previously considered.[1]

To find out how and why this change occurred we must examine the common assumptions of the wartime planners, and see how a creative politician at a peculiarly favourable juncture was able to replace these assumptions with new ones.

As we have tried to show, the war-time debates can be understood as processes of accommodation between various ways of organising medical care, characteristic of rather different socio-political outlooks. Historically the oldest was the upper- and middle-class emphasis on private practice in medicine. Doctors were *primarily* businessmen; the large and growing involvement of doctors with patients who could not afford to pay was mediated through public charities – voluntary hospitals which provided medical care for the poor, patronage for the rich and a means of professional education and differentiation to the medical profession. This model of medicine was dear to the bulk of the profession, to most conservative politicians and, probably, to a large proportion of the middle class. It had, however, already been hemmed in by the growth of different kinds of medical-care systems.

The compulsory public insurance system was, by the time of World War II, generally accepted as appropriate for the working classes. Its introduction had been opposed by the profession and the Tories, but by 1940 scarcely anyone objected to insurance cover being extended to include the families of workers as well as the working men themselves. The extension of the panel system to cover about 90 per cent of the population was the least that could be expected. In fact, Beveridge proposed, and the coalition government accepted, that the whole population should pay national insurance and that, in consequence, a medical service, free at the point of contact, should be available to all. This proposal affected hospitals as well as general practitioners for it was obvious to almost everyone that voluntary hospital contributions would be severely reduced. The inauguration of a complete national insurance scheme meant that in future medical care would be regarded in the same way as education. Both would be primarily public services run by government. Provided the national health service was adequate, the private sector would be very small, probably rather smaller than in education.

Once the government had accepted the Beveridge Report and had followed its logic by abandoning the proposal to charge 'hotel costs' to patients in hospital, then the real question in hospital planning was unavoidable: what sort of public authority should run hospitals? Before Beveridge the answer had been obvious to the officers and spokesmen of both local government and central government: the local authorities had been responsible for the public hospitals in their areas from 1930; they were responsible for clinic services and public health; they were beginning to play a role in financing, if not controlling, the voluntary hospitals; given time, the voluntary hospitals, starved of funds, would drop into their laps.

But after Beveridge the long term prospect was quite different.[2] If voluntary hospitals were to be funded from public monies then there would be no attrition; they would continue side by side with the municipal hospitals. Under the Brown proposals, the voluntary hospitals would have been paid for the work done under the Joint Authority plan; under Willinck's proposals, the voluntary hospitals would have had a major voice in the formulation of that policy, and would have been paid from central funds. Thus they would have been either an auxiliary to the local authority health services, or an additional hospital system. In either case the voluntary hospitals would have represented a third kind of relationship between medical care and public money; they would have been funded for doing a certain amount of public work, but the control over the way in which that work was done would have remained with the hospital authorities, i.e. the medical staff and a few interested lay people.

This modified syndicalism was very much to the fore when the British Medical Association attacked the Brown proposals and later. The profession wanted its voice to be predominant at all levels. They would have liked to see a Commission comparable to the BBC or University Grants Committee in charge of the nation's hospitals. The great advantage of all such corporate schemes was that they harnessed the experts and that they could operate according to the needs of the service, without reference to local government boundaries. The disadvantage, of course, was lack of democratic control.

All modern government seems to involve some kind of compromise between democratic control and the freedom of the expert to pursue policies dictated by criteria regarded as technical. In the wartime debates over the health services, this antithesis usually appeared in a form where expertise was linked with middle-class interests, voluntary hospitals and private practice. Democratic control was a goal cherished by left-wing politicians and some civil servants; for both groups, local government was the bearer of the democratic tradition.

This antithesis necessarily had a geographical dimension because of the way in which money and medical skill were distributed. The professional and middle-class case focused on regional hospitals because those were in cities and towns where medical specialists and their clients had congregated. By contrast, the democratic case concentrated on towns or population groupings large enough to support a few ordinary hospitals; the non-professionals tended to play down the importance of regional capitals and specialist skills, to emphasise that a far greater quantitative contribution was made by general hospitals.

Of course, this shift in focus also involved a political shift. In most towns, e.g. the larger cotton towns, the effective social pyramid was flatter than in regional capitals, partly because, at least in industrial regions, the rich and middle class tended to congregate in and around the larger cities; partly because those members of the upper classes whose homes were in the countryside or smaller towns often focused their influence on the regional capital, leaving more local questions to lower social strata. Thus to concentrate on towns rather than regions was to favour working-class rather than middle-class interests. The business world was hierarchical and so, increasingly, was the world of medical specialists. Economically and socially the two were bound closely together. Thus the 'expert' solution and the middle-class solution of the hospital problem were closely allied – the case for syndicalism and the case for private practice were interwoven. Set against this alliance, was the case for a non-hierarchical, democratically controlled system of municipal hospitals; a case based on proud democratic tradition, but lacking the technocratic appeal of its opponent.

Bevan, in the new dawn of the Labour government, fundamentally altered the terms of the discussion, by separating the issues from their 'carriers' in the previous debates. He did so by introducing elements above and below the level of professional and local government association. He presented a strong Minister of Health, himself, to a nation which had shown itself ready for radical initiatives.

Ernest Brown had defended the solutions of his Ministry, Henry Willinck had conciliated, Bevan saw himself as the creator of a brand new service. His predecessors had recognised the popularity of Beveridge's measures and had been happy to deliver a free health service, but for them, the form of the new service was to be determined largely by the various interested parties. The 'professionals' and their associates tempered their case by admitting central government powers and conceding that much of the hospital service would be left in local authority hands, for administration if not for planning. The democrats conceded the need for large joint authorities on functional grounds, and were ready to tolerate the continued existence of voluntary hospitals and private general practice. They were even ready to tolerate a considerable degree of professional and 'voluntary' control over the planning of the service, provided they could maintain and expand their municipal hospitals.

Bevan saw his chance to override the intermediate interests and present a service direct to the nation. The government enjoyed enough popular support and a big enough majority to launch a brand new plan. The Conservative opposition in parliament and outside, would not be strong enough to block it, but their attempts to do so would mollify any opposition from the Labour side. The situation and the Minister were uniquely suited to a radical initiative.

Bevan was able to plan for the people because he was a convinced parliamentarian. For him, parliament was by far the most powerful of the nation's democratic instruments. Provided that parliament had control over the new service, it would be a democratic service; there was no need to worry about large-scale organisation removing power from the people.[3]

For most of the previous 'chief-planners' – and they had *not* been Ministers of Health – the Ministry had always seemed too far from the hospitals to be the chief means of public control. The Ministry might be given a coordinating role; it might stimulate the more slothful local authorities; it might inspect and maintain technical standards and provide a vehicle for complaints. But, before Bevan, it was not seen as a creative force. The new outlook may have been, in part, a product of wartime experience. Some of Bevan's local authority-based opponents now took a more positive view of the potential of central government, after they had seen how well the wartime ministries had developed insurance and other personal services. However, Bevan himself never appealed to these precedents. His own view of the Ministry's potential sprang from his conviction that he was personally responsible for delivering the best possible medical care to the people of England and Wales.

Previous opposition to a centralised service had been overwhelming, not just because of fear but because of affection, a conviction that local government must be cherished and nurtured. To remove hospitals, let alone the whole range of health services, would, so almost everyone maintained, be to disembowel local authorities. The major purpose of the best authorities would be taken from them. Bevan did not share this sentiment. He considered that local government was overburdened and would remain so even if the power industries were to be nationalised and thus removed from local authorities. He looked forward to a full-scale examination of the relationship between central and local government, which would assign to each those functions for which it was most suitable. If local government could not properly carry the hospital service, then democracy gained nothing from its trying to do so.[4]

This shift of emphasis might have been related to the changes in the Ministry staff which Bevan brought about. Sir John Maude, the first secretary and a strong advocate of local government, left the Ministry in September 1945, replaced by Sir William Douglas, who rapidly became devoted in Bevan. The deputy secretary, Sir Arthur Rucker continued to supervise health matters, and it may be worth recalling here that Rucker, back in 1941, had expressed his preference for a regional system of hospital control. It seems likely that these changes, plus Bevan's fondness for discussions with top medical men played a part in effecting a fundamental change in focus, away from local government, towards a functionalist attitude.[5]

Certainly, Bevan's perspective was different from that of most Labour supporters who saw municipal hospitals as improvable and improving. Bevan saw municipal hospitals as grossly inadequate, excepting those belonging to a few major authorities. These exceptions were not accidental; only a few authorities, notably the London County Council, had the size, money and expertise to develop a top-class hospital system.

The difficulty had been recognised in the Brown plan by the proposal of Joint Authorities, with populations of large-city size. Bevan was convinced that these would not work. Everyone agreed that they were an unfortunate kind of authority, liable to become remote from the electors. The Ministry had long been aware that a single-tier system of this sort would necessitate much Ministry supervision, but for Bevan, in a hurry to create a new service, supervision was far too indirect a means of energising hospital authorities. Joint Authorities were too far removed from political power.[6]

They were also, and this is an argument in which Bevan concurred with the medical profession, too far removed from the sites of medical expertise. These were *regional*; there were only eleven medical schools, whereas there were to be about forty Joint Authorities. More than half of the Areas would not contain a major concentration of specialist expertise. Any good scheme would have to build up the expertise in these large towns, but it would be especially difficult to do so without regional control, if the Ministry had to work indirectly through Joint Authorities. Joint Authority areas were artificial, in medical and political terms. Bevan was convinced that they would be little better as hospital authorities than their constituent authorities had been.

To those Labour Ministers, like Herbert Morrison, who loved local government, Bevan's poor opinion of its performance in the hospital service seemed unfair. They were willing to try out Joint Authorities, even though they knew the drawbacks. Their opposition to centralisation was powerful and it might have blocked Bevan's path at cabinet level, but for his take-over of voluntary hospitals, something they had never dared to advocate and which they found very difficult to criticise. Bevan insisted on merging the municipal and voluntary hospitals; the removal of voluntary hospitals as an independent force was one of the major reasons for his plan and one of its major strengths.

Again the roots of Bevan's departure from precedent lay in his political nature. Where Morrison disliked voluntary hospitals because they were not local authority hospitals, Bevan hated what they stood for – the continued patronage and power of the propertied classes. This kind of charity was no substitute for social justice. He found it repulsive to see a nurse collecting money on the streets, or a specialist soliciting from businessmen – both were neglecting their real work to beg in support of health services which no civilised society would leave to chance.[7] Nor would it be satisfactory to provide public funds for voluntary hospitals unless they were put under public control. As a backbencher, Bevan had bitterly criticised the wartime government for doing just that.[8] But if the voluntary hospitals were to be taken over, it would be far easier under a national scheme than under the Joint Authority scheme. Much as the voluntary hospital and medical lobbies loathed state interference, they were far more horrified by the prospect of being 'put under' local authorities. Even had it been possible to overcome this resistance, the takeover would have imposed additional burdens and strains on Joint Authorities of doubtful capability.

For Bevan, the choice was clear; all hospitals ought to be nationalised. The Minister himself should take full responsibility for the new service. Bevan was then free to organise the administration along functional lines, bringing in experts and representatives of all the interests concerned. He proposed to set up regional and district councils, rather along the lines of the Nuffield Trust's proposals at the beginning of the war.

Because he was able to organise the administration of hospitals much as suggested by the more enlightened members of the voluntary hospital lobbies, he was sure of a measure of support from these influential figures. He minimised the opposition from hospitals and specialists by setting the large teaching hospitals outside the main framework of the regions; a move which pleased the London hospitals especially, and deprived the voluntary hospital lobby of their most effective leaders. This separation was unpopular with the left, and in many ways unfortunate. Bevan's stated reasons for excluding the teaching hospitals from the Regional Boards were either specious, or quite out of character.[9] As the Scottish example was to show, there was no functional reason for the split, and the English provinces would, in all probability, have accepted the Scottish pattern. The real reason was political – the London teaching hospitals had enormous influence. Their opposition, mediated through medical and political channels, could well have blocked the Bill. It was therefore expedient to allow the teaching hospitals their independence. To do so split the palaces of expertise from the workaday voluntary hospitals. The concession nicely illustrates the way in which Bevan began to separate the technocratic case from its alliance with 'professional' ideology.

Other concessions were also made, from the first announcement of the plan: a few private beds were to be allowed in hospitals, doctors were to be paid by capitation and little attempt was to be made to reform the mode of operation of general practice. Bevan concentrated his efforts on the massive reform of the hospital service.

The hostile reception of the plan by the British Medical Association has been nicely described in Michael Foot's biography of Bevan and elsewhere. It is a story of class politics and mistrust, the response of a middle-class profession to a supposed threat of governmental control. It is obvious from the initial response of the BMA that there was little to complain about, save that doctors were not in full control of a public service. The rest of their reservations were minor (that the Minister was also to control housing; that general practitioner services should be operated on a regional basis) or they were fears soon met by ministerial assurances.[10] In the end Bevan calmed the storm by reiterating his previous assurances that full-time salaried service and direction of labour would *not* be introduced. He could probably have softened the resistance sooner; he may well have chosen not to, because the emotional opposition of the BMA protected his left flank from those who disliked his concessions to the specialists and those who would have preferred a local government service.[11]

Throughout the long battle, which extended from January 1946 to July 1948, Bevan enjoyed the quiet collaboration of a number of distinguished specialists. The ex-syndicalist political high-flyer had built the experts into his hospital service and he enjoyed their support. There was a body of quiet testimony to the worth of the plan, evidenced for example when Dr Souttar, President of the BMA, bravely defied his members to defend Bevan's Bill: would Sir Ernest Rock Carling, Sir Henry Gray and Professor Gask support a hospital plan which was unsound or merely political? Of course not.[12]

Bevan was a clever tactician, but the specialist support was not won by tactics and concessions alone. Bevan, the technocratic centraliser, had cleared the field for the rationalisation of medical care. By doing so, he had separated the experts from the middle-class ethos of the profession and the voluntary hospitals. The choice for hospitals had once been presented as technical excellence in voluntary hospitals versus the inefficient democracy of municipalities. For those cool enough to see it, the choice now presented opposed an effective, co-ordinated hospital system under Parliament to out-dated parochial charity. The British Medical Association and the British Hospitals Association had become 'merely political'.[13]

The plan and the Cabinet

We have, as yet, relatively few sources for the critical period between the election of July 1945 and the Cabinet meeting of 11 October at which Bevan presented his plan for hospitals to his colleagues. From what we know of Bevan's habits of work, it is likely that the crucial decisions came in conversation with expert advisers and civil servants. Sir John Hawton, for example, recalled that at their first meeting Bevan put his finger on the weakness of the Willinck plan for hospitals.[14] We should not expect to find a series of memoranda and discussion papers like those which marked the progress of wartime planning and negotiations. Thus it is appropriate as well as necessary to present Bevan's hospital plan by outlining its rationale rather than its development. Cabinet discussions which followed the presentation of the plan, the parliamentary debates, the discussions with the profession changed little, and that little mostly concerned general practice rather than hospital services. The plan for hospitals remained as Bevan had first announced it.

The concessions to the specialists were there from the beginning. There was nothing to negotiate on the hospital side of the service; except the future control of voluntary hospital capital. But the context of the proposed hospital service was changed. In the first proposals, local authority clinic services were to be taken over by the Minister, and all medical services, other than those provided by general practitioners, were to be organised together.[15] Only later in the planning were local authority services divorced from the hospital service.

This split had serious consequences for the operation of the National Health Service. It involved the most powerful opponents of Bevan on the

Labour side, the advocates of local government. It is therefore worth examining how and when the split entered the Ministry proposals.

At the 11 October meeting Bevan did not present the whole of his National Health scheme, he concentrated on the nationalisation of hospitals, seeking agreement in principle, before he went on to plan the rest of the service.[16] This made sense, because the nationalisation of hospitals was Bevan's major new proposal and the basis of his plan. The procedure was also advantageous tactically, in Bevan's debate with his colleagues. Whether this advantage was sought or merely found, it is difficult to say.

By presenting hospitals in the foreground and relegating the rest of his plans to the darkness of future discussion, Bevan avoided questions about the integration of the new services. He was able to suggest that responsibility for all clinic and district nursing services should be taken over by the Minister who *might* then delegate powers to local authorities. This did not appreciably increase the disappointment of local government supporters for the hospitals were their major loss, but it gave Bevan the advantage of *all* the functionalist arguments about integration. For example, in a paper written for a Cabinet meeting of 18 October 1945, Bevan attacked the Joint Board scheme for the 'grave disadvantage of splitting the health service in half, leaving hospital services to be administered by the boards and other health services by individual authorities'.[17]

The Cabinet had already accepted the major proposals when the clinic and domiciliary services were 'given back' to the local authorities. By then it was difficult for local government defenders to mount an attack on the hospital–local authority split, the major functional defect in Bevan's plan. One of the strongest arguments for the development of integrated health services within local government had been rendered ineffective by the way in which Bevan's proposals had been presented.

Bevan's Cabinet opponents, notably Morrison and Greenwood, could not mobilise any technical arguments. They were very much on the defensive against a 'brilliant and imaginative paper' which had, it seems, taken them by surprise. Morrison was reduced to countering by a general defence of local politics. It was

> possible to argue that almost every local government function, taken by itself, could be administered more efficiently in the technical sense under a national system, but if we wish local government to thrive – as a school of political and democratic education as well as a method of administration – we must consider the general effect on local government of each particular proposal.[18]

Morrison was quite incapable of matching Bevan's imagination. Perhaps no advocate of a strong local government health service could have matched

Bevan's arguments at that time; the existing machinery of local authorities was too great an obstruction. Certainly Morrison's fears about the likely opposition and his advocacy of caution and delay were no song for a new dawn. Bevan had the support in Cabinet of Viscount Addison, G. A. Isaacs, Tom Williams, Ellen Wilkinson and J. J. Lawson. Morrison had support from Greenwood, Chuter Ede and Dalton.[19] Attlee on 11 October smoothed over the differences between Bevan's plan and the 1944 White Paper – in both cases, most of the money would come from the exchequer and most of the people in the administration would be the same: 'Whatever course was adopted there would inevitably be controversy, and the predominant feeling in the Cabinet seemed to him to be generally in favour of the solution proposed by the Minister of Health.'[20]

Bevan was given permission to develop his proposals and to work out the details with the Social Services Committee, before submitting an outline to the Cabinet. Except over the particular question of sale of practices, Bevan did not discuss his plans with the Committee until 17 December, when he met little opposition.[21] On 20 December the outline of the whole National Health Service was discussed by the Cabinet. Morrison and Greenwood tried to hold up the Bill and so delay the parliamentary debate to the next session; they were afraid of the likely opposition and the likely cost of the scheme.[22]

Bevan presented the Heads of his Bill to the Cabinet on 8 January 1946, and they were approved. Again, in March, Greenwood and Morrison tried to delay the Bill, claiming insufficient parliamentary time. But by then, the London County Council had given their support to the Bill and so reduced the likely opposition from the Labour side. The Bill was published and the debate began on 30 April.[23]

The split between local authority and hospital services
We may here leave the public process of debate and controversy to consider how, behind the scenes, the plans for the hospital services were elaborated. We shall consider, especially, the divisions within the proposed health service, and how the Ministry expected to deal with them.

By March 1946, the Ministry was already worried about the possible effects of separating hospitals from local authority health services. Dr John Charles, one of Jameson's two Deputy Medical Officers, presented a long paper to his chief outlining the relationship between hospital and domiciliary services. Sir Arthur Rucker was impressed:

> it shows plainly the weakness of our scheme in this regard. It is quite true that the hospital service will now be under our control and we can see that it is sweetly reasonable. But it takes two to make a partnership – as well as a quarrel – and I am afraid I don't believe we are going to have an easy time everywhere – for

example, with the LCC. I am particularly troubled about the split between hospital and domiciliary work in the mental field, with which Dr. Charles' paper does not deal. However the only real remedy is to entrust all the personal health services to the Regional Boards. That is not practical politics now but I believe it will have to come.[24]

Dr Charles suggested that close links be forged between the hospitals and the ante-natal and child welfare clinics. Hospital paediatricians and obstetricians should staff some of these clinics; local authority child welfare workers should be associated with the hospitals. Health visitors were to circulate between the child welfare centre and the hospitals. In addition, channels were to be established for exchange of information.

The links might be supervised, at regional level, by a co-ordinating committee drawn from the Board staff, and the Medical Officer of Health. The Regional Medical Officer of the Ministry might also play a role. At a local level the Medical Officer of Health might be given the right to attend the Hospital Management Committee and perhaps he could be invited to join the medical staffs committee of the hospital.[5]

All these provisions were to be achieved through administrative regulations, not through the Act, for the draftsmen of the Bill would surely resist any attempt to have them included.[26] None the less, there was room for hope, after all, the Regional Hospital Boards would *want* to get on with the local authorities, unlike some of the previous voluntary hospital boards.

The problem of co-ordination was discussed, on 13 March 1946, by Rucker and Dr Jameson, with Drs Frazer, Hall and Daley representing the medical officer of the Boroughs, Counties and London County Council respectively. Schemes were outlined as to how the hospital and local authorities might jointly staff the clinics for tuberculosis and venereal diseases. It was pointed out that Medical Officers of Health *might* be members of Hospital Management Committees or Regional Hospital Boards; there was no regulation to stop them, neither was there any positive directive. Though many of the problems had been fully described at the time the Bill appeared, the possible administrative remedies were implemented only late and in part.[27]

Nor were all the problems foreseen: it is a remarkable fact, revealing much about the abstract quality of planning, that no one had responded to Bevan's proposal by pointing out that all over the country municipal hospitals due for nationalisation were bound by bricks and mortar, heating systems and staff to the welfare services which remained under local government. Because the majority of data on hospitals had been collected during the war, when everyone assumed that municipal hospitals would remain as such, no one pointed out how very complicated it would be to separate hospital and welfare services, or undertook to examine the technical justification of these links.[28]

Once the Bill was published other bodies began to worry about the split. The Royal College of Obstetricians and Gynaecologists sent in a memo arguing that *all* obstetrical services should be controlled by a single regional authority on which local authorities would be represented. They produced evidence that low infant and maternal mortality was only found where unified services were operating, be they local authority based (e.g. Croydon) or voluntary hospital based (e.g. Guy's, London). In the new service, it was argued, all obstetrical services should be hospital based, with local authority representation on the maternity service committee for each area.[29]

Later, the Joint Tuberculosis Council became similarly concerned. It had taken decades to establish a unified tuberculosis service which covered all aspects of the disease; clinical, residential, convalescent, domiciliary, welfare, epidemiological; a service in which the *family* was the unit of concern. Now, under Bevan's plan, the whole edifice was to be broken up. Tuberculosis of the lung was to become a part of the responsibility of the chest physician; other kinds of tuberculosis belonged to different specialists. Local authority welfare and family services were separated from hospital services.[30]

The same points about tuberculosis were raised in a very cogent memo from the Medical Officers of Health of the County Borough and of the County of Nottingham. They were also worried about the rights of the Medical Officer of Health to admit pregnant women to hospital on social grounds. How, for example, could they deal with the homeless pregnancy unless they could, as of right, admit them to hospital.[31] For such cases, and for access to fever hospitals, the arrangements needed to be specified, not left to 'good-will'.

Again we see, in the concrete, the real links of hospitals with the medical services of the community. It is characteristic of the Bevan plan that the links become apparent in comments made *after* the form of the new service was decided. Only then did this major functionalist argument for local authority control emerge. The local government case had appeared to Bevan, indeed, had generally been presented, as a matter of precedent and local political life; perhaps because of the tendency to separate the technical from the sociopolitical, the real integration of hospital medicine in local life had been overlooked. The technical arguments that Bevan accepted and implemented came from medical and surgical specialists not Medical Officers of Health; the real merits and potential of municipal services were not fully recognised. It is no accident that the machinery set up under the socialist Minister of Health was that which had been proposed by the Nuffield Trust supported by the hospital consultants and the voluntary hospital lobby.

Notes and references

1. CAB 129–3, CP (45)205.
2. This was made very clear in the exchanges between Bevan and Morrison, 11 October 1945, CAB 128–1.
3. Michael Foot, *Aneurin Bevan*, vol. II, London, 1973, pp. 18–19.
4. CP (45)205; and Bevan's reply to Morrison, CP (45)231, 16 October 1945, CAB 129–3.
5. See Foot, *Bevan*, II, p. 39, and Neville M. Goodman, *Wilson Jameson, Architect of National Health*, London, 1970, pp. 121–2.
6. In CAB 129–3, CP (45)231, Bevan asked his Cabinet colleagues to choose between his scheme and Willinck's. Joint Boards were constitutionally objectionable.
7. Foot, *Bevan*, II, pp. 133–4.
8. 9 October 1941, CAB 117–211.
9. In CAB 129–3, CP (45)205 he put forward three reasons for treating teaching hospitals separately: (i) their exceptional standing; (ii) as a separate field for innovation and independent experiments in method and organisation; (iii) to avoid introducing direct state control into the educational field. As the Secretary of State for Scotland replied in his paper, CP (45)207: (i) exceptional standing was a reason for including teaching hospitals; (ii) there was room for initiative *in* the system; (iii) the Goodenough report had seen no objection to local authority teaching hospitals – ownership of the hospital had nothing to do with the curriculum.
10. See minutes of the meeting with the BMA, 6 February 1946, NHS (46)17 in MH 77–119.
11. Foot, *Bevan*, II, pp. 196–208.
12. Souttar sent a copy of his speech to Sir Arthur Rucker, 5 June 1946, MH 77–119.
13. One of Bevan's main aims was to find ways of bringing professional expertise into a fruitful relationship with government. See e.g. 'Proposals for a national health service', 13 December 1946, CP (45)339, para. 4.
14. Foot, *Bevan*, II, p. 130. The fullest account of the negotiations is now J. E. Pater, *The Making of the National Health Service*, King's Fund, London, 1981.
15. CAB 129–3, CP (45)205.
16. *Ibid.*
17. CAB 129–3, CP (45)231.
18. CAB 129–3, CP (45)227 by Morrison; Bevan replied in CP (45)231, both discussed at the Cabinet of 18 October 1945 as a result of Morrison's attempt to prevent Bevan from going ahead as had been decided on 11 October.
19. CAB 128–1, Cabinet 11, 18 October 1945.
20. CAB 128–1, Cabinet 11 October 1945.
21. CAB 134–697, SS (45)12.
22. CAB 128–2, Cabinet 20 December 1945; CAB 129–5, CP (45)339.
23. CAB 128–5, Cabinet 8 January, 8 March 1946; CP (46)3.
24. Rucker memo, 11 March 1946, MH 77–82.
25. Charles memo, MH 77–62.
26. Rucker memo.
27. Charles memo.
28. The problems of division will be discussed at length in a later section.
29. Memo by Royal College of Obstetricians & Gynaecologists, April 1946, MH 77–91.
30. 18 May 1946, MH 77–83.
31. MH 77–83.

Selected bibliography

Much of this work is based upon the manuscript and printed records of the institutions studied. For voluntary Dispensaries and Infirmaries, these were primarily the Annual Reports, but I have also used the minutes, souvenir programmes and newspaper clippings as well as the pamphlet or typescript histories which many institutions have produced at one time or another. Statutory institutions were generally less prolific, but committee meetings were often given detailed coverage in local newspapers, and the Annual Reports of Medical Officers of Health were invaluable for the hospitals run by public health authorities. For Manchester, especially, published articles, pamphlets or obituaries, by or of doctors or reformers, are very informative, especially about public debates. Where any of these sources have been used, references can be found in the footnotes. I have not listed them all in this bibliography, partly because we have recently published two extensive lists of relevant sources:

Liz Coyne, Dennis Doyle & John V. Pickstone, *A Guide to the Records of Health Services in the Manchester Region (Kendal to Crewe): Part One: Hospital Services, Part Two: Public Health and Domiciliary Services*, Department of History of Science & Technology, UMIST, 1981.

The medical press has been used in following up leads; *The Lancet* was surveyed more systematically for the two decades around 1900.

Government reports and central government papers formed a second major source, especially for the last section of the book. The chapters on the formation of the National Health Service derived largely from files in the MH series in the Public Record Offices, and from Cabinet Papers. Printed reports on which I have drawn substantially include:

Annual Reports of the Poor Law Commissioners, esp. 1841.
Annual Reports of the Medical Officer of the Privy Council, esp. 1862, 1866.
Annual Reports of the Medical Officer of the Local Government Board, esp. 1874, 1876.
Annual Reports of the Ministry of Health.
Reports of the Select Committee on the Poor Law Amendment Act, 1837–8.
Report of the Poor Law Commissioners on the Continuance of the Poor Law Commission and on some Further Amendments of the Laws relating to the Relief of the Poor, 1840.
Reports of the Select Committee on Medical Poor Relief, 1844.
Reports of the Royal Commission on the Health of Large Towns and Populous Districts, 1844.
Reports of the Select Committee on Poor Law Medical Relief, 1854.
Report on Existing Arrangements for the Care and Treatment of the Sick Poor in Provincial Workhouses, 1867 (Edward Smith).
Medical Officer of Health Report on The Use and Influence of Hospitals for Infectious Diseases, 1882 (R. Thorne Thorne).
Returns Relating to Sanitary Districts (Accommodation for Infectious Diseases), 1895.
Report of the Departmental Committee appointed by the President of the Local Government Board to enquire into the Nursing of the Sick Poor in Workhouses, 1902.
Report of the Medical Officer for 1905–6 on Sanatoria for Consumption ... 35th Annual Report of the Local Government Board, 1905–6.
Report of the Royal Commission on the Poor Laws and Relief of Distress, 1909.

SELECTED BIBLIOGRAPHY

Supplement to Forty-Second Annual Report of the Local Government Board: Second Annual Report on Infant and Child Mortality (1912–13).
Hospital Survey, The Hospital Services of the North-Western Area, Ministry of Health, 1945.

The bibliography which follows concentrates on secondary sources: books, articles and unpublished theses. It includes general sources, not specified in the notes. For further references on the social history of the region, readers are referred to:

John V. Pickstone, ed., *Health, Disease and Medicine in Lancashire 1750–1950*, Department of History of Science & Technology, UMIST, Manchester, 1980.
T. Wyke, ed., *A Checklist of Theses on the History of Lancashire*, Manchester Polytechnic, 1979.
Unity R. E. Lawler, *North-West Theses and Dissertations 1950–1978: A Bibliography*, Centre for North-West Regional Studies, University of Lancaster, 1981.

Books
Brian Abel-Smith, *A History of the Nursing Profession*, London, 1960.
Brian Abel-Smith, *The Hospitals, 1800–1948*, London, 1964.
W. R. Abram, *A History of Blackburn, Town and Parish*, Blackburn, 1877.
E. H. Ackerknecht, *Medicine at the Paris Hospital, 1794–1848*, Baltimore, 1967.
Paul Addison, *The Road to 1945*, London, 1975.
John Aikin, *Description of the Country Round Manchester*, London, 1795.
Anon, *Memoir of Thomas Turner, by a relative*, London, 1875.
T. S. Ashton, *Economic & Social Investigations in Manchester, 1833–1933*, London, 1934.
J. Aston, *A Picture of Manchester*, Manchester 1816.
J. A. Atkinson, *Memoir of the Rev. Canon Slade*, Bolton, 1892.
W. Axon, *Annals of Manchester*, Manchester, 1886.
G. M. Ayers, *England's First State Hospitals and the Metropolitan Asylums Board 1867–1930*, London, 1971.
E. Baines, *History, Directory and Gazetteer of the County Palatine of Lancashire*, 2 vols, Liverpool, 1824–5, reprinted 1968.
Samuel Bamford, *Early Days*, Dunkley Edition, London, 1893.
W. Bennett, *The History of Burnley from 1850*, Burnley, 1951.
Thomas H. Bickerton, *A Medical History of Liverpool from the Earliest Days to the year 1920*, London, 1936.
B. Bowker, *Lancashire Under the Hammer*, London, 1928.
W. M. Bowman, *England in Ashton under Lyne*, Altrincham, 1960.
J. L. Brand, *Doctors and the State: the British Medical Profession and Government Action in Public Health 1870–1912*, Baltimore, 1965.
J. W. Bride, *A Short History of the St. Mary's Hospitals, Manchester, 1790–1922*, Manchester, 1922.
Asa Briggs, *Victorian Cities*, London, 1963.
E. M. Brockbank, *Sketches of the Lives and Works of the Honorary Staff of the Manchester Infirmary from its Foundation in 1752 to 1830*, Manchester, 1904.
E. M. Brockbank, *A Short History of Cheadle Royal*, Manchester, 1934.
E. M. Brockbank, *The Foundation of Provincial Medical Education in England*, Manchester, 1936.
W. Brockbank, *Portrait of a Hospital, 1752–1948, To Commemorate the Bicentenary of the Royal Infirmary, Manchester*, London, 1952.
W. Brockbank, *The Honorary Medical Staff of the Manchester Royal Infirmary, 1830–1948*, Manchester, 1965.
W. Brockbank, *The History of Nursing at the MRI, 1752–1929*, Manchester, 1970.
Charles Brown, *Sixty-four Years a Doctor*, Preston, 1922.
E. Richard Brown, *Rockefeller Medical Men: Medicine and Capitalism in America*, Berkeley, 1979.
M. C. Buer, *Health, Wealth and Population in the Early Days of the Industrial Revolution*, London, 1926 (& 1968).

SELECTED BIBLIOGRAPHY

H.C. Burdett, *Cottage Hospitals, General, Fever & Convalescent*, London, 1896.
K.E. Carpenter, ed., *Conditions of Working and Living. Five pamphlets 1838–44*, Arno reprints, New York, 1972.
W. Chadwick, *Reminiscences of Mottram*, Glossop, 1870, reprinted 1972.
H.B. Charlton, *Portrait of a University, 1851–1951: to Commemorate the Centenary of Manchester University*, Manchester, 1952.
P.F. Clarke, *Lancashire and the New Liberalism*, Cambridge, 1971.
Frances Collier, *The Family Economy of the Working Classes in the Cotton Industry, 1784–1833*, Manchester, 1964.
J.R. Coulthart, *A Report on the Sanitary Condition of the Town of Ashton-under-Lyne*, Ashton, 1844.
Charles Creighton, *A History of Epidemics in Great Britain*, 2 vols., London, 1891–4, reprinted 1965.
M.A. Crowther, *The Workhouse System 1834–1929*, London, 1981 & 1983.
Marjorie Cruickshank, *Children and Industry*, Manchester, 1981.
M.J. Cullen, *The Statistical Movement in Early Victorian Britain*, London, 1975.
H.T. Darnton, *A Historical Sketch of the Origins of the District Infirmary*, Ashton-under-Lyne, 1877.
Warren R. Dawson, ed., *Grafton Elliot Smith*, London, 1938.
Jean Donnison, *Midwives and Medical Men*, New York, 1977.
C.L. Dunn, *The Emergency Medical Services*, 2 vols. (History of the Second World War), London, 1952–3.
M. Durey, *The Return of the Plague: British Society and the Cholera, 1831–2*, Dublin, 1979.
Sir F.M. Eden, *The State of the Poor, or an History of the Labouring Classes in England*, 3 vols., London, 1797.
N.C. Edsall, *The Anti-Poor Law Movement, 1833–44*, Manchester, 1971.
D.L. Emblen, *Peter Mark Roget: The Word and the Man*, London, 1970.
Leon Faucher, *Manchester in 1844: its Present Condition & Future Prospects*, London & Manchester, 1844.
John Ferriar, *Medical Histories and Reflections*, 3 vols., Warrington, 1792–8.
Edward Fiddes, *Chapters in the History of Owens College & of Manchester University 1851–1914*, Manchester, 1937.
S.E. Finer, *The Life and Times of Sir Edwin Chadwick*, London & New York, 1952, 1970.
Simon Flexner & J.T. Flexner, *William Henry Welch and the Heroic Age of American Medicine*, New York, 1941, reprinted 1966.
Michael Foot, *Aneurin Bevan*, 2 vols., London, 1962 & 1973.
J. Foster, *Class Struggle and the Industrial Revolution*, London, 1974.
Michel Foucault, *The Birth of the Clinic*, London, 1973.
Derek Fraser, *Urban Politics in Victorian England. The Structure of Politics in Victorian Cities*, Leicester, 1976.
Derek Fraser, *The Evolution of the British Welfare State*, London, 1973.
W.M. Frazer, *A History of English Public Health*, London, 1950.
A.H. Gale, *Epidemic Diseases*, London, 1959.
Peter Gaskell, *Artisans and Machinery*, London, 1836.
H. Gaulter, *The Origins and Progress of the Malignant Cholera in Manchester*, London, 1833.
Neville M. Goodman, *Wilson Jameson, Architect of National Health*, London, 1970.
Ruth Hall, *Marie Stopes*, London, 1978.
Henry Heginbotham, *Stockport Ancient and Modern*, 2 vols., London, 1882 [1887]–1892.
A. Hewitson, *History of Preston*, Wakefield, 1883, reprinted 1969.
G.B. Hindle, *Provision for the Relief of the Poor in Manchester, 1754–1826*, Manchester, 1975.
R.G. Hodgkinson, *The Origins of the National Health Service: Medical Services and the New Poor Law, 1834–1871*, London, 1967.
Frank Honigsbaum, *The Division in British Medicine*, London, 1973.
Michael Ignatieff, *A Just Measure of Pain. The Penitentiary in the Industrial Revolution*, London, 1978.

SELECTED BIBLIOGRAPHY

Angela James and Nina Hills, eds., *Mrs John Brown, 1847–1935*, London, 1937.
Kathleen Jones, *Lunacy, Law and Conscience, 1744–1845*, London, 1955.
F. W. Jordan, *Life of Joseph Jordan*, Manchester, 1904.
Patrick Joyce, *Work, Society and Politics: The Culture of the Factory in Later Victorian England*, Brighton, 1980.
R. H. Kargon, *Science in Victorian Manchester: Enterprise and Expertise*, Manchester, 1972.
Frida Knight, *The Strange Case of Thomas Walker*, London, 1957.
Royston Lambert, *Sir John Simon 1816–1904 and English Social Administration*, London, 1963.
T. W. Laqueur, *Religion and Respectability: Sunday Schools and English Working Class Culture, 1780–1850*, New Haven, 1976.
Jane Lewis, *The Politics of Motherhood*, London, 1980.
Almont Lindsey, *Socialised Medicine in England and Wales. The National Health Service, 1948–1961*, Chapel Hill, North Carolina, 1962.
O. MacDonagh, *Early Victorian Government*, London, 1977.
T. McKeown, *The Modern Rise of Population*, London, 1976.
A. S. McNalty, *The Civilian Health and Medical Services*, 2 vols (History of the Second World War), London, 1953–5.
W. G. Macpherson, *et al.*, *Surgery of the War* (History of the Great War), London, 1922.
Christopher Maggs, *The Origins of General Nursing*, London, 1982.
S. E. Maltby, *Manchester and the Movement for National Elementary Education, 1800–1870*, Manchester, 1918.
Jo Manton, *Sister Dora: The Life of Dorothy Pattison*, London, 1971.
J. D. Marshall, *Furness and the Industrial Revolution*, Barrow, 1958.
J. D. Marshall, ed., *The History of Lancashire County Council 1889 to 1974*, London, 1977.
E. C. Midwinter, *Social Administration in Lancashire, 1830–1860*, Manchester, 1969.
G. C. Miller, *Blackburn, the Evolution of a Cotton Town*, Blackburn, 1951.
Louis W. Moffitt, *England on the Eve of the Industrial Revolution: A Study of Economic and Social Conditions from 1740 to 1760 with special reference to Lancashire*, 1925, reprinted London, 1963.
R. J. Morris, *Cholera 1832: The Social Response to an Epidemic*, London, 1976.
Francis Nicholson & Ernest Axon, *The Older Non-Conformity in Kendal*, Kendal, 1915.
J. Niven, *Observations on the History of Public Health Effort in Manchester*, Manchester, 1923.
Oldham County Borough Council, *Oldham Centenary: A History of Local Government*, Oldham, 1949.
David Owen, *English Philanthropy (1660–1960)*, London, 1965.
E. Sylvia Pankhurst, *The Suffragette Movement*, London, 1931, reprinted 1977.
William Parry-Jones, *Trade in Lunacy: A Study of Private Madhouses in England in the Eighteenth and Nineteenth Centuries*, London, 1972.
W. Parson & W. White, *History Directory & Gazetteer of the Counties of Cumberland and Westmoreland, with that part of the Lake District in Lancashire etc.*, Leeds, 1829.
J. E. Pater, *The Making of the National Health Service*, King's Fund, London, 1981.
Margaret Pelling, *Cholera, Fever and English Medicine, 1825–1865*, Oxford, 1978.
M. Jeanne Peterson, *The Medical Profession in Mid-Victorian London*, Berkeley, 1978.
R. Pinker, *English Hospital Statistics, 1861–1938*, London, 1966.
Harry Platt, *Selected Papers*, London, 1963.
F. N. L. Poynter, ed., *Evolution of Hospitals in Britain*, London, 1958.
J. R. Poynter, *Society and Pauperism, English Ideas on Poor Relief, 1795–1834*, London, 1969.
Archibald Prentice, *Historical Sketches and Personal Recollections of Manchester*, London and Manchester, 1851, reprinted 1970.
Arthur Redford, *The History of Local Government in Manchester*, 3 vols, London, 1939–40.
Abraham Rees, *Cyclopedia or Universal Dictionary of Arts, Science and Literature*, 39 vols, London, 1819.
Frank Renaud, *A Short History of the 'House of Recovery' or Fever Hospital in Manchester*, Manchester, 1885.

SELECTED BIBLIOGRAPHY

Frank Renaud, *A Short History of the Rise and Progress of the Manchester Royal Infirmary from the year 1752 to 1877*, Manchester, 1898.
John Roberton, *Observations on the Mortality and Physical Management of Children*, London, 1827.
John Roberton, *Essays and Notes on the Physiology & Diseases of Women, and on Practical Midwifery*, London, 1851.
David Roberts, *Victorian Origins of the British Welfare State*, New Haven, 1960.
Elizabeth Roberts, *Working Class Barrow & Lancaster, 1890–1930*, Centre for North-West Regional Studies, occasional paper no. 2, 1976.
Nesta Roberts, *Cheadle Royal Hospital: A Bicentenary History*, Manchester, 1967.
William Robertson, *The Social and Political History of Rochdale*, Rochdale, 1889.
M. E. Rose, *The Relief of Poverty*, London, 1972.
George Rosen, *The Specialisation of Medicine with Particular Reference to Opthalmology*, New York, 1944.
George Rosen, *History of Public Health*, New York, 1958.
George Rosen, *From Medical Police to Social Medicine. Essays on the History of Health Care*, New York, 1974.
Andrew Scull, *Museums of Madness*, London, 1979.
G. Searle, *The Search for National Efficiency*, Oxford, 1971.
G. Searle, *Eugenics and Politics in Britain 1900–14*, Leyden, 1976.
M. B. Simey, *Charitable Effort in Liverpool in the Nineteenth Century*, Liverpool, 1951.
E. D. Simon, *A City Council from Within*, London, 1926, reprinted 1944.
John Simon, *English Sanitary Institutions*, London, 1890.
Sheena Simon, *A Century of City Government, Manchester, 1838–1938*, London, 1938.
F. Smith, *The Life and Work of Sir James Kay-Shuttleworth*, London, 1923.
F. B. Smith, *The People's Health 1830–1910*, London, 1979.
F. B. Smith, *Florence Nightingale: Reputation and Power*, London, 1982.
F. S. Stannicliffe, *The Manchester Royal Eye Hospital, 1814–1964*, Manchester, 1964.
J. D. Thompson & G. Goldin, *The Hospital, A Social and Architectural History*, New Haven, 1975.
R. M. Titmuss, *Problems of Social Policy*, London, 1950.
A. de Toqueville, *Journeys to England and Ireland* (1835), London, 1958.
Francois Vigier, *Change and Apathy. Liverpool and Manchester during the Industrial Revolution*, Cambridge, Mass., 1970.
John Vincent, *The Formation of the British Liberal Party 1857–68*, London, 1968, (Penguin, 1972).
W. R. Ward, *Religion and Society in England 1790–1850*, London, 1972.
Frederick Watson, *The Life of Sir Robert Jones*, London, 1934.
S. & B. Webb, *English Poor Law Policy*, London, (Cass Reprint), 1963.
J. Wheeler, *Manchester: Its Political, Social and Commercial History*, Manchester, 1836.
Charles White, *A Treatise on the Management of Pregnant and Lying-in Women*, London, 1773.
W. I. Wild, *The History of Stockport Sunday Schools*, London, 1891.
A. S. Wohl, *Endangered Lives, Public Health in Victorian Britain*, London, 1983.
John Woodward, *To Do the Sick no Harm: A Study of the British Voluntary Hospital System to 1875*, London, 1974.
John Woodward & David Richards, ed., *Health Care and Popular Medicine in Nineteenth Century England*, London, 1977.
Stephen Yeo, *Religion and Voluntary Organisations in Crisis*, London, 1976.
J. H. Young, *St. Mary's Hospitals Manchester, 1790–1963*, Edinburgh, 1964.

Articles

A. E. Barclay, 'Early days of radiology in Manchester', *Manchester University Medical School Gazette, 27* (1948), 115–21.
C. C. Booth, 'Doctors from the Yorkshire Dales', *Proceedings of the 23rd International Congress of the History of Medicine*, London, 1972, pp. 998–1001.

Rhodes Boyson, 'The New Poor Law in North-East Lancashire, 1834–1871', *Transactions of the Lancashire & Cheshire Antiquarian Society, 70* (1960), 35–56.

W. H. Chaloner, 'Manchester in the latter half of the eighteenth century', *Bulletin of the John Rylands Library, 42* (1959–60), 40–60.

G. P. Connolly, 'Little brother be at peace: the priest as holy man in the nineteenth-century ghetto', in W. J. Sheils, ed., *The Church & Healing, Studies in Church History*, vol. 19, Oxford, 1982.

G. W. Daniels, 'The cotton trade during the Revolutionary and Napoleonic Wars', *Transactions of the Manchester Statistical Society* (1915–16).

G. W. Daniels, 'The cotton trade at the close of the Napoleonic War', *Transactions of the Manchester Statistical Society* (1917–1918).

Anna Davin, 'Imperialism and motherhood', *History Workshop Journal, 5* (1978), 9–65.

M. J. Durey, 'Bodysnatchers and Benthamites: The implications of the Dead Body Bill for the London schools of anatomy, 1820–1842', *The London Journal, 2* (1976), 200–25.

H. I. Dutton & J. E. King, 'The limits of paternalism: the cotton tyrants of North Lancashire, 1836–54', *Social History, 7* (1982), 59–74.

W. V. Farrar, Kathleen Farrar and E. L. Scott, 'The Henrys of Manchester, Parts I–6', *Ambix, 20–24* (1973–7).

M. W. Flinn, 'Medical services under the New Poor Law', in D. Fraser, ed., *The New Poor Law in the Ninteenth Century*, London, 1976.

John Fulton, 'The Warrington Academy (1757–1786) and its influence upon medicine and science', *Bulletin of the Institute of the History of Medicine, 1* (1933), 50–80.

Patricia Gray, 'Grangethorpe Hospital Rusholme 1917–1929', *Transactions of the Lancashire & Cheshire Antiquarian Society, 78* (1975), 51–64.

David Hamilton, 'The nineteenth century surgical revolution – antisepsis or better nutrition?', *Bulletin of the History of Medicine, 56* (1982), 30–40.

Pauline Handforth, 'Manchester radical politics, 1789–1794', *Transactions of the Lancashire and Cheshire Antiquarian Society, 66* (1956), 87–106.

S. W. F. Holloway, 'The Apothecaries Act, 1815: a reinterpretation', *Medical History, 10* (107–29, 221–36.

W. Stanley Jevons, 'On the work of the Society in connection with the questions of the day', *Transactions of the Manchester Statistical Society* (1869–70), 1–14.

Joseph F. Kett, 'Provincial medical practice in England, 1730–1815', *Journal of the History of Medicine, 19* (1964), 17–29.

Anthony King, 'Hospital planning: revised thoughts on the origin of the pavilion principle in England', *Medical History, 10* (1966), 360–73.

R. Lawton, 'Population trends in Lancashire and Cheshire from 1801', *Transactions of the Historical Society of Lancashire & Cheshire, 114* (1962), 189–200.

I. S. L. Loudon, 'Historical importance of outpatients', *British Medical Journal, 1* (1978), 974–7.

I. S. L. Loudon, 'John Bunnell Davis and the Universal Dispensary for Children', *British Medical Journal, 1* (1979), 1191–4.

Norman McCord, 'Ratepayers and social policy', in P. Thane, ed., *The Origins of British Social Policy*, London, 1978.

T. A. I. McQuay 'The Blackburn General Dispensary 1824–1838', *The Practitioner, 196* (1966), 716–20.

A. W. Martin, 'The elimination of the unfit by the state, the evolution of a higher race and a third sex', *Public Health*, October 1907, 34–45.

C. F. Mullett, 'Public baths and health in England, 16th–18th century', *Supplement to the Bulletin of the History of Medicine*, 5, Baltimore, 1946, pp. 1–85.

Francis Nicholson, 'The Literary & Philosophical Society, 1781–1851', *Memoirs of the Manchester Literary and Philosophical Society, 68* (1924), 97–148.

SELECTED BIBLIOGRAPHY

Samuel Oleesky, 'Julius Dreschfeld and late nineteenth century medicine in Manchester', *Manchester Medical Gazette, 51* (1971–2), 14–17, 58–60, 96–9.

John V. Pickstone, 'What were dispensaries for? The Lancashire foundations during the industrial revolution' (Abstract), *Bulletin of the Society for the Social History of Medicine, 20* (1977).

John V. Pickstone, 'Establishment and dissent in nineteenth-century medicine: an exploration of some correspondence and connections between religious and medical belief-systems in early industrial England', in W. J. Sheils, ed., *The Church & Healing. Studies in Church History*, vol. 19, Oxford, 1982.

John V. Pickstone, 'Ferriar's fever to Kay's cholera: disease and social structure in Cottonopolis', *History of Science*, 1984.

John V. Pickstone & Stella V. F. Butler, 'The politics of medicine in the early industrial city; a study of hospital reform and medical relief in late eighteenth century Manchester', *Medical History, 28* (1984).

Roy Porter, 'Science, provincial culture and public opinion in enlightenment England', *The British Journal for Eighteenth Century Studies, 3* (1980), 20–46.

Winifred Proctor, 'Poor Law administration in Preston Union 1838–1848', *Transactions of the Historical Society of Lancashire & Cheshire, 117* (1965), 145–65.

Elizabeth Roberts, 'Oral history investigation of disease and its management by the Lancashire working class 1809–1939', in J. V. Pickstone, ed., *Health, Disease and Medicine in Lancashire 1750–1950*, Department of History of Science & Technology, UMIST, Manchester, 1980.

E. A. Rose, 'Cornelius Bayley and the Manchester Methodists', *Proceedings of the Wesley Historical Society, 34* (1964), 153–8.

Charles E. Rosenberg, 'Social class and medical care in nineteenth century America: the rise and fall of the Dispensary', *Journal of the History of Medicine, 29* (1974), 32–54.

Charles E. Rosenberg, 'And heal the sick: the hospital and patient in nineteenth century America', *Journal of Social History, 10* (1977), 428–47.

Charles E. Rosenberg, 'Inward vision and outward glance: the shaping of the American hospital, 1880–1914', *Bulletin of the History of Medicine, 53* (1979), 346–91.

Nora Schuster, 'Early days of Roentgen photography in Britain', *British Medical Journal, 2* (1962), 1164–6.

R. A. Sykes, 'Some aspects of working-class consciousness in Oldham, 1830–1842', *Historical Journal, 23* (1980), 167–79.

Arnold Thackray, 'Natural knowledge in a cultural context: the Manchester model', *American Historical Review, 79* (1974), 672–701.

M. C. Versluysen, 'Midwives, medical men and "poor women labouring of child": lying-in hospitals in eighteenth century London', in Helen Roberts, ed., *Women, Health and Reproduction*, London, 1981.

Charles Webster, 'The crisis of the hospitals during the industrial revolution', in E. G. Forbes, ed., *Human Implications of Scientific Advance, Proceedings of the XVth International Congress of the History of Science, Edinburgh, August, 1977*, Edinburgh, 1978, pp. 214–23.

T. J. Wyke, 'The Manchester and Salford Lock Hospital, 1818–1917', *Medical History, 19* (1975), 73–86.

J. H. Young, 'John Roberton (1797–1876), obstetrician and social reformer', *Manchester Medical Gazette, 46* (1967), 14–19.

Unpublished theses & typescripts

John Banks, 'Over a hundred years. The story of the local hospitals in N.-E. Lancashire, 1876–1976', typescript (Burnley Public Libraries).

S. V. F. Butler, 'Science and the education of doctors in the nineteenth century', PhD thesis, UMIST, 1982.

Mark Clifford, 'Medicine, politics and society: Manchester's 1832 cholera epidemic', BA thesis, History, University of California at Berkeley, 1979.

SELECTED BIBLIOGRAPHY

Rita Darling, 'The role of the medical profession in Manchester, 1790–1815', BA thesis, Modern History and Economics, Manchester University, 1977.

A. F. Davie, 'The government of Lancashire, 1798–1838', MA thesis, Manchester University, 1966.

P. J. Davies, 'Sir Arthur Schuster, FRS, 1851–1934', PhD thesis, UMIST, 1983.

Gerard Edwards, 'The road to Barlow Moor', typescript history of Withington hospital, 1975 (copy at Manchester central library).

Judith Emanuel, 'The politics of maternity in Manchester (1919–1939), a study from within a continuing campaign', MSc thesis, Community Medicine, Manchester University, 1982.

D. Gadian, 'A comparative study of popular movements in north-west industrial towns, 1830–50', PhD thesis, Lancaster University, 1976.

V. A. C. Gatrell, 'The commercial middle-class in Manchester, *c.* 1820–57', PhD thesis, Cambridge University, 1972.

John E. Harrison, 'The development of medical care and public health in nineteenth century Chorley', MSc thesis, UMIST, 1983.

R. B. Hope, 'Thomas Percival: a medical pioneer and social reformer, 1740–1804', MA thesis, Manchester University, 1947.

H. F. Hughes, 'The economics and administrative arrangements of statutory and voluntary anti-tuberculosis measures at home and abroad', unpublished thesis, Manchester University, 1936.

D. M. Jones, 'Local government policy towards the infant and child, with particular reference to the North-West, 1890–1914', MA thesis, Manchester University, 1983.

T. Jones, 'The cholera in Manchester', BA thesis, History, Manchester University, 1948.

Theresa P. Macdonald, 'Christie Hospital and Holt Radium Institute: foundation, development and achievements 1892–1962', MSc thesis, UMIST, 1977.

G. S. Messinger, 'Visions of Manchester: a study in the role of urban imagery in history, 1780–1878', PhD thesis, Harvard University, 1971.

Joan Mottram, 'The life and work of John Roberton MRCS LSA, (1797–1876)', forthcoming MSc thesis, UMIST.

P. A. Ryan, 'Public health and voluntary effort in nineteenth century Manchester', MA dissertation, History, Manchester University, 1974.

R. N. Thompson, 'The New Poor Law in Cumberland and Westmoreland', PhD thesis, Newcastle University, 1971.

J. E. M. Walker, 'John Ferrier of Manchester, MD: his life and work', MSc thesis, UMIST, 1973.

Katherine Webb, 'Medical Practitioners in Manchester, 1780–1860', forthcoming PhD thesis, UMIST.

J. R. Wood, 'The transition from the Old to the New Poor Law in Manchester, 1833–42', BA thesis, History, Manchester University, 1938.

Index

accident care, 4, 13, 50, 52, 68, 71, 74, 103, 110, 112–13, 142, 146–7, 150, 273, 286–9
Accrington, 151, 244
Acts of Parliament, 58, 156, 161, 173, 175, 184, 213, 223, 240–2, 244, 258, 272–3, 279, 290, 340–51
Addison, Viscount Christopher, 349
Adshead, Joseph, 102, 104, 107–9, 113, 125, 129, 130
Aikin, John, 16
Aitken, Mrs (Bury), 232
Altrincham, 208–9
American hospitals and influences, 185, 205, 208
Ancoats, 43, 52–3, 89, 98, 117, 130, 240; *see also* Manchester, Ardwick and Ancoats Dispensary and Infirmary
Arkwright, Daniel, 253
Arkwright, Richard, 69, 253
Armitage, Sir Elkanah, 109, 186
Ashby, Henry, 122, 192
Ashton, Margaret, 240
Ashton under Lyne, 25, 27, 39 n. 20, 73–5, 92, 141–2, 222, 239, 320–1, 325; infectious disease hospitals, 92, 174, 180; maternity homes, 244, 246; Poor Law, 88, 92, — workhouses, 92, 221–2, — infirmary (Lake), 260; voluntary, Infirmary, 113, 142
Association of Municipal Corporations, 313, 321
Attlee, Clement Richard, 349

Bamford, Samuel, 36, 37
Barclay, A. E., 200, 205
Bardsley, S. A., 50–1
Barnes, Robert, 130–1
Barnes, Rev Dr Thomas, 31
Barrington-Ward, Robert McGowan, 312
Barrow, 247, 255–6, 260–1, 320–1, 325; infectious disease hospital, 174–5, 233; maternity home, 244, 247; Poor Law infirmary (Roose), 261; voluntary,

North Lonsdale Hospital, 150–1, 255–6, 264
Battye, Thomas, 38
Bayley, Thomas Butterworth, 18, 25, 69
Bealey family, 244
Bevan, Aneurin, 285, 313, 336 n. 14, 340–9
Beveridge, Sir William, 310, 311, 342
Beveridge Report, 327, 341
Bevin, Ernest, 332
Birley family, 43, 52
Birley, Hugh, 188
Birley, Hugh Hornby, 52, 114
Birley, Richard, 103
Blackburn, 52, 72, 108, 142, 222, 255, 321, 325; infectious disease hospital (Park Lee), 165, 174–5, 177, 233; maternity homes (Springfield), 244; municipal hospital, Queen's Park Hospital (1930–), 262–3; Poor Law, 35, 72, 90–1, 165, — workhouses, 217, — infirmary (Queen's Park), 217; voluntary, Dispensary, 52, 72–3, 90–1, — (Royal) Infirmary, 72, 113, 125, 142–3, 154, 255, 262
Blackpool, 253, 255, 262, 264, 321, 325; infectious disease hospital, 165, 174, 233; voluntary, Victoria Hospital, 253, 255, 321–2
Bolton, 13, 71–2, 108, 141, 147, 170–1, 231–2, 255, 321, 325; infectious disease hospitals, 170–4, 180, 220, 231; maternity homes, 244, 246; municipal hospital, Townleys, 246, 263; Poor Law, 89, 93, 170–3, 225, 231–2, — workhouses (inc. Fishpool), 93, 160, 170–3, — infirmary (Townleys), 173, 220–1; voluntary, Dispensary, 71–2, 147, — Infirmary, 147, 155, 255
Borchardt, Louis, 116, 119–20
Boutflower family, 52
Boutflower, Rev H. C., 73, 74
Boycott, A. E., 203
Brackenbury, Miss, 146

[361]

INDEX

Bradley, Samuel M., 191
Brentnall, E. Stanley, 208, 257
Bright, John, 73, 139, 150
Bristowe and Holmes, Report, 128, 132, 164
British Hospitals Association, 266, 299, 310, 316–17, 321–2, 328–30, 347
British Medical Association, 48, 78, 88, 286–7, 304–5, 328, 338 n.42, 339 n.67, 341, 346–7
British Medical Journal, 218
Brock, Sir Lawrence, 311
Brown, C. Metcalfe, 283, 289
Brown, Charles, 144
Brown, Ernest, 327, 332, 336 n.14, 341, 343–4
Brown, John, 217
Brown, Mary, 218
Brumwell, Dr, 217–18
Bryce, Gordon, 288
Burdett, Sir Henry, 216
Burgess, A., 296–7
Burnley, 233, 239, 241, 255, 321–2, 325; infectious disease hospitals, 160, 166, 174–7, 180; maternity home (Bank Hall), 241, 243; Municipal Hospital (1930–), 244, 262–3; Poor Law, 89, 93, 160, — workhouses, 93, 217–18, — infirmary (Primrose Bank), 217–18; voluntary, Victoria Hospital, 151, 255, 262–3
Bury, 18, 25, 73–5, 92, 141, 147, 222, 232, 255, 321, 325; infectious disease hospitals, 169, 174, 176–7, 232, — sanatoria, 232; Poor Law, 85, 92, — workhouses, 92, 221, — infirmary (Jericho), 222, 260–1; voluntary, Dispensary, 73–5, 147–8, — Infirmary, 148, 255, 264
Bury, Judson Sykes, 191
Burrows, Arthur, 202
Buxton, 290, 297–8

Campbell, David, 65
cancer services, 194, 199–202, 290
Carling, Sir E. Rock, 317, 322, 326, 330, 333, 347
Chadwick, Edwin, 157
Chadwick, Samuel, 147
Chadwick, W., 281–2
Chamberlain, Neville, 258
Charles, John, 349
charity and abuse, 11, 14, 24–5, 35, 43, 57, 60, 63–4, 78–84, 90–1, 99–101, 105, 110, 114–17, 120, 138–41, 146, 151–3, 169, 187, 193–6, 209 n.9, *see also* economism, paternalism
Cheadle Royal Hospital, *see* Manchester (Royal) Infirmary
Cheshire County Council, 235, 260, 290, 303
Chester, 25–6
children, 53–4, 78, 115–22, 158, 161–2, 178–80, 192, 237–41, 249 n.54
Chisholm, Catherine, 240
Chorley, 73, 152–3, 176, 235, 253
Chorlton (S. Manchester), 43, 51–2, 108, 121; Poor Law, 51–2, 85–6, 122–7, 224, 237–8, — workhouses, 86, 122–7, — infirmary (Withington), 125–7, 161, 218, 224, 226, 229, 237, 242, 245; voluntary, Dispensary, 43, 51–2, 54, 57, 82; *see also* Manchester, Corporation, Withington Hospital
Christie, Richard Copley, 193
chronic sick, 35, 55–7, 86–7, 94, 123–6, 216, 258–64
Chrystal, George, 313
Clark, R. Veitch, 259, 274–5, 279, 281–3, 286, 296
Clarke, Ruscoe, 288
Clay, Charles, 117
Cobbett, Sir Walter, 275, 278–83, 304, 328, 329
Colne, 166, 175, 244
conflicts, especially lay–medical tensions, 19, 26, 47, 50, 74, 107, 115, 188–9, 197, 221, 224, 266, 275, 299, 313, 316–17, 328–36, 342–9
convalescent homes, 111, 129–30, 147
Cooper, Henry I., 225
costs of services, 66, 82, 88–90, 229, 252, 263
cottage hospitals. 3, 152–3, 253, 264–5
Cotton Famine, 6, 99, 122, 125, 139, 163
Coulthart, J.R., 142
County Councils Association, 308, 313, 320
Cox, Lissant, 233
Crewe, 244
Crossley Sanatorium, Delamere, 226–30, *see also* Manchester Hospital for Consumption
Crossley, W.J., 227–8
Crumpsall Hospital, *see* Manchester, Corporation
Cullingworth, C.J., 192
Currie, James, 65

[362]

INDEX

Daley, Sir A., 350
Dalton, Hugh, 349
Darbishire, Robert Dukinfield, 193, 194
Davies, Morriston, 235
Davyhulme, 260, 320
Dawson of Penn, Lord, 259
Delépine, Sheridan, 203, 226
Derby, Earl of, 69, 74, 92, 147, 148, 151
D'Ewart, J., 283
Dispensaries, 3, 16–20, 43, 51–4, 61 n. 35, 63–75, 81–4, 88–91
Docker, Sir Bernard, 328, 329, 333
Dougal, Daniel, 284, 285
Douglas, Sir William, 344
Dreschfeld, Julius, 190, 191, 192, 194, 197, 203
Duff Grant, Miss L. G., 296
Durnford, Rev Richard, 109

economism, 25, 29, 38, 57, 75, 84–94, 114–17, 148, 151, 165–77, 221, 245, 261, *see also* charity and abuse
Ede, Chuter, 349
Eden, Sir Fredrick, 36, 37, 65
Edwards, R. G., 258, 278, 281–3, 291
Elliott, Walter, 301
Elswick hospital (nr Kirkham), 234
Emergency Hospital Service, 288, 296–300
Etherton, Sir George, 316, 322
Ewing, Alexander, 291

Faulkner, George, 103–7
Ferguson, F. R., 291
Ferriar, John, 18, 24–5, 30, 39 n. 20 n. 31, 51, 60
fever hospitals and wards, 3, 17–20, 23–9, 59–60, 92, 93, 105–6, 131–2, 160–73, 215–17, 220, *see also* isolation hospitals
Fletcher, Matthew, 74, 75
Fletcher, Samuel, 103–8
Fletcher, Shepherd, 226
Fletcher-Shaw, Sir William, 281, 284
Foot, Michael, 346
Forber, Sir Edward, 310, 315 n. 41
Foster, Alex, 253
Fothergill, Anthony, 65
Fothergill, John, 65
Fothergill, W. E., 199
Frazer, W. M., 350
Friendly Societies, 65, 82, 229
Fylde, 176–7

Gask, Prof. George, 347
Gaskell, Peter, 56
Gamgee, Arthur, 187, 202
Gaulter, Henry, 59
German influences, 116, 119, 190, 192, 198, 224, 226
Gibson, John, 254
Goodenough, Sir W. M., 300, 312, 333
Gray, Sir Henry, 347
Greaves, George, 125
Greenwood, Arthur, 348–9
Greg, Eleanor, 240
Grindon, Leo, 188

Hall, F. (MOH), 350
Hall family, 18–19, 31
Handley, R. C., 254
Hardie, James, 191, 195, 197
Hare, Arthur, 194, 197
Harris, Thomas, 190–1
Hartley, William, 244
Haslam family, 221, 244
Haslam, J. P., 171–2
Hawton, Sir John, 347
Haygarth, John, 25, 65
Henry, Thomas, 16
Heywood, James, 125
Heywood, Oliver, 188
High Carley hospitals, Ulverston, 233–5
Hill, A. V., 203, 313
Hilton, J., 23, 38 n. 2
Hodgkinson, Alexander, 226
Holland, P. H., 104
Holme, Edward, 51
Holt, Sir Edward, 201–2
homoeopathy, 108–9, 149–50
hospital buildings, 14, 49–50, 71, 86–7, 99, 101–8, 111–13, 123–34, 142–3
hospital co-ordination, 173–4, 195–6, 230, 262–3, 272–93, 296–305, 319–27, 333–4, 348–51
'hospital diseases', 49, 103, 112–13, 128, 132–5, 179, 188, 197
hospital medical staff: honorary and consultants, 3, 11–12, 17–20, 27, 30, 47, 50, 70, 115–17, 122, 187–8, 190–3, 197, 257–8, 277–8, 318, 338 n. 49; honorary assistants, 17, 107, 187–8; residents, 11, 30, 37, 43, 51, 74, 87, 189–93, 206, 257–8, 318
Hospital Saturday Funds, *see* workpeople's payments
Howard, John, 16, 69

[363]

INDEX

Howard, Richard B., 104, 108
Hull, John, 45

infectious diseases, 4, 15, 54–5, 58, 104, 115, 131, 156–81; fever, 17–20, 23–9, 37, 55–7, 67, 92, 128, 130; cholera, 54, 57, 59–60, 130, 161; scarlet fever, 54, 158–62, 165, 180; diphtheria, 159, 164, 179–81; *see also* tuberculosis, smallpox
Isaacs, G.A., 349
isolation hospitals, 4, 131–2, 162, 165, 169–81, 232–3, 264–5, 276–7, *see also* fever hospitals

Jackson, James, 27
Jameson, Sir Wilson, 349–50
Jefferson, Geoffrey, 204, 207, 288
Jevons, W. Stanley, 209 n.9
Johnson, Sir Sydney, 312
Jones, Sir Robert, 199, 205–7, 234–5
Jones, Prof. Thomas, 191–2
Jordan, Joseph, 45–6, 48, 50, 186

Kay, J.P., 55, 78, 81–3, 146
Kay-Shuttleworth, Sir James P., *see* Kay, J.P.
Kendal, 17, 64–6, 255–6; infectious disease hospitals, 66, 169, 174; Poor Law, 91, — workhouses, 35, 214; voluntary, Dispensary, 64–6, 91, — Kendal Memorial Hospital, later Westmorland County Hospital, 141, 153 n.8, 255–6
Kletz, Norman, 208
Koch, Robert, 226

Lancashire County Council, 173–8, 232, 233–5, 260–1, 290, 303, 316, 320–2
Lancashire Mental Hospital Board, 291, 298
Lancaster, 10, 17, 64–6, 255–6, 321, 325; infectious disease hospitals, 66, 164–5, 174–5, 180, 235; voluntary, Dispensary, 64–6, — (Royal) Infirmary, 164–5, 255–6
Lancet, 209 n.9, 299–300
Latham, Lord Charles, 312, 335
Lawson, J.J., 349
Lea, A.W., 224
Leech, Daniel John, 190–4, 197
Leigh, 151–2
Leigh, John, 90, 104, 109, 110, 115, 121, 130–1, 158, 161–3, 170
Leigh, Robert Holt, 66
Lettsom, John C., 65
Little, David, 192
Liverpool, 10–13, 17, 44, 65–6, 129, 198–9, 207, 233–5, 260, 278, 287, 297–8, 302–4, 316–17, 322–6, 334, 336 n.5
Local Government Board, 132, 156, 166–9, 176–7, 180, 215–22, 237, 241
local health authorities, 25, 59–60, 70, 93, 130–2, 156–81, 224–5, 258–9, 305–14, 320–2, 331–2, 342–5, 348–51, *see also* Medical Officers of Health
London, hospitals and influences, 12–14, 16–17, 31, 46, 53, 65, 113, 128, 152, 187–8, 199, 201–2, 205, 207, 240, 243, 288, 297, 351
London County Council, 300, 309–10, 313, 331, 335–6, 344, 349–50
Lund, Edward, 187
Lyon, Edmund, 78–9
Lytham, 152

Macclesfield, infectious disease hospitals, 160, 175, 215; Poor Law and workhouses, 86, 93, 160, 215, — infirmary, 215–16, 260
Manchester, 5, 10, 13, 18, 42–3, 85–6, 98–9, 161–3, 201, 243, 255–6, 273–5, 297–8, 321, 325; public health, 4, 23–30, 54–60, 104–5, 108–11, 130–4, 161, 226, 239, 246, 264, 277
Manchester, Corporation, 161–3, 176, 179, 197, 226–31, 237–41, 245, 246, 258–60, 272–93, 296, 303, 329–30, 338 n.41, — infectious disease hospitals (Monsall), 127, 130–2, 160–3, 174, 178–80, 225, 243, 265, 276–7, — sanatoria 230–1, 238, 277, 288, 298, — smallpox hospitals, 176, 276–7; municipal hospitals: Booth Hall, 238–9, 245, 256–7, 265, 274–5, 280, 283–4, 287, *see also* Prestwich; Crumpsall Hospital (1930–), 256–9, 265, 274–5, 275–6, 280, 283–4, 287–8, 291, *see also* Manchester, Poor Law, infirmary; Withington Hospital (1930–), 256–9, 265, 273–5, 277, 283–4, 287–9, 292, 298, *see also* Chorlton

[364]

INDEX

Manchester, Poor Law, 35–8, 44, 85–90, 98, 105, 109–10, 122–7, 162–3, 237–8, 256, — workhouses, New Bridge Street, 35–8, 44, 86–8, 122–4, 127, 161, Crumpsall, 124–5, — infirmary (Crumpsall), 214–15, 226, 229, 242, 245, 256–9, see also Manchester, Corporation, Crumpsall Hospital

Manchester, voluntary hospitals:
 Ardwick and Ancoats Dispensary and Infirmary, 52–3, 55–6, 81–4, 89, 145–6, 197, 200, 205, 208, 257, 265, 280, 286–8, 290
 Babies' Hospital (Duchess of York), 240–1, 243, 251, 272, 280–1
 Children's Dispensary and Hospital (Pendlebury), 53–4, 78, 116–22, 161, 191–2, 238–9, 290
 Christie Hospital and Holt Radium Institute, 193–6, 199–202, 290
 ear hospitals, 193
 (Royal) Eye Hospital, 44–5, 114, 192, 198, 265
 Grangethorpe hospital, 207–8
 homoeopathic dispensaries and hospitals, 99–101, 108–9
 Hospital for Consumption, 226–30, see also Crossley Sanatorium, Delamere
 House of Recovery, 3, 23–30, 54, 57, 59, 65, 105–6, 158
 (Royal) Infirmary, 4, foundation, 10–15; lunatic hospital, 14–15, 27, 30, 103–7; reform, 15–20; French wars, 37; 1820s, 44–58, 80–3; rebuilding 1840s, 100–8; criticisms and rebuilding controversy, 110–13, 127–34, 145; convalescent home, 129–30; site question, 185–90, 194–8; medical staff, 187–202, 208, 240, 257; WWI, 206; TB, 226; interwar, 251, 257, 259, 265, 273–4; hospital coordination, 287–94; WWII and plans, 297
 Jewish Memorial Hospital, 265, 288
 Lock Hospital (St Luke's), 16, 44–6, 54, 193, 272, 280
 Lying-in Charity, later St Mary's, 31–4, 43–4, 47, 50, 58, 78–82, 114–20, 146, 187–8, 192, 194–6, 206, 242, 247, 265, 275–6, 281, 290, 292

 Northern Hospital (Clinical Hospital for Diseases of Children), 116–19, 242, 265, 291
 Skin Hospital, 54, 193, 194, 199–200, 251
 Southern Hospital, 121–2, 187, 192, 194–6, 242

Manchester, other organisations, see individual entries

Manchester, see also Chorlton, Prestwich, Stretford

Manchester Board of Health, 25, 30, 58–9

Manchester District Provident Society, 81–2, 187, 209

Manchester Guardian, 50, 56, 80, 107, 198, 201, 278

Manchester (Salford and Stretford) Joint Hospitals Advisory Board, 262, 281–93, 297, 302–4, 310, 322–3, 329–30

Manchester Ladies Health Society, 239

Manchester Literary and Philosophical Society, 15, 18, 30, 47

Manchester Medical Guild, 243

Manchester medical schools (proprietary), 44–7, 119, 186–7

Manchester medical school (Owens and University), 186–91, 194–7, 202–7, 226, 279–84

Manchester Medical Society, 199

Manchester Medico-Ethical Association, 109

Manchester Regional Hospital Board, 1, 296

Manchester Royal Institution, 104

Manchester and Salford Sanitary Association, 119, 126, 129, 161, 189, 198, 227

Manchester and Salford Town Mission, 81

Manchester Statistical Society, 81, 109–12

Manchester Strangers Friend Society, 24–5, 66

Manchester University, 202–5, 279–94, 322, 326, 330, see also Owens College, Manchester

Manchester Voluntary Hospitals Committee, 277, 279, 281

maternity services, 4, 6, 12, 16, 31–5, 43, 51, 54, 58, 65, 78, 89, 114–22, 124, 240–7, 275–6, 351

[365]

INDEX

McDougall, A., 225
McIntosh, T.S., 317–21, 326
McMurray, T. Porter, 235
McNicol, Niven, 317, 321–3, 326, 329
March, Dr (Rochdale), 150
Marshall, F.N., 296, 336 n.5
Martin, A.W., 236
Maude, Sir John, 310, 313, 326, 344
Meadowcroft, Cllr, 281–2
Meathop sanatorium (Westmorland Consumption Sanatorium), 231
Medical Officers of Health, 104, 121, 130–2, 157, 166–71, 178, 226–7, 236–7, 267, 274–6, 301, 319, 329–30, 350–1
medical practitioners, 32, 44, 48, 70, 78, 88–90, 109, 150–3, 170, 243, 247, 264, 304–5, 309, 328, 335, 338 n.42, 340, 346
medical Practitioners Union, 337 n.37
medical science, 120, 148, 159, 179–81, 184–5, 193–205, 226–8
medical teaching, 46–8, 107, 185–7, 190–3, 322, 346, 352 n.9
mental services, 14, 27, 37, 102–3, 217, 236–7, 274, 291, 298
Merei, Augustus Schoepf, 119, 120
Milligan, William, 193, 201
Ministry of Health, 231, 241, 262, 275–6, 286–7, 293, 296–314, 316–36, 343–51
Monsall Hospital, *see* Manchester, Corporation
Moore, F. Craven, 208
Morgan, J.E., 187
Morley, John, 282, 284, 286
Morrison, Herbert, 331, 332, 345, 348–9
Mumford, Lewis, 231
municipal general hospitals, 4, 110, 245–6, 274–8, 283–5
Murray, G.R., 203–4, 285

National Insurance, 225, 227, 229–30, 243
Needham, Sir Christopher, 281–3
Nelson, 175, 244, 253
Newell, R.L., 281, 286, 291, 304, 329
Nightingale, Florence, 99, 100, 111–12, 121, 125–9, 142, 167
Niven, James, 176, 225, 227, 231, 237
Noble, Daniel, 109–10
North of England Medical & Surgical Journal, 62 n.41, 47, 78–9

Nuffield, Lord, William Morris, 300, 312
Nuffield Provincial Hospital Trust, 289, 291, 293, 300–6, 311–14, 315 n.32, 317, 328, 351
nursing, 4, 11, 36, 50, 123, 126–7, 132, 172, 213, 217–9, 296

O'Hagan, Lady, 241
Oldham, 73–5, 139, 141, 222, 227, 234, 238, 243, 255, 321, 325, 334–5; infectious disease hospitals, 165–6, 174, 176, 180, 232, — sanatoria, 232–3, 238; maternity homes, 243–6; municipal, Boundary Park Hospital (1930–), 245–6, 262–3; Poor Law, 88, 91–2, — workhouses, 85, 92, 217, — infirmary (Boundary Park), 217, 238; voluntary (Royal) Infirmary, 150, 208, 255, 262, 334–5
Oldham, Samuel, 142
Oliver, T.H., 284
Ollerenshaw, Robert, 208
orthopaedics, 234–5, 238, 205–8, 234–5, 257, 277, 280, 286–8
Owens, John, 186
Owens College, Manchester, 107, 109, 132, 185–7, 193–201, *see also* Manchester University

Park Hospital, *see* Davyhulme
paternalism, 4, 6, 71, 73, 75, 99, 120, 138–41, 170–1
patients and patient numbers, 49–53, 76 n.11, 79, 83, 226, 230–1, 254–5, 272; home patients, 17, 23–9, 43, 53, 80, 158; in-patients, (MRI) 11, 29, 33–4, 103, 106, 129–33, (St Mary's) 117, 242–3, 276, (workhouses), 86–7, 122–6, 216–18, 221–3, 238–9, (infectious) 162, 168, 174, 179, (towns), 143–6, 254–6; out-patients, 11, 13, 19, 29, 53, 120–1
patient payments, 83, 114–17, 151, 162–4, 187, 312–13
payments, *see* patient payments, private patients, workpeople's payments; provident schemes
Peel family, 18
Peel Hall hospital (Lancs CC, nr Walkden), 234
Patrick, W.H.C., 296
Percival, Thomas, 16, 17, 25, 30
philanthropy, *see* charity

[366]

INDEX

Philips, Francis, 51, 68–9
Philips, J. L., 27, 29, 30–1, 47
Pickles, William, 301
Platt, Sir Harry, 204–7, 211 n.42, 235, 257, 273, 280–2, 286–7, 301, 304, 337 n.30
political affiliations, 5–6, 17–20, 24–9, 32, 36–8, 42, 60, 63–75, 84–6, 107, 138–53, 224–5; Labour, 268 n.19, 258–9, 274, 281, 309, 312–13, 340–9; Liberals, 49–50, 73, 85, 138–40, 147, 151, 254, 258; Radicals, 19–20, 29–30, 36, 49, 85, 98–9, 138–41, 147; Tories, 10, 18, 26, 36–8, 50, 64, 69, 70–4, 85, 107, 139–41, 335–6, 340; Whigs, 19, 86
Poor Law Commission, 224–5, 229
Poor Law medicine, 5, 35, 43, 51–2, 72, 84–91, 105, 109–11, 160–73, 212–25, 238–9, 256–64, 308
Poston, R.I., 208
Preston, 10, 13, 69–71, 75, 108, 163, 176, 222, 239, 247, 253–5, 261–2, 266–7, 316, 321–5; infectious disease hospitals, 70, 93, 163–4, 174–5, 180, — sanatoria, 233; maternity, 246–7; Municipal Hospital (Sharoe Green), 246, 261–2, 266–7; Poor Law, 70, 85, 91, 93, 143, 163–4, 174, — workhouses, 93–4; voluntary, Dispensary, 69–71, 91, 143, — (Royal) Infirmary, 143–4, 154, 163–4, 174, 253–5, 261–2, 266–7, 321–2
Prestwich, 122, 127, 238–9, *see* Manchester, Corporation, Booth Hall
private patients, 102–3, 164–6, 258–9, 265, 346
provident schemes, 82–3, 110, 146, 187, 252–6, 273, 307, 328
Provincial Medical and Surgical Association, *see* British Medical Association
public health, 17–29, 54–60, 104–5, 111–12, 130–4, 145, 156–81, 215, 220–47, 263–4, 298, 350–1

Radcliffe, 18, 244
Radcliffe, Netten, 132, 167, 188
Radford, Elizabeth, 114–5
Radford, Thomas, 114–8, 188
Ramsbottom, Albert, 281, 284
Ransome, Arthur, 209 n.9

Ransome, John A., 47, 49
Raper, Prof. H.S., 284
Rathbone, William, 126, 129
Raw, Nathan, 224
religious affiliations, 5–6, 17–20, 24–9, 32, 36–8, 42, 60, 63–75, 84–6, 107; Anglicans, 10, 18–19, 32, 36, 64, 68–74, 107, 150; Catholics, 31, 73, 80, 152–3; Dissenters, 12, 18–20, 21 n.28, 32, 36, 53, 64–6, 75, 107–8, 139–40; Methodists, 19, 32, 66–9; Quakers, 17, 49, 65, 67, 81, 107; Unitarians, 18, 31–2, 68, 193
Rhodes, J. Milson, 218
Roberton, John, 50, 56–8, 79–81, 99, 104, 109–10, 111, 113, 121, 125, 132, 142–3
Roberts, David Lloyd, 117–8, 192, 193
Roberts, Elizabeth, 247
Roberts, William, 187, 190
Rochdale, 5, 73, 141, 148–50, 222, 235, 247, 255, 321, 325; homoeopathy, 148–50, 266–7; infectious disease hospitals, 174, 180, 234–5, — sanatoria, 233–5; maternity, 245, 247; municipal hospital (Birch Hill), 238, 245, 262–3, 266–7; Poor Law, 85, 91, 93, — workhouses, 93, 221, – infirmary (Birch Hill), 221; voluntary, Dispensary, 73–4, 149–50, Infirmary, 149–50, 255, 262, 263, 266–7
Roget, P.M., 30, 47
Roscoe, Henry, 186
Ross, James, 190–2, 197, 203
Royalty, 68, 70, 151–2
Royston, William, 129–30
Rucker, Arthur, 309, 344, 349–50
Rufford hospital (Lancs CC), 234
Rutherford, Ernest, 200

St Anne's, 253
St Mary's hospital, *see* Manchester, voluntary hospitals
Salford, 52, 163, 166–9, 239, 241, 245, 247, 255, 262–3, 290, 321, 325; infectious disease hospitals, 166–9, 174, 180, 233, — sanatoria, 233; maternity, 241–2, 245, 247; municipal hospital (Hope), 245, 263, 288, 290, 297; Poor Law, 85, 122, 166–9, 237, — workhouses, 160–1, 242, — infirmary (Hope), 168, 216, 245;

INDEX

Salford (*contd.*) voluntary, Dispensary, 52, 73, 82; (Royal) Infirmary, 145, 255, 273, 288–9, 291, 297
Schuster, Arthur, 198–200
Schwabe, Salis, 119
Scottish influences, 12–13, 30–1, 190–3, 201, 309, 332
Sergeant, Edward, 170–1
Sillavan, James, 281–2
Simmons, William, 31, 46
Simon, John, 128, 157
Sinclair, W. Japp, 121, 192, 194
Skevington, W. E., 224
smallpox, 4, 34, 89, 128, 130, 158, 164–73, *see also* infectious diseases
Smith, G. Elliot, 204
Smith, Margaret Merry, 240, 243
Society for Bettering the Conditions of the Poor, 28
Southam, Frederick, 191
Souttar, H. S., 347
special hospitals (and dispensaries) and departments, 6, 16, 44–5, 54, 113–22, 188, 192–202, 255, 267, 286–91
Steel, Graham, 190–1, 197
Stewart, Alexander, 209 n. 9
Stirling, William, 202
Stockport, 68–70, 222, 235, 255–6, 321, 325; infectious disease hospitals, 68, 169, 174, — sanatoria, 235; municipal hospital (Stepping Hill), 233, 263; Poor Law, 85–6, — workhouses, 86, 219, — infirmary (Stepping Hill), 219, 222; voluntary, Dispensary, 68–90, — Infirmary, 68–9, 255–6
Stopes, Marie, 247
Stopford, John Sebastian Bach, 204, 207–8, 240, 279–82, 322
Stretford, 253, 262, 265, 282–3, 288
surgery, 133, 138, 148, 157, 191–3, 203–8, 254–5, 263, 286–9
Sutherland, D. P., 230
Sutton, John, 170

Tatham, J. F. W., 170, 227, 240
Telford, E. D., 281–6
Thorburn, John, 121, 187, 192, 209 n. 9
Thorburn, William, 203
Tocqueville, Alexis de, 42
Topping, Andrew, 247
tuberculosis and services, 4, 55, 199, 212–14, 225–35, 238, 351

Turner, Thomas, 47–8, 50, 186

Ulverston, 233–5

Victoria University, *see* Manchester University
voluntary hospital principle, 3, 11, 110, 138–53, 164, 222–3, 251–7, 263–7, 272–3, 282–5, 300–14, 321–2, 328–30, 335, 340–3, *see also* charity and abuse
Venereal disease hospitals, *see* special hospitals, *and* Manchester, voluntary hospitals

Wars: French, 28–9, 33–4, 37–8, 42, 46, 65–7; Crimean, 99, 111; Boer, 236; First World War, 205–8, 244, 246; Second World War, 296–306
Webb, Beatrice, 224
Webb, Sidney, 224
Westmorland County Council, 231
White, Charles, 11–13, 16, 18, 26, 31, 46, 47
White, family, 18, 19
Whitehaven, 17
Whitehead, James, 116, 119–20
Whitehead, Walter, 191–4
Whitworth, Sir Joseph, 193
Wigan, 10, 66, 108, 139, 141, 145, 149, 154, 166, 177, 321, 325; infectious disease hospitals, 166, 174, 177; maternity, 244, 246; Poor Law, workhouses, 221, 261, — infirmary (Billinge), 222, 261; voluntary, Dispensary, 56, 66–7 70, 76 n. 13, — Infirmary (Royal Albert Edward) 144–5, 154, 265
Wild, Prof. R. B., 201
Wilkinson, A. V., 155 n. 34
Wilkinson, Ellen, 349
Wilkinson, Thomas, 232
Williams, Tom, 349
Williamson, R. T., 203
Williamson, W. C., 193
Willinck, Henry, 332, 341, 343, 347
Wilson, William James, 44–5, 47–51
Windsor, Thomas, 192
Winsford, 152
Withington Hospital, *see* Chorlton; Manchester, Corporation
Withnell hospital (Lancs. County Council), 234

[368]

INDEX

women and medical services, 6, 34, 66, 114–22, 217–18, 240–7, 269 n. 28
Woolton, Lord, 232–3
workhouses (and Public Assistance Institutions), 3–4, 35–8, 43, 86–7, 91–4, 122–7, 160–1, 212–25, 214–5
workhouse infirmaries, 3–4, 122–7, 212–25
workpeople's payments, 6, 140–1, 144–5, 149, 153 n. 7, 154 n. 17, n. 22, 155 n. 26, 209 n. 9, 252–6, 273, 307 315, n. 42, 328
Workington, 17
Worthington, Thomas, 125–7, 154 n. 23
Wright, G. A., 191–2, 197
Wrightington hospital, 233–5
Wrigley, John, 307, 310